P9-DFN-167

The American
Immigration Collection

Filipino Immigration

BRUNO LASKER

Arno Press and The New York Times
NEW YORK 1969

*

Library of Congress Catalog Card No. 69-18783

*

Reprinted from a copy in the
Columbia University Libraries

*

Manufactured in the United States of America

FILIPINO IMMIGRATION

TO CONTINENTAL UNITED STATES AND TO HAWAII

Photo J. J. Billones

FILIPINOS, NEAR STOCKTON. PICKING STRAWBERRIES

Filipino Immigration

To Continental United States and to Hawaii

By

BRUNO LASKER

Published for the
AMERICAN COUNCIL
INSTITUTE OF PACIFIC RELATIONS
by
THE UNIVERSITY OF CHICAGO PRESS
CHICAGO, ILLINOIS

COMPOSED AND PRINTED BY QUINN & BODEN COMPANY, INC.
RAHWAY, N. J., U. S. A.

FOREWORD

FEW citizens are aware of the fact that the United States is facing a new problem of mass immigration, and even fewer understand its unique features. Even with a bill before the United States Congress since May 19, 1928,[1] for the exclusion of Filipinos from the territories of the United States—by the simple device of declaring them aliens—the amount of space given to the subject by the newspapers of the country, compared, for example, with that given to the tariff in relation to the Philippine Islands or to the agitation for Philippine independence, was almost negligible until recent agitation in California brought it to general attention. Yet, the subject of Filipino immigration [2] has for some years been widely and seriously discussed on the Pacific Coast; and the demand for its cessation through the passage of an exclusion law has been voiced vigorously in resolutions, first, of local and state federations of labor and of chapters of the American Legion and of other patriotic societies, then of the California Joint Immigration Committee, the American Federation of Labor,[3] the American Legion and other national patriotic associations, and finally the California state legislature.[4]

There is a widespread feeling in circles interested in immigration policy and in international relations that this proposal is both too serious in its direct consequences and related to too many other important questions of statecraft to be decided hastily and without careful examination of the possible results and implications of such an action. For one thing, it was obvious from the start that the agitation for Filipino exclusion would strengthen the claims of those demanding the independence of the Philippines. But the political consequences are even more far-reaching than this. Filipino exclusion would open anew, and in a setting unfavorable for

[1] H.R. 13799 (later H.R. 8708), introduced by Congressman R. J. Welch of California.

[2] Strictly speaking, the migration of persons from the Philippine Islands to the mainland of the United States and to Hawaii may not be "immigration"; but the term is popularly used and has the advantage of brevity.

[3] At the 1927, 1928 and 1929 conventions.

[4] Assembly Joint Resolution No. 15, May, 1929.

calm reflection, a discussion of American policy in general toward the peoples of the Far East. Furthermore, it is clear that any decision of Congress on the Filipino issue must react upon other open questions of immigration policy toward nations not now under the quota law and would carry a point nearer to definitiveness of declaration our American population policy for the distant future. Those who raise these questions in favor of a considered rather than a hasty answer to the question of Filipino immigration are not necessarily committed to one principle or another, but believe that the problems arising from that influx cannot satisfactorily be solved without relation to these larger issues. On the other hand, many of those who favor passage of the exclusion bill fear that delay may greatly increase the seriousness of the situation and, while willing to have the matter fully discussed in all its aspects, are averse to any procedure of inquiry which would unduly postpone decisive action.

It is for this reason that the American Council of the Institute of Pacific Relations, urged to take up the subject on the one hand by some who see this matter of Filipino immigration as one requiring immediate legislative attention, and on the other hand by those who regard the subject as one of international importance and in need of joint international study and discussion, decided to procure a rapid survey of the situation. The Research Committee of the American Council commissioned Bruno Lasker, of New York, to make this preliminary study, allotting three months for its completion—a period which, though later extended to five months, was obviously too short a time to permit of the collection of new quantitative data or of other extensive first-hand studies, but presumably sufficient, with the aid of the results of other studies already available, to secure a general picture of the situation, clarification of the problems involved in it, and indication of the major trends of current proposals for their solution.

The report which follows, though admittedly incomplete on many phases, has been accepted by the Research Committee as one of a series of publications which this committee intends to present to the China conference of the Institute in the fall of 1931, where new phases and developments of restrictive immigration policies will be one of the principal concerns of a round table on Migration and Race Problems. The American Council offers the following study as part of the informational background necessary for profitable discussion. The presentation of this material for consideration in the program does not, however, imply that either the Institute itself or its American Council assumes responsibility for statements of fact or opinion contained in the text. These remain as much the personal expression of the author as would be the case if the contribution were communicated orally.

JAMES T. SHOTWELL.

New York.

AUTHOR'S PREFACE

FOR a summary of findings the reader is referred to the concluding section (p. 323 *et seq.*). In presenting the results of the study of Filipino Immigration entrusted to him, the author has to meet, first of all, the immediate need for factual information on a controversial legislative issue. He also hopes, however, to contribute toward a better general understanding of the way in which a new migration movement begins, the problems which it occasions, and the new tasks which it imposes upon the policy of the receiving country.

The purpose of the report and the need for a rapid survey to make the findings available for a discussion of the present situation has precluded the employment of methods which would require laborious detailed research. On any single aspect of the subject, years of expert study would have been required to produce quantitative data that might serve as a basis for complete analysis. What this policy should be, the author is not called upon to advise. Nor does he claim for this study an exactitude and comprehensiveness of statement which might rightly be insisted upon if the purpose were primarily to make an original contribution to the scientific study of migration. For example, as is explained on p. 325, the information collected on causes of Filipino emigration does not suffice for a reliable statistical analysis with the aim of ascribing to each of the major causes its relative weight. In the absence of national statistics on such subjects as Filipino health or the employment of Filipinos in the civil service, a more extensive study would undoubtedly have produced more adequate data. Information given on the authority of individual specialists in the field of crime or employment or education could have been checked up by a more widespread inquiry. Attitudes, instead of being given on the basis of interviews, could have been ascertained by means of tests; opinions by means of questionnaires. But none of these methods were practicable within the limits of the present study.

Several important aspects of the general subject of migration from the Philippines to the mainland of the United States are not covered by the present study. In view of the acute controversy which has developed around the question of the ethnic character of the Filipino people—in connection both with the proposals for exclusion and with interpretations of the laws of several western states on racial intermarriage—it has not seemed advisable to include in the present survey such anthropological data as would necessarily have had to be taken at second hand and which are not generally accepted.

For a similar reason, no extended discussion is included of the legal status of the Philippine population as a subject people of the United States. There is at present no agreement as to the exact legal meaning of the designation of the Filipinos as "nationals" of the United States—a term applied first by the State Department to define inhabitants of the United States who are neither citizens nor subject to a foreign power. It is hoped that a full inquiry into the status of such nationals will soon be made by competent students.[1]

A third subject which it has not been found possible to include in the scope of the present survey is the political and economic situation in the Philippine Islands from which many influences must necessarily spring that make for and against the emigration of the archipelago's inhabitants. Material for a study of that situation has been collected during the progress of the present inquiry and will, it is hoped, take shape before long in a separate report.

A word is necessary also concerning the arrangement of the material. The present report differs from other monographs on particular immigrant groups or immigration problems in that it is intended not only to serve purposes of information but also very definitely purposes of discussion. For this reason an exposition is attempted which throws into relief the different interests at stake. Instead of describing in the more conventional order, to wind up with the author's conclusions and recommendations, first the sources of this movement and the characteristics of the migrant people, then the nature of its impact upon vocational and social conditions in the receiving country, with the problems arising from lacking or faulty adjustment, we shall, after a brief résumé of some major general factors, take up, separately, the problems occasioned by this movement, for the mainland of the United States, for the migrants themselves, and for the territory of Hawaii which has

[1] A formal request to this effect has been made to the American Council by the governing body—the Pacific Council—of the Institute of Pacific Relations. See Problems of the Pacific, 1929; Proceedings of the Third Conference of the Institute of Pacific Relations. University of Chicago Press, 1930, p. 649.

a different concern in the matter. After the reader has thus gained, it is hoped, a fairly accurate picture of the distinct problems that arise for larger interest groups from this movement of migration, he will find himself in need of further information on factors which affect all three major interests alike, in order to arrive, finally, at a point where he can, with added understanding for the variety of interests affected, weigh the remedies and plans proposed from different sides.

The reasons for such an arrangement will be clear to anyone who has followed the discussion of our subject in recent months. No agreement can be reached even on minor aspects of the matter so long as proponents and opponents of a measure select only those facts and interpretations that suit their own case; what we would get in this way would be an array of mutually contradictory and mutually exclusive statements that offer no basis for an integration of purposes and the possible adoption of measures by common consent. The peculiarity of Filipino immigration, as distinct from other immigration problems, is precisely that it does not lend itself to solutions dictated by sectional interests. Though it lies within the domain of domestic policy, the meaning of the word domestic in this case has to be considerably stretched if we remember the often declared solicitude of our government for the welfare of the Philippine Islands and their inhabitants—its own subjects and wards. It is for this very practical reason that, at the danger of seeming repetition, our present survey is looking at some of the outstanding facts from different points of view. One danger of this arrangement is that in the section dealing with the domestic problem of Filipino immigration for the mainland of the United States, it may give an exaggerated impression of the unfavorable effects of Filipino immigration, while the chapters describing the immigrant Filipino's problems on the mainland of the United States may seem to exaggerate his misfortunes. Such possible misinterpretation has been guarded against, so far as possible, by pointing out in appropriate places that the conflicts and difficulties of adjustment which accompany the introduction of Filipinos in a community resemble in many ways those conflicts and difficulties that have been experienced with other racial groups in the past, and that conversely the Filipino's troubles are, for the most part, incident to the situation in which he finds himself as a newcomer rather than a result of ill-will against him. The unprejudiced reader will soon discover, as the tale unfolds, that the *particular* problems associated with the Filipino as a racial group, apart from general problems of immigration and interracial contact, are not severe; and, on the other hand, that the immigrants' grievances are largely balanced by the friendly disposition toward them personally which newcomers of every race as individuals still find among us.

It is inevitable that some of the findings here presented, dealing with a new movement and with a rapidly changing situation, may have to be revised from time to time. But perhaps such value as this study may be found to have, will lie precisely in the fact that it was made during the incipient stage of a kind of movement which in the past has rarely been studied before earlier events had become overlaid with later happenings and been colored by attitudes later developed. The field study was completed in the United States and in Hawaii between November, 1929, and February, 1930; and significant additional data from the Philippine Islands were contributed by Frederick V. Field, assistant secretary of the American Council, and Mrs. Elizabeth Brown Field. They also are mainly responsible for the first-hand material contained in Chapters XIV-XVIII, and Appendices J and K.

The following report represents little more than a summary of an extensive documentation, made possible by the active cooperation of a large number of persons, only few of whom it has been possible to quote directly in the text. Apart from meetings held with groups, almost two hundred persons have been interviewed in the course of this study on the mainland of the United States, in Hawaii, and in the Philippines. About one-fifth of these were Americans well acquainted with conditions in the Philippine Islands. In Hawaii, public officials, teachers and organizational officers predominated among the informants; on the mainland the representatives of various economic interests formed a larger proportion. Filipinos, more frequently interviewed in groups, took part in one-half of the individual interviews in the Philippines and in about one-tenth on the mainland. In addition, about seventy sets of proofs were sent out to persons whose special knowledge and experience seemed valuable, and more than forty of them responded with detailed criticisms and amplifications. Indeed, the present volume could not have been written without the active collaboration of members of the American, Hawaiian, and Philippine Councils of the Institute, and of many others whose only reward—since they are too numerous for individual mention—is their part in such value as this volume may be found to possess. The author and his associates desire here to express their keen sense of indebtedness to all of them. While they alone are responsible for factual statements and interpretations not directly quoted, they cannot help feeling that the unusual amount of cooperation they have enjoyed—not only from those who had a primary interest in having the concerns and attitudes of specific groups fairly represented but also from social scientists and government officials, who in some cases have been at considerable pains to prepare statements on facts not easily available—has saved them from many blunders and insured a high degree of accuracy. No less grateful are they to the many persons who, often at great personal inconvenience, have placed their time and knowledge at their disposal on the field.

TABLE OF CONTENTS

PART V: POLICIES AND PROGRAMS

ILLUSTRATIONS

Maps

Plates

PART I

INTRODUCTION

PART I. INTRODUCTION

CHAPTER I

A NEW IMMIGRATION MOVEMENT

1. THE ARRIVAL OF THE FILIPINO

MOST Americans do not recognize a Filipino. Until about 1927 or 1928, only a small minority of them had become aware of the fact that tens of thousands of Filipinos were living in this country. For over 90 per cent of the population, a "Filipino problem" exists only through hearsay. College students and teachers were more familiar with them—particularly in the Far West. From many impressions of these early arrivals we gain this composite picture:

With family names difficult to pronounce, Juan, Mateo and Pedro heard themselves familiarly addressed by their first names and, with all the difficulties of residence in a strange country, these boys experienced warm hospitality and sincere friendship. Like American boys of their own age, they had to work their way through college; assigned as "house-boys" to the homes of faculty members or other neighboring families, they found friendly interest in their educational progress and expanded under sympathetic inquiries concerning their own country and their early life. Helpful fellow students and college officers made it possible for them to add substantially to their earnings during the summer vacation: Juan worked in a summer hotel; Mateo got his initiation into American country life by joining an American student friend on his father's ranch; Pedro made a round of Christian student conferences and, in addition to having his expenses paid, made profitable use of an art acquired the previous winter—the art of hair-cutting. Juan, Mateo and Pedro wrote home glowing accounts of their experiences; they saw an America that amply fulfilled the expectations given them by their reading and by the American school teachers in their distant island home town. While the work in kitchen or garden was hard at times, they felt that they were learning all the time, and since many of their fellow students did similar work, it did not take them long to overcome whatever reluctance they may have brought with them from the conventions of their set to engage in manual labor. At college they were treated like other "foreigners."

According to the more Asiatic or Caucasian character of their appearance, Filipino students were vaguely classed by their fellow-students either with Orientals or with Latin Americans. But outside the more educated circles, they were not so readily accepted. A Y.M.C.A. student secretary at a state university in the Middle West states that he has difficulty in explaining to boarding-house landladies, when in search of rooms for Filipino students, that these are not "Japs." A Filipino in New York finds that because he often speaks Spanish with his friends, many people class him, though aware of his nationality, with Latin-Americans—sometimes wondering a little why a person coming from somewhere in the West Indies, as they think, should have partly Oriental features.

Only a small proportion of the Filipinos in America are college students, now. But many are enrolled in high schools and in evening classes; and a majority of the others, too, are probably under twenty-five years of age. Those Americans who have known Filipinos only in the eastern part of the country are sometimes puzzled to understand what the difficulties reported from the West are about. They have known Filipinos as students or as waiters in some restaurant; they may have admired the good appearance and bearing of Filipino sailors on leave—wondering, perhaps, when unfamiliar with the facts, how so many "foreigners" have come to be in our American Navy. In short, these Filipinos are always seen as individuals or in small groups, as foreign visitors. They are all young, well groomed, cheerful. It does not occur to people to regard them as "immigrants."

Even in circles acquainted with the existence of a "Filipino problem" on the Pacific Coast, great uncertainty often prevails as regards basic facts. In the very heart of the region where its discussion was hottest, the investigator was not infrequently, in the course of the present study, asked for information which might easily have been obtained from responsible local sources. There is a disposition, on the one hand, to share in the regret of having to "ward off yet another Oriental invasion," and on the other hand, to be cautious in the acceptance of rumors suspiciously similar to those current in the past concerning other immigrant peoples. The more thoughtful citizens are sensitive to the reputation of the Pacific Coast in other parts of the country for exaggerated fears and for race prejudice. Yet, they do not always feel themselves in the possession of facts that would explain the situation. Again, while the cooperation extended to the investigator is evidence of a widespread desire to have all these facts made known, there is also an understandable eagerness to have these facts seen by the rest of the country, as the Pacific Coast is obliged to see them, in the light of the lessons learned from previous uncontrolled waves of Oriental immigration.

In the West, as in the East, Filipino newcomers were not at first popularly recognized as the harbingers of an incipient mass migration. Better acquainted with the Orient and more alert because of past experiences, people on the Pacific Coast were from the start less ignorant of the geographical, racial and political background of these newcomers; and it took them less time to realize the rapid increase of their numbers and its meaning. Moreover, a larger variety of Filipino types could be observed in the West. While the great majority of people east of the Rockies have even now never seen a Filipino laborer in working clothes, those on the Pacific Coast could not help seeing him, and, what is more, with those characteristic insignia of the immigrant, the blanket bundle and the cheap suitcase. Again, a composite picture may help to illustrate typical experiences:

Narciso, José and Manuel did not share the good fortune of the earlier student group. The reader is invited to meet them as they arrive at the San Francisco pier, for, alas, a few months later they may have become changed in outlook by their experiences.

Narciso is the oldest of the trio. He has left a wife and two children at home, in a village of Southern Ilocos. This is not his first trip abroad, for he has worked for three years on a sugar plantation in Hawaii. In fact, his children were born there; and he has taken his family back to his home town to buy a piece of land adjoining his father's farm. Now the savings are all invested or spent. Narciso is ambitious for his children. He has seen that in Hawaii the children of laborers go to high school, and that it is easy to become an *illustrado,* a member of the upper class, even when you have no money to start with. He does not want his children to slave all their lives; but he does not want to go back to Hawaii either, for there "a man has no freedom," and he is still young and wants to see something of the world. After all, California is not so much farther, and he has heard that one can earn four dollars a day there—enough to support the family and to have something over, in two or three years, to send the children to high school and, maybe, to buy a larger farm.

José is his younger brother and is brought along to help in this purpose. But José, at the age of fifteen, has ideas of his own. It took no urging to make him come along; but his mind is on the pictures he has seen of the great cities of America and on the stories he has read of the country where all men are free and equal, where a poor peasant may be President, and where one can learn to fly. He has thought it out many a time: What his country needs most is an airplane service from island to island, to make it truly one nation. To José his dreams are more real than the sordid reality of the long steerage passage; and as his eye sweeps over the sky-line of San Francisco, his heart leaps with joy.

Manuel has a cousin in Stockton. He has had many letters calling him across the ocean to that center of Filipino life in America. At first his family would not hear of it. But the decision of their neighbor Narciso to try the great experiment was the clinching argument. The cousin in Stockton had sent fifty dollars toward the passage money, to be paid back out of Manuel's wages. But it was not money nor the advantage of his older neighbor's protection during the trip that had fired Manuel's ambition. Rather it was the letters and photographs passed around among the young fellows at home that had long persuaded him—letters telling of automobiles bought on the instalment plan, photographs of girls. The work of cutting asparagus was hard, it appeared; but it brought more money in a week than at home one could earn in two months. And then one could take long trips in the winter and spring to the South where work was more pleasant—and visit Hollywood on the way.

Here they are, then, students and workers, boys and men, all of them dependent on their own efforts, for the most part full of hope and ambition, accustomed to meet life's hardships as they come, trustful—perhaps a little childlike in their simplicity. Some of them speak fluent English as well as Spanish, others who have not had much schooling little of either tongue.

There can be no doubt that at first these young Filipinos, nearly all of them under thirty years of age, made a good impression. They were not, of course, particularly noticed so long as their number remained small but merged into the cosmopolitan sections of the communities to which they were attracted. The recentness of our national awakening to the presence of these immigrants in considerable numbers may be illustrated with the fact that prior to 1928 one cannot recall a single article on Filipino immigration in a popular periodical. None of the textbooks on immigration mention this group except in passing. The subject did not, before 1929, appear on the agenda of any national organization interested in immigration or in social welfare, although Filipino students occasionally functioned at conferences which present speakers of different nationalities with the aim of fostering international understanding or of promoting the cause of small and oppressed nationalities.

2. PUBLIC OPINION AND THE FILIPINO

The distribution of the Filipinos on the mainland of the United States is such as to invite not only erroneous estimates of their number but also a repute based on too limited an observation. Concentration along the Pacific Coast—with minor nuclei in some of the large cities of the East—has created apprehension which, in turn, affects the view of what kind of people these newcomers are. Where Filipinos are few and inconspicuous, we usually find them well liked; and favorable descriptions of their qualities find ready credence among those not directly acquainted with them. Where Filipinos arrive in droves and seem suddenly to be inundating the streets and public places, unfavorable reports concerning them are more apt to be believed; and this suspicion and dislike often contribute toward the development of attitudes and forms of behavior among the Filipinos, which give still further occasion for their disrepute.

Much of the disparaging opinion held of the Filipino on the Coast has admittedly been fostered by propaganda. The Filipino is going through a cycle of appreciation and criticism similar to that experienced by other alien groups; [1] and both the favorable and unfavorable attitudes toward him, as in their case, are related more to the waxing and waning of numbers and to the circumstances of his absorption by different types of community than to actual observation of conduct and correct estimation of character. Of this further evidence will be given below. But it may here be stated that if observers in New York, Detroit, or Minneapolis are often differently impressed by the Filipino from observers in Seattle, San Francisco or Los Angeles, the reason is that in the one case the observation has been of a small group of newcomers, with a relatively large proportion of students and other exceptional personalities, attractive often by their very strangeness and their obvious need for friendship and protection; in the other it has been of a group of newcomers, sufficiently numerous to find an engrossing social life among themselves, composed more largely of persons of average and even inferior qualities and, through their very number if for no other reason, creating problems and apprehension.

[1] Emory S. Bogardus, A Race-Relations Cycle. *American Journal of Sociology*, January, 1930, p. 612 *et seq.* A comprehensive study of Californian attitudes toward Filipinos is under way, at the time of writing, at Stanford University, under the direction of Professor Charles N. Reynolds.

Sometimes changes in public opinion are attributed to changes in the type of the Filipinos who have been coming to this country since the migration started. With the changes in the composition of the Filipino group that have taken place, largely as a result of the larger proportion of immigrants who have come to the mainland by way of Hawaii since 1924 and of the changed methods of selection by the Hawaiian sugar planters (see page 165), certain differences are observable in the newer as compared with the earlier Filipino immigration. First, as to its age composition, though no accurate records are available, there is reason to believe that the age level has slightly risen.[2] But an older and steadier type of immigrant does not necessarily make for greater appreciation of the group. Less attractive in appearance, often less educated or able to speak English, the immigrant who is recognizably of the laboring class may produce more apprehension where he appears in considerable numbers than the young immigrant student or adventurous youth. The effect of differences in cultural background on the reception of Filipinos in America was frequently commented upon in connection with the present inquiry.

Some fifty per cent of the Filipinos now in this country are Ilocanos, writes Albert Ernest Jenks, professor of Anthropology at the University of Minnesota (former Chief of the Bureau of Ethnological Survey for the Philippines). They are hard workers; and it may be found by experience that they are better agricultural laborers than Mexicans. They are educationally ambitious toward American standards. But it is quite a mistake to believe that a majority of them come from homes with western standards of civilization. They still in their homes squat on the floor for meals and sleep on mats. Even students coming from the rural sections of Luzon are too well aware of the cultural differences between their homes and the life they find here to contemplate taking American wives to the Philippines.

In contrast, a Filipino graduate student maintains that the Filipino immigrants are closer to American than to Oriental cultural habits, except in the matter of diet. But too many are brought into contact with the least desirable traits of American life, and thus their culture complex disintegrates. . . . Many of them become suspicious of American conduct toward them; and as they are made more conscious of themselves as a group, with increasing numbers, they hold themselves more aloof from other groups.

Speaking more particularly of the Filipino student, a student of that race majoring in philosophy writes: He finds himself face to face with new situations. His environment is entirely strange, and it takes time to adapt himself to the surroundings. . . . He may come from a quiet town in the Philippine

[2] See p. 23.

Islands and suddenly find himself thrust into a great city. He is [obliged] to change for the time being the Spanish-Filipino etiquette into which he was reared for the American manners. Yes, he has many things to forget and many to remember and absorb while he is far from home.

I have never been able, writes Dr. Albert W. C. T. Herre, of Stanford University, who has lived in the Philippines for many years and visited every part of the islands, to discover noticeable differences in native intelligence between Ilocano, Tagalog, Visayan, or other language groups, although of course there are people of every grade of intelligence within each group. One can find natives of high intelligence and force of character in every part of the Philippines. Like all other races, the Filipino varies with his environmental conditions. The Ilocanos make good workmen because many of them come from a barren region where overpopulation requires hard work for a living. It is not true that they are more largely Chinese than other Filipino groups; there is no part of any Malay coast where at some time Chinese blood has not filtered into the racial stock. A young Visayan boy of limited school attainments has for nine years acted as my field collector and preparator; in any part of the Malay islands and of China he was able to learn enough of the language of the natives for marketing and other immediate requirements, and in three months he would speak like a native. The charge that they have difficulty in mastering a foreign language has always been made against newcomers. Another Filipino boy whom I brought over to the United States has trained himself, at first without suggestion in his spare time, to become a remarkably accurate and artistic draughtsman and has illustrated many publications.

The following resolution, passed by the Central Labor Council of Seattle in March, 1929, is typical of others: "Whereas the C.L.C. has been informed upon what it regards as good authority that many if not all of the Filipinos who are coming into Seattle are former inhabitants of the island of Luzon, where for many generations past there has been going on a mixing of the most undesirable elements of the Mongolian race. . . ."

When they have a mixture of Chinese blood, says a state official, the Filipinos are intelligent; when they are chiefly Malayan they are difficult to teach anything. This official blames the sugar planters of Hawaii for having selected, and thereby flooded also the mainland coast with, Filipinos of the lowest mentality.

Like other Malays, says a well known physician who has treated many Filipino patients, they are poor in capacity for mental development and physically unadapted to our climate . . . Successful Filipinos nearly always have a large proportion of Chinese blood.

The impression that Filipinos with Chinese blood are preferable to mestizos with white blood, replies Dr. Herre, has a simple environmental explanation: The Chinese who went to the Philippine Islands were usually of the initiative type; they married into the best families, made good husbands, and brought up their children well. Often they accumulated wealth; and after a generation or two their offspring became *illustrados* [the wealthy and socially prominent ruling class]. On the other hand, the children of American and English fathers were usually children of a soldier or sailor father with no sense of responsibility for his offspring. Literally thousands of mestizo children of such parentage have been deserted by their fathers, and the American Guardian Association has had a fearful problem in trying to care for them. Most of such children never have a chance. On the other hand, some of the handsomest and most intelligent young men and women I have known were the offspring of a superior American father and a high class Filipina, who gave their children a fine physical and mental heritage, plus every advantage of home and education.

The great diversity of opinion as to what the Filipino immigrant's typical behavior traits are requires an explanation not only with different degrees of personal knowledge on the part of various speakers but also with their different experiences of contact with Filipinos. Interracial attitudes may be due largely to predispositions with which different individuals and groups approach the judgment of another group. Thus, persons who habitually speak of the Filipino as a "nigger" or as a "monkey" because of his difference in skin color or physical structure, may have a background of unfavorable experience with other racial groups or apply to the newcomers prejudices formed through other race relations.

Different forms of contact and of association are bound to produce different attitudes. Thus it is but natural that, generally speaking, predominantly Catholic immigrant groups—Italians in the East and Mexicans in the West [3]—have more rapidly come to a friendly understanding with the Filipinos than Protestant groups. The Mexicans, moreover, sharing with the newcomers a history of Spanish domination and likewise being partly of Spanish blood, more quickly fraternize with them, even though there are differences in their dialects and though they often are in direct competition, both social and economic.

Previous contacts also affect attitudes. As Filipinos have inherited the exposure to anti-Oriental prejudices on the Pacific Coast, they, in their turn, often bring with them from the Philippine Islands a hostile attitude toward the Chinese, engendered by competition, especially in the small trades of the islands.[4] More economically settled and socially established, the Chinese and Japanese on the Coast, on the other hand, are apt to look down upon the

[3] The short term "West" is used in this book to designate the states of the Far West, specifically the three coast states.

[4] See page 235 *et seq.*

Filipinos where these occupy the least desirable occupations and living quarters in the community.

In the Alaska salmon canneries, there is almost no social contact between Chinese and Japanese; but Filipinos and Hawaiians get on well with either group. In the cities of the Pacific Coast, Filipinos are criticized for being aggressive in seeking social contact with whites; in Hawaii the Porto Ricans are sometimes subjected to this criticism, which is never heard in respect of Filipinos. The explanation here is, obviously, a marked difference in opportunities of contact.

Two Filipinos interviewed had remarkably contrasting attitudes toward the American Indian: One who had met members of that race at the fish canneries in Alaska considered them "too dirty and low to associate with." The other, who had worked with Indians in a theatrical venture, admired them. Differences in contact also explain the diversity of the attitudes of Filipinos to white Americans generally, which vary from open admiration to suppressed hostility. Often a compromise between an appreciative disposition and resentment of unworthy or contemptible behavior on the part of Americans is effected by the assumption that those unable to win respect "are not real Americans but low-class immigrants."

Japanese are well disposed toward Filipinos where their own status is assured; that is, where they have a monopoly on the better paid jobs because of their larger experience and recognition on the part of the white community. They display a sense of antagonism where they are more directly in competition, and also at times where their own prestige, as Orientals, seems to be impaired by the incoming of numerous other "Orientals" with lower social status.

To conclude, the reputation of the Filipino immigrant is no more uniform than that of any other immigrant group.[5] At most it can be said that a group as diverse in its composition as the Filipino is likely to show a corresponding diversity in its adjustments to new experiences of environment, work and treatment. A Visayan col-

[5] As a contribution to the present study, Professor R. D. McKenzie, of the University of Washington, asked a class of thirty students to list what they considered to be characteristic behavior traits of Filipinos. There was no agreement on any one trait. Professor E. S. Bogardus, of the University of Southern California, through a case study of the experiences of ninety persons, representing a considerable range of occupations and ages, with Filipinos, found a similar diversity, indicating "that there are gradations of Filipinos just the same as there are different levels among the members of every other race." *Sociology and Social Research,* vol. XIV, No. 1, September-October, 1929, p. 59 *et seq.*

lege athlete will react in one way, a Tagalog school teacher in another, and an Ilocano farm laborer in a third.

It may further be concluded from experience that, generally speaking, the immigrant school-boy will make more rapid social adjustments, the older laborer more rapid occupational ones. But all such generalizations must be held to admit of many exceptions and of further revisions of judgment in time.[6]

[6] See p. 182.

CHAPTER II

CASES OF ACUTE CONFLICT

NATIONAL attention was focused on the presence in our midst of a new racial group by a series of incidents in the summer and fall of 1929, which illustrated its resentment by residents on the Pacific Coast. These incidents, widely reported and commented upon, gave the impression, at first, of an all but unanimous antagonism toward the Filipinos, accentuated in many instances by social disorder and physical violence. Actually only in few of these incidents had violence been used in attempts to dislodge Filipino workers.

Most important of these happenings, in 1929, were the troubles which disturbed the peace of the Wenatchee and Yakima valleys of the State of Washington and of the small town of Exeter in the San Joaquin Valley of California. In the eastern part of Washington, Filipinos are employed during the harvest season in the potato and beet fields and also, to a considerable extent, in picking and packing apples and cutting hops. In these last named forms of work they do not seem to have given especial satisfaction but to have been introduced only when there was a threatened shortage of labor or when they happened to present themselves locally among other applicants for work. Because of considerable opposition to their employment in the apple orchards on the part of both resident and migrant white workers experienced in preceding years, relatively few of them seem to have been employed by the apple growers in 1929. Yet the flame of indignation against them burst out anew.[1]

In Exeter, itinerant white American workers started a riot in the last week of October, 1929. From one hundred to three hundred

[1] Because of the difficulty of securing accurate information on the most recent events in these areas, the more fully reported incidents of the year before in Wenatchee are described in Appendix E, 2, as an illustration of anti-Filipino action with a purely economic motive. Another detailed account of this case, made to the President of the American Federation of Labor by C. O. Young, general organizer, will be found in the report on the Hearings before the Committee on Immigration and Naturalization of the U. S. House of Representatives, May 7, 1930, p. 181.

of them banded together and visited every ranch where Filipinos were employed, to demand their dismissal or, failing in this, to smash the Filipino laborers' automobiles and wreak their vengeance on the employer's property. An inquiry made later by officers of the state Industrial Commission revealed that the objectors to the Filipinos' presence in practically all cases had later refused to take on the jobs from which they had desired to see these foreigners expelled. Conflicting accounts are given of the immediate occasion for this conflict which had been brewing for some time: One has it that some Filipino boys, mistaking the playful teasing of an Italian truck driver for deliberate insult, threw stones at him; that other white workers were drawn in, and in the mêlée the truck driver was slightly wounded with a knife; and that, under an impression that his injury was more serious than it actually was, a general movement to drive out the Filipinos ensued. Another account has it that the quarrel started with resentment over a Filipino's behavior toward a white girl; and a third that there was jealousy over a Filipino's attentions to a Mexican girl. There is no doubt that the trouble which required intervention by the authorities was the culmination of many molestations of Filipinos on the streets of Exeter in the preceding weeks. The cause of the hostility was unquestionably economic. On the ranch first visited by the mob, Filipinos were employed in the harvesting of figs, a job held in previous years by white transient laborers. The extent of the disturbance became somewhat exaggerated as the news travelled. According to a local sheriff, one automobile was smashed and one barn partly burned, with a total damage of less than one hundred dollars.[2]

It was early in 1930 that new cases of violence were reported from different parts of the Pacific Coast. The most important of these was the riot in Watsonville, California, which has been studied in some detail and is described in Appendix E, 1.[3] Here resident youths rather than migrant workers were implicated, and economic rivalry merely formed a background for a conflict which arose from the attention of Filipinos to white girls and the introduction of other white girls into the community for their entertainment. A mild echo of this case came before the local police court in August, 1930, when two white workers, an Italian and a Slav,

[2] For a fuller account see Facts About Filipino Immigration to California, State of California Department of Industrial Relations, Special Bulletin No. 3, April, 1930, p. 73.

[3] See also Anti-Filipino Race Riots, a report made to the Ingram Institute of Social Science, of San Diego, by E. S. Bogardus, University of Southern California, May 15, 1930, which contains an extensive account of the events and an analysis of the causes.

were fined for chasing Filipinos through the streets, armed with jack handles. Incited, unquestionably, by the prominence which this case received in the press of the country because of the unfortunate accidental killing, in connection with it, of a Filipino youth, similar disturbances, but of a milder character, occurred immediately afterwards in a number of localities. In San Francisco toward the end of January, 1930, two cases of assault by individual or small groups of whites upon individual Filipinos remained isolated instances of unprovoked fury. In one of these cases, two Filipino youths, on escorting two white women home from a theater —one of these the wife of one of them—were set upon by half a dozen hooligans after others had taunted the girls for appearing in public with Filipinos. The Americans got away as the police appeared, and the two Filipinos were arrested for disturbing the peace. In San Jose, an American was arrested for advocating a campaign of blasting Filipino homes and meeting places with dynamite. In the same city, four Filipinos had been convicted earlier for stabbing a white man in the course of a street brawl following the Watsonville affair. At that time, windows of Filipino clubs were broken in Santa Barbara and other places.

In Emeryville, four men, believed to be Filipinos, alighted from an automobile and assaulted two white men who had been drinking; the Filipinos were unable to give an explanatory account of the affair. In Fresno, a youthful plot to beat up a group of local Filipinos was prevented from materializing. Near Portland, Oregon, a Filipino was found on the roadside suffering from many cuts and abrasions. He said he had been attacked by eight white men in an automobile with a California license plate after he had refused to tell them the whereabouts of certain other Filipinos.

As yet unexplained is the bombing of the club house of the Filipino Federation of America in Stockton, California, which took place a week after the Watsonville killing. Since the explosion, produced by a dynamite bomb thrown from a passing automobile under the porch of this wooden building, destroyed only the porch and part of the front wall, none of the forty occupants of the house was injured. (The police at first were inclined to ascribe this fact to foreknowledge on the part of some in the building.) The explosion occurred at midnight and was followed next day by a few isolated street fights between whites and Filipinos; but no rioting or serious disturbance of the peace took place. The chief of police and the head of the detective department of Stockton held an extremely unfavorable opinion of the local Filipinos and formed the hypothesis that the explosion was the result of animosity between rival Filipino factions. This theory was not shared by other American groups close to the Filipinos. No good evidence could be found of the illicit presence of white women on the club premises; on the contrary, the federation here as in other communities has taken a foremost part in attacking vice and in opposing any form of behavior that might give rise to criticism. Furthermore, the Filipinos of Stockton, of whom there may have been two or three thousand at that time of year, are only incidentally in direct competition with white men, since they have taken the place of other Orientals and, by their increasing numbers, have made possible a large extension of vegetable cropping in the near-by San Joaquin Delta. The local labor people, in fact, have no special quarrel with the Filipinos—in spite of their occasional incursions into urban occupations which are fought with the usual union tactics—and went on record after the dynamite outrage to express their sympathy. There were no Filipino dance halls or dance halls admitting Filipinos in the city.

Only a few days before the bombing, the local press had been congratulating the city that, because of the good feeling existing between natives and immigrants, nothing like the rioting in Watsonville could happen there. The local Cosmopolitan Club, organized largely through the efforts of Filipino and Japanese leaders, had just been holding a successful Filipino night which was reported in the local papers. And these had carried articles commenting on the large financial returns of the local potato growers from the previous season's yields and the excellent prospects for the coming season. The public did not need to be told of the part which different racial groups in the community are playing in this gratifying result of cooperation. But there was some unemployment among local white workers, and these very reports of prosperity may have angered them against the Filipinos—the more so since it was also reported in the press that, because of the existing ill-feeling in other parts of the state, more Filipinos were congregating in Stockton. This report was probably false, for no substantial exodus has been reported from the Salinas or Pajaro valleys, and the winter population of Stockton is always relatively large. The whole circumstances point to a plot by a small, acutely hostile group rather than widespread animosity, which would have made itself felt in other ways also.

Three other clashes in the winter 1929-1930 are worth mentioning because they involved conflict of Filipinos with other immigrants rather than with native Americans. One resulted from the secret marriage of a Filipino with a Japanese girl in Stockton. The young bride was secreted by the father, who unsuccessfully tried to have the marriage annulled, not, he said later, because of any race feeling against Filipinos but because he felt deeply outraged by a form of marriage so contrary to the honored traditions of his family. Unable to get redress, the young Filipino managed to secure the adherence of large numbers of local Filipinos to a boycott of the local Japanese stores; and in some cases slight damage was done to Japanese property. The difference was, however, soon adjusted by a joint committee formed to avert just such strife, and the case was taken to adjudication by the courts. At El Centro, in the Imperial Valley, twenty-five Mexicans were arrested on January 10, 1930, for having caused a disturbance of the peace in endeavoring to arouse their fellow-workers in the lettuce fields to strike in protest against the presence of Filipinos competing with them for employment. The Filipinos did not retaliate to the insults meted out to them. At La Verne, in Southern California, rivalry between Mexican and Filipino workers led to a street battle in the course of which a Mexican was stabbed and a Filipino knocked unconscious.[4] Prompt intervention by the police here prevented further disturbances.[5]

In May, 1930, anti-Filipino agitation again appeared in Washington—this time in the White River Valley, south of Seattle, where forty or fifty white farm laborers, displaced by Filipino workers in their jobs of packing peas and lettuce, raided camps where some two hundred Filipinos were housed, kidnapped some of them and forced others to flee, without their belongings, to the near-by hills. The complaint here was that the Filipinos, for some time employed at harvesting the vegetables for white and Japanese growers, were being employed to pack vegetables for shipment, an occupation previously given to white workers, cutting the wage from 60 to 25 cents an hour. Though these wage rates lack confirmation, the motive obviously was one of resented competition, and the incident is in line with those experienced earlier in the lettuce regions of California.

[4] See p. 149.

[5] In addition, there has been, early in March, 1930, a murder of a young Filipino, as yet unidentified, on the Pacheco Pass highway near Los Baños, Merced County, which may or may not have been the outcome of a race clash.

Other outbreaks involving clashes between Filipinos and white itinerant workers occurred in the Sonoma, Yuba, Butte, and Sutter counties of Northern California in July, 1930. In Sonoma County, a ranch was raided near Santa Rosa by a mob demanding the discharge of Filipino workers engaged in apple drying. The employer declared that the Filipinos were paid the same wage as white workers, namely, 40 cents an hour, and that they were preferred because "whites won't stick to the job." While the disorder was checked by a posse hastily organized by the sheriff, most of the Filipino workers left the neighborhood within the week. In the more northern counties, after several minor clashes, a "peace committee," composed of two influential merchants and two white workers, endeavored to prevent serious disturbances by calling upon peach and apple growers who, it was rumored, were planning to employ Filipino packers. In Marysville, Butte, where thousands of orchard workers had congregated for the fruit-picking season, the authorities prohibited them from holding public meetings lest racial feeling be aroused; and from the apple country around Sebastopol a steady exodus of Filipino workers was reported at the end of July. At Dinuba, Fresno County, dynamite was thrown into a Filipino camp, fortunately without injury to life. In San Bernardino County, a Filipino, forbidden by a Caucasian mother to pay court to her fifteen-year-old daughter, slashed the daughter on face and body, disfiguring her for life, and barely escaped lynching.

In the Santa Clara Valley, the demand for Filipino exclusion became an important issue in the campaign for Congressional elections, in the summer of 1930. There were a few minor outbreaks of anti-Filipino feeling, and just before the pear harvest started, all the pear growers in a certain section of the valley were warned not to employ Filipinos or their trees would be destroyed. Similar warnings were also received by a large cannery in Sunnyvale. They had the desired effect, in some cases with considerable annoyance and loss for the contractors. Since, as in all such instances, the Filipino workers avoided trouble by moving off to regions where they expected a better welcome, other employers in the valley found it difficult to secure men to work for them.

In Salinas, there was a strike in September, 1930, stimulated, it is reported, by white workers, when local employers cut wages from 40 to 35 cents; this lasted a few days, and minor clashes occurred. On September 8, a Filipino was nearly beaten to death by eight whites before he was rescued by an American rancher's wife. Some eight hundred Filipino workers, from twenty-six camps, left the valley, and the growers who had made the reduction found it necessary to recruit labor from other parts of the state. The striking Filipinos did not, apparently, submit to the reduction, and the most recent news indicates that the wage rate of 40 cents was to be re-established. The striking Filipinos stressed the point that only by insisting on the traditional wage rate could they escape the violent opposition to their presence on the part of white workers.

On August 20, 1930, a serious clash was anticipated in Alta Loma where a young Filipino fruit picker, repulsed by a young American girl whom he desired to marry, broke into her parents' home and attacked her with a knife. He was subsequently apprehended and confessed to the crime. Owing to immediate steps taken by the local fruit growers to dismiss all their Filipino workers or transfer them to other areas, and the willingness of these workers to comply with the local sentiment, an incipient riot was prevented.

In the summer of 1930, anti-Filipino demonstrations were for the first time reported from more eastern states; one such outbreak occurred at Blackfoot, Idaho, and one in Utah. The year ended, as it had begun, with a serious incident in California, in the course of which a human life was lost: In spite of special vigilance on the part of the authorities to prevent itinerant agitators from stirring up antagonism between Americans, Mexicans, and Filipinos competing for jobs in the fruit- and lettuce-growing section of the Imperial Valley, racial feeling had been tense for some weeks when, on December 8, a Filipino rooming house at Imperial was bombed and one of its inmates killed. About sixty persons slept in the building, a converted stable, when the bomb was thrown from a speeding automobile. Three of the Filipino roomers were injured in addition to the one killed. Within a day, the police arrested an American as a suspect.

These various clashes point, of course, to the existence of tension which, if not relieved, must be expected to lead to other unfortunate incidents. And they indicate the presence of a variety of motives of antagonism which it will be necessary to examine in the course of the present inquiry. The causes of overt clashes are not always reported with sufficient detail to make possible a classification with reference to the major antecedent factors. But in most of them both economic and social motives seem to be present. V. S. McClatchy points out, in a letter to the author:

Mexicans offer in economic competition a very much more serious menace than do Filipinos; but there have been no such acts of violence on the part of whites against Mexicans—the reason being that the Mexicans do not offer similar provocation. . . . I venture to say that no act of extreme violence against Filipinos on the Coast [has taken place] but will be found to have had as its provoking cause the attitude of Filipinos and their acts against local white girls.[6]

Professor R. D. McKenzie, of the University of Washington, points out that the major clashes between Americans and Filipinos have, nearly all of them, taken place in villages and the smaller towns. This circumstance supports the theory that the city affords a more favorable communal setting for interracial symbiosis.[7] As earlier in the case of the Japanese,[8] so now in that of the Filipinos, a wide distribution provides more points of comparison and friction between individuals. Moreover, stereotypes have a larger hold on small communities,[9] and segregation carries with it larger social consequences.[10]

It should be added here that, with few exceptions, the citizens of California and of other Pacific Coast states and the leading newspapers have expressed their strong disapproval of mob violence in all these cases. Governor Young, of California, appealed to by numerous organizations to take exceptional measures to prevent such occurrences, promised the appointment of a commission of inquiry—for which later an inquiry by the State Department of Industrial Relations was substituted—at the same time vigorously denouncing those responsible for these disorders. Other law officers, including Attorney General U. S. Webb, while condemning these evidences of lawlessness, consider them inevitable under the circumstances and likely to recur—even on a larger scale.

[6] This cause of antagonism is further discussed below, p. 92 *et seq.*

[7] *Symbiosis* is the term commonly used by biologists to designate the living together of different species, irrespective of the nature of their relationship which may "range from mere contiguity of domicile to an actual fusion, involving the vital dependence or parasitism of a colony of one species on that of another." The term has been found useful by sociologists to designate the totality of group relations that make up a society, ranging from associations of mutual dependence to "accidental groupings formed of elements more or less specifically unlike, which convenience unites and not necessity." Robert E. Park and Ernest W. Burgess, Introduction to the Science of Sociology. University of Chicago Press, 1921, p. 167 *et seq.*

[8] R. D. McKenzie, The Oriental Invasion. *Journal of Applied Sociology,* vol. X, No. 2, November-December, 1925, pp. 127-128.

[9] John Moffatt Mecklin, The Ku Klux Klan, Harcourt, Brace & Co., 1924, p. 116 *et seq.*

[10] Jesse Frederick Steiner, The American Community in Action. Henry Holt & Co., 1928, p. 16.

CHAPTER III

THE MAIN FACTS OF FILIPINO MIGRATION TO THE MAINLAND OF THE UNITED STATES

I. NUMBER AND DISTRIBUTION

UNTIL the findings of the United States Census for 1930 are available, detailed statistics concerning the number, age and sex, occupations and distribution of Filipinos on the mainland of the United States cannot be given except on the basis of estimates that contain many elements of uncertainty. The census of 1920 enumerated 5,603 persons of that nationality on the mainland of the United States. Today there are about 56,000.[1] These are largely concentrated on the Pacific Coast. In the absence of sources of accurate information for practically the whole period of Filipino immigration since it began to exceed annual accessions in three figures, the estimate of the present Filipino population of this country just given is admittedly tentative.[2] Nor are there reliable estimates of the number of Filipinos in specific communities and regions. The reason for this is the exceptionally mobile character of the Filipino population.[3] Because of the unusual seasonal flow of Filipino labor, the trend of error in local estimates is probably in the direction of overstatement of numbers.

[1] See Appendix A, p. 347.

[2] Estimates of the number of Filipinos on the mainland of the United States collected in the course of the present study vary from 25,000 (that of a Filipino organization) to 80,000 (Seattle Central Labor Council and other exclusionists).

[3] For example, with a summer population of only a few hundred, Seattle in winter harbors around 3,500 Filipinos (one informant says 10,000). In Portland, the variation probably is between 350 and 700 (one informant says between 200 and 900). The further south one gets, the less unanimous become the local estimates because there is not even the basis of a more or less steady winter population, with opportunities of farm work hardly ceasing even in the heart of winter. Moreover, there is some confusion in such estimates between the city proper and the city with its surrounding region, with the result that for San Francisco (and Bay Region) estimates vary from 2,500 to 20,000, and for Los Angeles (city and county) from 3,000 to 6,000. In Stockton, the variation between summer and winter population accounts for estimates of Filipino population ranging from 1,000 as a minimum to 6,000 at the height of the asparagus season.

The unfortunate circumstance, says a Seattle paper, is that they [the Filipinos] tend to congregate at certain times of the year, enough to make it appear that there are more of them than their actual number.[4]

The estimate of 56,000 given above as the probable total number of Filipinos on the mainland of the United States is based on a study of the number of Filipinos migrating from the Philippine Islands to the United States between 1920 and 1929—producing a net increase of 48,480 of arrivals over departures from the mainland, to which is added the Filipino population of continental United States as revealed by the Census of 1920—5,603—and a rough estimate of 2,000 for the excess of arrivals from other foreign ports over departures to them. No data are available to estimate the probable balance between growth of the Filipino population on the mainland by birth and its decrease by death; but the age statistics collected for Filipino arrivals in California from 1920 to 1929 and the small proportion of woman immigrants make it probable that there is a small excess of deaths over births—possibly amounting to as much as 2,000.[5]

The estimate here given coincides with those made by other students of the subject, for example those of the Bureau of Insular Affairs[6] and of V. S. McClatchy, secretary of the California Joint Immigration Committee.[7] In this connection it is worth noting that labor spokesmen for Filipino exclusion have, in the spring of 1930, adopted a similar estimate after previously quoting much higher figures. Professor E. S. Bogardus, of the University of Southern California, in a study made in the early part of 1929, found an estimate of 60,000 for continental United States "conservative."[8]

In 1930, according to such reports as are available at the time of writing, there seems to have been a clear reflection of the prevailing economic depression in continental United States in the ratio between arrivals from and departures to the Philippines. While there is some discrepancy between various estimates advanced, the net increase of the Filipino population on the mainland of the United

[4] *Seattle Star,* January 4, 1929.
[5] See below, p. 23.
[6] Hearings on H.R. 8708 before the House Committee on Immigration and Naturalization, April 11, 1930, pp. 89, 123-124.
[7] *Ibid.,* April 10, 1930, p. 39.
[8] *Sociology and Social Research,* May-June, 1929, p. 475.

States from excess of immigration over emigration, appears to have been certainly less than 5,000 and possibly less than 4,000.[9]

2. SEX AND AGE COMPOSITION

Of the Filipinos now on the mainland of the United States, more than nine-tenths are males.[10] The proportion of female to male immigrants has steadily declined since 1922.[11] This decrease, as will be seen below, parallels a decrease in the proportion of Filipinos who have come to the mainland of the United States from Hawaii as compared with those embarked direct at Manila.

Of the Filipinos now on the mainland of the United States, the large majority are under thirty years of age.[12] The age composition of Filipinos on the mainland is gradually rising with the cumulative increase of arrivals over departures. There is also an impression that the age composition of immigrant Filipinos has risen with the larger proportion of those who come to the mainland for vocational rather than educational purposes. The following table for a typical group of Filipino steerage passengers arrived directly from the Philippine Islands shows that over one-half of the group are still under twenty-five years of age and one-quarter of them under twenty:

AGES AND PROVINCES OF ORIGIN OF FILIPINO STEERAGE PASSENGERS SAILING FROM MANILA FOR SEATTLE ON "S.S. PRESIDENT TAFT," JANUARY 16, 1930[13]

Province of Origin	*Number*	*Average Age*
Batangas	5	27
Bohol	31	25

[9] See testimony of Senator Hiram Bingham, of Connecticut, of Brigadier General Francis LeJ. Parker, Chief of the Bureau of Insular Affairs, U. S. War Department, and R. D. Mead, Vice President of the Hawaiian Sugar Planters' Association, before the Senate Committee on Immigration, on the proposal to suspend general immigration into the United States for two years. Hearings on S. J. Resolution 207, December 15-18, 1930, pp. 5, 8, 94, 99, 100.

[10] Of 31,092 Filipinos admitted through San Francisco and Los Angeles in the ten years 1920-1929, 29,013, or 93.3 per cent, were males, and 2,079, or 6.7 per cent, females. (Facts About Filipino Immigration into California. State of California Department of Industrial Relations, Special Bulletin No. 3, April, 1930, p. 32.)

[11] From 13.9 per cent in that year to 3.2 per cent in 1929 for those admitted through the two California ports. (*Ibid.*, p. 33.)

[12] Of 24,123 Filipinos, male and female, admitted through the two California ports in the five years 1925-1929, over four-fifths were under 30 years of age: 4.9 per cent were under 16, 32.5 per cent between 16 and 21 years, 46.9 per cent between 22 and 29 years, 11.8 per cent between 30 and 37 years, 2.9 per cent between 38 and 44 years, 1 per cent 45 years and over. (*Ibid.*, p. 38.)

[13] From the ship's manifest.

Province of Origin	*Number*	*Average Age*
Bulacan	4	23
Cagayan	2	22
Capiz	14	27
Cavite	1	18
Cebu	8	26
Ilocos Norte	10	22
Ilocos Sur	114	25
Iloilo	3	19
Isabela	2	23
Laguna	1	22
La Union	117	26
Leyte	2	32
Manila	1	19
Marinduque	1	24
Misamis	1	24
Nueva Ecija	2	19
Occidental Negros	2	24
Pangasinan	12	24
Rizal	6	26
Tarlac	2	27
Zambales	1	28
Unspecified	2	31
Total	344	25

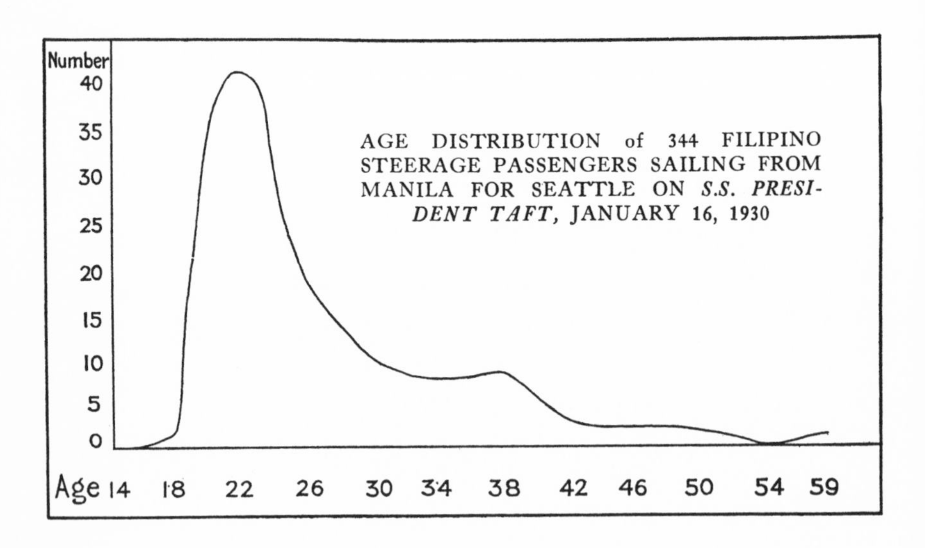

AGE DISTRIBUTION of 344 FILIPINO STEERAGE PASSENGERS SAILING FROM MANILA FOR SEATTLE ON *S.S. PRESIDENT TAFT,* JANUARY 16, 1930

It is safe to conjecture that the great majority of the female immigrants are dependents of men who come to the mainland with their families.[14]

A large majority of both male and female Filipinos in this country are unmarried. One out of every five of the Filipino immigrants coming to California in the five years 1925 to 1929 was married; the ratio of married Filipino women to married Filipino men among the arrivals was only one to every nine.[15]

3. POINTS OF ORIGIN

Among the earlier arrivals, an appreciable proportion—at first the great majority—were students who came to the mainland directly from the Philippine Islands to complete their training for professional careers, many of them with fellowships of the government, *pensionados,* and with the expectation of entering the government service. But at the end of the World War a different type commenced to appear on the mainland. These were men who had been enlisted in Manila for service in the Navy—the total of these recruits is estimated as about 25,000[16]—and managed to secure their discharge in continental ports, some of them taking service in the Navy yards and others finding their way into a considerable variety of occupations. Many of those who had served—and who have since served—in the Navy also have found employment in the mercantile marine.[17] In the first four years of the decade 1920-1929 there was a gradual increase in the proportion of Filipino migrants to the mainland of the United States who embarked in Hawaii; between 1925 and 1928 this proportion rapidly decreased in spite of an increase in the total number of Filipino arrivals at Pacific Coast ports.[18] The proportion of Filipinos now on the mainland of the United States who have come here by way of Hawaii is about one-fourth.[19]

While no figures are available showing the provincial origins of Filipino migrants to the mainland, there is reason to believe that

[14] Of female Filipino arrivals at the two California ports in the five years 1925-1929, 35.3 per cent were under 16 and 21.9 per cent between 16 and 21 years of age. (Facts About Filipino Immigration to California, p. 38.)

[15] *Ibid.*, p. 43.

[16] Statement of Brig. Gen. F. LeJ. Parker, Chief of the Bureau of Insular Affairs, before the House Committee on Immigration and Naturalization, Hearings on H.R. 8708, April 11, 1930, p. 88. See also below, p. 61.

[17] See below, p. 58 *et seq.*

[18] Facts About Filipino Immigration into California, p. 24.

[19] See Appendix A, p. 348.

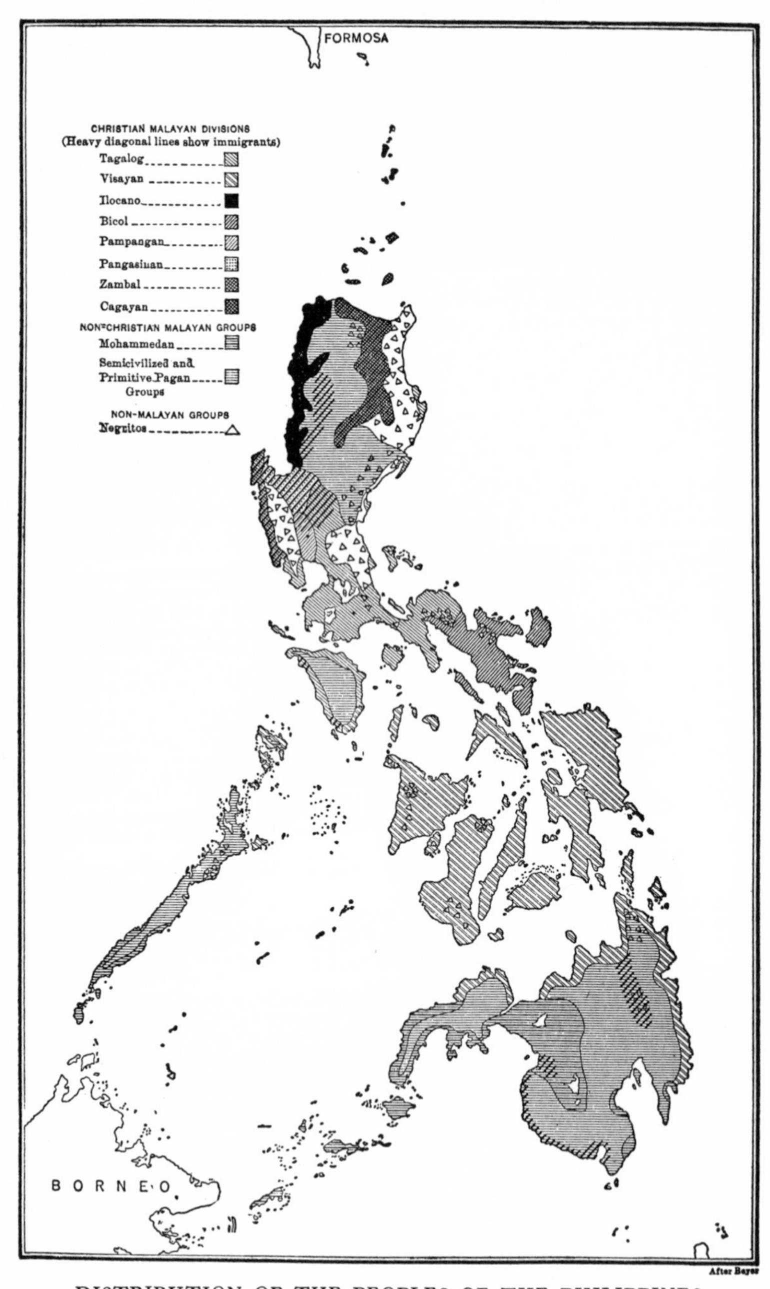

DISTRIBUTION OF THE PEOPLES OF THE PHILIPPINES

Through the courtesy of Ginn & Co., from Intermediate Geography by Hugo H. Miller and Mary E. Polley

at first the great majority were Tagalogs, with a sprinkling of Visayans, but that in later years, as the movement was transmitted from the student to the laboring class, Ilocanos have become predominant in the composition of the newcomers. The proportion of Hawaiian-born Filipinos in the total number of arrivals on the mainland has remained small for the male immigrants but is surprisingly large, about two-thirds, for the female immigrants,[20] indicating that the proportion of married men accompanied by dependents is much larger among Filipino migrants to the Pacific Coast coming from Hawaii than among those coming directly from the Philippine Islands.

[20] Facts About Filipino Immigration into California, pp. 29 and 33.

CHAPTER IV

THE MAIN FACTS OF FILIPINO IMMIGRATION TO HAWAII

1. THE ETHNIC SETTING

WE have already commented on the part played by Hawaii in the migration of Filipinos to the mainland of the United States. (See p. 23.) But that is not the aspect of our subject which is of major consequence to Hawaii itself. Indeed, it is chiefly because of their reaction upon its own labor conditions that Hawaii is intensely interested in the problems of the mainland occasioned by Filipino migration. With a population of 368,336 as against a total for our three coastal states of seven million, Hawaii has a larger immediate concern in large-scale immigration.

Its native population does not suffice to carry on the gigantic enterprise which it set going half a century ago. As its production of sugar is the outstanding economic fact in Hawaii, so its racially mixed population, the result of half a century of foreign recruitment of plantation labor, is the outstanding social fact. The capitalist group itself has evolved from intermarriages among American, English and German pioneers. Germans, Scotsmen, Scandinavians and Russians were among the first plantation workers—recruited often without knowing anything of the hardships that awaited them. (Many of their children still are on the plantations as overseers or technicians and in other positions of importance.) After them came Spaniards and Portuguese, again rapidly followed, as the sugar industry grew, by thousands of Chinese.

When Hawaii was annexed to the United States, in 1898, there were in the territory 25,654 Japanese and 5,969 Chinese. The Chinese exclusion law, which took effect in 1900, had little effect on the labor situation; but the Gentlemen's Agreement with Japan, in 1907, forced the sugar planters of the islands to look for a new supply of labor. From that time on, the population of the Hawaiian Islands was diffused through further experiments with the employment of different racial groups. As many of these contract workers subsequently settled on the Hawaiian Islands, these now have one of the most remarkably mixed populations to be found anywhere in the world. For, the more successful of these groups, even when they have in large number returned to their home countries or extended their migration to the mainland of the United States, have deposited a residuum of prosperous and progressive people who have entered into the general life of the island communities, and in addition to their continued association with their main agricultural industries, also engage in many other types of business and industry. The children of these earlier comers, Chinese, Japanese, Portuguese, Korean, with lesser contingents of Porto Ricans and Malaysians, now form a large and constantly increasing part of the American-born population, educated in the best public schools which American enterprise has been able to devise, and brought up, generally, under American standards of life.

This native-born population, including of course also the Hawaiians themselves, now largely intermarried with both Caucasian and Asiatic immigrants, only rarely are content with the status of laborer on a plantation under a semi-industrial form of management. They largely make up the ranks of foremen and of the skilled and semi-skilled operators who handle farm machinery, run the transportation system and perform the skilled work in the mills. But the common labor, traditionally performed by immigrants, still is almost exclusively in immigrant hands.

Since the Gentlemen's Agreement with Japan,[1] the only two large potential reservoirs of labor were Porto Rico and the Philippine Islands: Because they were under the American flag, these countries seemed free from the danger of being suddenly closed by restrictive immigration laws. Porto Ricans had been introduced in considerable numbers about 1901, but their influx did not again assume a large volume until about 1922. Filipinos, at first tentatively introduced in 1907, soon came to be looked upon as the most available of all potential labor supplies.

According to the latest estimate, for 1929, the racial distribution of the territory's population is as follows:[2]

Racial Ancestry	*Amer. Citizens*	*Aliens*	*Total*
American, British, German, Russian	37,165	841	38,006

[1] See below, p. 162, note 7.
[2] Annual Report of the Governor of Hawaii for the year ended June 30, 1929, p. 46.

Racial Ancestry	*Amer. Citizens*	*Aliens*	*Total*
Hawaiian	20,479	—	20,479
Asiatic-Hawaiian	10,598	—	10,598
Caucasian-Hawaiian	16,687	—	16,687
Portuguese	26,933	2,784	29,717
Porto Rican	6,923	—	6,923
Spanish	1,217	634	1,851
Japanese	87,748	49,659	137,407
Chinese	15,625	9,586	25,211
Filipino	9,176	54,693	63,869
Korean	3,643	2,750	6,393
All others	383	125	508
Total	236,577	121,072	357,649

The Porto Rican, it will be seen, has remained a small factor, taking the territorial population as a whole; the Filipino has risen to the position of the second largest group. The rapidity with which this influx took place, after the first few experimental years, will be seen as we compare the proportion of each racial group in the total population in 1920 and in 1929:

PERCENTAGE OF DIFFERENT RACIAL GROUPS IN THE TOTAL POPULATION OF HAWAII

Racial Ancestry	*1920*	*1929* *
American, British, German, Russian	7.8	10.6
Hawaiian	9.3	5.7
Asiatic-Hawaiian	2.7	3.0
Caucasian-Hawaiian	4.3	4.7
Portuguese	10.6	8.3
Porto Rican	2.2	2.0
Spanish	1.0	0.6
Japanese	42.7	38.5
Chinese	9.2	7.0
Filipino	8.2	18.0
Korean	1.9	1.5
All others	0.1	0.1

* Based on table of estimated population in Annual Report of the Governor of Hawaii for the year ended June 30, 1929, p. 46.

As will be seen, there has been in these ten years a relative decrease in the proportion of all groups except the Caucasians and the Filipinos. None of the changes have been striking except the marked decrease in the proportion, already small in 1920, of pure Hawaiians and the relative increase of the Filipinos by more than one-half.

2. THE INTRODUCTION OF FILIPINO PLANTATION WORKERS

The actual increase in the number of Filipinos in the territory has been computed by Professor Romanzo Adams, of the University of Hawaii, by a critical analysis of the principal source, namely the steerage passenger lists of arrivals and departures.[3] Dividing the movement of Filipino immigration into three periods, corresponding to the effects of different immigration policies, he arrives at the following net gains of Filipino population:

	*1907-1919** *12½ years*	*1920-1924* *5 years*	*1925-1929* *5 years*	*Total* *22½ years*
Net Gain from Philippines . .	24,113	21,049	26,432	71,594
Net Loss to Continental U.S.A.	2,335	3,571	9,097	15,003
Total Net Gain for Hawaii .	21,778	17,478	17,335	56,591

* Filipino immigration may be said to have started with the introduction of about 200 laborers in 1906-07 by the sugar planters.

A glance at Professor Adams' detailed tables shows an uneven increase in the number of Filipino arrivals during the first period.[4] In the second period, a notable rise in 1922 marked a labor shortage produced by industrial developments in the territory which had drawn considerable numbers of former plantation workers into other pursuits.[5] There had been a strike of Japanese in 1920, as a result of which the planters employed only 16,992 persons of that nationality in 1922, as compared with 24,791 in 1919. In 1923 and 1924, a labor shortage in California further drew upon the labor force of the Hawaiian plantations. This led to the large increase of Filipino migration to Hawaii at the beginning of the third period, in 1925, a movement slightly accentuated by the plan-

[3] See Appendix B, p. 350.

[4] The figure for 1911, however, is for six months only.

[5] Congressional relief was sought for this situation through measures designed to permit bringing alien labor to Hawaii under temporary arrangements. See Senate Joint Resolution 82, 1921, and House J. R. 158 and 171, 67th Congress, and relevant Hearings before the House and Senate Committees on Immigration.

tation strike of 1924.[6] From that time on the figures remain high, but with marked variations. The tables also show that the annual movement of Filipinos from Hawaii to the mainland of the United States remained under one thousand and, in fact, only once reached 500, until 1923 and 1924, when it was stimulated by a strike in the sugar plantations. It reached its highest point in 1926 and 1927—partly through artificial stimulation by Filipino labor organizations. The discrepancy between the final figure thus arrived at for the number of Filipinos by Professor Adams and that computed by the Bureau of Vital Statistics of the Board of Health is in part explained by arrivals other than by steerage, by the presence in Hawaii of Filipinos before 1907, and by Professor Adams' inclusion of some Filipinos who sailed from Hongkong. There are also probably small errors to account for differences. But the two estimates sufficiently confirm each other for all practical purposes. It is sufficient to recognize that the Filipinos now form the second largest racial group in the Hawaiian population, not excluding the Caucasian groups put all together, and that there are probably more of them in Hawaii today than on the mainland of the United States.[7]

[6] The delay in securing Filipinos was due to lack of steamship service—the disruption due to the war not yet having been made good.

[7] The sudden increase in the arrival of Filipino women in 1923 marks a change in policy on the part of the planters. A larger proportion of married workers was expected to have a steadying influence. Later the arrival of women decreased because plantation workers found it more economical to support their families at home. For this reason the birth rate of Filipinos (in proportion to total Filipino population) in Hawaii has been decreasing from 40.61 in 1924 to 22.77 in 1929.

CHAPTER V

THE DEMAND FOR EXCLUSION

THE demand for the exclusion of Filipinos from the mainland of the United States, which has given occasion to the present study, is part of a larger movement to restrict immigration and, especially, to prevent the infiltration of non-Caucasian races into the blood stream of the population of the United States. It is significant that several of the spokesmen of organizations desiring to go on record before the House Committee on Immigration and Naturalization as in favor of Filipino exclusion admitted that they had not been especially instructed what stand to take on this measure, but that their general instructions on all legislation concerning immigration covered this case.[1] Moreover, a large number of organizations, affiliated with the American Coalition, a group organized with headquarters in Washington, D. C., to promote restrictive immigration legislation, are taking joint action on a variety of legislative proposals without, apparently, referring each separate proposal back to the constituent bodies for the instruction of delegates. These patriotic and fraternal societies, united for the most part through cooperation in past campaigns, know that essentially their policies are represented, and are satisfied to leave the formulation of programs and methods to an advisory board. The impetus behind the exclusion proposal, then, is decidedly national and not limited to any section of the country. It is important to keep this fact in mind because, with the experience of this particular problem in one part of the country—the Pacific Coast—and with a discussion of the problem naturally somewhat colored by the resulting special interest in that section, the erroneous impression may easily gain ground that the demand for Filipino exclusion is localized.

As a matter of fact, there have in recent years been two nuclei of sentiment for restrictive immigration legislation, the Pacific Coast and New England. Both have succeeded in influencing public

[1] Hearings on H.R. 8708 before the House Committee on Immigration and Naturalization, April, 1930.

opinion to such an extent that at present, while each section has its distinctive problems, the support for the restriction movement generally—as represented by the patriotic bodies and by organized labor—has become national in extent and supports with equal unity restrictive legislative proposals facing toward Europe and those facing toward the Orient. On the other hand, there is practically no national organization consistently working for a liberalization of our immigration statutes. While on certain matters affecting the interests of alien residents—such as the alien registration bills—many organizations representing the interests of specific national groups may be acting in harmony, it is not the avowed object of any national organization to work for a lifting of bars to immigration generally or for the admission of racial or national groups not already powerfully represented in our population. Industrial interests, considering themselves in need of alien labor, are not at present pushing their claims against the rising tide of exclusionist sentiment.

So much for the general situation. The demand for Filipino exclusion specifically was first raised in the state with the largest Filipino population, California, and by that group which is most directly affected by this immigration, organized labor. The bill first introduced in May, 1928, by Congressman Richard J. Welsh, of California (H.R. 13,900), was in conformity with the demands, primarily, of his labor constituents. Under the vigorous leadership of the secretary-treasurer of the California State Federation of Labor, Paul Scharrenberg, other groups in that state and organized labor in the neighboring Pacific Coast states, Oregon and Washington, were brought into line behind this proposal. The same forces that had worked for the exclusion of the Japanese soon became active for that of the Filipinos. In the meantime, the California Joint Immigration Committee, the chief embodiment of this cooperative effort, under the direction of its secretary, V. S. McClatchy, had joined forces with that larger national body, the American Coalition, with a program aiming at "restriction of immigration into the United States whereby racial and political solidarity may be accomplished with the least delay." Among the officers of the Coalition are such well-known restrictionists as Captain John B. Trevor, Mrs. A. J. Brosseau, and Fred R. Marvin. With a program directed toward the strengthening and enlargement of all legal provisions and administrative machinery for restricting immigration, the Coalition is most concerned at the present time in the exclusion of those groups which it considers least assimilable or least desirable as additions to the racial composition of the United States population. It is for this reason rather than for any special interest in the West and Southwest that the immediate activities of the organizations are focussed on measures for the exclusion of Mexicans and of Filipinos—the two ethnic groups which, not being under the quota law, are for the present producing the largest "menace" of unlimited immigration of groups racially distinct from the predominant Caucasian stock.

While the interest of organized labor in restrictive immigration legislation on economic grounds is easily understandable, this major motive becomes somewhat confused when labor spokesmen join with those of other restrictionist groups in basing their demands on the "unassimilability" of specific foreign peoples, including the Filipinos. It is sometimes difficult to discern from the arguments advanced whether what is meant is only the legal prohibition of race fusion in certain western states or biological or cultural inability to assimilate with the predominant Caucasian majority. So far as cultural assimilation is concerned, the statement that they are unassimilable is made as strongly concerning the Filipinos as it was made concerning the Chinese and the Japanese who formed strongly organized foreign bodies within the American communities in which they settled.[2] As to biological assimilation, no proof has ever been advanced that the unions between Americans and Orientals, or between Caucasians and Mongolians or Malays are sterile, or that their offspring is physically or mentally inferior to the parent stocks. What is true is that racial mixture introduces a new diversity of types with larger opportunities for the survival of characteristics which previously were infrequent and, consequently, a change, eventually, of the predominant racial character.[3]

As a matter of fact, there has not, in the discussion of Filipino

[2] See further below, p. 331. It is worth noting that failure to assimilate is quite as often charged against Caucasian immigrant groups as against non-Caucasians. It is observed whenever for one reason or another members of the dominant group feel dissatisfied with the behavior or the presence of a minority, whether it be composed of Italian laborers at a time of widespread unemployment, or of Germans during a war in which sympathies were with her enemies. See Henry Pratt Fairchild, Immigration. Macmillan Co., 1925, chapter XVIII.

[3] Anthropological opinion today emphasizes the environmental circumstances under which race fusion usually takes place and which nearly always place the mixed stock at a considerable disadvantage. Nevertheless, the opinion prevails that, considering the necessity of adaptation to conditions controlled by the dominant race, the results of interbreeding, especially between members of the Caucasian and Mongoloid stocks, are decidedly dysgenic. See Charles B. Davenport, The Mingling of Races; Human Biology and Racial Welfare, edited by E. V. Cowdry. Paul B. Hoeber, 1930, chap.

immigration, so far been evident an effort to appraise, by reference to the results of experience with similar race mixtures in the past, the biological contribution which, if that movement were to lead to settlement and intermarriage, it would make to the stock of our population. The assertion of non-assimilability is made usually not in the factual meaning of that term but merely as implying that assimilation would be undesirable as interfering with the perpetuation of the dominant race with its present characteristics. Implied in this attitude is a strong preference for the preservation of the Caucasian race *on this continent,* but not necessarily a sense of Caucasian superiority as measured by ideal standards. Indeed, spokesmen for the exclusion of non-Caucasian races frequently state that they claim no superiority for Caucasians but consider the colored races superior in certain matters. But, to quote Mr. McClatchy:

> There is a basic racial or biological difference which does not permit of assimilation or absorption of one race by the other, and therefore the presence in either country of large groups of the other race must create friction and possible international difficulty. The fault in such cases lies with neither race. The usual dislike of one race for another, frequently assumed to be purely a matter of prejudice, is perhaps really a wise provision of Nature, acting as a safeguard against miscegenation.

With that view public opinion has been widely impregnated in recent years; and contrary or critical attitudes toward that view are popularly looked upon as unpatriotic.

Against this background of general suspicion of the Filipino as an Oriental immigrant endangering the economic status of the workers, the cultural traditions of the country, and the character of its people, other distinct apprehensions have developed to strengthen the demand for exclusion. These will be further discussed below. At this point it is only necessary to note that the issues of disease, crime, immorality, and so on, are secondary as regards the place they occupy in the movement for exclusion. This is recognized by those exclusionists who make ineligibility to citizenship rather than any specific trait of the Filipino people the main

XXIII. S. J. Holmes, The Trend of the Race. Harcourt, Brace & Co., 1921, p. 247 *et seq.* R. Ruggles Gates, Heredity and Eugenics. Constable & Co., Ltd., London, 1923, p. 222 *et seq.* Earl Finch, The Effects of Racial Miscegenation. Papers on Inter-Racial Problems; Proceedings of First Universal Races Congress. P. S. King & Son, London, 1911, p. 108 *et seq.* Ellsworth Huntington, The Character of Races. Charles Scribner's Sons, 1924, p. 336. A. L. Kroeber, Anthropology. Harcourt, Brace & Co., 1923, p. 79. Edward M. East, Heredity and Human Affairs. Charles Scribner's Sons, 1927, pp. 183-184.

argument of their case. Nor is present competition the most important factor. There is little hostility shown today toward the Japanese on the Pacific Coast, although they outnumber the Filipinos three to one. The reason is that their presence offers measurable problems that can be faced objectively with due regard to all rights and interests involved. The door has been definitely closed to further Japanese immigration. The prevailing attitude toward the Filipinos, on the contrary, is affected by the possibility that the influx may rapidly grow. "If we must eventually exclude these people to protect ourselves," say the spokesmen of the majority opinion on the Coast, "why wait until we have to absorb 150,000 of them? Let's do it now. The resistance we shall meet will be the same this year or five years hence."

Since the fall of 1929, the movement for exclusion has taken a new turn from a sudden revival in the United States of active support for the Philippine independence movement. The occasion was largely independent of the immigration question but partly at least a result of the agitation for exclusion; for it became clear to many supporters of that measure that its constitutionality and its appeal to the conscience of Americans would be greatly enhanced if the independence of the Philippine Islands were at least definitely guaranteed if not immediately consummated. A decided change in emphasis took place, more particularly in the movement of public education on this question promoted by organized labor. In earlier resolutions, expressions of sympathy for the national political aspirations of the Filipinos had been tacked on to strong declarations in favor of their exclusion. More recently, the demand for Philippine independence has moved into the foreground of labor's demands. This change in emphasis also brought with it a change of tone in the campaign for Filipino exclusion. While this group is still described in no uncertain terms as a wholly undesirable addition to the mainland population, greater care is taken not to offend sensibilities by exaggerations of unfavorable traits, exaggerations which might have the effect of weakening the case for independence.

In the fall of 1930, the severe industrial depression through which the country was then passing greatly strengthened the general sentiment for immigration restriction, and a number of emergency measures were before the country for reducing immigration to a minimum for a number of years. One of these measures, a bill introduced by Senator David A. Reed of Pennsylvania,[4] expressly

[4] S. J. Resolution 207, 71st Congress, third session, December 2, 1930.

includes "citizens of the islands under the jurisdiction of the United States who are not citizens of the United States" in a two years' suspension of general immigration into the United States—excluding, however, the admission of citizens of the Philippine Islands to the Territory of Hawaii "under such regulations as the Secretary of Labor may adopt to prevent the further migration of such persons into continental United States."

As a later chapter will more fully explore other elements in this situation and the major reasons advanced in opposition to the passage of the Welsh bill [5] it need here be stated only that this opposition arises from a variety of motives and is in part directed against the form of the proposed exclusion measure rather than its object or substance. Distinctive group interests, such as have in the past often played a decisive part in the shaping of our immigration legislation [6] have played a relatively small part, so far, in this opposition.[7] There are, however, special interests in the maintenance of the political status quo of the Philippine Islands which look with disfavor on anything that might foster their claim for independence. But the strongest of the motives in opposition to the exclusion bill is the desire to have the essential purpose of that measure accomplished by means less derogatory to Filipino pride and to Oriental race-sensitiveness generally. There is a widespread feeling that the exclusion procedure adopted in the case of Japanese immigration has greatly harmed American interests in the Far East, both by giving occasion for the development of a dangerous Pan-Asiatic movement, conscious of thwarted interests and of injury to prestige in world affairs, and by making more difficult cooperation across the Pacific on matters unconnected with migration but of equally vital importance. It is feared that a further exhibition of what will seem an American assertion of racial superiority will injure the friendly relations of the United States with countries not directly concerned in the immediate issue as well as render more difficult an honorable, peaceful and mutually advantageous settlement of the issue of Philippine independence.[8]

[5] See Chapter XVIII, p. 273 *et seq.*

[6] The interest of employers desirous of cheap labor, of co-religionists, of sympathizers with foreign liberal and revolutionary movements, of regions in need of homesteaders or of settlement in defense against encroachments of other less desirable groups.

[7] See p. 306.

[8] See p. 306.

PART II

THE DOMESTIC PROBLEM OF FILIPINO IMMIGRATION FOR THE MAINLAND OF THE UNITED STATES

PART II. THE DOMESTIC PROBLEM OF FILIPINO IMMIGRATION FOR THE MAINLAND OF THE UNITED STATES

CHAPTER VI

ECONOMIC PROBLEMS FOR THE UNITED STATES

EAST of the Rocky Mountains, there is no serious problem of economic competition by this new immigrant group. On the Pacific Coast, the area of direct competition between Filipino and American labor is so far relatively small. But just because for the most part it is limited to a few occupations, and these in a few states, this competition is serious for those who feel it.

It must not be thought that, supposing there are 56,000 adult Filipinos on this continent,[1] 56,000 other workers are deprived of a corresponding number of jobs. For, a large proportion, possibly a majority, of these workers are engaged upon work which, but for their presence and their willingness to accept the conditions under which it is carried out, would not be done at all. It is obvious, for example, that in the eastern states, where no large immigrant groups are available for domestic service, a much smaller proportion of households are able to keep servants than in the West. Here the Filipino houseboy, earning from $10 to $15 a week and his board, is only to some extent in competition with other available domestic workers but more often releases a housewife who otherwise would do the work herself. Similarly, as a rule, the Filipino "stoop" worker in the lettuce and carrot fields does not displace other workers, but his presence and willingness to accept the terms offered make possible the conversion of hay fields for forms of production which, under present conditions, have no other available supply of labor. As Professor R. D. McKenzie, of the University of Washington, points out, our economic system, in contrast with that of most other countries, provides so many opportunities of preferred work that those occupations which are menial

[1] The number of Filipinos in Canada and Mexico is negligible.

or require irksome hand labor must rely upon immigrant or subject racial groups. As soon as one of these groups is displaced, another comes in to fill the vacuum. Work now done by Filipinos would more largely be done by Mexicans; and if Mexicans also were rejected, probably Negroes would be attracted to it by slight improvements over their condition in the South. The problem, as he sees it, is that society cannot function, *as at present organized,* unless the high level of educational and economic opportunity at the top is held in balance by groups willing and permitted to perform, at the bottom, the labor essential for the maintenance of its standards.

To this it may be answered, of course, that such a social system, by assuming divided functions in society in accordance with race or length of residence, is not in keeping with the American principle of democracy, and that it should be replaced by a system making it possible for all the essential work of society to be done by labor now engaged upon less essential tasks. This, indeed, is the position of organized labor. But it is not likely that all the necessary jobs in fruit and vegetable growing, for example, would be filled by white American men if immigrant and colored labor were excluded. Since they are in competition with other food industries, there is no question that some of these forms of food production could not adjust themselves to such methods and conditions of labor as native-born white American workers would be willing to accept.[2]

Nevertheless, competition between immigrant and American labor exists if industrial developments which would give employment to the latter are held in check by too ample a supply of "common" labor.

National and international causes not directly related to the labor costs have contributed to recent changes in the consumption of agricultural products, which have transferred a relatively large demand for labor from cereal production to that of fruits, vegetables, and sugar beets; and this transference, coming at a time of labor shortage—especially during the World War—coincided with the introduction of more efficient methods of production.[3] In this situation, a shift comparable with that incidental to mechanization in industry took place: Where large-scale production of fruits, vegetables and sugar took the place of general farming, more op-

[2] See further below, p. 72.

[3] See O. E. Baker, Changes in Production and Consumption of Our Farm Products and the Trend in Population. *Annals of the American Academy of Political and Social Science,* vol. CXLII, No. 231, March, 1929, p. 97 *et seq.*

portunities of high-class employment were undoubtedly provided for some of the resident, experienced working population; but it was possible to introduce inexperienced and unskilled labor in many field operations at wage levels out of keeping with the established standards. This subdivision of processes, therefore, had the two-fold effect of boosting up some of the resident working population to better positions and, on the other hand, of cutting out men with American traditions of life and labor from a large part of the new opportunities for common labor. Instead of saying, "Americans are no longer interested in farm labor," it would be truer to say in this instance, "Farm management is no longer interested in American labor."

1. AREAS OF DIRECT COMPETITION

Until recently, comprehensive data on the occupations and wages of Filipino workers on the Pacific Coast have not been available, and at times exceptional situations have been played up as though typical for the whole area and for the larger number of Filipinos gainfully employed.[4] The report produced by Dr. Louis Bloch, statistician of the California Department of Industrial Relations, on Facts about Filipino Immigration into California[5] gives us the first budget of reliable data on a sufficient scale to make possible a conspectus of the types of occupation filled by Filipino workers and knowledge of their earnings. Since these data were obtained from licensed employment agencies, the sample of placements examined may not be typical of the total volume of Filipino employment since many employers hire their help directly. This is evident from the fact that distinctly industrial occupations are not included.

a. *In Culinary, Institutional, Hotel and Domestic Work.*

Taking 1,392 jobs sold to Filipinos by Filipino employment agencies during 1929, Dr. Bloch finds the following averages:

	Total jobs tabulated	*Average wage rates*
Hourly wage rates	97	$0.55
With board only	17	.51
Without room or board	80	.57

[4] See, for instance, Hearings before the Committee on Immigration and Naturalization of the U. S. House of Representatives, seventy-first Congress, Second Session, on H.R. 8708, April 10, 1930, p. 3.

[5] Special Bulletin No. 3, April, 1930, p. 48 *et seq.*

	Total jobs tabulated	*Average wage rates*
Daily wage rates	34	$2.89
With board only	25	2.69
Without room and board . .	9	3.44
Weekly wage rates	503	$15.94
With room and board	94	11.20
With room only	46	17.71
With board only	288	16.96
Without room or board . .	75	18.11
Monthly wage rates	758	$67.40
With room and board	492	66.68
With room only	108	51.39
With board only	90	86.76
Without room and board . .	68	73.82

The significant figures, as affecting the largest numbers, are the average weekly wage rate of $16.96, with board, and the monthly wage rate of $66.68, with room and board. Taking separately three major occupations, it appears that the average monthly wage for cooks (with room and board) is roughly $80, for dishwashers (with room and board) $55, and for janitors (with room only) $75. However, the variations are considerable: Of the cooks, 19.4 per cent received $70 or less; of the dishwashers, 11.3 per cent were paid $35 to $45; of the janitors, 22.7 per cent earned between $25 and $50.

In a large proportion of the occupations listed, the Filipino wage-earner is evidently in competition with American women rather than with American men. Perhaps because of the large proportion of students among the earlier Filipino immigrants, many of them first secured work at occupations similar to those also held by American students, except in so far as the newcomers were disqualified by their often inadequate knowledge of the language. Thus, in a typical university town, Filipino students will have great difficulty in securing jobs away from the campus but will be apt to give considerable satisfaction in house work or gardening. With an established reputation in this field, gained by their clean habits, nice manners, good appearance and conscientious effort, most newcomers of the group were drawn into these occupations. At first only in competition with American students, increasingly the Filipinos came to compete with professional women workers in these and allied fields, until today the occupations named have become one of the most serious fields of actual competition.

This statement may seem peculiar in view of the known shortage of domestic labor in many parts of the country; but the concentration of Filipinos on the Pacific Coast and their congestion especially in a few cities means that the symbiosis previously existing between different age groups is destroyed: There are many complaints that the Filipino successfully competes with the elderly person whose range of possible employments is as limited as his own. Moreover, a competition which started in a small way as between individuals has gradually entered the phase of group employment, so that large institutional concerns, hotels, clubs and restaurants today often secure a large part of their total personnel from Filipino employment agencies. Negro leaders complain that the chances of employment in these occupations have been seriously curtailed for members of their race through Filipino competition. In San Francisco, Salvation Army officers complain that for the same reason they have increased difficulty in placing middle-aged couples. Employment of Filipinos on elevators in hotels, office buildings and institutions, as janitors in apartment houses, and as kitchen helpers, has been deeply resented because in some cases it deprived of employment elderly people difficult to place in any work. Throughout the country, one of the greatest of present difficulties in industry is the fact that increased mechanization has hit most heavily those in the lower labor groups whose speed declines with age while their experience no longer has a market value. According to such testimony, it has never been so hard for elderly people to get or hold a job.[6] While, therefore, the Filipino is perhaps often unjustly blamed for a situation which he has not created, it is true nevertheless that his competition is concentrated on the sorest spot in the whole industrial system.

Apart from these special cases, there is a feeling that Filipinos are entering in too large numbers domestic, institutional and hotel and culinary employments, often at wages below those acceptable to American workers, male or female. A union official estimates that they are paid from 50 cents to $1 a day less than white workers in restaurant work. Employment agencies in the Bay region of

[6] Recent Economic Changes in the United States, Report of the Committee on Recent Economic Changes of the President's Conference on Unemployment. McGraw-Hill Book Co., 1929, vol. II, pp. 516-517, 522, and 877.

California have additional difficulty, since 1927, in placing women in housework, tea rooms, hotels, restaurants and clubs. In Stockton, a union official in a typical case found that, after having started with Filipino bus boys, a local restaurant gradually substituted Filipino for white American workers in other departments of work, paying a frying cook $18 as against a standard wage of $40, a pantry boy $14 instead of $18, and so on.

Employers in the hotel and restaurant business often deny that Filipinos are employed at appreciably lower wages than those paid white or colored workers for the same work, or that they have affected the standard rates of wages. Several of them expressed to the writer their preference for Filipinos because of their qualities of neatness, courtesy and prompt obedience, because they are more manageable than American workers, and, in some cases, because they are more permanent. This last named argument was found especially in institutional work which for white workers often is merely a stop-gap between more desirable jobs.

In the classes of work which we are here considering, rates of wages so largely depend on the type of establishment that comparisons are difficult.[7] For example, wages for Filipino bus boys in San Francisco vary from $30 a month (and food) in the most modest restaurants to $65 at one club and $75 in a first-class hotel.[8] In Portland, where there are fewer Filipinos and where there is less competition generally for this type of work, $60 is said to be the average wage of bus boys. In the larger cities of the Pacific Coast, houseboys often earn $15, with room and board; but in the smaller college cities, with their keener competition for the few available jobs, $10 represents the most frequent wage for this kind of work.[9] In short, there seems to be a sharp division between the wages earned by newcomers and by those who have acquired experience and a working knowledge of the English language. These differences rather than racial discrimination seem to be the decisive factors also in comparative earnings as between American and Filipino workers.

The competition would affect general wages even less if organized labor took steps to organize these Filipino workers. It is

[7] Dr. Bloch draws attention to the difficulty of comparing wage rates in many cases where it is not certain that the occupations followed by American and immigrant workers really are identical. *Op. cit.*, p. 49.

[8] The average monthly wage of bus boys for California given in Dr. Bloch's report is $46.67.

[9] The average weekly wage for Filipino houseboys in California given by Dr. Bloch is $9.54.

true, at times a little support has been given to movements among the Filipinos themselves to organize an inclusive union, under their own leadership, but because of the extreme mobility of these men, such movements have never been continuous enough to succeed. On the other hand, the international unions affiliated with the American Federation of Labor—including the Hotel and Restaurant Employees—are prevented from organizing Filipinos under constitutional rules limiting enrollment to persons eligible to citizenship. Thus repeatedly, when Filipino workers of their own accord applied for membership in local chapters, they have courteously been turned away—sometimes much to the regret of the local officers of the union, especially in localities where the culinary and service trades cannot at present be so fully organized as to force the elimination of non-union workers.

b. *In Fruit and Vegetable Growing.*

Because of their seasonal and unorganized character, labor opportunities in the fruit and vegetable growing industries of the Pacific Coast are a haven of refuge for the members of any group that is finding difficulty in securing work of a permanent and remunerative character in industry. Thus it was only natural that young Filipinos, prevented partly by their own ambition and partly by lack of opportunity from filling permanent positions in the cities, drifted to the land and made those operations for which they are physically equipped a large source of their earnings while in the United States. Later this movement to the land—always alternating with periods either of study or of urban employment—was fostered by deliberate efforts of labor agents to draft Filipinos to those sections where their labor was in demand. At the same time, the new movement of Filipino immigrants to the Pacific Coast from Hawaii since 1924 contained a large proportion of workers accustomed to hard work on the land, for whom high earnings rather than the attractions of city life were the dominating objective; and these were the more easily persuaded, often before they had left the pier, to let themselves be carried away to the field labor awaiting them in different parts of the coast states.

As the possible needs of these rural operations for foreign labor will be further discussed below, we shall here limit ourselves to a discussion of the extent to which Filipino labor in this kind of work is actually in competition with American labor.

Several cases in which Filipino workers were forcibly evicted by white American workers have been so widely quoted as to give an impression of severe competition. As a matter of fact, however, the area of such competition is limited, and propaganda of groups hostile to Filipino immigration has exploited these incidents to make it appear as though white American wage-earners were largely being deprived of desirable work opportunities by these immigrants.[10]

In this connection it is interesting to note that recently, when a delegation of white farmers in the Marysville section of California visited the Salvation Army in San Francisco, asking for emergency help to save the peach crop, none of the unemployed workers were willing to do this work which they considered too heavy.

The employment of Filipinos in the fruit orchards offers a more serious form of competition when the work is taken away from families with small farms of their own who need the seasonal work for wages on the larger holdings to eke out a meager livelihood. Even now it is not uncommon to see a whole family work in an orchard or on a berry patch. Similarly, the cutting and drying of apricots and prunes is still done largely by families from the small towns. The young people sometimes make a sort of holiday of it even though they work hard. Orchardists have, however, increasingly come to favor Oriental laborers—and more recently Filipinos—for this class of work because they can hire them in organized gangs and need not provide amusements for them. It is this type of competition that has been largely responsible for some of the more violent attacks on Filipinos described in an earlier chapter.

There is no question that in many parts of California Filipinos now are employed on seasonal labors previously performed by foreign white workers. The report of the Department of Industrial Relations in this connection mentions especially the picking of peaches, apricots, and cherries.[11] In the tomato district, for example, Portuguese, Spanish, Mexican and Italian workers have largely been replaced by Filipinos. Likewise in the asparagus fields and in hop picking. They have replaced Japanese workers in potato picking and in other stoop labor. Generally speaking, it may be said that there is no active competition between Filipino and white American workers in any of the vegetable growing and picking operations, but that there is, in some cases, such competition in fruit

[10] These cases have already been described above (p. 13 *et seq.*) and in Appendix E, p. 358.
[11] Facts About Filipino Immigration into California, p. 73.

Photo J. J. Billones

Photo J. J. Billones

Above: FILIPINOS CUTTING ASPARAGUS IN THE SAN JOAQUIN DELTA
Below: FILIPINO CONTRACTOR TAKING A CREW OF FIELD WORKERS TO RANCH FROM STOCKTON

Photo J. J. Billones

Photo Hobart N. Young

Above: FILIPINOS PICKING GRAPES IN SAN JOAQUIN VALLEY
Below: FILIPINOS PICKING CARROTS IN SALINAS VALLEY

orchards. Not always, for the great majority of Filipinos on the land are not employed in these orchards but on intensive and extensive truck farms and ranches, especially in the San Joaquin Delta, in the Salinas Valley, and in the Imperial Valley. In most of these areas, an almost binding understanding concerning the limits within which Filipino workers may be employed is recognized by the employers. In Salinas, for example, the field work in the lettuce and carrot fields is done almost exclusively by Filipino workers, under Filipino contractors. The packing in the packing sheds for eastern shipment and refrigeration is entirely in the hands of white American workers. It is contended by some employers that the extension of lettuce growing, made possible by Filipino labor, has greatly increased the employment opportunities in the valley for white labor.[12] For some time it was conceded by public opinion that a packer, when short of labor, might in an emergency employ Filipino gangs in the packing houses at night work. The community, in other words, was not so much concerned in barring the Filipino from this additional source of revenue as it was from preventing his working with American workers—particularly with women and girls. But more recently, the opposition to Filipinos has stiffened, and apprehension of their gradual introduction to forms of employment previously held by white Americans has increased to such an extent that few employers now would risk crossing the forbidden line.

Briefly, then, Filipino workers can be said to be in competition with white workers on a considerable scale only when it is assumed that an offer of higher wages on the part of the growers would attract white labor. In that sense, the Filipinos, as other foreign workers before them and now, are undercutting wages. But it is far more correct to say that the white and other resident foreign groups have been able to raise their standards of wages and, while theoretically available for farm labor, are not willing to do work on the land under the present conditions of forced speed which continue so long as any source of available "cheap" labor remains.

For California, Dr. Bloch has obtained from the camp inspectors of the Division of Housing and Sanitation of the Department of Industrial Relations the following list of occupations held by Filipinos in the camps visited in 1928:[13]

[12] See Hearings before the Committee on Immigration and Naturalization on H.R. 8708, May 7, 1930, pp. 210 and 213.

[13] Facts About Filipino Immigration into California, p. 57.

Counties	*Occupations of Filipinos*
Alameda	General ranch laborers
Butte	Harvesting rice
	Picking peaches
Contra Costa	Asparagus cutters and washers
	Fruit pickers
	Sugar beet laborers
Glenn	General ranch laborers
Imperial	Grape pickers
	Melon pickers
	Tomato pickers
Kern	General farm laborers
	Grape pickers
	Other fruit pickers
Monterey	Thinning and harvesting lettuce
Sacramento	Asparagus cutters and washers
	Asparagus sorters
	Grape pickers
	Pear pickers
San Joaquin	Asparagus cutters
	Grape pickers
	Celery planting
San Luis Obispo . . .	Laborers on vegetable ranches
Santa Barbara . . .	Laborers on vegetable ranches
	Irrigators
	Cooks
Santa Rosa	Hop pickers
Solano	Apricot pickers and cutters
	Asparagus cutters and washers
	Cherry pickers
Sonoma	Hop pickers
Stanislaus	Grape pickers
	Peach pickers and laborers
Sutter	Asparagus cutters
	Beet hoers
Yolo	Beet hoers
	Lettuce harvesters [14]

In the White River Valley of Washington, Filipinos now are increasingly drawn into general farm work previously performed almost entirely by Japanese hands. Even the Japanese farmers in

[14] This list omits to mention the activities of Filipinos in the Santa Clara Valley, which consists of tomato, pea, bean, and fruit picking and general work in the vegetable fields. The largest rose-growing nursery in the world here exclusively employs Filipinos in budding roses.

these areas are employing Filipinos whose wages are substantially lower than those which Japanese laborers are now willing to accept. Indeed, many Japanese growers maintain that they cannot get Japanese laborers at any wage. The recent disturbances in that region (see page 16) result from the introduction of a new Oriental labor group after a period in which fear of Japanese labor competition had been greatly lessened. Only rare examples can be found of Filipinos offering to work for less than standard rates of wages or of being introduced deliberately for the purpose of cutting existing wage scales. The system of the Agricultural Labor Bureau of the San Joaquin Valley may be quoted as an example. The board of directors of this organization, which represents the cotton and fruit growers of five counties, once a year, after full discussion, fixes the standard rates of wages for all major operations. The resulting schedule, published throughout the valley, while not binding, has the effect of so standardizing wages that in the fourteen years since the system was inaugurated there has never been a complaint of large-scale undercutting. All races and nationalities, in so far as they compete for the same jobs, are paid the same wages without discrimination.

Taking the Pacific Coast as a whole, farm wages of course vary enormously. For example, individual Filipino students at the University of California complained that at summer work lasting from three to six months they were unable to average more than from $2 to $2.50 a day. On the other hand, when no deduction is made for room and board, the average daily earnings more nearly approach $3.50 or $4 for asparagus cutting near Stockton and for lettuce and carrot picking in the Salinas and Pajaro valleys. In the Santa Clara Valley, the prevailing wage rate is $4 per day. However, wherever possible, the work is put on a piece work basis—for instance, for picking tomatoes, peas, and beans.

The asparagus industry offers a striking illustration of the effect of increasing numbers on wages. Although competition with other racial and national groups has decreased rather than increased since the coming of the Filipinos into this work, average daily earnings, according to a special inquiry made by the California Department of Industrial Relations, have steadily fallen in the five years, 1925 to 1929, from $6.06 to $3.75—and this in spite of the fact that during this period Filipino contractors have unquestionably stabilised their position and now bargain with the growers on a decent business footing. The explanation given by a representative employer is the increase in the number of men employed. "With the arrival of Filipinos in the asparagus fields, the growers are using more men per acre of asparagus [*i.e.* as cutters]. This makes it possible to have the fields gone over more thoroughly, although it decreases the earning capacities of the men employed." [15]

Detailed data concerning the hourly rates of wages earned by Filipino farm laborers employed on certain California ranches in 1928 are given in the California report.[16] Of 708 farm laborers in the camps visited, nearly one half, 47.6 per cent, were paid at the rate of 40 cents an hour, and only 2.8 per cent received from 45 to 50 cents. On the other hand, less than 10 per cent earned less than 35 cents an hour. Of 203 fruit pickers, paid by the hour, 35.5 per cent received 40 cents and 52.2 per cent less than 40 cents. Of 341 fruit pickers receiving a daily wage, 37.5 per cent earned $4 and more.

The report points out that wage rates vary considerably with the quality and volume of the crop to be harvested and other local circumstances:

> For instance, if there is a bumper fruit crop to be picked, the workers are willing to work for lower piece rates, because they can earn more wages during the day than they would earn harvesting a poor crop at higher piece rates. The ready availability or lack of workers in a given locality affects the wage rates which the growers, or owners of the ranches, are willing to pay. The daily wage rates are, of course, also influenced by the number of hours per day the laborers are called upon to work.
>
> Still another factor influencing wage rates is the time of the season when the laborers are hired. In the picking of cantaloupes, for instance, it sometimes becomes necessary for a grower to secure extra help towards the end of the season when the picking is thin, and when workers are unwilling to work at the same piece rates which were paid during the height of the season. In such cases the grower is likely to hire laborers at much higher daily rates than he would ordinarily pay.[17]

Another cause of considerable variety in wages rates is the difference in charges deducted for room, board, and sometimes daily transportation. When a wage of $2 or $2.50 is mentioned, this usually represents the money earnings without the perquisites.

[15] Facts About Filipino Immigration into California, p. 69.

[16] *Ibid.*, p. 57 *et seq.* See also Mexicans in California, Report of Governor Young's Fact-Finding Committee, October, 1930, p. 168 *et seq.*

[17] Facts About Filipino Immigration into California, p. 58.

Moreover, individual Filipino youths roaming the countryside and taken on as extra helpers are apt to fare worse than the members of crews engaged to harvest a crop from the start. The Filipino transient worker unquestionably is paid less than white American workers engaged in similar work; but then he is employed only, as a rule, when white American workers cannot be secured.

c. *In Alaskan Fish Canning.*

Although it constitutes one of the most coveted forms of breadwinning for certain classes of Filipino workers, their seasonal employment in the salmon canneries of Alaska does not constitute direct competition with white labor.

In 1921, the total number of Filipinos engaged in Alaska in the salmon canning industry was 957. It gradually increased to 2,869 in 1927 and then took a jump to 3,939 in 1928, constituting almost one-seventh of the total number of employees and the third largest group (whites, 12,039, natives, 4,298). But, as a matter of fact, in most of the operations no Filipinos are employed. Only 16 of them were fishermen, 7 transporters; and of the 3,916 employed as shoremen (out of a total of 16,017) only very few were engaged in the handling of machinery and other technical operations giving employment to the 5,971 whites employed on shore. In the hand work of cleaning, cutting, trimming, filling, etc., upon which the great majority of them are employed, the Filipinos are in competition with 2,027 natives, 1,065 Chinese, 1,445 Japanese, 1,269 Mexicans and negligible numbers of Negroes, Kanakas, Porto Ricans, Koreans and Arabs.[18]

Summer work in Alaska is a principal attraction for Filipinos because it provides continuous employment for three or four months, during the recess of school or university; and because the earnings suffice to make possible savings, to be expended on educational pursuits, to be sent home, to pay for the return journey to the Philippine Islands, or to make possible further adventures on the American continent without prospect of regular work in winter. Although the conditions often are far from satisfactory and for many the hardships encountered cast a shadow over their whole experience of American life, nevertheless it is probably true that this source of employment is freest from the handicaps that beset others, and freest from the charge of undue competition with white American workers. The Filipino workers are recruited by

[18] For full statistics see Appendix D, p. 356.

Chinese, Japanese or, increasingly, Filipino contractors who pay them an agreed monthly wage, ranging from $60 to $100—the average closer to the lower figure—often with a bonus for overwork. The contractor is paid by the company 35 to 65 cents per case, say 50 cents, and the company has no direct dealings with the contract worker but is responsible only for furnishing him with camp accommodation, while the contractor furnishes food. The contractor is guaranteed a minimum number of cases but paid for the actual quantity of fish canned when above that minimum. The Filipinos have come into this work at a time when the number of Chinese is rapidly decreasing and those who offer themselves for this kind of work, though experienced and appreciated, often are too old for rapid work, while the Japanese are increasingly emancipating themselves from the economic need of working seasonally for other employers. Mexican workers are not increasing in number, not being considered as desirable as Filipinos and, because of their different food habits, not easily mixed with Orientals.

While labor leaders often point to the Alaska salmon canning industry as an example of Filipino competition, no one contends that Filipinos often take the positions of white American machinists, electricians, process men and operators of every kind hired directly by the canners at their own risk. As in the fruit packing industry, the line between jobs open and not open to Orientals and Filipinos is tightly drawn. Neither the work performed nor the wages earned by the latter have so far proved attractive to American itinerant workers.

An important effect of the Alaskan fish canning industry on Filipino immigration is its stimulation of the influx at one time of year. As the following figures, reported by the Philippine Islands Bureau of Customs, show, migration to the mainland of the United States is at the present time highly concentrated upon the spring months. While this is partly due to conditions in the Philippine Islands, the concentration of the exodus on that time of year is undoubtedly helped by the fact that then the Filipino worker feels reasonably assured of a job in Alaska, with chances of further work in the harvesting of crops on the Pacific Coast for the later part of the summer and the fall:[19]

[19] See also p. 242 and Appendix J, p. 406.

NUMBER OF FILIPINO MIGRANTS TO AND FROM THE MAINLAND OF THE UNITED STATES IN 1929, BY MONTHS

Month	*Departures to the United States*	*Arrivals from the United States*	*Excess of Departures over Arrivals*
January	600	74	526
February	857	51	806
March	1,533	55	1,478
April	1,834	66	1,768
May	1,672	62	1,610
June	714	46	668
July	469	53	416
August	149	95	54
September	129	91	38
October	152	95	57
November	151	299	–148
December	300*	300*	—
Total	8,560	1,287	7,273

* Estimates by the chief of the Statistical Division, P. I. Bureau of Customs, admittedly below probable actuality.

d. *In Saw Mills and Other Industrial Plants.*

The Filipino in industry (in the narrower sense) is as yet a rare sight. With few exceptions, no industrial plant on the Pacific Coast or elsewhere in the United States depends upon Filipino labor. Factory and mill employers are indifferent to Filipino immigration or exclusion. While trade union conventions have in the strongest terms demanded the latter, evidence that union members seriously suffer from the competition of Filipinos is confined to a few isolated localities, such as Grays Harbor, Washington.

Filipinos do not in any considerable numbers enter mechanical occupations for obvious reasons: Industrial employers are more selective than rural ones;[20] Industrial labor opportunities are more coveted and more strongly defended by white American workers than are jobs on the land. The great majority of Filipinos are young and inexperienced; whether they have come to the United States for education or for adventure, they rarely wish to engage in all-year-round work in the same place; they are not often physi-

[20] The present investigator was impressed with the unconcern with which even large employers in the vegetable and fruit growing areas of California pick up any stray workers in pool rooms and rooming houses, and place them on work in which unskilled hands can do considerable damage without as much as asking for their previous experience.

cally capable of work requiring heavy physical exertion—or, if they are, most likely come from primitive farming communities and prefer to work in the open.

The few existing industrial opportunities are chiefly in those industries that require seasonal labor and in those carried on under Filipino and Oriental auspices.[21] To take the last-named first, it is obvious that a Filipino, especially when a recent arrival and dependent on his *paisanos* (countrymen) for advice, will willingly enter into the employment of a countryman without unduly comparing the wages and terms of employment offered him with those of other occupations that may be open to him. However, there are very few such industries, and the largest of them, employing up to five hundred persons, is exceptional, while most are small tailors' or printers' establishments, automobile repair shops and the like.

Of partly seasonal industries employing Filipinos, saw mills and box factories are most frequently mentioned. Here also the mechanical work is almost always done by white workers. Very few Filipinos have acquired training for the most skilled part of the work. When they have had such experience—usually through previous work in navy yards—they are likely to be employed at responsible work for wages little better than those of unskilled laborers. A Filipino student in Oregon who has taken extensive notes of his experiences and observations states that in the saw mills Filipinos are paid $3.25 a day as against $3.50 paid white workers engaged on similar work; but he modifies the statement by adding that even white workers, when engaged temporarily as extra hands—the only condition under which Filipinos are employed—are paid at the lower rate. But occasionally there is direct undercutting of wage scales by the use of Filipino labor. Thus in 1927, a box factory in Stockton employed a large group of Filipinos at 35 cents an hour when the previous wage for common labor had been 40 cents. As soon as they learned of this discrimination, the workers went on strike. Under the constitution of the International, the local union was unable to grant the Filipinos' desire to be organized. The American workers employed upon the more skilled and higher paid jobs in this factory did not join in the strike.

Since Filipinos are nearly always newcomers, they usually are given the hardest work at the lowest piece rates. In this they compete with Chinese and Japanese rather than with white labor. At table-pulling, a job of sorting that has to be done very fast, a quick

[21] Employment in transportation is separately discussed below (p. 58 *et seq.*).

worker may earn as much as $5 and even $6 a day; but the job is so wearing that few can stand it for long.

The building industry offers another opportunity to Filipinos, although as yet only on a small scale. According to trade union leaders, Filipinos are employed in San Francisco and in Los Angeles in those unskilled occupations which have been open to other unorganized immigrants before. Their competition is not to any extent with native white Americans and in skilled trades—though Filipino painters, concrete mixers, and electricians are mentioned—and their employment is resented as much on racial as on economic grounds.

The transition from field work to industrial work is, of course, facilitated where both operate in close proximity. Thus in the canning and boxing of vegetables and fruit there have been, in recent years, the most severe disputes as to the limits within which employers on the Pacific Coast owe it to the community to hold to the tradition that American labor only may be employed.[22] In a time of emergency, when enough hands cannot be found at short notice to can a perishing fruit crop or to crate lettuce for eastern shipment, the packer is easily tempted to put on a gang of Filipino laborers of whom plenty can be had. Even though he may be paying these workers the standard price per box (which was reported to be the case in several California incidents), this employer invites strong criticism on the part of the whole community. For this reason, as we have seen (p. 49), employment of Orientals or Mexicans in the packing sheds has remained surprisingly infrequent when the potential supplies of cheap labor are considered.

In summary, when organized labor on the Pacific Coast is apprehensive of serious Filipino competition in industry, its case rests upon relatively few striking instances of such competition rather than upon a widespread condition.[23] It is only after years of tryout, with many failures, and a slow breaking down of the barriers of tradition, that the members of a new immigrant group find the occupations in which they give satisfaction to employers and, therefore, enter into active competition with native workers. Where a systematic trying out of abilities is substituted for this hit-and-miss

[22] See pp. 17 and 49.

[23] Although the same fear was expressed in the past concerning the Japanese, Orientals never have entered American industry to any great extent. See H. A. Millis, The Japanese Problem in the United States (Macmillan Co., 1915, Chapter II), and Eliot Grinnell Mears, Resident Orientals on the American Pacific Coast (University of Chicago Press, 1928, Chapter XII).

process, and where traditions limiting the employer's area of choice are few, this period may be cut short. Thus, for instance, the relatively few Filipinos employed in the Ford plants at Dearborn and River Rouge give entire satisfaction to their employers, earn good wages (so that hundreds of others are always on the waiting list), and naturally are in competition with workers of many other races and nationalities, including those of American stock. The explanation is that the Ford system of management provides for a systematic fitting of worker and job, so that it is not infrequent for a Filipino worker to have worked in half a dozen departments in as many months before he is finally judged to have found an operation at which he can give satisfaction without overexerting himself.

A process which here is concentrated into a few months normally takes years—with a larger proportion of failures, that is, men who always remain misfits. But eventually those few hundreds or thousands of young Filipinos in industry who are not now in direct competition with American workers may be expected to enter into such competition with them.

There are, however, two factors that *may* falsify this prediction: In the first place, industrial work is only a make-shift for many of those Filipinos who are engaged in it; they are surrounded with so many limitations, experience so much discrimination, and see so little prospect of a career (see further below, p. 81 *et seq.*), that only an exceptional individual stays in industry. In the second place, almost every one of those few hundred who are enjoying higher opportunities in industry desires eventually to return to the Philippines (see below, p. 152) and will be better able than his compatriots in agriculture or domestic service to gratify that desire.

e. *In Transportation.*

i. *Mercantile Marine.* American workers in the mercantile marine were the first to suffer from Filipino competition. Filipinos, like other foreigners, are employed because they are cheaper. Lack of muscular strength does not close many opportunities for Filipinos on modern oil-burning liners. As in other trades, Filipinos have on occasion appeared at union offices and expressed their desire to be organized—a request that could not be granted under the present constitution of the International. The occasional replacement of whole crews, when expressing dissatisfaction, by Filipinos, and memories of a long continued combat for the employment of Americans in the mercantile marine of both oceans, has rendered the opposition of organized labor to the Filipino particularly bitter in this industry. It is interesting to note that, as is so often the case, employers endeavored to justify the infiltration of cheaper workers with the statement that white workers could not stand the heat—in this case of boiler rooms in tropical shipping. But when lines have been compelled, under the terms of the Postal Subsidy Act, to employ American citizens for part of the crew, it was not found impossible so to improve the conditions of work as to make them bearable to white men.

On the qualities of the Filipino as a seaman no objective testimony is obtainable. Andrew Furuseth, president of the International Seamen's Union, in giving evidence before the House Committee on Immigration and Housing,[24] could not find words strong enough to describe the inefficiency and undesirability of the "Manila man." On the other hand, James H. MacLafferty, vice president of the Pacific American Steamship Association and of the Shipowners' Association of the Pacific Coast, lauded the Filipinos as "very excellent sailors in any position.[25] This was also the view taken by the Hon. Victor K. Houston, the delegate in Congress from the Territory of Hawaii, speaking from thirty-two years' experience in the Navy service.[26] The actual number of Filipinos in the mercantile industry it was found impossible within the limits of the present study to ascertain. But we do know the proportion. According to the most recent report of the United States Bureau of Navigation,[27] 7,305 Filipinos were signed on by Shipping Commissioners in the year ended June 30, 1929, out of a total of 280,428 seamen, other than officers, *i.e.*, constituting 2.5 per cent of the total number. The figure stated, however, does not represent the number of individuals signed on for the year which, according to the Commissioner of Navigation, is probably considerably less than one-half, since most seamen are signed on for one voyage only, with a smaller number for a period of time, rarely exceeding six months. In addition to the 7,305 Filipinos signed on by Shipping Commissioners, 498 were signed on by Collectors of

[24] Hearings on H.R. 8708, May 8, 1930, p. 235 *et seq.*

[25] *Ibid.*, May 7, 1930, p. 171.

[26] *Ibid.*, May 8, 1930, p. 250. An American scientist who makes frequent trips to the Orient writes: "Several times when crossing the Pacific I have been interested to hear the captain of the ship say he had no sailors in his crew and would be glad when he reached Manila, so he could 'pick up a few real sailors, Manila men, able to do all the necessary work.' "

[27] Merchant Marine Statistics, 1929. U. S. Department of Commerce, Bureau of Navigation, p. 59.

Customs and 87 by American Consuls, making in all 7,890 Filipinos shipped, out of a total of 325,120, or 2.4 per cent. Of the 7,890 Filipinos signed on, 5,590 were in the overseas and foreign trade and 2,300 in the coasting trade.[28]

However, in this particular industry something more than competition of numbers is the issue. The Pacific Ocean is as yet an expanse with few steamship lanes. Its commerce is more recent than that of the Atlantic and Mediterranean; and one decisive element in the development of the carrying trade for the future will be the availability of a supply of skilled seamen. It is for this reason that the American mercantile marine cannot be uninterested in the building up of a tradition of seamanship on the Pacific Coast. Competition of Filipinos—as yet largely in the lowest ranks—therefore, is not simply a matter of bread and butter for an equivalent number of white American workers, but is regarded by many as a serious menace to the future of American shipping.

ii. *Railroads.* Experiments with the employment of Filipinos by the railroads is another subject upon which little authentic information can be found. No statistics whatever are available on the number of Filipinos employed by American railroad companies. In 1925, the Pullman Company introduced Filipino porters and also some Chinese maids—chiefly on the Pennsylvania lines and on transcontinental trains. It is said to be employing about two hundred Filipino porters and attendants now. The Brotherhood of Sleeping Car Porters, although almost entirely composed of Negroes, is not opposed to taking Filipinos into the union. Hostility toward the group is engendered, however, by the practice of the company to disregard seniority rights in the allocation of jobs to Filipino workers.

Filipinos have recently been employed in small numbers as section hands by five or six of the western railroads. They are supplied by Oriental employment agencies, in most cases, and their total number is estimated at about five hundred, with possibly an additional five hundred or more for occasional work during the summer

[28] Andrew Furuseth, president of the International Seamen's Union, not only interprets the figure of 7,890 as representing the number actually employed at one time (instead of being merely those signed up in the course of one year), but states, in his testimony before the House Committee on Immigration and Naturalization (Hearings on H.R. 8708, May 8, 1930, p. 235), that it does not include all Filipinos employed in coastwise shipping whose number he estimates as between seven and eight thousand.

months.[29] The Southern Pacific Company, in the early summer of 1930, employed 89 Filipinos out of a total of 12,528 section hands. A. F. Stout, national legislative representative of the Brotherhood of Maintenance of Way Employees, in testifying before the House Committee on Immigration and Naturalization,[30] stated that at that time 36 Filipinos were employed in the maintenance of way department of the Spokane, Portland & Seattle Railroad. He did not contend, nor do others believe, that the Filipino is at present an important factor in this type of work. His employment seems to be more in the nature of a try-out, especially with a view to the possibility that Congressional legislation may in the near future greatly curtail the number of Mexican workers who now make up —because of their special qualifications for it—almost two-thirds of the section work in the West and Southwest, with increasing opportunities also in other parts of the United States.[31]

f. *In Public Employment.*

During the war, when patriotism ran high, and nowhere more so than in the Philippine Islands, it was but natural that these islanders should offer more than their proportionate share to the naval forces of the United States. Some 25,000 Filipinos served as volunteers in the armed forces of the United States during the war, and other thousands were employed in the Navy yards of Manila. There are now in the United States Navy about four thousand Filipinos.

FILIPINOS SERVING IN THE UNITED STATES NAVY[32]

Year ended June 30	*No. of Filipinos*	*Total Number of Navy Men*	*Percentage of Filipinos*
1925	4,193	84,289	4.9
1926	4,240	82,161	5.2
1927	3,949	83,566	4.7
1928	4,087	84,355	4.8
1929	4,227	85,321	4.7

[29] Statistics collected by Professor Paul S. Taylor, of the University of California, for nine western railroads, show that of a total of 38,369 common laborers employed in maintenance of way departments in 1928-1929, only 287, or 0.7 per cent, were Filipinos, compared with 22,824 (59.5 per cent) Mexicans and 12,020 (31.3 per cent) American and miscellaneous Whites. Chinese and other Oriental workers have almost wholly disappeared from this occupation. *Journal of Political Economy*, vol. XXXVIII, No. 5, October, 1930, p. 611.

[30] Hearings on H.R. 8708, May 7, 1930, p. 187.

[31] Report of Governor Young's Fact-Finding Committee on Mexicans in California. State Printing Office, October, 1930, p. 91.

[32] From Annual Reports of the Secretary of the Navy.

These men serve for the most part as mess attendants under a rule adopted since the war which bars them from admission to other ratings. There are still in the service a few petty officers enlisted during the war. The navy maintains a training school for mess attendants at Manila, and enrollment is for four or six years. At the end of this period a majority re-enlist, the enlistment of new men in Manila being limited to twenty-five, or about 7.5 per cent of the total number. The average rating of the Filipino mess men in the Navy is in the first mess class, with a pay of $67.50 a month. Some advance to the officers' steward class, with a maximum pay of $105 a month, after sixteen years' service. About 400 of the total of 4,227 Filipinos in the Navy are in general service ratings. Some of these have given satisfaction particularly in mechanical assignments, and men with this background of training can occasionally be found in American industry.

Enlistment of Filipinos on the mainland of the United States is limited to re-enlistment of men who have previously served. Such re-enlistment is very popular with Filipino ex-service men because their pay in the Navy compares favorably with the earnings they can obtain in private employment. Many of them, with the aid of their savings, have become substantial citizens of their home community. The social status conferred by the navy uniform and the absence of all discrimination in treatment from other men of the same ratings also are attractions. But with their excellent training, Filipino ex-navy men also secure preferred positions in hotels, clubs and domestic employment. As a result, many of them waive their claim to home transportation and take their discharge in American ports—notably in Los Angeles, where many of them find work as butlers, waiters and hospital attendants.

Some of the ex-service men are to be found also among the several hundred Filipinos employed in the Navy yards of the United States.[33] No exact record is obtainable of their number, as a large proportion of these men is employed on a temporary basis by the local commanding officers, also because the Aid for Navy Yards Bureau on principle disregards in its records the race, national origin and religious affiliation of men employed. It has been observed that both in the Navy and in the Navy yards Filipinos, with

[33] Under a special ruling (Sec. 401 of Statutes at Large, July 12, 1921), Filipinos have been excluded from employment as mechanics and laborers at the Navy yard of Pearl Harbor, Hawaii.

the present limitation of their chances of promotion, live and work on excellent terms with their American mates.

Most of the men in the Navy and in the Navy yards are men who have completed their primary education in the Philippine Islands. With the definite racial stops to their promotion, the more ambitious of these men, by attending evening schools, endeavor to prepare themselves for other work. Owing to the fact that their employment in the Navy yards is subject to civil service rules, the Filipinos often set to work to prepare themselves for other civil service examinations; this explains the relatively large proportion of them who enter the United States Post Office in eastern cities. Under civil service regulations, it is impossible for local officials to refuse appointments of Filipinos or colored men on grounds of local race attitudes. But apparently the intentions of the civil service law do not altogether prevail against the traditions of racial relations in different parts of the United States. Thus, while the Chicago Post Office, with a total local Filipino population of 2,500, employs an average of three hundred Filipinos, the San Francisco Post Office employed only eighteen in May, 1930; that of Los Angeles seven, while none were known to the Seattle Post Office. In addition, a few Filipinos are usually employed with extra crews for holiday seasons.

The astonishingly large number of Filipinos in the Chicago Post Office is partly explained by their preference for night work which does not interfere with their studies at the local colleges. Nearly all of them are employed as distributors, but a few because of their lack of English take work, also under civil service rules, as laborers. While the examination ensures competency for the job, the Postmaster finds that the Filipinos, because of a slight language handicap, are not quite so fast workers as are American distributors. Practically none of the Filipinos engaged in this work look upon it as a career; rather, it is a make-shift employment, especially for those who are preparing for professional careers or who at least hope for opportunities in business, either here or on their return to their home land.

The Civil Service Commission has no information on the racial and national composition of the civil service personnel and, at the time of the present study, was asking for a special appropriation for a statistical analysis of its records from this point of view.

Under practically all state laws, non-citizens are ineligible to positions as teachers in public schools. Under a decision rendered by Attorney General U. S. Webb of California, a Stockton Filipino's application for a teacher's license was refused on March 4, 1930, on the ground that Filipinos, while not aliens, are not citizens either.

SUMMARY

In summary, then, the tendency of Filipino wage earners to undercut American wage standards and to create unemployment is real but limited. For the Filipino, whether he comes directly from his home country or from the sugar plantations of Hawaii, even the lowest of established standard rates of wages on the Pacific Coast look large, and it is often only after some years that he realizes their inadequacy when intermittent employment and American living costs enter into the consideration. It may be expected, therefore, that the Filipino's presence and acceptance of lower wage scales has a depressing effect upon wages in related industries —and this particularly in the food industries which, in a sense, all are in competition with each other. This influence is mitigated, however, by the small number of Filipinos who enter industry and by the fact that few rise above the level of common labor.

To say that certain industries cannot maintain themselves except for cheap labor, obviously is no answer to the contention that these industries are parasitical. But as a matter of fact the larger employing groups entirely deny the charge; the one phrase heard over and over again in the course of the present investigation, both from employers and from independent agricultural experts, is that Filipino labor is not cheap—in the sense that Chinese coolie labor once was cheap. The Filipinos arrived at a time of real labor shortage and, on the whole, have entered those occupations in which the need for any kind of willing labor was greatest. Their competition with other Orientals and with Mexicans is only apparent when all these groups together cannot supply the labor needs of the West. Hence it will be worth while to inquire a little more fully what these labor needs are.

CHAPTER VII

ECONOMIC PROBLEMS FOR THE UNITED STATES (*Continued*)

2. THE NEED FOR FILIPINO LABOR

THE discerning reader will have concluded from the preceding pages that Filipinos fill a function in the economic life of the Pacific Coast similar to that which different waves of immigration always have filled on the Atlantic Coast. Their difference from the earlier Atlantic Coast groups is, however, that they are too distinct in appearance ever to be mistaken for Americans or members of an assimilated group, and that they have made their entrance upon a scene which but recently was the battleground of anti-Oriental agitation. The Filipinos have not been called to the mainland to help out employers at a time of labor disturbance or to man new industries for which they are exceptionally qualified. Nor is their employment to any large extent due to a desire to cut wages, although this incidentally often is its effect. They simply flow in to fill a vacuum created at the bottom of our economic life by the gradual rise of every stratum. The question is, do the Filipinos now in this country fill a real economic need, or might their uninvited presence be terminated without injury to any important interest?

a. *In Urban Occupations.*

It is obvious that the employment of Filipinos in domestic, institutional and culinary services satisfies no primary economic need. As these necessary demands of society have already adapted themselves largely to a shortage of labor, they will increasingly do so. On the other hand, if the Filipinos were to develop new skills of a high standard, hitherto unavailable, they might become acceptable specialists, adding as much to the amenities of American life as, shall we say, French cooks, English butlers, German waiters, and Russian musicians have added, or—in slightly different fields—

Swedish masseurs, Irish policemen, Italian barbers. As a matter of fact, there are Filipino specialists in the field of entertainment whom few will want to exclude or deport from our shores.

b. *On the Land.*

A more serious question confronts us when we survey Filipino employment on the land. Opinions are sharply divided whether, in the first place, agriculture on the Pacific Coast requires immigrant workers—and, if so, whether for permanent employment or for seasonal work only—and secondly, whether the Filipinos have "made good." The Agriculture Department of the Chamber of Commerce of California demands the exclusion of the Filipinos.[1] On the other hand, groups of employers in the San Joaquin Valley, the Salinas Valley, the Imperial Valley and the Santa Clara Valley are by no means sure that they can dispense with the timely aid which Filipino immigration has brought them after the doors were closed upon Oriental immigration, and indeed, wonder what would become of them, in competition with other food industries, if they were deprived of their Filipino workers.

Such employers point out that "availability" of a type of workers means more than just their physical presence. In any given region and for any particular operation, before it can be said that sufficient labor is available, experience must have proved that employment at mutually satisfying conditions is possible. This is not only a question of wages; many other elements enter in: The workers must be teachable, willing to stick until the season is over, either willing to work with members of other groups or in large enough numbers to make up complete crews. They must be fast and able to endure whatever the climatic conditions are, careful in the handling of perishable crops and of crops harvested periodically over the same fields—such as cantaloupes or asparagus; they must be honest where weight affects payment. Although they speak of mutuality, such employers often do not sufficiently consider interests of the workers that also enter into their "availability"—such as relative pleasantness or unpleasantness of the work, the kind of local housing and board to be had, methods of foremanship, nearness to other chances of work when the season is over, contacts with members of other races, and so on. And, as we have seen,

[1] See below, p. 302.

the interests and prejudices of the community in regard to different racial groups cannot be neglected.[2]

Now, all these conditions are in flux. The Chinese at one time were popular farm workers on the Pacific Coast; but today few of them are to be had. The Japanese, likewise, are now available only in small numbers for field labor on seasonal crops. The Mexican workers find themselves in greater demand not only because of the decrease in the number of available Orientals and restrictions on European immigration but because they have increasingly adapted themselves to the needs of employers and learned to handle new kinds of crop and new methods. They have also become better accustomed to the more northern climates and, therefore, steadier and more reliable. The Filipinos' desirability, therefore, is always relative: Even where differences in wage scale do not enter in, what shape the employer's attitude are above all the different degrees in which, in particular areas and in relation to particular operations, Filipino workers have already gained experience or have provided their employers with experience in managing them.

Thus, in Salinas, one foreman of a large ranch explained the different judgments of the Filipino by different employers with their methods of employing them: According to his judgment, where an employer is careful in the choice of his contractor, that is, employs a man who knows how to train his boys to do careful work, who stands high in their esteem and manages to keep them steadily at work, his results will be favorable. Where an employer hires chance crews, under indifferent leadership and with no prospect of fairly continuous employment, his results will be unfavorable. In a few cases in which the present writer was told of unsatisfactory experience with Filipino workers, further questions brought out that the judgment was formed on a first contact with previously untrained Filipino workers under conditions which could not but produce errors, lack of responsibility, and ill-feeling. Thus, near Fresno, a Filipino gang under a contractor of their own nationality had been given a contract for drying raisins. When the fruit arrived at the packing house, it was found that it was not properly dried. The grower complained that this was done deliberately to secure an extra gain on the additional weight and returned the

[2] For an illuminating exposition of what constitutes availability of labor from a Californian rural employer's point of view see a report contributed to Governor Young's Mexican Fact-Finding Committee by Dr. R. L. Adams of the University of California, Mexicans in California, October, 1930, p. 161 *et seq.*

fruit to be dried properly. This grower declares he will not employ Filipinos again. Another grower, commenting on this incident, suggested that the blame for the faulty work may justly fall on an incapable or fraudulent foreman-contractor, but not necessarily on the rank and file of the Filipino boys. (Some 2,000 to 2,500 Filipinos were employed in that region picking grapes in 1929.)

"Once—and never again," when it qualifies an adverse judgment of a labor group, it was found, often represents a first judgment on the basis of an experience without proper selection, supervision or mutual understanding. Where Filipino workers are "preferred," the explanation often is that from the start the employment of members of that group took place under conditions favorable to intelligent effort on their part. One Filipino worker in the State of Washington gave it as his opinion that Filipinos probably would not be found successful in the beet fields in the long run, and explained this prophecy with the statement that only newcomers went east to work in this industry since old timers found the work less pleasant than other work they could get at similar wages. Therefore, he expected, the growers' judgment of the beet industry's need for Filipino workers would be likely to be found negative. Yet, a labor agent of large experience in California found that Filipino workers in the beet fields of the Salinas Valley were just as satisfactory as those of any other race or nationality when under experienced contractors in whom they had complete confidence. In the Yakima Valley, Filipinos are considered almost indispensable by some of the potato growers—and for this reason: When Japanese workers were first employed on potato picking, they improved on the method previously used by white workers, greatly speeding up the process. When Filipino boys were brought in by Japanese contractors, they naturally learned this improved method and invented further improvements to compete in speed with the Japanese workers. Now white workers, seeing the chances of good earnings at this sort of work greatly enhanced, again compete for this field of labor; and this, by the way, is one of the reasons for the feeling against Filipinos which prevails in that region. (See p. 365 *et seq.*)

Special physical fitness is often given as the reason for the Filipinos' success in lettuce picking.[3] Their ability to work on wet

[3] Small stature is claimed by employers to be an advantage not only in "squat" labor, such as thinning lettuce, and thinning and cutting asparagus, but also in picking

ground and in wet weather is given as a reason for preferring Filipinos in the Delta Region of the San Joaquin Valley. Being small and agile, they are considered more handy and better able to bear the strain of long continued stoop work than most other groups—except other Orientals, and these are not available in sufficient numbers. On the other hand, special physical fitness for cotton picking—one expert says that because of his smaller hands the Filipino could be trained to do this work faster than Mexicans—has not so far created a large demand for Filipino labor in that industry. The main reason for this, he suggested, is that this occupation and the conditions surrounding it are not sufficiently attractive to Filipino workers so long as they can find other work.

Sometimes the same employer prefers one national group for one operation and another for that following it, or finds that he must break up his operations because the group most available for one kind of work will not do the other. Thus in the Delta of the San Joaquin, the work of irrigation and cultivation is often in the hands of Hindus while Filipinos do the thinning and harvesting of asparagus and potatoes. Sometimes Japanese are employed especially as washers. Sugar beet growers sometimes prefer Filipinos for thinning, because of their smallness, when they employ Mexicans for pulling, topping and loading.

Size of operations also plays its part. Filipinos are more often employed on large than on small farms because of the special advantage of being able to hire them in gangs through a contractor, while the Mexican, travelling as an individual, gets the jobs on small farms.[4]

An official of a large vegetable growers' association draws attention to the fact that the present age composition of the Filipino group offers special advantages to employers which cannot be expected to continue when, with advancing years, many will become unfit for the heavy stoop labor they are now doing. He personally believes that a very large majority will return to the Philippines before, for this reason, they become competitors for other forms of labor; but in efforts to assess the economic and social value of a new source of common labor the age factor must not be overlooked.

Again, social factors play a much larger rôle than is usually

the fallen fruit—often from under low branches—which constitute a substantial part of the pear harvest, for example.

[4] Mexicans in California, p. 160.

thought. In the lettuce and asparagus regions, Filipinos are sometimes preferred to Mexicans because the latter bring their families with them and are apt to create problems of dependency; also some employers have had unfavorable experiences with Mexicans drinking to excess and, when drunk, quarrelling. On the other hand, one of the strongest objections to Filipinos in certain regions is that they do *not* have families and wish to mix socially with the white community—and especially the fair sex.[5]

A confusion of thought between mobility and instability often characterizes the opinions expressed about Filipino workers. In Salinas, according to a good authority, Mexican workers are considered "less stable" than Filipino workers; but the fact is that they follow a larger range of seasonal occupations and so do not stay around at all times of the year when an employer may need them. Likewise, the manager of an important farm bureau federation in the San Joaquin Valley explained a preference of local employers for Filipinos with the astonishing statement, "the Filipinos do not migrate much." What he meant, he explained, was that many of them stay around Stockton when the Mexicans, almost as a body, move South to pick cotton, as soon as they can—and that often is before the local crops are all harvested. Contrariwise, in districts with a relatively short cropping season, employers, finding their Filipino laborers leave the neighborhood when the "cream has been taken off," often think of them as the most unreliable of workers. Sometimes they forget that in the past they have made the same charge against other groups. These were replaced with Filipino greenhorns precisely because they made trouble when the daily earnings decreased toward the end of the season or when an inflation of the personnel, profitable to the grower, proved disastrous to the individual earnings of the men.[6]

From the mobility of the alien workers on which the agricultural West must depend to have its crops harvested, must be distinguished a tendency to break contracts which is said to be characteristic of Filipinos (though many employers state, on the contrary, that they stay better on their jobs than transient white workers). It is natural that irresponsibility toward the employer should be frequent in a newly immigrant group. The complaint used to be

[5] But in this respect, curiously enough, also judgments differ. One employer of American girls prefers Filipino to white male help because the latter "fool around with the girls, make dates with them and unfit themselves for work next day," while the former "keep themselves to themselves."

[6] See Facts About Filipino Immigration into California, p. 71.

made with the same bitterness against Japanese workers whose fulfillment of contractual obligations apparently improved with the length of their American experience.[7] According to a large grower in Stockton, it is rare for a Filipino contractor to break his contract. Where Filipinos are taken on individually, without an experienced contractor to manage and advise them, their behavior more nearly resembles that of other transients who are easily lured by prospects of higher earnings elsewhere; but even then their lesser knowledge of opportunities and their temperate habits make them slightly more reliable than workers of other racial groups. In general, the evidence supports the conclusion that local circumstances and methods of management are the determining factors in the labor turnover of a given ranch or a given district.

And this brings up another question which influences the "desirability" of one group rather than of another. It seems that in some areas, notably in the San Joaquin Valley, Filipino workers, ably led, have gone on strike for better conditions at times when crops had to be picked and no emergency labor supplies were in sight. The hostile attitude of employers toward the workers in these cases and, in consequence, toward Filipinos in general, is easily understandable.

While the subject of social disqualifications will be taken up more fully in a later section, it is impossible to dissociate these extraneous factors from the economic problem with which we are here concerned, for they create attitudes and pre-judgments that interfere with a purely economic point of view. Thus, the question whether western agriculture needs the Filipino moves from the realm of economics into that of psychology.

It is fairly evident, then, that no considerable branch of agriculture has as yet become dependent upon Filipino labor, though Filipinos are preferred in some regions and by individual growers to members of other groups. Where at present Filipino workers are a substantial part of the available labor force, especially in the cultivation and cropping of vegetables and cantaloupes, they have not introduced methods peculiar to them and their special qualifications but can be supplanted by other workers—if other workers can be found. In the great majority of cases—whether looked at regionally or by types of production—the Mexican worker is unquestionably preferred to the Filipino. Where the Filipino is emphatically

[7] H. A. Millis, The Japanese Problem in the United States. Macmillan Co., 1915, p. 245. See also similar complaints against Mexicans, in Mexicans in California, p. 93.

preferred, this is often for qualities associated with his newness as an immigrant which in time will disappear.

The question of the need for Filipino workers really is part of a broader question, namely the large and still increasing dependence of California and the Southwest upon seasonal labor which at present cannot be supplied from the ranks of white American labor. It is thus linked, on the one side, with questions of Mexican immigration, and on the other with questions of the relative worthwhileness of food industries dependent on intermittent supplies of cheap labor in comparison with other food industries. Certain groups frankly state that if some of the special crops which now make up so large a part of Californian production require a specialization of labor involving processes at which white laborers refuse to work, it were better to abandon these crops. Others are less consistent or continue to claim, in the face of all experience, that there is no work on the land which white workers would not be willing to do if they were not forced to labor side by side with members of the colored races.

It is not always realized that those branches of food production in the West and Southwest which most clearly depend upon seasonal labor are recent in their present magnitude. Vegetable fields cover areas but recently cropped for hay or entirely uncultivated. The mushroom growth of the grape growing industry since the war is a familiar story.[8] It is sometimes argued that only by the maintenance of these and other forms of intensive cultivation can the West buy the staples necessary for the maintenance of its population with a surplus large enough for the purchase of industrial products on the present scale. But it is not impossible that with the development of industrial power under the Hoover Dam project the larger economic balance of the region in its relation to the whole country may be maintained, even at the sacrifice of some of its present types of food production. The problem of California, as some of its economists see it, is not one of unsatisfied labor needs. It is rather implied in the precarious situation which confronts this rich state when it so largely depends for its economic existence on the production of specialties. The economics of food substitution are as yet so undeveloped that we do not know exactly at what point in the scale of prices any given specialty enters into competition with others; but it is clear that an

[8] See Commerce Yearbook, 1929. U. S. Government Printing Office, vol. I, p. 274 *et seq.*

indefinite expansion of high-class fruit and vegetable production is possible only by increasing cost reductions which bring them within the reach of new classes of consumers. In this sense only, that is, assuming the desirability or necessity of making these specialty crops the main supports of western prosperity, is a *relatively* cheap labor supply an inescapable condition of success. Now, because of its climatic advantages, the West is attracting workers from every part of the United States. Only a rapid expansion of agriculture has made possible the maintenance of a high wage standard in spite of this constant influx. With wages already higher than those of most food-producing regions, the Pacific Coast is forced to proceed with the development of new types of production that can afford to employ skilled workers at relatively high wages by having the less skilled labor performed by inexperienced workers satisfied with wages which the white American worker finds unacceptable.

The present reporter, unfortunately, cannot pursue this important subject of inquiry within the frame of the study committed to him, and merely raises it in order to suggest the unwisdom of trying to settle the question of Filipino immigration without reference to some of the larger economic issues necessarily involved in it.

c. *In the Alaska Fish Canneries.*

The part played by the Filipino in the salmon canneries of Alaska deserves special consideration. It is one of the few industries that welcome the Filipino in large numbers and might seem in danger of being hard hit by his exclusion. On account of the highly seasonal nature of the operation, it would be impossible to interest American laborers to perform the common labor in the canneries at a price which, in competition with other food industries (see p. 54) the canners could possibly afford to pay. But no such views are urged by the leaders of the industry, and the matter had apparently not, until the time of the present inquiry, been discussed by them at all, either formally or informally. In fact, the salmon industry has no labor policy. Since its beginning, because of the large risks involved, it has been willing to let the risk connected with the supply of common labor fall upon Oriental contractors who, on their part, are not averse to a little gamble in fish when potential returns are as lucrative as they have often proved. Of course, the necessary trained labor, usually on a monthly wage basis, has always been predominantly white and employed directly at wages sufficient to attract men of the requisite skill—for operating boats, large and small, fishing, store keeping, farming, can making, machine processes, and as carpenters, electricians, clerks, engineers, etc.

In the old days, salmon fishing expeditions were outfitted like any other adventurous maritime enterprise; the boats went out fully equipped with all necessary apparatus for canning as well as for catching the fish. Even today, fifty per cent of the cost, or more, is incurred before a fish is seen. While, to protect their investment, employers have a direct interest in the hiring of mechanics of every kind, they are glad to be able to share the risk in the employment of common labor with others. And, on the whole, they have fared well under this arrangement. Chinese, Japanese, Mexicans, increasingly Alaskan Indian natives, and in recent years also Alaskan residents of other races have been recruited by the contractors. The Chinese have always been most highly regarded by the salmon canners as laborers. Then came the Filipinos, needing money to go to school, often without a cent, eager to take advantage of the opportunity to go off during the summer months when schools and colleges are closed, to earn a substantial part of their keep for the winter months. The students' success attracted other students. In spite of their growing proportion in the total labor supply, Filipinos are not as yet regarded as an essential necessity to get the fish canned. One reason is that employers, owing to their past success in getting what they needed, have apparently given no thought to their future labor requirements. Another reason is that the whole industry is very precarious anyhow; and it is probable that, with further restrictions imposed upon salmon fishing by the government, some of the smaller or less remunerative enterprises will have to cease operating, with the result of a lessened total demand for labor.[9] But it is also realized by the more progressive concerns that the limits of profitable mechanization have not yet been reached, and that, to some extent, difficulties in securing common labor might be met by introducing more labor-saving appliances. In the last few years many such devices have been introduced. Closing machines now operate 120 to 125 cans per minute where previously they operated 60. All filling, in the

[9] On account of over-production, especially of pink salmon, during the past two or three years, the price in 1930 fell below average production cost, and several companies went bankrupt. Another cause of precariousness is the strict administration of the Pure Food Law, under which all salmon is seized and condemned if it contains more than a trace of tainted fish, in conjunction with the Alaska Fisheries Law of 1924, under which the U. S. Bureau of Fisheries heavily fines—and may even send to jail—any canner who wastes salmon.

past done by hand, is now done by machine. The speed of this operation has increased in three or four years from 60 or 70 to 125 cans a minute. One rapid cutting machine has been substituted for two of the older type. Through a new vacuum device on the filling machine, the old exhaust box, requiring separate operation, has been done away with. Cans are brought in collapsible form from Seattle, saving dozens of men. In short, the need for common labor is diminishing, and the demand for skilled mechanics is increasing—of course in much smaller proportions.

At the same time, the cost of labor has to be carefully watched. The salmon cannery industry has not only in recent years experienced additional competition from the development of new fish canning industries in California, in British Columbia and in Siberia (conducted by Japanese enterprise) but it is always in competition with the canning of sardines, mackerel and tuna, and, indeed, with many other food industries. As the price of canned fish reaches certain points, it comes into competition with frozen fish and with meat.

It is safe to say, then, that, present appearances notwithstanding, the salmon canning industry is not in any real sense dependent upon cheap Oriental or Filipino labor. Apart from the possibility that present efforts to train Alaskan natives for this work may meet with increasing success, it is probable that a reduction in the total volume of the industry will follow the necessity of larger investments in machinery and the necessity to pay more in wages for skilled labor.

SUMMARY

It must be stated, then, in conclusion, that there can be no absolute answer to the question whether there is a need for Filipino labor on the mainland of the United States. Too many considerations enter into the picture, even in those few industries and forms of service that most fully avail themselves of this labor supply, to make possible any but a conditioned statement. Nor can the immediate advantages and disadvantages of employing Filipinos be dissociated from questions of future requirements. The Filipino on the Pacific Coast at present occupies the first of three stages in a natural shift in the occupational history of Oriental immigrants which, unless new controlling factors enter in, leads up to new problems.[10] The immigrant worker is a man with normal motivations. He does not stay on the rung of the ladder of advancement which first he grasps on his arrival, however much satisfaction he may give in fulfilling those functions which are readily assigned to him. Already, in the cities, Filipinos aspire to vocational choices which the social traditions of the community and a sharper competition for jobs refuse to grant them. Increased hostility to the presence of a group easily distinguishable by differences in appearance is bound to arise in the course of time as that group gains in versatility and sureness of economic footing.

[10] Professor R. D. McKenzie, in summarizing the findings of the Oriental Survey on the Pacific Coast, distinguishes between three well defined stages in the Orientals' competition for jobs: first, a period of contract labor and camp life, with considerable mobility within a zone close to the port of entry; second, a period of occupational exploration, concentration in certain occupations, segregation and establishment of a communal life; third, a tendency toward wider occupational and territorial distribution. *Survey Graphic* for May, 1926, p. 151.

CHAPTER VIII

ECONOMIC PROBLEMS OF THE FILIPINO IMMIGRANTS

THE problems occasioned by Filipino immigration have up to this point been considered entirely from the point of view of American welfare, as though limited to that of the mainland of the United States. But that is not the only one from which the situation must be considered. The Philippine Islands, subject to American rule, may perhaps from one point of view be expected to share the fate of all conquered territories and to acquiesce in policies that are for the benefit of the conquering nation rather than their own. But the many and diverse declarations and testimonies of our acceptance of a position of guardianship over the welfare of the islanders preclude that interpretation.

It is for this reason, if not for others, that, contrary to precedent, the question of Filipino immigration cannot profitably be discussed as one of purely domestic interest for the United States. In order to emphasize this mutuality of interest, the present report has been so arranged as to permit of a separate consideration of those problems arising from Filipino immigration which, though they are our problems also, may perhaps be regarded as primarily involving the interests of the Filipinos themselves.

What are the experiences of Filipino immigrants on the mainland of the United States that give rise to questioning and anxiety or to satisfaction and the desire to continue the flux of young manhood from the Philippine Islands to our western shore?

I. LACK OF OPPORTUNITY

The question on which thoughtful Filipinos in the United States are most likely to agree is whether for most of those who have come here from the Philippine Islands the expectation of what they would find of opportunity has been fully realized. They will say that, on the whole, the contrary has been the case: For a large proportion of Filipino immigrants their actual experiences here are a sad disappointment. And this only in part because, with youthful enthusiasm, difficulties to be expected had been minimized in anticipation: These difficulties are so rapidly growing that accounts of their experiences by those who have returned from America three or five years ago no longer represent the facts.

a. *Limitations of Ability.*

First, as numbers increase, it is no longer the exceptionally equipped individual who confronts American opportunities, but a more normal and representative group of young men, including also its quota of the subnormal and less fit. This is true both as to physical and as to mental ability. The bright son for whom the family has made sacrifices, so that he might travel to the great land of opportunity, draws after him if he is fairly successful less brilliant brothers, nephews or cousins. And because the newcomers flock where success has been achieved, vocations found inviting in the first instance become overcrowded. A cheerful, bright, good-looking young Filipino in a bellhop's uniform will be an attraction where such have not been seen before, and will be treated accordingly. But when there are scores of such Filipino boys to choose from and many of the applicants no longer are as fine in personality as were the first comers, the interest is likely to wane; wage and treatment will tend to conform to the new relation between supply and demand.

In assessing the Filipino immigrants' ability to adjust themselves to the requirements of American vocational life, it is important to remember that almost none of them have come to this country with any special skill or trade experience. While this has kept down their reputation as a racial group, it has minimized the area of their competition and made them the more valuable to employers who dislike employees who are dissatisfied because employed at tasks lower in prestige than those which they have formerly had. This lack of previous training explains both the absence among our Filipinos of a group rapidly winning its way to success and their general willingness to take any vocational chances that may be offered them, no matter how unpromising.

Opportunity is circumscribed by the individual's ability to learn. The complaint of immigrants that they are not advanced to the better paying positions often is due, not to prejudice, but to their own limitations—in the case of Filipinos frequently an imperfect command of the English language. A group of Filipinos interviewed at a club in San Francisco expressed themselves as favorable to an immigration system subjecting Filipinos to at least the same standards of desirability to which aliens are subjected and, in addition, refusing those unable to speak English. "The failures of Filipinos here," they said, "are largely of those who do not speak English." An industrial concern in San Francisco, employing about one hundred Filipinos—mostly young and recent arrivals—in a total personnel of about five hundred, insists that these employees must be able to read and write English, although they are employed at unskilled work which they can quickly learn.

It is sometimes stated that Filipinos have particular difficulty in learning to speak English. But the wish here probably is father of the thought; for precisely the same statement has always been made against undesired foreigners, since Germans first landed in considerable number in Pennsylvania one hundred years ago.[1] As a matter of fact, while many Filipinos have a faulty pronunciation, there are many others who could not, judged by their language alone, be taken for foreigners.

Physical disability for many types of work, likewise, often is more imaginary than real. Those who have seen the young Filipino only on the city streets, perhaps hurrying from school to a job in an all-night restaurant, should see him a few months later out in the asparagus fields, a finely proportioned, muscular body, the shade of dark bronze, stripped to the sun. Thus in the Philippine Islands, the pale *illustrado,* effeminate, elegant, limp, hardly seems to belong to the same race as the sturdy, heavily muscled fisherman—lean, hard, a very model of splendid manhood.

It is frequently asserted that the mainland of the United States receives the "leavings" after the sugar planters of Hawaii have had their pick of physically desirable specimens among those who wish to emigrate from the Philippine Islands. Unquestionably, the rigid system of selection administered by the Hawaiian planters[2] does rule out those who are physically unfit; and some of these may find their way directly to the Pacific Coast. But they do not, at most, constitute more than a small proportion of those who come over here. One cannot single out from a mixed group of Filipinos in an American city those who have come here directly from the Philippine Islands and those who have come here after a period

[1] Edith Abbott, Historical Aspects of the Immigration Problem. Chicago University Press, 1926, p. 411.
[2] See p. 165 *et seq.*

of work in Hawaii. In the large, these distinctions do not exist. Nor is it easy to distinguish by differences in physical efficiency those who come from different parts of the Islands or those belonging to different race mixtures—except, of course, that different degrees of Chinese, Malay and Spanish blood admixture often are pronounced enough to be visible.

The fact is that a physical difference—such as small stature, lack of physical strength, agility—is apt to be accentuated by the occupations to which it first gives claim. Assigned to domestic employments fitting these physical characteristics, the Filipino often is prevented from developing into an athlete; and while the tall Swede, as lumberman, becomes taller, rougher, more angular and muscular, the small and wiry Filipino becomes adapted to the ways of the city and the requirements of polite and refined service in hotel, club, and restaurant. Having drifted into a given function in society, each group tends to adapt itself more and more to that function and to grow into it. While usually this process takes generations, it is interesting to note in the case of the Filipino an incipient adaptation of this kind. In fact, he has already made a new occupation for himself—at least in nomenclature—called "school-boy." The need for this kind of job, originally that of a youngster attending school and in his spare time earning something toward his keep by working in a garden or household, on the part of the penniless Filipino boy who has come to this country to complete his high-school education, and his special aptitude for this work have made "school-boy" a recognized occupation, listed on the slates of employment agencies and taken by young Filipinos, whether at the time they happen to be enrolled in a school or merely hope to be so in the future.

While many employers prefer Japanese or Chinese if they can get them, these two groups are increasingly able to secure more rewarding chances than those offered by domestic employment.

The tradition that a Filipino can only do light work often works injustice to individuals. Thus a highly educated Filipino in New York, who had to work his way through college, comments on the fact that because Filipinos generally dislike factory employment they are now as a group considered unsuitable for it and not given a chance when they apply for it.[3] Or when, in exceptional cases,

[3] The attitude toward skilled Filipino mechanics is somewhat different from that frequently shown toward skilled Negro or Mexican workers who may be considered "unsuitable" for skilled employment merely because the great majority of them are known to be engaged in unskilled occupations.

they are employed in industry with white or colored American workers, it is assumed that they can and will only do light work. Thus, when he sought work in a furniture factory in order to gain industrial experience, he was refused other than light work at painting.

It must be concluded, therefore, that, from the Filipino's point of view, economic prospects on the American mainland are less bright than those of other immigrant groups: He is disqualified for too many occupations by his slight physique. Opportunity in this country has always been by way of physical work. Employments requiring qualifications of quick mental adaptation, for which a large proportion of Filipino immigrants are at least potentially candidates, are precisely those that are longest and most emphatically denied to the newcomer.

2. OCCUPATIONAL DISCRIMINATIONS

The saddest experience of the Filipino, in fact, is to find himself excluded from chances of employment at work for which he knows himself well prepared. This experience is, of course, most frequent on the West Coast because of the effect of large numbers—including a preponderant majority of persons by no means qualified for other than menial work—and because of its history. But the difficulty of raising money for railroad fares, the natural desire to be with others of their group (and especially with relatives and friends who have earlier come to this country), and sometimes climatic considerations have so far mitigated against a wider distribution of the Filipino immigrants.

> Filipinos often tell me, says the wife of a missionary in Ilocos South, that they want to go to Chicago or even further East. I always ask them if they have enough money, and they say yes. Then I ask them if they know that it costs another hundred dollars or so to get from Seattle to Chicago, and they always say vaguely that they have plenty of money. . . . Then a few months later I get a letter from them from Seattle saying that they have had to stop there and get a job in order to have enough money to go on to Chicago. I have had a number of such letters.

As a result, because they get there in so much smaller numbers, we find a larger proportion of them given opportunities at skilled, technical and clerical work in the East than in the West.

Mention has already been made of the larger number who pass civil service examinations and are employed in the Post Offices of eastern cities. While in the Pacific Coast cities it would be hard to find a Filipino employed as a salesman or clerk in a store, as accountant, electrician, bank clerk, newspaper reporter, druggist, mechanical engineer, carpenter, nurse, insurance agent, tailor, foreign correspondent, librarian, physical director, social worker, all such jobs are held by Filipinos in the cities of the East. Not many of them, to be sure, but just enough to prevent the growth of a sense on the part of the local Filipinos in these cities that they are denied all access to the more remunerative and reputable forms of employment.

But standards of achievement are relative, and a Filipino in New York complains that "no matter how highly qualified he may be, clerical work is practically the only kind a Filipino student can secure." In Detroit, a Filipino engaged in skilled work in an automobile plant deplores that "Filipinos cannot get work in banks or law offices." In Chicago, a young Filipino who is practically managing the dining room in an institution, with several workers under him, sneers at the lack of ambition in his countrymen who are content to work as carpenters in furniture shops or to set up small barber shops, restaurants, cafeterias and pool rooms for their own countrymen. In the same city, a Filipino journalist, with a steady job on a large daily paper, complains that in the local business houses Filipino clerks, even when they have graduated from schools of commerce, are not admitted to the better jobs; and that many who have educationally qualified themselves for a profession have to engage in domestic and club employments.

It is probable, therefore, that in the Middle West and in the East, as well as on the Pacific Coast, the Filipinos' increase in numbers has so far militated against their chances. They are not yet numerous enough or prosperous enough to have developed many business and professional opportunities in their own group, but on the contrary their prestige has suffered. Thus a prominent government official in the Philippines says:

I went to the United States in 1901, when the Islands were still in a state of war, to learn English. I stayed for nine months at Berkeley and then went on to Washington, D. C., and, after three years, took a law degree. At that time there were few Filipinos in America. We were well treated. The Filipinos had not made a bad name for themselves. I returned to the United States in 1920. The difference was great. There were many Filipinos many of whom were not making good. . . . We called a meeting of all the Filipinos

Photo J. J. Billones

Above: FILIPINOS TAKING CARE OF BOILERS IN BEAN CANNERY
Below: NEW YORK FILIPINO INVENTOR-MANUFACTURER IN HIS SHOP

Photo J. J. Billones

Photo J. J. Billones

Above: FILIPINO CLUB HOUSE IN STOCKTON AFTER BOMB OUTRAGE WHICH REMOVED PORCH
Below: PROTEST MEETING ON GROUNDS OF BOMBED STOCKTON CLUB

in San Francisco, and I spoke to them of the bad name they were getting; but it did no good.

Many Filipinos describe as absurd the arrangement under which they are permitted to attend our high schools, technical schools and colleges and then refused to gain the practical experience at their chosen profession without which the training received must be largely wasted; for in the Philippine Islands they can get that practical experience much less than they can get the academic training.

Here, for instance, is a high-school graduate in Seattle who has specialized in mechanical drawing and electro-engineering but, as an Oriental, cannot get into any shop in the city on an ordinary trade basis. When interviewed, he was in a privately owned automobile school where a percentage payment for work done on the cars of customers pays for the tuition fees.

College authorities and friends of the Filipinos complain that too many of them study law and prepare for a political career.[4] But these students know that in that field (and in a few others, especially teaching) practical experience can be gained later in their own country; while the engineer, the agronomist, the journalist, the chemist, and the technician generally too often have to return "half-baked" without the prospect of finding at home those opportunities for practical training which abound in the United States—for all but him.

One peculiarity of this situation is that Filipino students often continue their graduate studies simply because they are unable to find work in their chosen field and have not yet given up hope to do so. Thus a student of journalism went to work on a farm after graduating and then went back to college to study some more—alternating with periods of farm work—always trusting that something in his line would turn up. Sometimes such trust is rewarded; but more often it leads to ultimate discouragement, and sometimes to complete demoralization. Of course, cases are not lacking in which the forced discontinuation of a professional career has proved a blessing; but in these cases we usually find exceptionally resourceful and self-confident men who are able to turn every misfortune to their advantage. Again, others, denied opportunities of completing their vocational training through practical experi-

[4] In California, and probably in other states, Filipinos are not permitted to practice law on the ground that they are not admissible to citizenship. See Eliot G. Mears, Resident Orientals on the American Pacific Coast. Chicago University Press, 1928, p. 318.

ence in this country, unquestionably have benefited their home country by returning to it at a relatively early age.

While the larger questions of prejudice and discrimination will be further considered below, it may here be noted that, in the opinion of the more reasonable Filipinos in this country, two causes of lack of opportunity operate in their group exactly as one must expect from the previous history of American race relations. First, it is frequently observed that what stamps the Filipino as undesirable for many jobs is his dark color. This does not, however, operate in unskilled field employments traditionally associated in people's minds with the darker races. The second cause, the effect of numbers, has already been mentioned. Even as far east as Chicago, it has considerably reduced the chances of Filipino work-seekers. In one of the plants of that city a hundred Filipinos were employed three years ago, now a bare dozen. Another fairly large employer of Filipino labor some years ago, at the last count had only two. Two mail-order houses, in the past well disposed toward the Filipino, now employ only a very few. A large electrical-supply house which a few years ago gave work to about ten Filipino clerks has passed a rule not to employ any more. Filipinos look upon all instances of this kind as evidences of unreasonable discrimination although they may sometimes be incident to a general business depression during which the demand that preference be given to local citizens tends to be especially strong.

Attorney General U. S. Webb, of California, in giving evidence before the House Committee on Immigration and Naturalization in Washington on April 11, 1930, expressed the view that even if inequality of wages did not enter into the argument and if there were work for all, still the white workers of California would refuse to work with Filipino workers. While in this generalized form the statement is contrary to the facts in almost any city along the Pacific Coast, nevertheless, the Filipino worker is justified in believing that to a large extent it is not the part he plays in the economic life of America but a social exclusiveness which classes him as a member of an inferior race, that stands in the way of his acceptance and of his opportunity.

It is believed, not only by Filipino workers but also by some of their employers who have been interviewed, that the Filipino holds his position in the better class hotels, restaurants and clubs only because of real superiority—in the qualities that count—over other available help. This is not, of course, true of his employment in the automobile industry, where Mr. Ford some years ago set the example of giving all foreign races and nationalities a chance—and of insisting that this principle be applied also in equality of treatment—definitely as an experiment in industrial management and a contribution to effective Americanization.

The experience of discrimination in wage rates and other terms of employment is frequent, as indeed it is the common experience of all immigrant groups coming for the first time into the industrial field. Even in unorganized occupations it is common for employers to offer less favorable conditions to Filipino applicants for work than they would offer to Americans or European immigrants of groups long established in American industry. Not only on the Pacific Coast but also on the Atlantic Coast, which has no pronounced anti-Oriental attitude, Filipinos are barred from deserved promotion and often receive lower wages than others doing similar work in the same concern. In the West, Filipinos frequently receive less favorable treatment than other, more settled groups of Orientals. But, as the number of Japanese laborers is decreasing and even Japanese farmers are becoming more dependent upon Filipino help, the wages of these newcomers are gradually rising. "We have no wish to destroy labor standards here," an intelligent Filipino worker said in San Francisco, "but we are forced to accept the wages we can get, since, without the aid of organized labor, we are quite unable to hold out for more."

In short, the Filipino is in very much the same position in which other immigrants have found themselves before their own national group had become strongly established. In each case, the contemptuous attitude toward the newcomer expressed itself in the denial of equal treatment. This experience of the Filipino in industry is in striking contrast with his experience in agriculture which, with few temporary exceptions, places him on an equality, as regards wages, with others doing the same class of work. The explanation for this difference is, of course, the need for labor on the land.

3. EXPLOITATION BY EMPLOYERS, CONTRACTORS, AND AGENTS

Like every other group of new immigrants, the Filipinos are taken advantage of by unscrupulous persons—often of their own nationality—who deceive them about their choices of available work, their rights, the conditions of an offered job. Usually arriving with very little money and obliged to secure work at once (even when their intention is to go to school or college), they are an easy prey to sharks who, parading as free labor agents, cart off as many as they can gather either to an employer whose hirelings they are or to some distant place where there are no chances of continuous employment, often merely for the bus fare and other incidental charges.

Most of those who arrive want to go to relatives or friends. But the chances of finding them by their own efforts are sometimes misrepresented by runners of hotels, a double-line of taxis, and labor agents who may have ready at the pier the trucks or stages on which the newcomers are to be herded away from enlightening contacts to some distant scene of underpaid or insecure labor. In San Francisco, the fights for the luggage of these unfortunates—"who holds the bundle has as good as secured the man"—at one time assumed such proportion that at last the steamship companies themselves had to intervene, so that a somewhat more orderly system now prevails, a system, however, which by no means insures that the new arrival really has a larger opportunity of weighing competing offers and testing or being assured of the accuracy of promises received. The attraction of a place they have heard of before as the location of a Filipino colony enables taxi drivers to round up a car-load of immigrants and take them there at an exorbitant fee. Thus a charge of $10 for the trip from San Francisco to Stockton for each of seven passengers is common; and sometimes the driver manages to extract from his fares as much as $20 for this trip. (The stage fare is $2.70.) News of these conditions evidently has spread in the Islands. For, a Filipino student and social organizer, who used to meet incoming boats to be of what help he could to those without a definite destination, states that nowadays he is often met with a wholesome suspicion of his well intended services on the part of these arrivals.

In San Francisco, two blocks from Chinatown, and in the parts of other cities where the new arrivals congregate, they are picked up afterwards by fraudulent padrones who play false to both employers and wage-earners by misrepresenting to the one the number of Filipino workers over whose seasonal itinerary they can dispose and to the other the earnings or the period of work for which they are to be hired. Collusion between foremen and labor agents sometimes occurs. Willing workers find themselves discharged after a week or two to make possible the earning of another employment fee, split between the two functionaries named. (This state of things, however, seems to be more true of industrial establishments, such as lumber yards and box factories, than of field employment.)

In Seattle, agents recruiting workers for the canneries in Alaska and for the hop yards and orchards in the Yakima Valley almost denude the rooming houses of available Filipino labor supplies during the weeks of pressure—in spite of the fact that hundreds of Filipinos come to that city to sign up for these summer jobs. One local agency, although legitimate in its major operations, is said to be the main cause of an overflooding of the hop yards, and occasionally of other areas of seasonal demand, with unwanted Filipinos. Centralization of the growers' own hiring activities for part of the San Joaquin Valley, in the Agricultural Labor Bureau, already mentioned in another connection (see p. 70), has tended to minimize this hardship for the Filipino work-seeker (as for others) for one important area and indicates a way in which the abuse may be corrected elsewhere. Obviously it is not to the interest of such an association when it is sending out its own scouts to ports of entry and other places where workers may be found to misrepresent the conditions and create trouble for itself.

It is rumored that agencies from the mainland are often sending agents to the Philippine Islands themselves to compete with the Hawaiian Sugar Planters' Association in attracting the most desirable type of workers. But only one actual case—that of a Filipino contractor with a well established clientele—has become known to the present writer, in which such annual recruiting trip was reported. The Philippine law requiring a fee of $3,000 additional to a $500 fee for each province in which foreign contract labor is recruited seems effective to prevent such activity.[5]

The most serious chance run by the Filipino wage-earner is that the contractor to whom he is selling his services may misrepresent the conditions under which he is to work or to live, or that he is made a participant in risks of which he is not told in advance. For instance, workers who took a five months' contract for field work in the State of Washington were told at the end of the season that, because the crop did not realize the anticipated price, the contractor could not afford to pay them anything beyond the rooming and board they had already had. Of course, this was illegal; but a gang of young fellows, some of them anxious to return to their

[5] See p. 392.

studies, surrounded by unsympathetic foreigners, do not find it possible to fight for their rights.

The California law requires that "upon application of either the employer or the employee, the wages earned in seasonal labor shall be paid in the presence of the commissioner of the bureau of labor statistics or an examiner appointed by him," and that "the commissioner shall hear and decide all disputes arising from wages earned in seasonal labor" and "shall allow or reject any deductions from such wages; provided, however, that he shall reject all deductions made for gambling debts incurred by the employee during such employment and for liquor sold to the employee during such employment." A large proportion of the deductions allowed by the commissioner in the years 1926 and 1927 was for clothing and other merchandise supplied. In the Biennial Report for 1925-1926, the commissioner of labor, after reporting some of the difficulties experienced in protecting men recruited for the Alaska fisheries against exorbitant charges, stated:

> The legislature should afford greater protection to the men who are hired annually to be sent to Alaska. These men are induced to sign contracts which they do not understand and which bind them to hard labor and unfair working conditions for a period of six months. They are always preyed upon by labor contractors and merchants who exploit the ignorance of these workers for their own selfish uses.[6]

The Washington state law likewise contains stringent conditions (section 7604) concerning contracts for seasonal labor, which must be in writing and must contain any arrangements made for the advances of moneys to be earned or for the furnishing of supplies before or during the season. (P.C. 3552-2.) The labor commissioner is empowered to hear and determine disputes (section 7606) and to allow or reject deductions made from wages for moneys advanced or supplies furnished. Under section 2624 of the Washington state labor law, every employment agent or broker who misstates or misrepresents material relating to the demand for labor, conditions of employment, or wages, is guilty of a misdemeanor.

Where the workers are remote from helpful government agencies, the chance of defrauding them is especially great. Fraud does not usually take the form, however, of an outright denial of the wage agreed upon but rather of indirect methods to part the youthful

[6] Twenty-second Biennial Report of the Bureau of Labor Statistics of the State of California, p. 84.

wage-earner and his money. Thus, it was for long the practice of Alaskan contractors to provide the workers with a decidedly unappetizing diet on board the ship and at camp, but to place on the table at each meal tempting canned foods upon the sale of which they made a heavy profit. It also used to be charged that contractors induced the wage-earners to participate in gambling games during which they would adroitly possess themselves of their anticipated earnings in advance of pay-day. Whether these charges are based on more than exceptional experiences it would be difficult to discover; but they seem to have been more frequent five years ago than they are now—possibly because each year a larger number of Filipino workers take part in the fish canning expeditions who have had previous experience, because there is greater watchfulness also on the part of the authorities, and because substantial contracting firms, with a reputation for fair dealing to maintain, are more and more taking the place of mushroom concerns consisting of some individual, previously a wage-earner himself, who often managed to get together a fairly large gang of greenhorns and contract for their labor.

In two rural areas of California where Filipinos are employed during the season in considerable numbers, around Stockton and Salinas, the system usually is that the company has an American white foreman who is responsible for the production and, responsible to him, a foreign straw boss or contractor who independently does all the hiring and firing. In Stockton this contractor often is Japanese, in Salinas nearly always Filipino. The contractor either moves with his gang of workers into a camp provided by the company, or he has a camp of his own from which he sends the workers each morning by truck to the employer for whom they are to work. There is little complaint against the Japanese contractors, who fulfill their contracts to both employers and men. (It is said, however, that their discipline is not always perfect because the Filipino workers are not afraid of them and when harshly spoken to are apt to leave in a bunch.) Against Filipino contractors complaints are plentiful.[7] This is, perhaps, partly due to the fact that they are more recent in the game and themselves unsettled—often, as has been said before, little more than workers of two or three years' experience who manage to escape the hard labor of field work by becoming small-scale entrepreneurs, requiring very little capital which, moreover, they can sometimes borrow from a grower who

[7] See Facts About Filipino Immigration into California, p. 62.

is anxious to secure a definite supply of labor when needed. Often, however, according to chiefs of police and other witnesses, these men are not of good character but make more profits from running pool rooms and gambling tables on the side than from the work for which they contract. It is significant that in speaking of his work as labor manager for a large beet sugar concern some years before, a trustworthy witness incidentally remarked that during a period of several years "only" one Filipino contractor had decamped with the pay roll, while another one had made a deduction for himself from the workers' pay, as an extra commission to which he was not entitled, occasioning the company a loss of several hundred dollars made good to the workers after the man's departure.

A large fruit grower in Fresno, a college graduate, good business man and racially unprejudiced, decided to employ no more Filipinos after three years' experience with them because too often "the bosses ran away with the wages, and the boys did not prove land-minded." In that neighborhood, a few weeks before the present writer's visit, a Filipino contractor claimed to have been held up after calling at the bank and to have lost the whole of his workers' wages. In this case, the boys had gone to the local police court; the contractor was arrested, confessed and later restored some of the money. (He was put on probation on promising to make good the loss and was later reported to be running a gambling house.) Another contractor in that region ran away with a Mexican girl, taking the workers' pay for several weeks with him. The boys rebelled against his successor, installed by the Agricultural Labor Bureau, because he had been "too friendly" with the absconding boss and they had no confidence in his willingness to help them actively to apprehend him; only after reassurance on this point by a trusted official did they consent to stay and finish the contract. These and similar cases seem to point to the probability that injustices of this sort have been among the main causes of the Filipino worker's reputation for instability. Too often a quick move on, while work is still to be had in the neighborhood, is the only practicable way of eluding a cheating boss.

Another circumstance which has recently tended to mitigate the evils here described is the increasing willingness of Filipino contractors to associate for the maintenance of ethical standards and for their mutual protection. One such association, due to the devoted efforts of an experienced Filipino contractor and a Filipino minister in Salinas, has a membership of thirty-five Filipino contractors in that region. Of course, some of the less intelligent employers are furious when they discover that one of the results of such association is that mutual price-cutting is eliminated, and sometimes picture these men to the public as veritable pirates and conspirators against the common good. As a matter of fact, the association of contractors, in this case, has led to a considerable stabilization of the whole seasonal working force in the Salinas Valley and to a distinct improvement of the relations between the growers and the Filipino workers. It was due to this association, also, that a voluntary agreement was arrived at in that region for the elimination of Filipino workers from the packing sheds and, therewith, the principal cause of anti-Filipino agitation in the neighborhood.

CHAPTER IX

SOCIAL PROBLEMS

1. SEX RELATIONS

MANY of those who in the last two years have commented on the problems produced by Filipino immigration, including outstanding trade unionists, have referred with special emphasis upon the *social* problems as more serious than the economic ones. As Chester H. Rowell says:

> Racial aliens may undercut us, take away our jobs, surpass us in business competition, or commit crimes against our laws, and we will be only a little harder on them than we would be on aliens from Europe of our own race. But let them start to associate with our women and we see red.[1]

The objective of racial purity, widely diffused among all classes on the Pacific Coast, expresses itself formally in laws against racial intermarriage[2] and informally in a sense of unease and suspicion whenever a member of a non-Caucasian race is seen in the company of a white woman. The difficulty in which the Filipino finds himself is, largely, that he ignores this traditional taboo but also that, to a considerable extent, white Americans ignore it *in his case*. Thus conversations with many officers of colleges, religious organizations, of courts and social agencies, revealed that the attitudes of young women toward Filipinos are not normally those of abhorrence or distrust, such as one would expect where a social taboo is complete, but, on the contrary, often attitudes of maternal interest if not of sex attraction. And if the Filipino is charged with being too aggressive in the pursuit of American women, it is generally conceded that, on the whole, he has met with success.

The social attitudes toward the Filipino were set by the appearance and behavior of the earlier arrivals. These were not laborers but students. They often resembled Spanish-Americans, whose language they spoke, rather than Japanese or Chinese. Many of

[1] *San Francisco Chronicle,* February 10, 1930.
[2] See p. 117.

them, when obliged to work for their living, obviously represented a higher social status than that indicated by their occupation. They were neat and clean, with a leaning toward good if occasionally too showy clothes, musical, considerate, eager to please, good dancers. All of them were under twenty-five years old, many of them good-looking. They were romantic and cheerful—or a little pathetic in their loneliness so far from home. Girls liked them. Mature women liked them. Everybody liked them.

That liking has had to struggle against new feelings as the Filipinos appeared in larger numbers and with a larger admixture of less desirable behavior traits and less attractive physical types. Experience showed that it was inexpedient to treat the Filipino boy as one would an American boy; that, having heard of the freedom permitted to American women, compared with which their own social system is iron-bound, the young Filipino immigrant is sometimes exploring the unknown limits of the permissible in intimacy with a member of the other sex; that the American girl, unaware of the Filipino's ignorance, too often inadvertently encourages a courtship which she does not desire. Remembering now that the Filipino was an Oriental, many tried to stop this social relationship altogether. Those who did not see the beginnings of the Filipino's reception in America but became aware of him only when he was already an economic problem, did not recognize the vagueness of his social standing but accused him of insolence in speaking to an American woman at all.

The immigrant Filipinos in many cases contributed to their unfavorable reputation by accepting as a challenge the increasing rigor of the social taboo, and by going out of their way to demonstrate their contempt for it in as public a manner as possible. While the great majority of immigrant Filipinos are most careful not to give offence, the rowdier element too often loudly proclaim their interest in white American girls and their insistence on freedom to associate with whom they like.

Out of this change of situation new attitudes have arisen which, in a sense, are at the basis of the Filipino "problem" on the Pacific Coast: namely, the sense of intense dislike for any social success on the part of the Filipino, over-sensitiveness to his presence, insistence on his racial identification with other Orientals and on the maintenance in his treatment of past traditions concerning relations with Orientals. Yet, in spite of such agitation, there is still a widespread feeling that the Filipino cannot simply be classed with the Chinese and the Japanese as an Oriental to whom a recognized traditional code of behavior must be applied. Public opinion has become aware that all the Filipino immigrants do not belong to the same class; and that the members of this group represent a wide range of traits, calling for a similarly expanded range of social opportunities. Of course, this recognition expresses itself in conduct rather than in verbal explanations. While sentiment on the Pacific Coast is strong for Filipino exclusion, common sense and a decent regard for the amenities usually characterize the behavior toward individual Filipinos.

Perhaps the outstanding factor in this situation is the exceedingly small number of Filipino women on the American continent —variously estimated as 3 or 4 per cent of the total number of resident Filipinos.[3] Persons unaware of this condition sometimes speak of a preference of Filipinos for American women, when, as a matter of fact, the Filipino immigrant has no choice, as a rule, between these and women of his own nationality if he seeks female companionship at all. Their Spanish-Catholic traditions make it impossible for Filipino women, especially those of the better classes, to travel, unless under the care of father or husband; and few have as yet emancipated themselves from these traditions to take advantage of American educational opportunities. The large majority of Filipino immigrants look upon their eventual marriage to a Filipina at home as a matter of course—a matter, moreover, much more of parental and less of personal choice than is always realized by persons brought up in a western country. But this does not prevent them from seeking the companionship of American women. The motive here is about the same as that of an American student or worker abroad who for his entertainment, his education or his comfort, and most often with no conscious objective at all, seeks the acquaintanceship of women in the social environment in which he finds himself for the time being—with this difference, that with the great admiration for Americans in the East, acquaintanceship and intimacy with an American woman lends a special prestige to the Filipino emigrant among his fellows.

Marriages, of course, occasionally result from these contacts, but they are relatively rare, and there is no sign of a considerable increase in their number. Such marriages in the past have usually been with immigrant women or daughters of immigrants; but more recently it is reported that many marriages contemplated or ac-

[3] See p. 23.

complished (through legal subterfuge or otherwise) have been with American girls born and raised in the middle west or east. Often they take place with women who either have no strong family ties or whose social or intellectual status is somewhat below that of the immigrant husband.

It is not surprising that the sex behavior of an immigrant group almost entirely composed of young men receives watchful attention. And when that attention has for its background a sense of the impropriety of all social contacts that might lead to interracial unions, it easily finds cause for alarm in trifling circumstances.[4] Not every Filipino who smiles at a waitress or a fellow-student has either honorable or sinister designs upon her; yet the behavior of Filipinos in the presence of American women is often so interpreted. He is said to be "fresh" or "aggressive" when he takes the liberty of every normal young man to try to get to know some member of the opposite sex. But here the investigator deals with purely subjective evidence. After reading the present chapter in its original form, one western teacher of sociology wrote:

> I have never, in my ten years of acquaintance with Filipino students, heard a remark in regard to their sex aggressiveness. I recently made inquiry from sorority groups that employ Filipino students, and all testify that the students show no indication of "freshness." In fact this is one reason why they are preferred to white boys.

In a middle-western university, a Y.M.C.A. secretary stated the more prevalent opinion, that Filipino students are "most persistent in following up casual introductions." For this reason, many of the better dance halls in the city have been closed to them. The dean of women here found it necessary to warn girl students frequently seen in the company of Filipinos.

> More than anything, said the matron of a Christian institution at a western university, do the Filipino students like to be with American girls. This is a constant source of trouble. There is no such situation in regard to other Oriental students.[5]

Here also special observations of behavior were made and women students were warned to guard their reputation.

[4] It is not contended that the circumstances are always trifling. The special problems occasioned by the Filipino's standards of sex morality are described in the following section.

[5] Yet this same statement has frequently been made in the past concerning other foreign students, and their treatment is often based on the assumption that it is dangerous to open to them normal opportunities of social life. See The Foreign Student in America. Association Press, 1925, p. 136 *et seq.*

Catholic and Protestant clergymen who interest themselves in young Filipinos, policewomen and social workers tell a like story. Complaints of Filipino aggressiveness come from women teachers in evening schools and from employees in hotels and restaurants. Frequently they come from parents, brothers and friends of young women who disregard the prevailing feeling that friendly relations with Filipinos are undesirable.

2. IMMORALITY

Unfavorable attitudes toward a group of immigrants invariably lead to suspicions and to misinterpretations of observable facts concerning their behavior. When the Chinese drew upon themselves popular antagonism on the Pacific Coast, there developed a view of Chinatown as essentially an abode of vice, which is still perpetuated in our moving pictures and cheap fiction magazines.[6] The Japanese were accused widely of taking advantage of the custom to admit picture brides to bring to this country women for immoral purposes. Exaggerated statements were current concerning their dishonesty in business and their propensity to gambling. Particularly interesting is the repetition, in the case of the Filipinos, of what was said about the Japanese, expressions of the "general feeling that those who begin in an inferior economic position should remain in it and that [they] are 'cocky.' . . . They frequently spend over much on dress. When they appear in up-to-date suits and possibly patent leather shoes, they at once are said to be 'cocky.' "[7] The statement was frequently made that the presence of Japanese boys in the public schools was creating a moral problem.[8]

Not only Orientals but many other immigrant groups have in the early stages of their residence, both East and West, given rise to unfavorable judgments of their moral traits. This has especially been the case when a new immigration movement was composed of young men without women of their own nationality.[9] The

[6] Mary Roberts Coolidge, Chinese Immigration. Henry Holt & Co., 1909, p. 401 *et seq.*

[7] H. A. Millis, The Japanese Problem in the United States. Macmillan Co., 1915, p. 247.

[8] Herbert B. Johnson, Discrimination against Japanese in California. Courier Publishing Co., Berkeley, 1907, p. 22 *et seq.*

[9] Where a new group continues a family and social life of its own in an American community, usually public opinion considers "clannishness" one of its distinctive characteristics. See H. A. Millis, *op. cit.*, p. 247. Also John Daniels, America via

following statement, made some years ago about the Greeks in America, applies almost exactly to the reputation of the Filipinos now:

When we turn to sexual immorality, it appears that the effect of American life upon the immigrants is injurious, rather than the reverse. This is in part due, no doubt, to the fact that the Greek colonies are largely composed of young men, freed from the restraints of family ties and the surroundings of home, where the close watch kept upon the women prevents active immorality to a large extent. Through the scarcity of women of their own race these young men in America are prevented from contracting marriages in a normal way. Furthermore, the liberty of American life in regard to the relations of young people is construed by the Greeks as license. The innocent, friendly comradeship of young people of opposite sexes is something so foreign to their experience that they do not understand it. . . . Unfortunately, the women with whom the average Greek in this country has the opportunity to become familiarly acquainted, are not usually such as to raise his standard of morality or his opinion of womankind.[10]

Similar problems are reported from English port cities which in recent years have experienced an influx of West Africans, mostly former seamen. A report of the Liverpool Association for the Welfare of Half-caste Children states:

The Negro, usually well dressed, generous with what money he has, a good singer and dancer, shows to advantage and makes a good impression on the girls in the poor and overcrowded district he frequents. In his own country the Negro's relations with women are restricted by a rigid tribal discipline; in this country he is cut adrift from these restrictions before he has developed the restraint of Western civilization. The Negro thus tends to be promiscuous in his relations with white women. The women almost invariably come to regret their alliance with Negroes . . . especially when they find their colored children unable to get work, but are rarely able to cut adrift from their mode of life. . . .

The women first meet the men in cocoa rooms where they are waitresses, in public houses, and at dances in the cellars of houses frequented by colored men. Once a woman has lived with a colored man, the house appears to become a sort of club for any colored man in port.[11]

the Neighborhood. Harper & Brothers, 1920, p. 91 *et seq.* American residents abroad share this criticism.

[10] Henry Pratt Fairchild, Greek Immigration to the United States. Yale University Press, 1911, p. 206. See also p. 115 insert. Similar has been the experience with Russian immigration before the war when it was 86 per cent male. See Jerome Davis, The Russian Immigrant. Macmillan Co., 1922, p. 78.

[11] *London Times,* June 15, 1930.

Compare these statements with the testimony of Dr. David P. Barrows, of the University of California, formerly director of the educational system in the Philippines:

> Their [the Filipinos'] vices are almost entirely based on sexual passion. . . . The evidence is very clear that, having no wholesome society of his own, he is drawn into the lowest and least fortunate associations. He usually frequents the poorer quarters of our towns and spends the residue of his savings in brothels and dance-halls, which in spite of our laws exist to minister to his lower nature. Everything in our rapid, pleasure-seeking life and the more or less shameless exhibitionism which accompanies it contributes to overwhelm these young men who, in most cases, are only a few years removed from the even, placid life of a primitive native barrio.[12]

It is not difficult to see how the members of such a group may be drawn into unwholesome associations and into vice. In the absence of a normal family life and without the opportunity for normal sex relations, often crowded together in small houses or apartments that hardly deserve the name of home, or in camps just a little above that level of insanitation at which they would be condemned by the health authorities, often without means of wholesome recreation, engaged for long hours in tedious work to which many of them are not accustomed by their previous mode of life—such boys and young men all too readily become the easy mark for the provenders of commercial vice.

Such vice, in many countries, goes together with high standards of family life. There is some prostitution in the Philippine Islands, and a rigorous maintenance of purity in that great majority of homes in which the influence of the Church has taken root. Those who come here in youth, according to a medical examiner, are for the most part venereally clean.

When the charge of vice is sifted with the aid of competent public officials and social workers, it appears that the number of sex offenses among the Filipinos in the United States in proportion to their number is no larger than that of Americans of the same age group. But these offenses take unusual forms: For example, a group of four or five young Filipino workers may occasionally be found amicably living in a single household with a single woman—usually a former dance hall habituée or professional prostitute. Again, it is sometimes found that a Filipino will seduce a girl by ingratiating himself with her whole family; and in some cases ir-

[12] Hearings of House Committee on Immigration, Seventy-first Congress, Second Session, on H.R. 8708, p. 35.

regular unions are found to have the sanction of the parents—always, of course, families of a low type. Though unimportant in numbers, those court cases in which Filipinos are charged with seducing girls under age create special difficulty because under western state laws marriage is not a permissible way out.[13] In several cities dance halls have been closed, not so much because their patrons were in danger from immoral Filipinos, but because professional prostitutes invaded these places in large numbers attracted by the presence of unsophisticated Filipino patrons, who are known as lavish spenders. Thus, in a western university town, the chief of police said, concerning the dance-hall problem, that a unique situation had arisen from the aggressive pursuit of Filipino patrons by immoral women frequenting these places. And a similar opinion was expressed by the dance-hall supervisor in a middle-western city.

It is widely conceded, among those whose business it is to watch their behavior, that the Filipinos are unusually considerate in their dealings with women. The statement has repeatedly been heard in the course of the present inquiry that the type of girl that frequents cheap dance halls is both better treated by the Filipino and safer with him than by and with other men who go to these places.[14] In different cities it was reported that such women would live with Filipinos, sometimes even get married to them, to rob them of all they have, then disappear.

Two circumstances must be kept in mind when the Filipino's addiction to "night life" is under discussion: first, that like sailors between trips, seasonal workers returning from Alaska or from a profitable summer on the ranches are apt to throw their money about in an attempt to enjoy life; second, that young foreigners, far from home, in every climate and in every civiliza-

[13] Being classed as Mongolian, the Filipino is legally deprived of the right to marry a white woman in California, Arizona, Idaho, Nevada, and Oregon. (This subject is further discussed below, p. 117.) This sometimes leads to anthropological curiosities: In one case, a Filipino, of almost pure Spanish type with a trace of Malay but not of Chinese in his appearance, desired to marry a Mexican girl of distinctly Indian features. But as he was declared a Mongolian and she a white, the marriage was refused. See Eliot G. Mears, Resident Orientals on the American Pacific Coast. University of Chicago Press, 1928, p. 145 *et seq.*

[14] Particularly interesting in this connection is the case of the taxi-dancers in Los Angeles. These are very largely girls who have been attracted to Southern California from all over the country by the desire to become movie stars. Unadjusted at home, run-away, lonely and penniless, they adopt a profession which is always open to attractive girls. In these dance-halls, many patrons treat them on the assumption that they are "bad." But the Filipino, in a situation himself that is not very different, behaves both sympathetically and generously—often with dire ultimate results for both boy and girl.

tion, have been the principal patrons of illegitimate resorts. Often the "cheap dance-hall girl" is the only person who will take a personal interest in these boys, learning to speak a few sentences in their language and giving them a good time. Or, as a Filipino in Stockton plaintively observed: "A fine automobile stops at the corner and invites the boys to jump in and come out to a roadhouse where there are girls and drinks. No other American has ever invited them to anything. Will they go?"

The policewomen in some of the cities visited in connection with the present study do not find the Filipino a special problem—except in so far as public agitation has made it one. That is, as soon as he sees a Filipino with a white American girl, the propagandized citizen is apt to assume the existence of a questionable relationship; and this air of suspicion is sometimes as large a source of trouble as real misconduct. One prominent police officer, throughout an interview, referred to the Filipinos as "niggers"; one of the chief exponents of labor's antagonism to the Filipino is a southerner with a similar attitude; and underneath the charge of immorality diffused by such men as these it is easy to detect a race attitude lacking in discrimination; for they class as equal moral offences misconduct and marriage.

Another reason for the prevalent charge against the Filipinos is, of course, that in the large cities they are often prevented by the prevailing prejudice from renting rooms or apartments in decent neighborhoods. They are conspicuous on the streets because, unlike the Chinese and Japanese, who have families, they are obliged by the congestion of their "homes" to spend practically all their leisure time in public places.[15]

Through association with bad characters in the cheap pool rooms, in the dance halls (where they are permitted to attend them) and in restaurants of low reputation, young Filipinos often come into contact with the underworld and, through ignorance, through loneliness, or through general disappointment with the conditions of life in America, are led astray.

3. CRIME

Considering their age and sex and their economic and social status, the Filipino immigrants of the United States do not appear

[15] See further below, p. 126 *et seq.*

to have an unusually high crime rate.[16] Take, for example, the convictions of Filipinos in the Police Court of Seattle for the four years, January, 1924–January, 1928:

Offense	*No. of Convictions*	*Occupations*	
Grand larceny	4	Cannery Worker	8
Petty larceny	4	Farmer	1
Investment	2	Laborer	11
Disorderly conduct	17	Dishwasher	3
Pickpocket	1	Bus boy	1
Desertion	1	Mess boy	2
Burglary	4	Navy	3
Fugitive	2	Waiter	3
Forgery	1	Mechanic	1
Delinquency	1	Cook	2
Concealed Arms	1	Unknown	1
Robbery	1	Student	2
		Shoeshine	1

Or take two sample months—one during the season of minimum and one during that of maximum residence of itinerant workers—of arrests in San Francisco.[17]

CAUSES OF ARRESTS OF FILIPINOS IN SAN FRANCISCO IN TWO MONTHS OF 1929

Offense charged	*Number*	
	July *	*October* *
Disturbance of peace	—	2
State revolver law	1	5
Abandonment and neglect of wife	1	—
Vagrancy	2	6
Ordered into custody (bail)	—	1
Pimp law	1	—
Visits to houses of ill fame	—	20
Gambling house visiting	1	78
Cal. Vehicle Act (chiefly speeding)	2	3

* These months were chosen as typical of seasons of minimum and maximum Filipino residence.

16 For purposes of this report, statistics of convictions have been gathered in so far as this was possible, rather than of arrests. But as the police chief of one city with a large Filipino colony points out, convictions measure the crime rate of foreign groups even less adequately than among Americans, because with the inability of many witnesses to identify members of a group who "all look alike," the difficulty of securing convictions is increased.

17 The conviction sheets in San Francisco carry no nationality records; hence the following extracts were made from records of arrest in the police department.

Offense charged	Number July *	October *
Assault	—	1
Assault with deadly weapon	—	2
En route	—	1
Rape	—	1
Keeping gambling place	—	2
Lottery place visited	2	1
Petit theft	1	1
Drunk	2	2
Pandering	1	—
Threat to kill	1	—
Battery	1	—
Barber law	1	—
Total	17	126
Total for City	4,722	5,387
Total for American Citizens	2,442	

* These months were chosen as typical of seasons of minimum and maximum Filipino residence.

In Los Angeles County, the sheriff estimates that between 120 and 150 Filipinos are booked in the county jail each year—or less than 1 per cent of the total number of prisoners booked.[18] Statistics of court convictions by national groups are unfortunately not available for that city or county.

A police captain reputed to have the most intimate and long continued knowledge of the Filipino population in San Francisco states that Filipinos are less given to theft than certain other immigrant groups because of a longer history of civilization behind them. Also they are restrained by a higher respect for law and order as represented by the police.[19]

While Filipinos are sometimes reputed to be less honest than Chinese and Japanese in domestic service, most of the thefts reported are from Filipinos. The chief trouble the police department has with Filipinos is through their contacts with vice and gam-

[18] This proportion is, of course, no indication of the relative crime rate when corrections of the raw statistics are made for total male population between the ages, say, of twenty and forty. Unfortunately, even with accurate census figures no completely satisfactory comparison will be possible because of the constant shift of the Filipino population.

[19] Owing to this respect, Filipinos, though sometimes charged with "inability to distinguish between truth and falsehood," are said to present less trouble to courts than members of other foreign groups. One court officer states that Filipino offenders almost invariably make an immediate and complete confession.

bling.[20] In contrast with this, one of the chief enforcement officers of the vice laws in San Francisco finds cases in which girls bring charges against Filipinos rare, in proportion to the number and age distribution of the resident Filipinos. Part of the explanation lies in the fact that Filipinos, whether married or not, are reputed to be always "good to" the women they live with, so that charges are rarely made except at the instigation of parents or others.

Federal officers declare that Filipinos have never been found involved in cases of illicit dealing in narcotics.

Arrests for the possession of firearms are said to be on the increase in 1930 and sufficiently explained by the use of violence against Filipinos on many occasions and their complaint of insufficient police protection on some of them.

Apart from criminal exploitation of each other (see above, p. 85 *et seq.*), minor theft is the main cause of complaint. Often it is associated with the Filipino's desire for good clothes.

It is interesting to note that leading Filipinos are making the same complaint about the treatment of Filipino crime by the press that Negro leaders are making in the East. Says one of them:

> When a Filipino boy is in trouble, the newspapers print big headlines about it. When a white man does wrong, they print small articles, saying that Jones, Brown or Johnson did such and such a thing. They do not say that a Swede committed a crime. But they always pick on the Filipinos.

Another cause of undeserved unfavorable publicity is the proneness of police officers to make false arrests of members of any group against which public opinion is prejudiced. For example, during a moral clean-up campaign in Seattle recently, a policeman arrested a group of eight Filipinos for standing at a street corner late at night, charging them with accosting women. Since the policeman could not produce a single witness, and the boys declared that after coming home late from work they had no other place to congregate before going home than the street, the magistrate immediately dismissed the charge. A probation officer in California writes:

> Three Filipino boys were recently arrested here for molesting two white girls on the street. I doubt that they had any intention to do so but believe that the girls became frightened and, perhaps, still more alarmed when the Filipinos tried to keep them from causing trouble. The boys were given fifty days in jail.

[20] This latter subject, since it is a problem for the Filipinos themselves and only indirectly a source of crime, will be taken up below, p. 133 *et seq.* See also p. 191.

Unfortunately no sufficient body of comparable statistics is available to discover whether the circumstances under which Filipinos live in different types of communities affect their crime rate. A high police officer in California believes this to be the case and complains that his city is getting a particularly low type of Filipino, with a relatively high rate of convictions for every kind of larceny. It is probably true that to this area there come thousands of workers of little education and relatively low intelligence; for, by opportunities of particularly heavy and disagreeable agricultural occupations, it attracts a racial mixture unusual even for the Pacific Coast; and since the laborers are able to make good earnings, they are exploited by many varieties of quacks, fakers and hangers-on—usually of their own race and nationality.

Californians familiar with social conditions believe that the statistics of arrests and convictions give too favorable a picture of the Filipino, not only as regards the relative amount of his crime but also as regards its nature. Cases of sex delinquency, they say, are rarely brought into court. But they become known in the locality and, just because charges often cannot be pressed, inflame public opinion.[21]

4. DESTITUTION

Public officials and social workers close to the Filipinos often comment upon the remarkable degree of mutual aid among the Filipinos, who rarely, if ever, become a burden to the local charities. In some of the cities visited in connection with the present inquiry, the more important welfare agencies could barely remember having handled cases involving Filipinos. A religious social worker who is keeping close contact with hundreds of Filipinos says that nearly always a boy, when he gets into financial difficulties, has relatives or close friends who will help him out. He has never come across a Filipino who did not have shelter and the bare necessities, even when he was out of work. One explanation is that probably a majority of the Filipinos now in this country have brothers, uncles, or cousins here; and that most of them are members of organizations which, though mutual aid is not always part of their objec-

[21] Similarly, social workers in New Bedford, Mass., reported that standards of sex morality among immigrant Portuguese were very low. "When it was replied that criminal records in Fall River did not bear out this claim, they answered that most offenses of this nature were unknown to the general community and that arrests for them were infrequent." In this case, further inquiry by the investigator failed to prove the validity of the assertion. Donald R. Taft, Two Portuguese Communities in New England. Columbia University Studies in History, Economics and Public Law, vol. CVII, No. 1, 1923, p. 329.

tive, yet usually have members coming from the same region in the Philippines, even from the same town and neighborhood, so that the sense of mutual obligation is keen.

The large degree of self-help among the Filipinos is the more remarkable since very few of them arrive in this country with a substantial nest-egg to fall back upon; or if they do have money are even more rapidly than other immigrants deprived of it. For the youth and inexperience of the Filipino laborer, his unbounded faith in the land of opportunity and childlike trust in those who are kind to him make him a frequent victim for every kind of confidence game.[22]

The few cases in which Filipinos figure that come under the survey of welfare societies usually are cases of domestic maladjustment or desertion. But it is interesting to note in this connection that desertion of a Filipino husband and children by an American wife is more frequent—or rather, less infrequent—than the reverse.[23] And even fewer are the cases of Filipino desertion of a Filipino wife. Typical cases are those in which an American girl, after having married a Filipino here and gone with him to the Philippine Islands, finds life over there unbearable and returns alone to live as best she can in an American environment.

In short, frequent statements to the contrary notwithstanding, it may be said with certainty that under present circumstances—that is, with the given age and sex composition of the group—the Filipinos in America do not tend to become a public charge and do not throw a heavy burden upon organized charity.

The different situation, in this regard, in which private and public welfare agencies find themselves in facing Mexican immigration is often commented upon. In Los Angeles, where they make up about 12 per cent of the population, Mexicans absorb about 25 per cent of the budgets provided for charity and other forms of relief.[24] Because of insanitary living conditions, the Mexican quarters in western cities frequently are the foci of epidemics. Preventable sickness is more prevalent among them than among their neighbors. Delinquency also is out of proportion among Mexicans to their share in the total population.[25] In all these respects, differ-

[22] The same is true in Hawaii. See p. 191.

[23] See below, p. 195.

[24] Mexicans in California. Report of Governor C. C. Young's Fact-Finding Committee, October, 1930, p. 190.

[25] Robert N. McLean, Mexican Workers in the United States. Proceedings of National Conference of Social Work, 1929, p. 536 *et seq.* Mexicans in California, p. 202.

ences in age distribution and in cultural background rather than in racial traits suffice to account for the much larger liability of the Mexican to the American community compared with that of the Filipino.

5. HEALTH

"Practically all of them have become afflicted with loathsome diseases." This statement repeatedly occurred in statements and resolutions concerning the Filipinos during the summer of 1929; it is contrary to fact. The great majority of Filipinos who come to this country are free from contagious diseases. Nevertheless, because of their tropical origin and their manner of living, which makes their resistance and susceptibility to various infections different from that of the native population, they do contribute health problems with which public health officers are rapidly becoming familiar.

The immediate occasion for a wide spread of unfavorable reports concerning the health of the Filipino immigrants was the meningitis epidemic of the spring of 1929.

a. *Cerebro-Spinal Meningitis.*

The relation of this outbreak to the immigration of Filipinos has been so competently described in the medical press [26] that it is not necessary here to repeat or to analyse it. Unfortunately, a mistaken early statement of a public health officer in San Francisco, to the effect that immigrant Filipinos were responsible for this epidemic, attracted the attention of circles hostile to the Filipino's coming to this country and was widely diffused throughout the country, while the corrective information, since circulated by federal and state health officers and competent epidemiologists, has not yet caught up with it.

An editorial article in the *Journal of the American Medical Association* (June 15, 1929, Vol. 92, No. 24, p. 2022) states:

> California as well as Oregon and Washington reported a decided rise in the number of cases in 1926. In fact, this increase was manifest in Oregon in 1925. The important thing to observe is that the increased incidence was maintained for 1927 and 1928 for reported cases and deaths. Likewise, cases were continuously being reported throughout the summer months. For instance, Washington in 1925 reported 55 cases and 39 deaths; in 1926, 190

[26] *Journal of American Medical Association* for June 15, 1929, p. 2022, August 10, 1929, p. 462, September 7, 1929, p. 774.

cases and 84 deaths; in 1928, 123 cases and 95 deaths; and for January and February, 1929, 48 cases and 8 deaths, the latter figure being incomplete. Oregon in 1925 reported 46 cases and 37 deaths; in 1926, 99 cases and 65 deaths; in 1927, 89 cases and 35 deaths; in 1928, 76 cases and 36 deaths, and for January, February and March, 1929, 22 cases and 24 deaths. California in 1925 reported 97 cases and 30 deaths; in 1926, 192 cases and 91 deaths; in 1927, 222 cases and 91 deaths, and for January, February and March, 1929, 260 cases and 127 deaths.

The situation as to cases in steerage passengers did not at first appear to be serious and gave little concern to health and shipping officials. The disease was practically prevalent in one nationality, the Filipino, whose individual resistance to the causative strain of organism was probably low. . . . It is known that Filipino steerage passengers were at first allowed freedom in all ports of call.

In August, the *Journal* reported that the measures advocated by health officials and presumably adopted by the American shipping company concerned had apparently been efficacious, as all ships sailing from Manila as far back as May 11 had arrived "clean"—that is, without a single case of meningitis.[27] In September it further reported that the epidemic was under control. In Shanghai probably about 10,000 had succumbed to the disease.[28] In December, the steerage passenger agent of the Dollar Steamship Company in Manila stated that the last nine or ten boats to the United States ports had all gone in "clean."

In July, the Public Health Service followed up a Presidential order, issued in June, with a drastic regulation under the Navigation Act of 1882, reducing steerage capacity to one-fourth of the cubic space. This regulation was amended in October, 1929, permitting the use of one-half of the steerage capacity.

In short, so far as transmission of this disease from the Orient to the United States is concerned, these facts show that the protective measures taken by the government and by the steamship company have been effective. With further measures that are advocated by medical authorities for a more complete system of information on the prevalence of the disease in different parts of the world,[29] for further port facilities to handle communicable disease,

[27] *Journal of the American Medical Association* for August 10, 1929, Vol. 93, No. 6, p. 462.

[28] *Journal of the American Medical Association* for September 7, 1929, Vol. 93, No. 10, p. 774.

[29] Through its Far Eastern Epidemiological Intelligence Bureau, the Health Organization of the League of Nations has been able to effect, in 1929 and 1930, considerable improvements in its epidemiological information service to shipping. The

and for the training of medical officers skilled in taking effective action in an emergency, we need not here concern ourselves.

Dr. J. C. Geiger, professor of epidemiology at the Hooper Foundation for Medical Research, University of California, and other authorities believe that, while the epidemic did not originate with the Filipinos, low resistance on their part may have made them especially liable to become its victims on the passage and contact between Shanghai and, especially, American ports; their mortality was greater than that of other racial groups. The epidemic in California probably was aggravated by the fact that unrecognized cases among immigrant Filipinos acted as an additional source of infection.[30]

b. *Venereal Diseases.*

Perhaps the "loathsome diseases" of the labor resolutions mean venereal diseases, with which it is widely stated that Filipinos are greatly afflicted. But the syphilis rate is very low. The gonorrhea rate, according to one Filipino bacteriologist who has the opportunity of seeing a large number of Filipino patients, is fairly high; that is, about 60 per cent of patients examined in the hospitals of San Francisco have had it. But the rate of occurrence varies with the length of residence, being highest among those who have been longest in the United States. Gonorrhea is less common in the Philippine Islands than in this country. And there are few cases among those who have recently arrived from Hawaii.[31] Not more than 15 or 20 per cent of these new arrivals, according to one authority, have had sex experience before coming to the United States, partly because of the supervision exercised over the workers there and their careful selection. As elsewhere, the disease in the Philippine Islands is more prevalent among urban than among rural populations. Also, as in other parts of the world, the venereal rate is high among sailors.

I believe that if the vital statistics of the Philippine Islands are consulted, said Dr. H. H. Darling at a meeting of the Commonwealth Club of California, you will find that venereal disease is as rare in those Islands as it is

recent epidemic of cerebro-spinal meningitis, in this connection, received special attention by the international advisory committee, on which the Philippine Islands are represented.

[30] See also an editorial in the *Journal of the American Medical Association* for August 16, 1930, and a full account of "Epidemic Cerebrospinal Fever on the Pacific Coast," by Dr. Geiger in *California and Western Medicine*, May, 1930, vol. XXXII, No. 5.

[31] See p. 189.

in any country in the world. When Filipinos have venereal disease, they get it here in the United States, or they get it in the Hawaiian Islands. It is not common in the Philippine Islands.[32]

A number of venereal clinics have been visited in connection with the present inquiry to secure information on the relative proportion of Filipinos among their patients. In Seattle, with a large and constantly changing Filipino population, many of them housed in the vicinity of the red light district, nevertheless the municipal clinic finds no larger number of Filipino clients in proportion to their number than clients of other racial groups. An examination by a federal health officer of all Filipinos going from Seattle to Alaska for work in the salmon canneries, following the meningitis scare, revealed a very small proportion with active venereal diseases. This officer believes that venereal infection is decidedly less prevalent among Filipinos than among white Americans of the same class and age group. The federal health officer at San Francisco likewise states that the rejection of Filipino immigrants because of venereal infections is rare. The total number of Filipino cases on the files of the municipal venereal clinic of San Francisco from January 1 to December 5, 1929, was two.

Of course, these statistics are not convincing because Filipinos may prefer to visit private physicians—especially those of their own race and Japanese—when in need of treatment. For this reason the opinions already reported above were checked. A physician who sees many Filipino cases at the Hospital of the University of California states that most recently arrived Filipinos are venereally clean, but that they tend to get infected here through absence of normal sex opportunities. A physician in San Francisco with a considerable insurance practice states that mild forms of gonorrhea are prevalent among Filipinos. Lastly, inquiry produced the interesting fact that, with twenty-six Filipinos employed in the kitchen department of one of the large San Francisco hospitals, involving, because of the labor turnover, the medical examination of probably at least twice that number in the course of a year, only three were rejected in twelve months because of positive reaction to the Wassermann test.

c. *Diseases of the Respiratory Organs.*

Tuberculosis and other respiratory diseases are common in the Philippine Islands, probably, according to the best medical authori-

[32] *The Commonwealth,* Vol. V, No. 45, November 5, 1929, p. 375.

ties, because of unhygienic living conditions: congestion in homes, inadequate diet and, in the cities and among the more affluent classes—with a Latin tradition of the mode of life in consonance with their social status—lack of physical exercise. With the difference in work habits and largely because of the selective character of voluntary migration, tuberculosis is known to be less prevalent among the Filipinos in the United States than it is in their home country.[33] A physician in San Francisco, with a record of several hundred of Filipino patients examined, had among them only ten cases of tuberculosis.

In Seattle, the tuberculosis rate among Filipinos is believed to be slightly higher than the average for the city population—the causes given being overcrowding, frequent unemployment and malnutrition. A federal health officer states that in that city large numbers of Filipinos congregate in the cheapest lodging houses, often as many as eight or ten occupying one small room, sometimes sleeping in shifts because of their poverty and thus eking out a most unhealthy existence. No more favorable environment for the spread of tuberculosis and other communicable diseases could be conceived. The supervising nurse of the tuberculosis division of the city health department believes that, in addition to the causes just named, the Filipinos experience a special danger of infection by being, in the Alaska salmon canneries, brought in contact with the natives of that territory who have an exceptionally low resistance to the disease, first introduced there by white men. The rate at which tuberculosis develops among Filipinos tends to be faster than among Americans. (This, of course, would speak against the theory of a higher tuberculosis rate in the Philippine Islands as compared with the United States, except on the assumption that there also, as in Alaska, the disease has but recently been introduced by white men so that the population has not yet become immune to any extent.)

In San Francisco, the total number of Filipino tuberculosis cases on the active list of the municipal clinic in November, 1929, was 5; the total number under treatment between January 1 and

[33] A scientist who has long resided in the Philippines and there has had access to all classes of the population also blames faulty modes of living for the prevalence of tuberculosis. While nipa-bamboo huts let in a certain amount of air, they are often grossly overcrowded. It is not infrequent to see in a hut with a floor space of 10 feet by 8 feet every inch occupied by persons sleeping on the floor. Every window and door is tightly closed to keep out the *asuang*—the dreaded "night-air." In his opinion, Filipinos have developed a high tolerance in the cities, because of constant exposure.

October 31 of that year, 11.[34] During the period from January 1, 1919, to November 30, 1929, out of a total of 4,150 patients listed in the Chest Clinic of the Hospital of the University of California, in the same city, only 28 were Filipinos, and of these only 8 diagnosed as definitely afflicted with pulmonary tuberculosis. Of a total of 2,585 subsidized patients in the county tuberculosis hospitals of California in 1927, 36 were Filipinos.[35]

As in Seattle, so also in San Francisco, many stories are told of the appalling congestion in which Filipinos are at times found to live. The assistant health officer, Dr. Herbert F. True, blames lack of heating in winter in many cheap apartment and rooming houses as a special cause of overcrowding. Poverty is another. In one case of sickness, a health inspector found four Filipinos occupying a small room with one bed, two using it at night and the other two in day time. In another case, an inspector of hospital orderlies reported finding 24 Filipinos occupying a house which the landlady had rented to two of them. A physician especially familiar with Filipino health through insurance practice confirms the opinion above mentioned that in men of that race the disease is very difficult to arrest. In the county hospital, in spite of fairly good results with American tuberculosis patients, the Filipinos affected with the disease much more frequently fade away and die.

Investigation of the causes of tuberculosis among the Filipino immigrants is rendered difficult by the impossibility, in most cases, of securing a complete case history. Usually the patients have been in this country at least a year or two before tuberculosis develops; but it does not follow that their infection is due to conditions here. Questioning occasionally reveals that other members of the family have died of the disease at home in the Philippine Islands. Malaria and colds contracted at some time in the past are sometimes admitted; but a much larger number of Filipino tuberculosis patients have at some time suffered from malaria than are aware of the fact.

In the case of pneumonia as in that of tuberculosis, Filipino immigrants have a low resistance. Here also bad living conditions and unsuitable habits are at least contributing factors. Dr. J. C. Perry, Senior Surgeon of the United States Public Health Service in San

[34] As in the case of the venereal clinic figures, these statistics are no measure of the total incidence of the disease because it is not known to what extent Filipinos avail themselves of the city's facilities for treatment.

[35] Thirtieth Biennial Report, California Department of Public Health, 1926-1928, p. 131.

Francisco, reports that during the epidemic of cerebro-spinal meningitis numerous cases of pneumonia likewise developed among Filipino steerage passengers.

> It was noted from a study of data and observation at the Quarantine Station that there had been an unusual prevalence of upper respiratory infections among arriving steerage passengers, and that in many cases those vessels which had had many cases of meningitis had concurrent epidemics of pneumonia and influenza.
>
> In crowded steerage quarters under the conditions prevailing there is abundant opportunity for the direct exchange of nose and throat secretions, and the consequent spread of communicable diseases.[36]

There is, then, no experience on which the statement could be based that the Filipinos are unadapted to the American climate. Arguments of that kind, whether related to Filipinos or some other race, are received with scepticism by the medical profession; for it is now well known that both in the tropics and in colder zones climatic change is a minor influence on health conditions compared with unwise or incomplete adaptations of modes of living to climate. The spread of influenza [37] and pneumonia among natives of tropical regions when transplanted to colder regions is probably due not to cold but to lack of ventilation, congestion, unsuitable clothing and unsuitable food habits. But particularly it is due to contagion against which immunity has not been acquired in the previous history of the race.

The effect of climatic change on Filipinos in many respects is similar to that on Negroes. And just as in the early days after the war the northward migration of Negroes brought with it a large increase in deaths from diseases of the respiratory organs, and as in their case the return of a certain proportion to the South to escape the hard winters of the North gave currency to the belief that Negroes could not stand the northern winter, so the southward migration of Filipinos on the Pacific Coast in the fall and early winter has given rise to the belief—also sometimes among themselves—that their health requires a warm climate.[38] But in both cases experience is disproving this notion.

[36] Filipino Immigration. Transactions of the Commonwealth Club of California, vol. XXVI, No. 7, Nov. 5, 1929, p. 362.

[37] Low resistance to influenza in the Philippine Islands, due to the recentness of its introduction, has made this disease as fatal as all our common infections have proved in turn, from Greenland to the South Sea Islands, when they found no previously acquired immunity.

[38] Dr. Milton J. Rosenau, quoted in Charles S. Johnson, The Negro in American

d. *Intestinal Parasites.*

Opponents of Filipino immigration make much of the fact that the spread of dysentery in San Quentin prison and elsewhere has been traced to Filipino carriers. As a matter of fact, there is always some of this disease in the United States. Tropical parasites are indigenous with the Philippine Islands, where probably 80 per cent of the population are infected. The source of infection, as elsewhere, is often associated with the absence of proper sewage systems. Going barefoot is another, perhaps even larger, cause.

A physician familiar with the amœba problem and with large numbers of Filipino patients in the United States believes about 8 per cent of them to be affected by it. Amœbic dysentery has been found in Americans who have never left the United States.

e. *Other Diseases and General State of Health.*

The fungus *coccidioidal granuloma,* which brings about conditions similar to those produced by tuberculosis, is more common in California than anywhere else in the world.[39] One hundred and forty-seven cases of this disease have been studied in California, and of these eight, or 5.44 per cent, occurred among Filipinos. This disease, always serious, has proved particularly fatal to Filipinos and Negroes.[40]

Trachoma, which has been largely instrumental in shaping the port inspection methods of our public health service, rarely occurs among Filipinos.

Hookworm is an important indirect factor in the general effect which the Filipino immigrant has on American health conditions, in that, with about 25 per cent of the Philippine population infected (through lack of sewer systems, even in fairly large towns), it has a devitalizing effect on the whole population of the Islands and exposes them to the inroads of other diseases. Yet, the eradication of hookworm has made remarkable progress in recent years, and Vice-Governor General Eugene Allen Gilmore was able to report to the White House Conference on Child Welfare in February,

Civilization. Henry Holt & Co., 1930, p. 181. The same opinion has also often been expressed about Mexican workers in the more northern states.

39 Alfred C. Reed, Tropical Medicine, *Scientific Monthly,* November, 1929, vol. XXIX, p. 460.

40 Thirtieth Biennial Report of the Department of Public Health of California, 1926-1928, p. 40.

1930, that the results of its conquest are noticeable in the increased mental alertness of the Islands' school population.[41]

There is still considerable leprosy in the Philippine Islands; but any passenger arriving on the Pacific Coast suffering from this disease, if detected, would promptly be returned under the provisions of our quarantine law. Even if the disease should develop or be recognized after landing, the sufferer would be sent to the National Leprosarium or returned.[42]

This section would not be complete without mention of the fact that as regards all the diseases discussed above, conditions in the Philippine Islands are improving. The public health service, partly through lack of funds, leaves a great deal to be desired, but the influence of education, both through the elementary schools and the institutions of higher learning, already has been considerable.[43]

We sometimes forget how recent is our own American preoccupation with personal hygiene. For all classes of Filipinos to learn the value of physical exercise, the dangers of insanitation and the devitalizing effect of every kind of excess, will take time. Dr. George W. McCoy, director of the National Health Institute of the Public Health Service, at one time stationed in the Philippines, and other health authorities testify to the remarkable reaction of seemingly physically poor Filipinos when subjected to a proper diet.

The cultural habits which the Filipinos must learn to overcome if they would enjoy good health, it is thought by some of those who have studied their condition at first hand, are partly those handed down through the ages by their ancestors of Malay blood and partly those inherited from the Spanish régime. Some causes of ill health are attributed to the Spanish inheritance, and therefore largely limited to the higher social classes: the cultivation of

[41] For many years the medical tests in the Philippines of applicants for contract labor in Hawaii included stool examinations for hookworm. This was discontinued several years ago because the number of hookworm carriers found was negligible among the people otherwise eligible.

[42] Dr. J. C. Perry, *loc. cit.*, p. 361.

[43] Progress in this connection largely depends on a rise in prosperity and taxable property. Even in cities with a population of 40,000, writes a correspondent from Manila, there is usually no system of sewerage, and only a score or so of their most affluent citizens will be found to possess modern toilets. Hookworm, according to some authorities, can only be eradicated by costly sanitary measures. Therefore, lack of money seems to be the most important factor. But there is also much criticism of the public health service since its "Filipinization"; and it is pointed out that the conservative resistance to health reforms which must normally be expected cannot as effectively be broken down by local as by national health officers or by Filipino officials as by the militant representatives of the American régime.

indolence as a mark of social superiority, too large a transference of expenditure from proper food and wholesome habitation to personal adornment and social graces.

Yet, even these failings may easily be exaggerated; and the impression that Filipinos are of ill health may largely be due to the normal physical appearance of the Malay type—pale, slight, with high cheek-bones that suggest tuberculosis—compared with the more robust Americans among whom they are seen. A comparison of the Filipino student type with the splendid color and admirable physique of a group of young Filipinos after they have worked for a season in the fields suggests that the observer may readily be led into erroneous generalizations unless he remembers that there are as many differences in the physical conditions of classes and regions in the Philippine Islands as there are here. And it is unquestionably true, as we shall see in a later section, that with a more careful selection of immigrants fitted for the particular work to be done, the planters of Hawaii are securing a physically much more desirable type of Filipino worker than the American employer on the continent, who has no policy of selection and management at all.[44]

From many statements by lay people and resolutions passed by diverse bodies, it is clear that there is a widespread feeling that life in the tropics is unhealthy, and that those coming from tropical regions are necessarily inferior in physical efficiency to those bred in moderate climates. But, as Dr. Alfred C. Reed points out:

> In California especially we have all the essentials of a tropical climate, and . . . diseases ordinarily considered tropical are found native to this state.[45]

Moreover, some diseases popularly looked upon as typically tropical really have originated in the temperate zone:

> An instance of how an ancient and dangerous disease has deserted cold climates and become truly a tropical disease is seen in the case of leprosy.[46]

Dr. Albert W. C. T. Herre, a zoölogist and anthropologist who has lived for many years in the Philippine Islands, believes that all the traditional impediments to full physical efficiency in the tropics can be, and increasingly are being, eliminated:

[44] See Appendix H, p. 384.
[45] Tropical Medicine. *Scientific Monthly,* November, 1929, vol. XXIX, p. 458.
[46] *Ibid.,* p. 459.

It is axiomatic that until we eliminate intestinal and other parasites, which in some places infest an enormous percentage of the people, and likewise overcome the effects of an impoverished diet, . . . we can know nothing of the results due to a tropical climate. It has been the mode to impute the lack of physical strength and the lack of energy of many people native to the tropics to the ill effects of the climate, when as a matter of fact they have been weakened by hookworm, malaria, filariasis, amœbic dysentery and other infestations and infections. . . .

Wherever we find native workmen sufficiently well fed and leading an active life we find them well muscled, capable of great exertion and able to do efficient work. One could not ask for better specimens physically than the longshoremen and sailors of the Philippine ports, or the lean hard Samals who not so long ago were the most dreaded of pirates. On the other hand, many of the tao and illustrado classes alike are miserably puny specimens, equally deficient in muscle and vitality. But this is due to many causes, some of them already cited, others having to do with social traditions and customs, but none traceable to climate.[47]

As we shall see, these contentions are fully corroborated by the experience of Hawaii with Filipino laborers.[48]

In conclusion, mention should be made of an increasing tendency to question the whole basis on which comparisons have in the past been made between standards of health in tropical countries and those of temperate climate. Caucasians in tropical countries have experienced among themselves as well as among the natives that a lower basic metabolism, expressing itself in lessened vigor, is a symptom of successful adaptation rather than of lower vitality in the sense of physical failure.[49] Recognition of the need for adaptation does not, of course, lessen the health problems produced by migration; but it transfers their consideration from preoccupations with racial factors to those with factors of general validity.

[47] *Scientific Monthly*, September, 1923, vol. XVII, No. 3, p. 214.

[48] See p. 188 *et seq.*

[49] Several Americans, trained in scientific observation, declare that they are able to maintain in the tropics indefinitely an optimum of physical and mental energy.

CHAPTER X

SOCIAL PROBLEMS OF THE FILIPINO

I. LACK OF NORMAL HOME LIFE

WHILE, for the sake of convenience, we have separated the economic handicaps of the Filipino in America, it has already been seen that these are very closely related to social handicaps. The excessive mobility of the Filipino laborer is that of a group of men without homes. The fact that he has no family to support enables him to undercut wages when in competition with other men; the fact that he has no family *to support him,* puts him at a disadvantage in competition with other boys.

In a way, the Filipino only experiences what other immigrant groups have experienced before him in the earlier years of their American residence:

> Fully two-thirds of our incoming immigrants have always been men. This sex disparity brings problems of its own. Many of the men are unmarried; others have left their families at home, hoping to be able some day to send for them. The young men who come are of marriageable age, but owing to language and other barriers, find scant opportunity to meet young women whom they can marry.[1]

Why does not the Filipino create a satisfying home life for himself? For the same reason that other young foreigners who intend to return to their country make no such effort. The proportion of Filipinos who marry in this country is exceedingly small, as the census returns will soon reveal. From estimates collected in the cities with larger Filipino colonies, it is probable that the total number of Filipinos with dependents in the United States may be less than one thousand. And this prevalence of bachelorhood is due not only to the desire of the great majority to return to their own country but also to exceptionally close home ties which usually mean that the family is considered to have a say in the choice of a young man's wife. Moreover, the marital choices of the Filipino are lim-

[1] Annie Marion MacLean, Modern Immigration. J. B. Lippincott Co., 1925, p. 51.

ited by state law in California, Oregon, Arizona, Idaho, and Nevada.[2]

Until lately, there has been much uncertainty concerning the Filipino's "official" race in states that impose restrictions upon the marriages between Mongolians and whites. Marriages between Filipinos and white women were frequent; and it was left, apparently, to the discretion of county clerks in issuing licenses to decide on the racial membership of applicants. Sometimes the Filipino's status in a California county changed over-night as new county clerks were appointed whose anthropological ideas differed from those of their predecessors. Thus in Santa Barbara, county clerk D. F. Hunt, several years ago, decided that Filipinos were Mongolians and has consistently held to this decision in the face of heated arguments and of the fact that many couples which first presented themselves before him later secured marriage licenses in some other county. Other county clerks took the same stand. The majority of officials seem, without any recourse to science at all, to have married Filipinos indiscriminately with white and with Japanese and Chinese girls, thus exposing themselves to the possible charge that if Filipinos should through some court decision be declared to be white, then their marriages to the Asiatic girls would be illegal.

The issue received much public attention from a case decided in the Superior Court at Los Angeles in February, 1930, when the mother of a white girl secured, first a temporary and later a permanent, injunction against the county clerk of Los Angeles to restrain him from issuing a marriage license for her daughter and a Filipino. Evidence as to the Filipino's race adduced by the County's counsel and by the attorneys representing the mother ranged over the whole of anthropological literature, from Linnæus and Cuvier in the eighteenth century down to recognized textbook writers of today. The former argued that, according to the best authorities, Filipinos are Malays, and that Malays are not Mongolians; the latter, assisted by expert testimony, argued that all the brown races are Mongolian. The County's counsel was further able to back up his case with an opinion rendered in 1921 on the operation of section 69 of the California Civil Code, enacted in 1884, which provides that no marriage between a white person and a Mongolian or a Negro shall be performed in that state; on that occasion the opinion had been upheld that the legislature did not intend to

[2] See p. 99.

prohibit the marriage of people of the Malay race with white persons. However, Judge Smith, in making the final decision in the present case in favor of the mother, seems to have been influenced by a later opinion given by Attorney General U. S. Webb, to the effect that Filipinos are Mongolians. While this decision may be further challenged, as things stand at present, the County of Los Angeles, which had the largest number of applications from Filipinos for marriage licenses in the state, is refusing them all, and other county officers, to avoid litigation, are following suit.

A question which remains for decision is whether all marriages performed between Filipinos and white women in the State of California since 1881 must be considered illegal. There are said to be several hundred of them,[3] and their cancellation at this time obviously would create serious hardship. On the other hand, it is impossible to consider these marriages legally valid until some court has passed upon the question or special legislation has declared them so.

For the Filipino, to be officially classed as a Mongolian, has a serious social significance quite apart from these marriages. He has never considered himself as such and, in fact, has not been accepted as an "Oriental" in Chinese and Japanese society. The group life of the Chinese is too close-knit to permit of the admission of an outsider on terms of intimacy. This is even more strongly the case with the Japanese colonies in western communities; these live entirely apart and uphold to the best of their ability the cultural traditions of their country even to the third generation of American residence.

Some of the most successful Filipino marriages are those where the wives are Mexican. Partly because of a similarity of cultural background and of language, often also of common membership in the Catholic Church, Filipinos of a desirable type are accepted into the best Mexican families, and there is no tradition of social superiority on either side. However, cases are not infrequent in which a Mexican girl, after marrying a Filipino, is ostracized; and these marriages, usually brought about by a lavish expenditure of the groom during the period of courtship, are prone to end in the divorce court. Since Mexicans of all shades of Indian admixture are considered white under American law, many of these marriages probably are also illegal, except where they have been brought

[3] Possibly an exaggeration. No accurate statistics are available until Census returns are published.

about through temporary residence in a state without legal restrictions against racial intermarriage. Similarity of cultural background and likeness of religious faith also are the reasons why, in the eastern cities, marriages between Filipinos and girls of Italian parentage are said to be those most likely to conduce to happiness. Filipino marriages with Indian women in Alaska and with Negro women are very rare. In all the mixed marriages, contacts with the wife's family are usually not strong. American-born women, more particularly, who marry Filipinos are nearly always unattached.

Except occasionally as a student, the Filipino has practically no direct contact with American home life. The American women he is permitted to know intimately are either frequenters of dance halls or fellow-employees in hotels and restaurants. As we have seen, even among women in humble walks of life it has become increasingly difficult for a Filipino to make acquaintances without having his right to them challenged. Under the circumstances, it is not surprising that among the small number of Filipino marriages with American women, those between college students play a conspicuous part. And these are also the most likely to endure—so long as the couple remains in this country. An educated woman marrying a Filipino is almost certain to take a keen interest in the husband's social and national ambitions—perhaps frankly countering ostracism of her own set by espousing the cause of Philippine nationalism or of "oppressed" peoples generally.

Lack of stability also marks Filipino marriages with women of their own nationality. Because of the scarcity of Filipino women in the United States, the temptations for them of lack of fidelity are considerable; and it is noteworthy that social agencies, while they occasionally have to adjust the affairs of deserted Filipino husbands with children, rarely find themselves burdened with the care of deserted Filipino women.[4]

Among many Filipinos interviewed on this subject few were found who did not prefer, if they had the choice, Filipino to American wives. The main reason is that the great majority intend at one time or other to return to the Philippine Islands, and they fear —their apprehension is born out by actual experience—that Ameri-

[4] For exactly the same reason, an abnormal sex ratio, desertion by wives also appears frequently among Mexican immigrants, especially in the North. It was also observed among Russian immigrants before the War. See Jerome Davis, The Russian Immigrant. Macmillan Co., 1922, p. 78.

can girls will find it too difficult to adjust themselves to Filipino ideas of home life.

A former American official in the Philippine Islands ascribes the unhappy outcome of so many marriages between emigrants and American wives to a tendency on the part of such emigrants to exaggerate the attractions of their homeland and the status of their families when courting an American girl: "They paint elaborate pictures of palm trees and music, great estates and titles of old Spanish families. Then, when their wives arrive here, they have to eat terrible food, live with an entire Filipino family, and have no social life of their own. A few of these women leave their husbands but remain in the Philippines, trading their way around. We have had to help dozens of them to return to America."

In the relatively few cases where American wives are reported to have succeeded in making happy homes for their Filipino husbands in the Philippine Islands, the reason is that they have sacrificed their preconceived tastes and ideas and that, because they brought knowledge, perhaps even specialized training, to the affairs of the husband's home, they won recognition from his family. Of course, the strongest reason for not desiring to marry American women is that the intelligent Filipino is usually aware of his inability, in his home country, to earn enough to maintain a family according to American standards.

It is worth noting also that the number of children in Filipino-American marriages is usually small. It is probable that low earnings and the practice of birth control are the reasons.

Why are there not more Filipino women in this country? The answer most frequently heard is that it is contrary to the traditions of the Islands to have girls emigrate or travel alone. But this explanation is insufficient; for it does not explain why whole families do not emigrate. Truer explanations probably are that the cost of transportation is exceptionally high; that Filipino migration to the mainland of the United States is relatively recent and so still in the stage of experimentation on the part of the Islands' young manhood; and that until recently Hawaiian sugar planters have encouraged migration of single men rather than of families to Hawaii.

Of the single Filipino women now on the mainland of the United States, almost all have come as students; and many of them marry educated Filipinos here before returning to their country to practice their profession—usually nursing or teaching. Of the non-student Filipinas in the United States most have been married before they came to this country and have accompanied their husbands here from Hawaii. Their total number is probably only a few hundred.

Not only absence of women of their own nationality is a major cause of difficulty. Lack of home life may be compensated for by a strong group cohesion under male leadership. But because of the circumstances of their migration, older men of experience, enjoying general prestige, are few. There are, in the larger cities with Filipino colonies, mature men of that nationality in business and in the professions; but often these have yet to spend much of their energy to maintain their own status. In a few instances, men of this caliber have become true leaders. In one city, Detroit, the more mature and married Filipinos associated, several years ago, largely for the purpose of establishing a nucleus of wholesome community life for the younger members of the colony.

A very natural further cause of lack of cohesion is the tribal division of the Philippine Islands, which expresses itself in the formation of small groups of those who come from the same regions and speak the same dialect. This tendency to separation exists in all our larger immigrant groups but is particularly strong among the Filipinos because of the recency of their national consciousness and the distinctness of their dialects.[5] There is as yet no common background of tradition, and in the more intimate concerns of life the immigrant associates with those who share his habits and tastes, however genuine may be his loyalty to the national cause.

In this connection mention must also be made of the fact that organized religion does not usually have a strong hold on the young Filipino in the United States. Although in several cities, notably in Seattle, Portland, San Francisco and Los Angeles, Catholic organizations have by admirable leadership won the respect and loyalty of considerable numbers of Filipino youths, it is probably more largely to the friendly services rendered than to a sense of religious duty that these memberships are primarily due. A trend of Filipino youth away from the Mother Church, observed in the Philippine Islands, is usually attributed to the influence of the America-oriented school system.

The Filipino who comes to this country, while calling himself a Catholic, knows little, if anything, about his Faith; he is easy prey for maleficent secret

[5] In this respect, the experience of the Filipinos parallels that of the earlier Italian immigrants whose excessive group division has likewise been ascribed to the recentness of their national consciousness. See Robert F. Foerster, The Italian Emigration of Our Times. Harvard University Press, 1919, p. 37 *et seq.*

organizations which affirm they will better his economic state, and for professional proselyters who would deflect him from his Faith by promise of social connection. Yet the faith of generations is not totally destroyed.[6]

One reason for the energy which some Protestant churches have displayed in their activities on behalf of local Filipino immigrants is a previous connection with missionary enterprise in the Philippines or through the chance circumstance that the minister or some other church worker has at one time lived in the Philippines. The charge of proselytism among Catholics is generally denied. The difficulty lies in the Philippine Islands where, for historical reasons, Catholic church membership, while it is still general, has become so weakened in intensity that it retains little hold on the young men who emigrate and often but vaguely realize that participation in the advantages offered by Protestant institutions in the United States (and in certain lodges) impairs their good standing in the Church.[7] There is no definitely anti-Catholic movement among the young Filipinos in this country. The success of the Filipino organization managed by the Society of Saint Vincent de Paul of Portland, and of the Catholic Filipino Clubs in Seattle, San Francisco, and Los Angeles, in securing and holding their membership would seem to show that efforts of Catholic organizations on behalf of their welfare are greatly appreciated by these young immigrants.

Owing to the extent of American missionary enterprise in the Philippine Islands, many young Filipinos coming to this country are predisposed to membership in a Protestant church. But as a rule only a minority of the Filipinos in the community are reached by Protestant churches or church institutions; and here, it is true, the social and recreational elements are the main attraction.

It is only just to add that among the Filipino leaders, both on the Pacific Coast and in the inland and eastern cities, those who have the most wholesome influence on their young countrymen usually are themselves deeply religious and, through continuous contact with Christian organizations, both Catholic and Protestant, fired with a desire to serve their fellow men. In this connection, the Y.M.C.A.—with a few outstanding exceptions—plays a less

[6] Andrew G. Haley in *America,* the Catholic weekly, for February 15, 1930. This writer further deplores that so few Filipinos coming to this country for higher education go to Catholic colleges.

[7] One important historical factor has been the establishment of an independent, national Catholic Church, by secession from Rome, which, though hard hit by a decision of the American Supreme Court, depriving it of most of its property, has gradually regained its strength.

conspicuous part than the youth of the Filipino immigrants would suggest as likely. The explanation probably is that individual churches with a background of traditional missionary interest in the Philippine Islands have a stronger motive of helpfulness and, since they can more easily limit the nature of their services to the Filipino immigrant, face fewer difficulties in rendering these in the face of a community sentiment antagonistic to the Filipino.

Be that as it may, in connection with our present topic it is worth noting that absence of a well regulated home life, the lack of mature leaders, and the slackness of religious affiliations are three distinct causes of unadjustment for the Filipino immigrant.

2. EXCESSIVE MOBILITY

A fourth cause is the mobility of the Filipino worker, which stands in the way of strong and lasting group organization. It has already been noted that the popular impression as to the size of Filipino population on the Pacific Coast is an exaggerated one because its members are constantly on the move. A stream passes along the highways, flows around the cheap rooming houses for transients, fills the seats in stage and railroad stations—seems to be everywhere. This flux, brought about by the intermittent nature of the Filipino's principal sources of livelihood, also is reflected in the temporary nature of his organizational bonds.[8]

Filipino leaders frequently exhort their countrymen to be more loyal to the many fraternal orders, associations and clubs which seem to be constantly forming and dissolving. Strong editorials in Filipino papers deplore the mushroom appearance of new societies and the frequent splitting off of new societies from old ones. Outsiders point to the frequent quarrels between rival Filipino organizations and their managers as evidences of an inherent fault of race character.[9]

And yet, it is all very easy to explain. For, the Filipino group has not as yet, except in isolated cases, acquired a permanently resident leadership. Organizations break up often because all of the officers have removed within a year or two after their in-

[8] A similar instability has also been observed among Mexican mutual benefit societies, in Southern California and in Chicago.

[9] Dr. Manuel Gamio points out that such a diversified group organization of immigrants may be beneficent in its general effect by educating for social cooperation. Mexican Immigration to the United States. University of Chicago Press, 1930, pp. 135-136.

auguration. Sometimes the inclusion of larger numbers of a dialect group previously represented only by a few individuals makes for schism. Moreover, the members are all young, in most cases; distinctions of prestige that make for election to posts of authority are acquired by fleeting recognition of ability—especially oratorical ability—and not by measurable services to the cause over a number of years. Hence jealousies are natural. Furthermore, deprived of many chances of remunerative employment except through hard labor, the emoluments of office are more attractive than they would be for members of other sets. The president of a Filipino club, even when conspicuously honest, has valuable patronage to distribute among his friends. The prestige which his office gives him may be just enough, for example, to make the issue of yet another Filipino newspaper a promising venture. (Of such papers there is no end, and many do not outlast the first three numbers.) He may engage in business, set up as a contractor, maybe, and so gradually entrench his position as an outstanding member of the colony. Of all the Americanisms which Filipinos of some years' residence on this continent have absorbed, the pursuit of personal success is perhaps the most noteworthy; and so it must here be recorded in passing that leadership too often is associated in that group with shady methods of self-enrichment. Hence scepticism as to motives plays no small part in the more intelligent or educated Filipino worker's attitude toward organized effort.

In short, excessive mobility keeps the Filipino apart to a considerable extent from the finer elements in American community life, exposes him to exploitation, and gives him a false notion of the values of western civilization. It prevents the growth of steadying influences on the younger members of the group, produces homesickness, recklessness, and much preventable unhappiness.

3. BAD HOUSING CONDITIONS

Both in town and country, many, perhaps a majority of, Filipino immigrants are wretchedly housed. This is due in part to the negligent attitude of community and employers toward itinerant labor, in part to poverty, in part to a wrong budgeting of incomes, and in part to unpreparedness for the demands of American climate and of physical efficiency.

Take Seattle: Although Filipinos here often return with hundreds of dollars in their pockets from the salmon fisheries, and from lucrative employment also in the rich fruit districts of eastern Washington, many of them crowd together in the least desirable section of the big city, in close proximity to Chinatown and the cheap rooming houses of white itinerant laborers. Sometimes a dozen or more together rent an apartment or an unpainted and unrepaired wooden house amid the litter and waste lots of a once fashionable residential hillside. Unwelcome in more desirable parts of the city, even students and men of fairly profitable local employments here congregate, standing in pool-rooms and on the streets until late into the night to avoid as long as possible the depressing atmosphere of their abodes. In San Francisco, most Filipinos live in the heart of the city, again close to Chinatown amid the clatter of street cars and the shrill noises of motor traffic charging the hillside in second. In Stockton, Filipinos share with Asiatics and Mexicans a few congested blocks, living over cheap stores and restaurants, sometimes in fairly well kept "hotels" that are subject to frequent inspection by the local health authorities, but also often in rooming houses and private apartments whose cleanliness, to judge from outer appearance, may be suspected to leave much to be desired. In Los Angeles, again, a few streets near the Plaza seem to house the great majority of Filipinos. Here the streets are wide and well kept, however; and occasionally the owners of substantial residences in good upkeep take Filipino boarders. In the smaller towns, Filipinos usually live in houses owned by contractors who deduct the room rent from their wages and, forced perhaps by the shortage of available homes in the areas where "Orientals" are tolerated, give little accommodation in return.

It is because of these living conditions that Filipinos are often unjustly accused of personal uncleanliness. But they are merely tainted by their environment, as other residents in such places were tainted before them. As a labor official observes:

> The sections of the cities occupied by Orientals are usually the "tenderloins," the "hobohemias," where all the odds and ends of city population live without any community life. The American people have associated these places with crime, vice, poverty, and the like, so that any resident therein cannot but get the taint of such discrimination. . . . It is natural to suppose that all people living in such places are of the same class. . . . The depravities attributed to or associated with Japanese and Chinese in the height of the agitation are now associated with Filipinos.[10]

[10] C. O. Young in the *Seattle Star* for January 4, 1929.

Many of the houses occupied by Filipinos in California are unheated. This, of course, makes for more congestion, as it is natural for shivering human beings to crowd together for warmth and comfort.[11] Perhaps partly for this reason, the overcrowding in the more southern California centers of Filipino life is accentuated in the winter months, even when opportunities of employment there are no greater and living costs are higher than in the cities more centrally situated for early spring work in the fields. And again it is said that one reason why Filipinos congregate in the cities of the Pacific Coast is that they have heard of the low temperatures in the cities of the North and East, possibly without always knowing of the universal custom in the colder regions of heating houses with furnaces.[12]

Not social discrimination, refusing to Filipinos a wider dispersion over the city area, but the desire to be near to possible sources of employment sometimes is the cause of overcrowding. In Los Angeles, for example, informed persons doubt the inability of Filipinos to find homes, either individually or in groups, in many other parts of the city besides that which so many of them choose. But nearness to the employment offices, and of course also to the pool-rooms, barber shops and restaurants of their countrymen, to their clubs and recreation centers, forms an attraction against which more desirable surroundings weigh too lightly in the scale.

It must further be admitted that adequate food and housing accommodation play too small a part in the traditional culture pattern to which these young men are accustomed. Room overcrowding is as common in the Philippine Islands as it is in the Chinatowns of our Pacific Coast cities. There as here, too large a part of the income is spent on gaudy raiment, too little on house room. Unfortunately, kept too far apart from the domestic life of Americans of modest means, Filipino immigrants do not become sufficiently aware of our American scales of value in material comforts and enjoyments, and their measures of prosperity remain too superficial.

Housing conditions on the ranches are another chapter, for here not individual tastes but the responsibility of employer and com-

[11] Incidentally, this was one of the major causes in the high sickness rate among Filipino steerage passengers, since corrected by an order of the federal government compelling an increase of the space allotted to these passengers and by greater attention of the steamship companies themselves to proper heating and ventilation.

[12] There is no movement of Filipinos from the eastern parts of the United States to the South for the winter months.

munity play the largest part in determining prevailing standards.[13] Complaints of insanitary camp conditions for itinerant workers are an old story on the Pacific Coast, with which state legislatures and administrations have endeavored to cope for a long time. The California Commission of Immigration and Housing, now superseded in this effort by the Division of Housing and Sanitation of the Department of Industrial Relations, has been instrumental in immensely improving these conditions through a rigorous system of inspection and prosecution of defaulting owners. Nevertheless, the general standard, even though complying with elementary demands of sanitation, is distinctly low—especially if one may compare it with the conditions provided on the sugar plantations of Hawaii from which so many Filipino workers migrate to the Pacific Coast.[14]

The camp habits of Filipino workers, according to R. W. Kearney, chief of that division, are clean; but in the camps occupied by Filipinos the worst cases of overcrowding are observed. Often the camps, or rather shacks, that give occasion to this criticism are owned and managed, not by ranch owners or farmers, but by Filipino contractors who, as we have seen, find it profitable to house gangs of Filipino workers in camps of their own from where they can easily dispatch them daily to fields within a considerable radius. One such contractor in the Salinas region was recently arrested for housing an incredible number of workers in a four-room house. The excuse here, as in similar cases, was that house provision was unable to keep pace with the rapidly expanding area under crops demanding handling by Filipino laborers.

Polluted water, especially in the Delta Region of the San Joaquin Valley, is sometimes the cause of sickness and of deaths from typhoid and other contagious diseases. Even more than in the case of the Filipino's urban habitations, lack of heating is a frequent cause of throat and lung diseases, while poor construction, permitting drafts of air, are a cause of huddling even in comparatively mild weather.

A number of camps in the Salinas area were visited in the course of the present investigation. One camp, housing thirty boys in the

[13] For a description of labor camps in the Delta Region of the San Joaquin Valley, housing from 5,000 to 6,000 Filipinos during the asparagus season, see Facts About Filipino Immigration into California, p. 66 *et seq.*

[14] Will J. French, director of the California State Department of Industrial Relations, in his monthly report for May, 1929, refers to the fact that out of more than nine thousand workers housed in 352 of the state's labor camps recently visited 2,199 were Filipinos, as against 4,343 Americans and 1,195 Mexicans.

busy season, consisted of a series of rooms opening to the outside, under one long roof, with kitchen and bathroom at one end. The bath was a square tank in a dirty outhouse, roughly constructed, it seemed, by the workers themselves, with an open space underneath for a wood fire to heat the water—a most insanitary arrangement because of the temptation it holds out for many persons to use the same water instead of waiting between baths until more can be heated. (See illustration facing p. 130.) The building was unpainted, and the cots were as close together as they would go.

The second camp inspected was a little better. It is reached by a wooden bridge over a stagnant pond, almost certainly a mosquito breeder, perhaps three hundred feet from the buildings. This camp, belonging to one of the more important lettuce growing companies, consisted of a large sleeping shed, fairly well built, with a separate kitchen and a bath house equipped with a shower and sanitary plumbing. The yard was extremely dirty and evidently had never been considered worth tidying up.

A third camp, belonging to a large carrot producing firm, is considered a model. In addition to a well constructed bunk house, it had an airy dining room, a kitchen with modern boilers and scullery, and a bath house with cement floor and five showers. The water here is heated in ample volume by a coal furnace.

There are two reasons why camp conditions generally are so unsatisfactory: Where contractors are responsible, they often are too poor to pay for proper equipment and furthermore are tempted to cut down on every kind of expenditure. With a small margin of profit on field work, the earnings from providing the workers with camp accommodation—including a separate rent for cots—and board often are a substantial part of the contractor's income to which all too often he adds through less legitimate means. The second reason is that the owners of those ranches that provide camps for their seasonal workers usually are absentees. The tenant who has taken a three years' lease finds it cheaper to pay a fine than to invest in expensive camp buildings or equipment. Illustrative of their attitude was the response of a rancher, far from a Filipino settlement, who was asked by the contractor he had engaged for the field work where the workers were to be put up: "Here are 160 acres; take your choice." A large rancher in the San Joaquin Valley gave a contractor for sixty to seventy-five men two abandoned barns in which to house his men. In another case, twenty men were housed under the roof of a barn, the beam six feet high, all sleeping on the floor. The ground floor of the same barn housed forty more laborers.

Sometimes employers when faced with criticism contend that the willingness of Oriental workers to put up with rough accommodation of this kind during the few weeks of harvesting the crop is the chief reason for their employment. If camps suitable for white workers had to be erected, they say, there would be no dearth of white labor—but the cost would be prohibitive. In contrast, a case of cooperation between a Filipino contractor and local ranchers was mentioned by several informants which shows that the economic obstacles to good housing of field workers can be overcome. This man, in the Salinas Valley, obtained loans from the farmers with which to build a model camp at a point, in the open country, from which many of their ranches could be reached. This camp occupies five acres, taken on a ten-year lease. The shacks and other buildings are substantially constructed and heated.

Under the present California law, every contractor for labor must have an employment agency license and be bonded, whether he charges a fee or reimburses himself for his trouble by profit on transporting, boarding, or housing workers. These licenses can be revoked, and the contractor holding a license is subject to inspection. As the bond is fairly high, $2,000, the contractor has to obtain help, usually, from a surety company or, sometimes, from a grower for whom he contracts. Since under the California law the employer is held responsible for the payment of wages to individual workers even when these have been obtained through a contractor who acts as foreman, the larger growers often insure voluntarily for even larger sums against possible defalcations on the part of the contractors. (See p. 87.) In this way, it is hoped that some of the smaller and less honest contractors, especially those who have been profiteering on the side earnings of their legitimate business, will gradually be eliminated. So far as the bunk houses on individual farms are concerned, it is believed that the improvement of roads and the cheap automobile and second-hand truck will gradually eliminate them altogether. A distance of ten or fifteen miles between camp and workplace is no longer unusual. The resulting concentration of workers' accommodation in larger units will, it is thought by many, result not only in a great improvement of the housing standards but also in a social camp life counteracting the temptations of the near-by city. It is worth noting also that in the fruit districts, where ranchers are more accustomed to

Photo Hobart N. Young

Photo Hobart N. Young

Above: ONE OF THE WORST CAMPS FOR FILIPINO LETTUCE WORKERS, SALINAS VALLEY. (Note open-air bath at right.)
Below: TYPICAL CAMP FOR FILIPINO LETTUCE WORKERS, SALINAS VALLEY

Photo J. J. Billones

Photo J. J. Billones

Above: FILIPINO POOL PARLOR IN STOCKTON. (Proprietress center right.)
Below: A FILIPINO LODGE DANCE IN STOCKTON. (A majority of the participants are field laborers.)

dealing with itinerant white workers, the conditions for Filipinos and Mexicans also tend to be better than they are in the areas specializing in work which for long has been done exclusively by Orientals. A peculiarity of the Filipinos is that they seem to prefer to live together in a large room, provided they can also have a large dining and recreation hall and hot and cold showers, while Mexicans desire individual shacks and prefer to buy and cook their own food, not caring at all for recreation facilities.

Fruit growers, even when seriously crippled by shortage of labor, often take the attitude that the cost of providing model camps for their seasonal workers would be prohibitive. As one of them expressed it, "the paternal interest of the rancher in his workers that prevailed in California during Spanish days has permanently given place to the American way." And that, in his eyes and those of many others, seemed to imply providing no more than the minimum the law requires. The question whether unsatisfactory housing accommodation had anything to do with their labor difficulties was answered negatively whenever it was put in these conversations.

4. LACK OF THE RECREATIONAL FACILITIES

One of the special cares of the American school system in the Philippine Islands has been to awaken the people to the values of physical exercise and, particularly, outdoor recreation. According to the older social tenets it was not dignified to exert oneself; the children of *illustrados,* that is, of the more well-to-do, had even their books carried to school by servants. But such has been the eagerness with which American ideas have been observed that today there is probably no spot on earth where games and athletics are valued more highly or participated in so eagerly by the youth of all classes than in the Philippines.[15]

As one talks with Filipino immigrants, one becomes impressed with the fact that many of them come to the United States in a spirit of adventure. They not only seek new experiences but also wish to measure their skills and prowess against those of Americans. They are prepared for competition as the way to success. Whether it be due, as has been stated, to the long history of their island people as a history of inter-tribal warfare and of seamanship or to the American school and playground, wherever conditions are

[15] See Charles Edward Russell, The Outlook for the Philippines. Century Co., 1922, chapter XVI. See also p. 439.

favorable we find Filipino youths in the United States engaged in outdoor sport.

Filipinos have been successful aspirants to athletic honors in high schools and colleges. A graduate of the University of Chicago had distinguished himself at tennis, basketball and marathon running, before being appointed physical director of the national university in Manila. Another one recently was the all-around champion swimmer and won his varsity letters in tennis and other sports at practically all major sports (except golf and polo) on the Pacific Coast and in the Middle West. At the end of January, 1930, the chairman of the California State Boxing Commission ruled that Filipinos in that state must be excluded from boxing contests because their presence in the ring was inflaming public opinion.[16] As in the case of similar rulings against Negroes in other parts of the country, their pugilistic success is feared, not their failure. To quote from the *Cleveland Plain Dealer:*

> The Filipinos have taken to prize fighting like the proverbial duck to water. They have repeatedly beaten the Nordic, the Latin, the Celt and the Semite in the American realm of pugilism. And in the greater part of the United States their successful efforts have been popular.

In Hawaii, the present writer was informed that Filipinos had "gone crazy" over football.

Yet, in spite of this propensity and in spite of his youth, the Filipino immigrant does not usually enjoy normal recreational opportunities in this country. Herded as a steerage passenger, again herded on a stage to take him to his destination here, herded into an overcrowded rooming house, with often nothing but a dismal and congested street for his use out of doors, the opportunity for wholesome individual spare-time occupation often never enters into his life at all. Of course, it may be said that this is a big country, and if Filipinos herd together that is their own fault. Other immigrant groups have done the same; and, of course, our American poor are far from being provided with adequate facilities for outdoor recreation. But the Filipinos' experiences in this respect on the mainland are often sharply at variance with their own earlier opportunities and with their tastes.

The Filipino likes company; he is naturally drawn to those places where he can hear his mother tongue spoken and where things

[16] This ban seems to have been lifted in February; for, in that month several bouts between Filipinos and Americans were reported from different parts of the state, which were attended by mixed crowds without the occurrence of disorder.

familiar greet his eye. Hence the congregations at street corners and in pool-rooms; hence also the ease with which large numbers can be induced to gamble, to visit dance halls, to assemble in celebration of some holiday or other. It would be as easy to get large numbers of them to attend a baseball game, to take part in athletic contests, to do almost anything that American youth likes to do. But unfortunately, public opinion assumes that they share the tastes of other Orientals, and their cultural exclusiveness. It takes no account of the fact that these youths have often been brought up in American schools and on American playgrounds, and that they would readily mix with American youths in outdoor games if given that chance. There is no more dreary region than Seattle's Chinatown where practically nothing is going on, especially since the police closed the dance halls. With the exception of a cheap moving picture house, the Filipino worker finds nothing here to keep him out of those iniquitous places where Chinese owners and those of his own nationality lie in wait to deprive him of his money in one way or another. One can walk the streets all evening and hear no music or any of the sounds that indicate innocent gayety.

The Filipinos' amusements in America and their deteriorating effects are frequently described at great length in illustrated articles contributed from America to the *Philippine Free Press* of Manila, a paper edited more particularly in the interests of educated Filipinos. The descriptions given coincide very largely with those given by American observers.

Those Filipinos who send money home are the "blanket boys." These have steady jobs on the farm. . . . The pastime of the "blanket boys" is playing cards. After a day's work they assemble around the improvised table and play cards till late at night. Poker and black jack are the popular games. Their hard-earned money is easily lost. In the town or city the *Pinoys* may be found in the billiard rooms and pool-halls from after breakfast till late at night.

There are many gambling houses, mostly managed and controlled by Chinese. They are popularly known as "sikoy-sikoys." The Filipinos who are usually there are called "sikoy-sikoy boys."

In Stockton there is one gambling house managed and controlled by white men. It is for Filipinos. It is one mile south from the heart of the city. Anyone who wants to go there gets a free ride back and forth. These hired automobiles are owned by Filipinos.

In Walnut Grove there are six "sikoy-sikoys"; in Isleton there are four; in Dinuba one; in Redley four, and so on. All these gambling houses are patronized by Filipinos and a few Mexicans.

The gambling houses in Walnut Grove and Isleton serve free meals: breakfast at eight o'clock; dinner at twelve; supper at five; coffee and bread at ten in the evening.

These gambling houses are hard to raid. Outside are guards who give the warning when they see suspicious-looking characters. . . .[17]

The Filipinos are too poor and too unorganized to provide a high type of indoor recreation for themselves. In Chicago, the clubhouse of the Filipino Association is a dismal place on a dismal street. In Detroit the single Filipino dance hall was objected to by social workers, not for moral reasons but because of its shabbiness. (Yet, in this city the Filipinos are not admitted to the better dance halls.) In San Francisco, Los Angeles and Portland, religious agencies have come to the aid and provided club rooms for those willing to abide by the rules of membership. In a few places, the Y.M.C.A. permits the use of its premises by all, irrespective of race or nationality; but few Filipinos except those of the student type seem to be attracted. Here the difficulty sometimes is that, deprived of a normal home life and unwelcome elsewhere, Filipino members take too enthusiastically advantage of what is offered them and all but monopolize the premises. This, together with too aggressive an assertion of their social equality, does not tend to make the Filipinos popular among others of their own age, especially since nearly always social recognition is almost at once taken advantage of in efforts to meet and pay court to American girls.[18]

But we are here speaking of the Filipino's problems and not those of the institutions that are trying to help him. He finds himself classed in the public mind with a group whose recreations he is forced to adopt, whether he shared them at home or not, the Orientals. Dance halls are increasingly closed to him; and other opportunities to meet women of the better type are largely

[17] The quotation is followed by a detailed description of the way in which the secrecy of these places is maintained. *Philippine Free Press,* February 23, 1929. Other articles, giving first-hand accounts of Filipino experiences in the night-life of Los Angeles and of Chicago are given in the *Press* for June 8 and November 16, 1929.

[18] The relationship between acquaintance with American girls and social prestige among the Filipino immigrants was graphically described by the American director of a Catholic Filipino organization: "On one occasion when a party was to be held, the question was timidly advanced whether dancing would be allowed [on the premises of a religious institution]. When I had assured them that they might, some suggested it would be difficult to find girls, and it was intimated that I might perhaps find women partners for the dance. When I refused, twelve of the seventy-five boys managed to find lady companions for the event. These were given special seats during the earlier part of the entertainment and treated with the greatest deference. The boys who had managed to persuade girls to accept the invitation at once rose to the summit of admiration among their fellows."

denied. He is often forced, between jobs, to spend days and weeks in idleness, yet is given no facilities of an educational character to turn these periods to his advantage.

Filipino leaders are the severest critics of their young countrymen's misuse of their leisure time. The Filipino Federation of America and other organizations with large membership make the inculcation of habits of clean living and the substitution of harmless amusements for vice an important plank in their platforms. The night life of the big cities is often denounced in the American Filipino press, and efforts are made to keep the young Filipinos away from resorts of questionable reputation. But these endeavors, in the large, are too negative in nature to have much success. So long as country life offers no distractions, the majority of Filipino workers, after a remunerative job, will ride off to the nearest city to meet with *paisanos,* perhaps from their home town, to buy new clothes, if possible to make the acquaintance of girls, and generally to have a good time. And, like other transient laborers, they will spend in hectic recreations what has been earned through hectic work.

The larger the numbers of their countrymen, the greater of course is the attraction of the urban aggregations. The complaint is sometimes heard that in the past Filipino college students were content with the recreations which campus life afforded but that now they spend too much of their time "downtown," especially at dance halls. The explanation is twofold: Not only are there now, with larger numbers of Filipinos in the city, opportunities for a glimpse of the homeland and for common diversions which did not formerly exist; but the very increase in the number of Filipino residents of the wage-earning type also has had an adverse influence on the Filipino student's prestige among his fellow students; so that some campus privileges formerly enjoyed are now withheld or must be fought for. Perhaps the time has been too short, since the arrival of Filipinos in large numbers, to focus attention upon their recreational needs; but already individual men and women, social agencies and churches are deeply concerned in these needs and considering means of more adequately meeting them.

5. SOCIAL DISCRIMINATION

As has already been seen, natural outlets for the Filipino's surplus energies often are barred by prejudice. Social discrimination, however, is not limited only to recreation and must, therefore, briefly be considered separately as one of the main problems which the Filipino immigrant faces in the American community.

This discrimination is not limited to the Pacific Coast, although naturally in that part of the country, with its memories of anti-Oriental agitations, it takes on more virulent forms. In New York, a Filipino inventor who at one time employed a not inconsiderable personnel in a manufacturing establishment of his own, throughout his business career has found it difficult to have himself taken seriously by other business men. With their fixed ideas, many people when calling on him simply cannot believe that this small man, of slightly Oriental appearance, is the inventor-manufacturer they have come to see. He and his wife repeatedly have been refused apartments in the assumption that they were Chinese or Japanese. Like dark-hued West Indians they have at times had to speak Spanish to each other in the presence of others to be recognized as educated foreigners.

Also in eastern cities, Filipinos have had the experience of being refused service in restaurants, even though Filipino waiters are an appreciated novelty. In the colleges, east as well as west, Filipino students sometimes find themselves ostracised and prevented from taking part in campus activities. Cases of open insult are not, however, as general east of the Rockies as they are in the West; and in such cities as Detroit and Chicago as well as on the Atlantic seaboard, Filipinos may be seen in the best hotels, in the best seats at theaters, as guests in the best families and welcome as members of churches, religious associations and clubs of many kinds. Discrimination on college campuses against Filipinos in the East and Middle West is exceptional.

It is reported, however, by Filipino students that in the last two years or so there has been a slight change in the attitudes displayed toward them. They are apt to find themselves unwelcome at dances; co-eds seen with them on the campus more often are under criticism. Religious associations endeavoring to find invitations for them in private homes for holidays have more difficulty. This is attributed partly to the hostile propaganda from the West which has gradually reached eastern cities.[19]

Even on the Pacific Coast, social discrimination appears only

[19] For a systematic statement of American Attitudes Towards Filipinos, see an article with that title by Professor Emory S. Bogardus in *Sociology and Social Research* for September-October, 1929, p. 59.

in patches. An interesting illustration of the cumulative force with which public opinion reacts upon the social opportunities of an immigrant group is the experience of Filipino students at a western state university. A number of circumstances here combined to lower their reputation. Large numbers of Filipinos had lately come into the city twice a year between seasonal jobs and, in a community already a center of migrant labor, had come into severe competition for all available minor jobs. At the university itself the number of Filipino students had rapidly increased. Through agitation, partly brought forth by the objectionable behavior of some of the laboring Filipinos, the rumor spread that men of that race were immoral. An effort of the Filipino students to provide for themselves a club-house near the campus was frustrated by neighborhood opinion, which forced the owner of a house who had already made a preliminary lease contract to cancel it. The fact that some Filipino students, finding it difficult to secure remunerative employment to help them through college, were employed as servants in fraternity houses, further lowered their social status, for these drew a sharp line against admitting any of their number to membership, even though many American students also are engaged in these jobs. Denied recreational opportunities elsewhere, the Filipino students tended to monopolize the facilities of the campus Y.M.C.A., thereby further displeasing their fellow students. Owing to misjudgment, that institution did not at once employ tactics calculated to disarm criticism against itself and to create a better understanding between American and Filipino students; with the result that, for months after, the rumor was current in Filipino circles that this particular university and Y.M.C.A. had passed rules discriminating against Filipino students, while at the same time American students criticized that institution as unduly favoring the Filipinos and demanding that separate accommodation be provided for them—a measure which, of course, would have made matters worse by practically implying a declaration of the Filipino's social inferiority.

It is noteworthy that even in this city discrimination against Filipinos is not sharply drawn but largely dependent upon the personal appearance and behavior of individuals of the minority group and the particular shade of prejudice in members of the majority group. One particular cause of criticism is that Filipinos who wished to attend high schools in the more desirable portions of the city (usually because they have jobs as part-time houseboys there) have been discouraged by the school principals and are forced to travel long distances to be enrolled in less exclusive neighborhoods.

More frequent than charges of institutional discrimination are those against individuals. At another state university, a Filipino student who had not previously given any thought to his social standing felt deeply offended when, on his entering a café, known as a favorite rendezvous of students, American fellow students left the counter without finishing their meal to make him feel that his presence was regarded as an intrusion. More often an innocent comradeship with a co-ed, starting with attendance at the same classes or perhaps some aid rendered in the college library, is rudely terminated by official and unofficial denunciations of its impropriety—often launched with a publicity deeply damaging to the Filipino's social standing. It may be doubted whether, where feelings already run high, the discussion of such incidents in sociology classes and the taking of racial attitude tests contribute toward the smoothing out of these difficulties. In at least one case where expressions of race attitudes were invited, the Filipino students—perhaps unconsciously saving their self-respect—discovered in themselves all sorts of prejudices against other peoples of which previously no one, they themselves included, had been aware! [20]

Like other immigrants of colored races, Filipinos suffer certain minor discriminations: There are many moving picture houses that will admit them—and presumably other Orientals likewise—only to the gallery. In San Francisco one photographer advertises that he does not desire Filipino clients; other business and professional men show their preference for an exclusive white patronage by "dirty looks" when non-Caucasians enter the door. One has to be a connoisseur of such things to be able to anticipate whether a certain barber shop is likely to serve one and whether it is safe to enter a certain restaurant. For it is by no means only or always the most expensive places that draw race lines.

Sometimes it is not service but the choice of a seat that requires an elaborate knowledge of etiquette: For example, one may be asked to sit at the back rather than in the front of the café, in a booth rather than at the counter. On the bathing beaches there are similar restrictions, often incomprehensible to a foreigner but recently arrived from a much simpler environment and perhaps

[20] There is, however, a genuine antagonism of Filipinos in the Philippine Islands toward the Chinese, comparable to the feeling against successfully competing immigrants elsewhere. See p. 237.

conditioned at school for an immense abhorrence for the evils of class distinctions under the old Spanish régime and with reverence for American democracy. In one place it may be perfectly all right to mingle with other bathers; in another, for no perceptible reason, it will invite evil glances, even physical violence. Or again in the same city, a social taboo may be rigorously kept, suddenly to be broken wide open by some special event—as for example in one of the smaller agricultural towns where no white barber would dream of cutting a Filipino's hair and no waiter other than in the Oriental section wait on him, but where the acceptance by some American notables of invitations to a Filipino banquet opened the dining room of the best hotel in town to the lowliest of Filipino farm laborers. And as to attendance of dance halls, every city seems to have its own rules—from permissible complete promiscuity to the closing of all public dance halls because a white citizenry prefer to forego that form of entertainment rather than to mix with Filipino patrons.

While social discrimination offers no problems comparable in seriousness with that of being refused a job or a room in a decent neighborhood, nevertheless it cannot but have a detrimental effect on the solution of these larger difficulties. For these experiences of denial of equality create a bitterness of attitude particularly among those who, because of larger means or better education, form the social nucleus from which Filipino leadership will emerge in the years to come. No people lightly accepts a status of social inferiority—but even less than others are the Filipinos willing to take the place of permanent inferiority assigned to them, because they have been taught to regard themselves as Americans, are conscious of a longer historical background of European culture than many other national groups that now play a conspicuous part in American life, and desire no permanent hold upon the right to be here, such as might predispose them to accept a lower status at the start.

Their resentment takes many forms—chiefly, as might be expected in a group of young men, that of open antagonism. There is, as a well-known Filipino religious worker expressed it, "an intense sense of injustice" when statements are made on the public platform and in the public press concerning Filipino morality that are demonstrably contrary to fact. Troubles between Filipinos and their fellow workers in a Detroit automobile plant, according to the employment manager, are often due to the Filipinos' resentment of nicknames of the sort which the members of other national groups, longer established in American life, have learned to recognize as harmless and not intended seriously in a derogatory sense. Similarly a business woman who employs a considerable number of Filipinos has found them excessively sensitive to verbal offences; they somehow have a way of interpreting cuss-words addressed to them by way of remonstrance as reflecting upon their personal honor and that of their nation. This same response to rough language has been observed by farm employers, both on the mainland and in Hawaii, who often have found themselves obliged to replace foremen or straw bosses simply because these could not restrain their expletives and caused an unrest among the Filipino laborers quite out of proportion to the occasion.

Similarly, the reaction of Filipinos to treatment which they regard as unjust is sometimes of astonishing violence. Even a single experience of social discrimination, when it comes unexpectedly, may produce an acute hatred of everything American, when but a little while before the individual seemed thoroughly reconciled to the way of life which America had to offer him. In several cases, students yet in their teens expressed themselves to the writer in such terms of intense hatred for those who, perhaps inadvertently, had injured their feelings as to suggest some mental abnormality.

The underlying reason for this phenomenon is, indeed, an abnormality which, however, must be sought not in the racial predisposition of these individuals, but in the totality of their experiences. The transition from joyful anticipation to the reality of their reception in America often is too sudden to permit of a balanced adjustment to the conditions which they are called upon to tolerate. This may, perhaps, be illustrated by a few sentences from a student paper. After having described the lure of America as first it came to his distant village in the Philippines through letters of Filipino sailors discharged in the United States, and then from personal witnesses who had lived on the American continent through the period of labor shortage and high wages immediately after the war, then also through the stories of passenger agents for the steamship companies—promising a very miracle of transformation from indigence on a barren farm to wealth amid the glittering night life of cosmopolitan cities—he proceeds to the events of the voyage itself: the uncleanliness of steerage accommodation, friction with fellow travellers from the Far East, unappetizing food, and sickness. Then the arrival:

Arrival is one of the gloomiest parts of the trip. The journey has sapped joy out of most of them, and aside from this impending problems have to be met. . . . There are the custom officials . . . Some are met by friends or relatives. . . . Most of them are brought by taxi drivers to cheap rooming houses. . . . Then the problem of work . . . Many face the autumn and winter without any penny, and for support they have to turn to their friends and acquaintances.

Hopes are high while on the journey, writes another; but when our destination, Seattle, was reached, they seem to dwindle. Stranded in a strange place, alone and short of means, affected everyone's point of view. Wandering through streets where people looked at you askance and in indifference seemed too depressing a situation. Then, too, where to live was a problem. With just a little money in hand, it would be natural for us to seek a place where our purse would fit into. This would lead us to cheap rooming houses. Facing such circumstances would altogether seem difficult for our age and experience. But the crisis had to be faced.

Disappointment after disappointment; at last the dreary camp on the edge of a bleak expanse of farm land; dirty work of a kind to which some of them have not been accustomed; lack of amusements; the constant drive to speed up in their work; and then white Americans of a type they have never met before, coarse, arrogant, expecting the silent docility of slaves. In the town they are taken in hand by a countryman who explains to them where they may go and where they may not go, what they may do and what not. The smiling countryman who introduces them to a gambling game and takes their hard-earned savings; memory of his boasting before he left home, of the family's expectations. Sense of his loneliness amid the crowd; first experiences of friendly approaches received with the cold shoulder; eventually, as he has yielded to temptation and squandered money that was meant to send a brother through school, sense of guilt; a wild desire to find the hidden cause of his misfortunes, of his inability to climb even the first step to success and affluence; then on some occasion when he is least prepared for it, an insulting epithet. Suddenly, accumulated anger vents itself, blow is returned with blow.

CHAPTER XI

EDUCATIONAL PROBLEMS OF THE FILIPINO

THE immigrant Filipinos' frequent assertion that they have come to America in search of an education cannot simply be disposed of by pointing to the fact that a large majority of them are not enrolled in any educational institution but engaged only in earning their livelihood. There can be no question that a large proportion of these young men think of themselves as in a preliminary stage of a student career, intent on accumulating savings toward high-school and college attendance. Actually, Filipinos are now, next to the Chinese (who still enjoy the benefits of the remitted Boxer indemnity) and to the Canadians, the largest national group among foreign students in the universities and colleges accredited by the Association of American Universities.[1] There has been a marked increase of Filipino students since 1926.

The simplest explanation for the trend of Filipino students toward the United States is to be found in the natural ties between their country and ours and in the educational and social successes of their pioneers, mostly sons of good families or equipped with government fellowships, who have drawn others after them. It may be true that for many young Filipinos the claim that they have come to study is but an attitudinizing with the aim of gaining social recognition. Yet, the motives of large numbers in coming here include education as at least one of the elements.[2] In the Philippine Islands the prestige of the college graduate is high. Families will make severe sacrifices over many years to have a son go through school because a learned son sheds lustre over all his kin. American teachers first, and later the native system of

[1] The four largest groups in the academic year, 1928-1929, were Chinese 1,287, Canadians 1,122, Filipinos 1,073, Japanese 814. All other groups were under the 400 mark. These figures vary somewhat from those listed by the Committee on Friendly Relations Among Foreign Students which include many of the smaller institutions. For the academic year, 1929-1930, this committee gives the following figures: Canada 1,294, China 1,263, Japan 987, and Philippines 887. Another cause of discrepancies is the fact that some colleges register their students by nationality, others by previous residence and still others by mother tongue.

[2] See p. 376 *et seq.*

public education which they have inaugurated, encourage this tendency; and so, where there is a certificate of college attendance in a home, it hangs framed in a place of honor.[3]

Correspondingly, the Filipino student feels a more than usual sense of gratitude and obligation toward the parents, grandparents, uncles and aunts who have made it possible for him to go through school and to make the trip to America, here further to add to his educational attainments. "Memory of the family's sacrifices," writes one who has investigated this phase, "in many cases is regarded as a sacred trust and highest stimulus to ambition." A large percentage of Filipino immigrants' savings go toward the education of a younger brother or other member of the family. Cases are not uncommon in which two brothers or cousins travel together to this country, one to go to school, the other to earn enough for the keep of both. Groups of students interviewed at different colleges in connection with the present inquiry place the proportion of Filipino immigrants who have come here primarily to study between 30 and 90 per cent. There is no factual basis for these guesses; probably the proportion is smaller even than the lower of these figures since the mainland of America has received so large an influx of Filipino laborers from Hawaii; but it is a mistake to assume that all those who have worked in the sugar plantations of that territory and then proceed to the mainland are motivated solely by a desire for financial gain. Often a period of labor in Hawaii is the intentional preliminary for an extended period of study in American schools and colleges.

We shall presently see that this educational ambition is not always realized. But for our immediate purpose, of showing the intensity of that ambition, it may be worth while to quote a paragraph from a student paper:

> On the ship I came to know a great many boys on the same journey and with the same purpose, and that is to go to work and to attend school. It would be interesting moment to hear the boys talk about their ambition, an ambition which ranges in many varying degrees. One may hear of careers such as lawyers, doctors, engineers, and business administration, and also teachers. Hearing them talk of such high ideals, one would naturally think that all would come true. But the extent toward which these ideals are carried, one never knows, not even the speaker himself.

[3] See further, p. 258 *et seq.*

In another class paper, the same student writes:

> Many come because they want to continue their schooling. Young men and women have learned that American institutions are better than those that exist there [in the Philippine Islands]. They have heard, too, that there are more chances for one to follow a career, due to more number of institutions and due to the probability to work one's way through school. These young men have been influenced by those that first came to study and who have come back with some type of a college degree, not to mention of the prestige that they got from their fellow countrymen as well as the privilege of higher pay.

A government official in Seattle who has come close to arriving Filipino immigrants over a number of years states:

> My impression is that most of the Filipinos landing here come primarily for education; all say they do. This is not true to the same extent of those who go directly to San Francisco.

The Filipino president of a manufacturing company in San Francisco said on this point:

> One reason for our desiring a large number of Filipinos here in the United States is our belief in the superiority of American sanitation and the advantage of associating with educated Americans for which there is no opportunity in the Philippine Islands. The only Americans Filipinos see there are rough men who sleep on the sidewalks. Here they meet a different type; and it is good for Filipinos to acquaint themselves with their customs.
>
> I am not much concerned with the fact that few actually finish school or go to college, or that educational opportunities in the Philippine Islands are improving. To see and observe American conditions of life seems to me the most important educational factor.

Even informed critics of the Filipino, from an American employer's point of view, do not fail to recognize the reality—unfortunate as they consider it—of the immigrant's educational aspirations. Says one of the sharpest opponents of Filipino immigration:

> The Filipino scorns factory labor and wants easy jobs. In the Philippine Islands the educational system never gives wholesome respect for work on the land. It rather fosters the bombastic tendencies of the Filipino. Filipinos come here, not to study as they say, but to become lawyers to exploit their fellows. They fill the evening courses and subscribe to correspondence extension courses for which they pay as much as $100. Often they enter these courses when they have passed only the sixth grade.

A western teacher of political science who has lived in the Philippine Islands and is taking a personal interest in the fortunes of young Filipinos here, spoke of having recently met with two or three hundred Filipinos in a middle western city, largely young fellows who were studying in night school, only a few of them in college; but not 30 per cent of them were actually enrolled at any one time. This estimate is almost identical with that of a minister in Los Angeles, formerly a missionary in the Philippine Islands, who is in charge of a center for Filipinos in that city:

> Some 85 per cent of the Filipinos say they have come here for study. The actual proportion is probably about one-third. The rest have come here to make money. The boys' own estimate that over four-fifths of them have been to higher schools before going to Hawaii and the mainland of the United States also is probably a considerable over-estimate.

He finds a difference between the educational ambitions of Filipinos in the city and those he meets on the ranches outside. Of those who attend his religious meetings at the camps very few respond to offers to help connect them up with educational institutions; of those who attend religious meetings in the city nearly all say they want to go to school as soon as they are financially able to do so.

The secretary of the Filipino Federation of America, E. C. Pecson, states that the great majority of their members have gone to school in the Philippine Islands and left between the seventh grade and the first year in high school:

> Many of them come to the United States to study because there is no chance for self-supporting study in the Philippine Islands. Arriving here with $100 to $200, the greenhorn soon has his money spent, however, and then begs for work, saves a little, spends more. Thus it may take him years before he actually saves enough to start going to school. Many boys who are working now are right in considering themselves students. As soon as they can they enter an automobile school or a business school if not high school or college. All aspire to elevate themselves, but few earn enough. When they have earned enough they enroll for three months' or a year's schooling; at the end of that time they are again "broke."

Four evils or problems appear when the Filipino's educational experiences in the United States are analyzed:

1. LACK OF ADEQUATE PREPARATION

It is the all but universal testimony of teachers of Filipinos that they are ill prepared for the grade in our educational system to which they consider themselves entitled. Policies vary from a kindly desire to grade these students as nearly as possible in accordance with the standing they have attained in the school system of their own country and to help them as best may be to pass, to a rigorous re-grading which often means that those who consider themselves entitled to college entrance are obliged to re-enter high school for one year or more. There is complaint not only of the Filipino's lack of fluency in the use of the English language but also of his immaturity of outlook and lack of elementary essentials, sometimes due to the fact that the schools from which the students matriculate are inadequately equipped. Several of the western universities have of late been compelled to adopt more rigorous entrance examinations, and these often fall with special severity upon foreign students, including the Filipinos. The President of the University of Oregon, during the progress of the present inquiry, appointed a special faculty committee to consider the case of the Filipino students, their economic background (with a view to their ability to pay tuition fees), their school rating, their standing in English, and their means of self-support. This committee, presided over by Professor W. D. Smith, dean of the Department of Geology, reported on this point:

> Their economic and social background in the Philippine Islands leads us to believe that we are not getting the cream of the Philippine students who come to the United States for an education, and that many of these boys have come to the United States primarily to better their economic conditions rather than to improve their educational advantages. In many ways the University of the Philippines might provide these boys with an education better suited to their future needs than can be obtained in this country, as the instructors of the University of the Philippines are better acquainted with the social, economic and mental background of the Filipinos than any University faculty in this country.

The same view is taken by Professor Stephen P. Duggan, director of the Institute of International Education, who is familiar with the subject not only from his studies at American universities but also from a survey of the educational situation in the Philippines, made a few years ago.[4] In a letter recently addressed to the presidents of a number of western universities, he says:

> . . . They come in many cases with almost no money and without proper scholastic qualifications for admission to our colleges and universities. . . .

[4] A Survey of the Educational System of the Philippine Islands. Government Department of Public Instruction, Manila, 1925.

My stand on this question is the same as the stand I take with reference to Far Eastern students generally, and Hindu and Latin American students, namely, that they should receive their undergraduate instruction at home and come to the United States only for graduate, technical and professional training. Having been a member of the Educational Commission sent to the Philippines in 1925, I know that such institutions as the University of the Philippines, the University of Santo Tomás, the Ateneo and others provide all the facilities necessary for the number of college graduates who can be absorbed by the population of the Philippines. No one more heartily approves of the advent to this country of the Filipino *pensionados* and other graduate students than I.[5]

2. LACK OF EDUCATIONAL AND VOCATIONAL GUIDANCE

Filipinos desirous of continuing their education in the United States drift almost casually to the schools which they attend and to the subjects in which they decide to major. An extreme case was told on one of the plantations in Hawaii where a group of boys had broken their contract to go to school in St. Louis—for the only reason that "Lindbergh lives there." Too many are influenced in their choices by the relative prestige of different professions in the Philippine Islands rather than by their own qualifications.[6] Many students interviewed in the course of the present inquiry were unable to distinguish personal ambition from the needs of their country for trained talents in many fields of effort. If they chose the law or political science it was too often the prominence of lawyers and politicians in the affairs of their homeland rather than a considered weighing of the chances for success in a larger variety of possible callings that determined the choice.[7] In a few

[5] For a concrete suggestion of action to be taken in this matter by American universities see below, p. 311.

[6] The major courses of study selected by 896 Filipino students in the United States are given in Appendix F, p. 374.

[7] The Educational Survey Commission in the Philippines was impressed with a similar lack of harmony between the courses of study chosen at the University of the Philippines and the professional needs of the country. In addition to stressing the needs of the College of Agriculture for further developments, they also point to possibilities of the College of Engineering as a source of much needed "all-around technical experts of sound practical judgment." Furthermore, the figures showing the enrollment of students in the Medical School and the other medical departments indicate an obvious discrepancy between the number of those preparing themselves for a medical career and the needs of a country of twelve million inhabitants, distributed in small communities over a large island archipelago. The explanation lies, in part, in the organization of this as of other Philippine institutions of higher education on European models answering a very different set of conditions and, in part, in a natural drift, in a poor country just awakening to the values of scientific expertness in many fields of endeavor, toward professions in which proficiency and status can be obtained without too strenuous and long-continued a training.

exceptional cases, however, such a deliberate choice was found to have been made on the highest patriotic grounds, often not only with a view to the country's needs but with one to the needs of the immediate locality from which these students come. There seems to be more of a trend recently toward the study of mechanical engineering, of agronomy and of other practical sciences of which the Philippine Islands are certainly in need, no matter what their political future.[8]

It is unfortunate that no machinery exists so far that would aid the great majority of Filipino students in the United States who have no definite professional preferences or outstanding talents in arriving at a choice of courses. Such counsel would have to take into consideration not only all those points which enter into the vocational guidance open to American high-school graduates, but in addition the special difficulties of foreigners and the careers open in the Philippine Islands. It is unfortunate, further, that for purely financial reasons a few universities are overcrowded with Filipino students, when often other institutions could give these men more nearly what they need in specialized training and personal help, as well as wider opportunities of vocational self-help during the years of college attendance.[9]

3. DISCRIMINATION AND DISCOURAGEMENT

There is no evidence that schools and colleges deliberately discriminate against Filipinos in their requirements of admission or in their grading and treatment after admission. Yet many Filipinos, unable otherwise to interpret their unfortunate collegiate experiences, believe this to be the case. Accustomed in the past to special leniency in the interpretation of residence requirements for the relinquishment of school fees, they are inclined to look upon more rigorous enforcement of these rules as specially directed against them.

The charge is also occasionally made that high-school and college teachers, animated by prejudice, deliberately discourage Filipino students from continuing their studies. But of this no proof has been found—other than in the case, already mentioned, of some

[8] See p. 374 *et seq.*

[9] Forty-two per cent of the Filipino students in America are congregated in the three Pacific Coast states. One-half of the Filipino students are in attendance at eleven colleges and universities. See Appendix F, p. 369.

high-school principals in the more exclusive residential districts of one or two western cities who evidently feel that Filipino students will be better helped and happier in schools with a larger proportion of children of foreign, specifically Oriental, parentage.

In this connection, it may perhaps also be stated that the attitude of many young Filipinos toward their experience in the United States is favorably colored by the kindness and solicitude for their educational progress on the part of American families in which they are employed on a part-time basis as house-boys.

There is, of course, discouragement also in the unfavorable attitude of fellow students. A Filipino student of philosophy in a middle-western college writes:

> In many activities in schools and colleges what is latent in the best Filipino cannot be given expression simply because he is shown and sometimes told in terms that are unmistakable that he cannot equal his white classmates because of his color. This disheartens many, but there are a few Filipino young men and women that are emboldened by such an outrage, and not infrequently have they shown their mettle in physical and mental contests and won laurels.

At one western university, members of the faculty are trying to induce the American fraternities to consider the feasibility of occasionally inviting Filipino students to dinner—a gesture of friendliness which might create a better feeling on the campus.

The Oregon report, previously quoted, states on this point:

> In spite of their generally pleasant demeanor and uniformly good manners, we find a general discrimination against them on the campus. This is not overt or due to ill will, it is simply indifference. Probably we cannot blame anyone for this. It is a matter of race and color prejudice which is extremely strong in the native American.

The general attitude of the population also is discouraging. Accustomed to seeing Orientals in the rôle of laborers and servants, many people cannot reconcile themselves to the sight of these particular Orientals with books and briefcases. The clash between Filipinos and Mexicans in La Verne (see p. 17) is said to have been caused by the jeering remarks hurled by the latter at Filipino schoolboys. Too often these boys and young men, when they dress and behave according to the manner of American college students, are accused of "aping" their betters.[10] While probably few have

[10] It is, of course, true that often Filipino youths who have long ceased to attend school or have never even yet begun to enroll in any educational institution, try to preserve their self-esteem by dressing the part of students—just as our own store clerks are apt to be more "collegiate" in their make-up and manners than those who

been dissuaded by insults of this sort from attending school, nevertheless having to face them adds yet another strain to a by no means easy position in a strange environment.

> As it appears to me now, writes a Filipino student at the end of a long letter setting forth his difficulties and those of his colleagues, I fear that we might no longer enjoy the unmolested life of a student here, for now and then we might be mistreated by some class of people who might entertain some racial or labor ill-feelings, just because they happen to read the articles about the local troubles now happening in some towns in California.[11]

4. DEMORALIZATION AS A RESULT OF FRUSTRATED AMBITION

By far the most serious circumstance in this connection is the psychological effect upon many young Filipinos of their inability to continue their education, begun often with so much real ambition. If one remembers that one of the chief reasons for coming to study in the United States is the reputed ease with which an immigrant can work his way through school and college here, one will readily see that changes in this primary condition of success produce deep disappointment.

But has that condition changed? Earlier Filipino students at American universities undoubtedly did find it possible without undue hardship to make both ends meet by taking part-time jobs and a job at good hard labor during the summer vacations. Thousands of American students were doing the same thing. But these earlier students were not in most cases entirely dependent upon their earnings. They were either *pensionados,* in receipt of a government fellowship, or members of families that could afford to contribute toward their expenses. The present Filipino student contingent in the United States represents a much larger variety of classes; there are now few government fellows, but the school system in the Philippine Islands has made such strides that much larger numbers consider themselves, and are considered by their teachers, qualified to enroll in an American college. In addition, there are large numbers who, after holding teaching positions in the Islands—often without having graduated from a normal school—find it inconvenient to return to school at home to complete their education and

actually attend college. Typical is the story, everywhere told, of the Filipino window-washer who carries his rags in an elegant briefcase. There was also a case of a Filipino who had the name of some American college inscribed on his calling cards—hoping some day to enroll there!

[11] *Detroit Free Press,* February 27, 1930.

prefer to do so in the United States where periods of school attendance can, according to current rumor, be alternated with remunerative work and where, in this way, graduation and entrance to a college or university seem the more assured.

Now, this system, so satisfactory in theory, does not work very well. First, there is an impression among college teachers that the grade of students coming from the Philippine Islands is not as high as it used to be. This is quite possible; for a larger proportion of the earlier students had a background of culture at home and, moreover, as pioneers, while the acquisition of an American college degree was as yet a rare distinction, may have been more ambitious. But they also had an easier time; not only because more of them received financial help from home but also because, with lesser numbers, they found less prejudice against themselves and correspondingly had the choice of a larger variety of occupational openings, in addition to receiving as individuals a great deal of personal attention and kindness from well-disposed Americans.

Today, the typical Filipino student receives no help from home, but on the contrary is expected as soon as possible to re-pay debts incurred on his behalf or to help some other member of the family get an education. The presence of larger numbers of Filipinos, both within and without college, has the effect of depressing wage-earning opportunities and also—this is perhaps even more important—of offering a constant run of distractions from the serious business of life. This means not only loss of time but also larger expenditure on clothes, tributes toward social prestige among one's *paisanos,* whether it be part ownership in an automobile, going out with girls, participation in such hazardous enterprises as the publication of a periodical, or the organization of a new club. With the increase in expenditures comes the temptation to spend more time on remunerative work and less on study. A fairly agreeable job that can be made permanent is retained after school begins. An anticipated interruption for one terms becomes a prolonged cessation of school attendance until, finally, only the vaguest expectation remains of returning some time or other to continue the interrupted course of study. Thus it comes that at the very least two-thirds of those who still regard themselves as students and are so regarded by their fellows may pretty definitely be considered as having dropped out. In addition to these, there is perhaps an even larger number of Filipinos who come here with the intention of studying but never even get a start by a first enrollment. These are the boys who, arriving here with practically no money at all, undertake to work for a year and with the accumulated savings go to school. Either work is too intermittent or the temptation to spend the earnings is too irresistible to permit realization of that plan. Sometimes the educational ambition is entirely supplanted by an economic one; and the boy who set out to bring the prestige of a profession to his family instead succeeds in paying off the mortgage on the paternal farm, to buy a new piece of land, or to send brothers and sisters at home through high school.

A "chaotic state of mind" sometimes is the description which American social and religious workers give of their young Filipino friends' attitudes toward their careers. Even when long established in an occupation in which they may be expected to make a good livelihood, they will speak of going home after having secured some college degree or other. Others confess themselves failures and unable to face the people at home because they have neither made money nor secured the coveted degree. Yet others are continually wavering between these conflicting aims. One Filipino graduate student, an exceptionally able young sociologist, calculated that the average Philippine high school graduate, even when ambitious and not lightly deflected from his educational undertaking, ought to allow nine years for his stay in the United States; for he would have to take at least another two years in high school here before being able to take full advantage of any college course and would need at least three years' whole-time work in addition to part-time and summer-work during the rest of the period to earn his living before being able to graduate. Now, most Filipino students coming to the United States neither are aware of the necessity for a long-time program of this sort nor have the necessary stamina to carry it through. Instead, they either fail to enter seriously upon their studies at all or drift between job and school attendance without becoming conscious of the particular point at which they no longer can justify their claim to being students. With this drifting there usually comes a profound sense of dissatisfaction; letters home are fewer; temptations to extravagance are more easily yielded to; superficial symbols of distinction, such as titles and honorary positions in group organizations, or displays of affluence are substituted for the search for real superiority.

Why do not these disappointed young Filipinos go home? Nearly all of them talk of eventually going home as a foregone conclusion. Here is one student's explanation. He is an exceptionally able young man in the department of education of a western college:

All Filipinos I know want to go home to the Philippine Islands. The difficulty is that many of them do not graduate: Much is expected of them, and they fear they will be sneered at if they return home without a degree. Most of the boys here now do not go to school. Some of them are even ashamed to write home. The cause of their failure is that self-support is too hard for all but the most persevering. In Alaska, for two months' work in the fish canneries—and that is all a student can do—earnings come to about $150; of this the school or college takes $100 or $125 in tuition fees. The houseboy usually has to work four or five hours a day. Housework is easier than most accessible jobs, and earnings are higher, namely $15 a week in addition to room and board. It is also easier to get. Those who work outside as night extras in hotels and restaurants earn about $30, out of which $15 goes for room.

Many boys, under these circumstances, have been driven out of the schools as soon as tuition fees were charged. The academic work is heavy and hard to keep up with. Filipinos are traditionally fond of good clothes—in the Philippine Islands just as much as here, and farmers' boys as much as city boys. . . .

Practically all these boys have promised their people at home to study in the United States; and their largest problem—he had been talking of diverse forms of occupational and social discrimination suffered by Filipinos in America—is their inability to keep this promise.

Two students interviewed at a large state university told almost the identical story:

Love of pleasure is not the cause why many Filipinos discontinue their studies, but the economic situation: There are not enough jobs. The students stick to their studies even when they are out of work so long as they feel that they may soon be able to land a job. The first comers, at the end of the summer, get the best jobs; those who come late, even when more experienced, often must be content with odd jobs only or with inferior jobs. . . . [Details as to earnings and expenditures, much as above.]

Filipinos cannot get away from spending money on clothes. Even in small towns and on the farms of Luzon good clothes come first. We could not go even to high school in the Philippine Islands dressed as we are here.

All of the Filipino students here will go back to the Islands. They know that their services are needed there. But it takes a whole summer's work in Alaska or on the farms to earn money enough for transportation. And few wish to return empty-handed. Some of the boys in Washington have taken their A.B. and A.M. degrees from two to four years ago but go on working instead of returning immediately because they want to make more money first. They say they are "about ready to go home" but need a little capital before they can be sure of doing well at home. Others send home the extra money they earn beyond what they need to live on and so are forced to stay on to earn more.

Even those who seem to have given up the idea of ever going back to school often have the serious intention of returning to the Philippine Islands when they have saved money. The family ties are very strong. That is also one reason why so few Filipino women are here. Filipinos who might be in a position to marry would not want to settle here even if life were easier. . . .

Students who get discouraged are usually those who have been misled by advertising of the ease with which a living can be made here. They find the work too hard. All try to make good before they go back and feel that they cannot go home until they have done so. The biggest problem for the Filipinos here is how to get back to the Philippine Islands those who have not finished their education and have not made good financially either.

Repeatedly young Filipinos when questioned on their opinion concerning the pending exclusion bill came out at once with the remarkable reply: "Immigration here should be stopped; there are too many Filipinos here that are failures." On the other hand, the secretary of a large Filipino organization believes that expressions of this sort should be taken with a grain of salt:

We do not consider the unhappy type of immigrant a particular problem. It is only natural that there is such a type among so many boys in a foreign country. Many of them, especially those who come from good families, think of themselves as self-supporting students, get broken-hearted by the difficulty of continuing their studies, drift for a time—but eventually go home. Many of those who do most of the complaining have a nest-egg hidden away somewhere. Anyhow, this dissatisfaction among the boys is not so general as to be a real problem. They easily get discouraged when they suffer hardship. I know several boys who were drifting in this way five or seven years ago but are now doing fairly well—earning money and saving it. When I hear of a fellow drifting now, I feel fairly sure he will come out right in the end.

Few earn enough to send money home. When they have worked on a farm for three or six months, they usually spend their money—buy an automobile, for example. While the money lasts, they are not dissatisfied with this mode of life. Then they go out to earn more and to get more experiences. Students usually work hard to save several hundred dollars to continue their studies; when that is spent, they are broke again—and nearly always, of course, at the end of their studies, so that they cannot then go home.

Father Thomas O'Dwyer, head of the Catholic Welfare Bureau of Los Angeles, who is conducting a Filipino center, also took up this theme:

When they come here, the young Filipinos are enthusiastic over their prospects. They immediately write back home, almost as though they had found gold on the streets. A wage of $50 a month looks enormous until they find out how much it costs to live. Many start to go to school and college, then find out that they cannot meet the cost and fall out, to take the whole-time work. Our principal problem, for this and other reasons, is the moral situation. Loneliness and disappointment give a special attraction to vice: First loneliness, then the sense of failure when studies have to be discontinued, discouragement leading on to gambling and the dance halls. Nothing so bad about the conduct of these necessarily but for the acquaintances made there. . . .

These boys live from hand to mouth and rarely earn enough to go home. They are ashamed, after their first enthusiastic letters to their families, to tell of their real experiences. They stay on.

In short, then, whichever way one looks at it, the conditions under which at present Filipinos pursue undergraduate studies in American schools do not conduce to the best results. Inadequately prepared, often, without sufficient guidance—especially during the frequent periods away from school and college—subject to discouragement because of the prevailing popular attitudes toward them as "Orientals," in too large a proportion forced to discontinue their studies altogether or drifting off into menial occupational careers through lack of persistence, many self-confessed failures, others embittered against a country that has failed to fulfill its promises, few able to return immediately upon the completion of their studies to take a satisfying part in the affairs of their country or home-town—the Filipino students as a body do not constitute that helpful link between the United States and the Philippine Islands which the rich educational facilities of the one and the keen desire for contact with western culture in the other might forge under happier circumstances.

PART III

THE FILIPINO PROBLEM OF HAWAII

PART III. THE FILIPINO PROBLEM OF HAWAII

CHAPTER XII

ECONOMIC PROBLEMS

1. FILIPINOS IN THE MAJOR INDUSTRIES

HAWAII'S main interest in Filipino immigration is so different from that of continental United States as to require separate treatment. While the labor situation of Hawaii, as we have seen, is closely linked up with that on the mainland, the part played by the Filipino immigrant is wholly different. For, out of a total of 64,000 Filipinos, 34,000 Filipinos, with 10,000 dependents, are productively employed in Hawaii's principal industries where they form over two-thirds of the total labor supply, as will be seen from the following figures:

NUMBER AND PROPORTION OF MEMBERS OF DIFFERENT RACIAL GROUPS AMONG THE EMPLOYEES OF 41 PLANTATIONS OF THE HAWAIIAN SUGAR PLANTERS' ASSOCIATION, IN JUNE, 1929.[1]

Classification *	*Total Male Employees on Pay Roll* †	*Percentage*
American	1,269	2.5
Japanese	9,197	18.5
Filipino	34,345	69.3
Chinese	946	1.9
Korean	520	1.1
Porto Rican	810	1.6
Portuguese	1,682	3.4
Spanish	76	0.2
Hawaiian	574	1.2
All others	160	0.3
Total	49,579	100.0

* This classification is based upon racial ancestry, not upon citizenship.

† There were also on payroll Women: Japanese 1,472
All Others 261
Minors: Regular 461
School 4,889

[1] Annual Report of the Governor of Hawaii for Fiscal Year ended June 30, 1929, p. 47. The figures include the field labor of the large pineapple growers of Hawaii.

Although the great majority of these employees are young, unmarried men, the total number of Filipinos dependent for their livelihood on the sugar plantations at that time was 43,433, or about 68 per cent of the total Filipino population in the territory. In addition, about 5,000 Filipino laborers are regularly employed by the pineapple companies, with a maximum of about 9,000 during the height of the season. Applying to them the same ratio of dependents as found on the sugar plantations, the pineapple industry probably supports from 6,500 to 12,000 Filipinos. Assuming a similar age and sex composition for the 12,000 or so Filipinos in Hawaii thus unaccounted for, probably between 7,000 and 9,000 are engaged in other farm and plantation work,[2] in civilian employments at the army and navy stations, as stevedores (about 300), truckdrivers, yardboys, bootblacks, in institutional, restaurant and hotel service, and in construction work, with perhaps a few hundred in business, unemployed and living on casual jobs.[3]

While the large majority of Filipinos in Hawaii have been brought there by the sugar planters, a relatively small additional number—possibly a thousand or so—came of their own accord. Since 1925 the knowledge has become more widespread in the Philippines that there is little chance of getting into the sugar plantations except through the regular channel. The H.S.P.A. (Hawaiian Sugar Planters' Association), both in its own interest and that of the community, strongly desires to have only selected Filipinos come to Hawaii, to reduce to a minimum the risks of contagious disease and of physical mal-adaptation. Moreover, while in larger countries employers are able to throw the burden of unemployment upon the community, in Hawaii the sugar and pineapple growers, as the largest taxpayers, are deeply concerned to prevent it. Hence their constant opposition to labor shipments from the Philippines outside the carefully estimated supplies to fill the territory's actual needs. But there were large numbers of Filipinos who wanted to come, among them many who had been rejected by the representatives of the H.S.P.A. on medical or other grounds. Unscrupulous individuals took advantage of this situation and began an independent venture with the chartering of a vessel and, in some instances, the

[2] The total number of men employed in the coffee industry at the height of the picking season is only about 1,200. Not more than 500 Filipinos work in rice fields. They are barred from the fishing industry, which is entirely in the hands of the Japanese.

[3] Other Orientals are preferred in domestic work; yet the Philippine Labor Bureau estimates that roughly 200 Filipinos in Hawaii are employed as house- and yardboys.

fraudulent sale of passages.[4] The last organized attempt to ship several hundred Filipinos to Hawaii outside the system of the H.S.P.A., but with vague promises that work on the sugar plantations would be found for them, took place in 1928 when a Philippine concern chartered two ships and brought some six hundred Filipinos to Honolulu.

With a view to deterring such independent ventures, which would be seriously to the disadvantage of the community and also of the Filipinos in creating a surplus of labor, the H.S.P.A. did not immediately employ the men who arrived in Hawaii on these independent ventures. Mr. Ligot, the Philippines labor commissioner, in consultation with the H.S.P.A., advised the newcomers where they were most likely to find temporary or permanent employment; and gradually, after subjecting themselves to the customary medical examinations, most of them were absorbed. Others managed to obtain employment on the pineapple fields or in the canneries. The pineapple producers are in mutual competition and have no cooperative agency. They are not in a position to stabilize employment chiefly, however, because of the much shorter duration of the periods demanding field labor, compared with those of the cane fields, with a maximum demand for labor during the harvesting season of ten weeks. Cannery work is also necessarily intermittent, averaging only four months a year. The number of Filipinos employed by the largest of these concerns, the Hawaiian Pineapple Company, in 1929, was as follows:

	Plantations	*Cannery*	*Total*
Summer:			
Male	2,287	579	2,866
Female	40	87	127
Total	2,327	666	2,993
Off-Season:			
Male	1,234	312	1,546
Female	13	33	46
Total	1,247	345	1,592

Compared with the relative value of its product, the pineapple industry absorbs but a small proportion of the Islands' labor resources. The Filipino's opportunities in this industry are some-

[4] See further below, p. 142.

what limited by the fact that jobs in the canneries must largely be reserved for the native-born, often youths of school age who depend on this summer employment for a necessary contribution to the family income.[5]

Under an arrangement now in force a number of years, the leading pineapple growers recognize their indebtedness to the sugar planters for bringing to their doors the largest source of their permanent labor supply, namely, the Filipinos, by paying their pro rata share for workers assigned to them by the H.S.P.A.[6]

The question arises, why does Hawaii employ so large a number and proportion of immigrant workers? And why do the Filipinos take first place among these? It should be understood that both in public and private employment native Hawaiians are always employed whenever this is possible. For example, they are given preference by the government in employment on public works. Only the demands of economic development forced the planters to look for supplementary labor sources. When the Japanese government decided to curtail further migration of its citizens to Hawaii,[7] the Hawaiian sugar and pineapple planters were faced with the choice between either so changing their whole labor system as to make possible the employment of native-born workers or introducing other immigrant groups to take their place. As both European and Asiatic labor had been, or was in process of being, cut off, the choice really lay between the transformation of the industry and the employment of either Porto Rican or Filipino labor —the only two large sources of immigrant common labor remaining open.[8] Experiments had already been made with workers of

[5] In the summer of 1928, 1,299 boys and 1,211 girls enrolled in public schools worked in the pineapple canneries or in other mechanical operations of the industry. (Report of the Governor of Hawaii for the year ended June 30, 1929, p. 74.)

[6] The minimum wage for picking pineapples on one plantation is $2 a day; and the more experienced men can make $3.50 and $4. Wage rates for parallel occupations are approximately the same on sugar and pineapple plantations. Average earnings, however, are lower than those of workers permanently employed on sugar plantations because of the intermittency of the work and the difficulty to find equally remunerative employment in the off-season, when many of the pineapple workers are employed on cane fields and others on casual jobs in the cities, while quite a large proportion are temporarily unemployed.

[7] The "Gentlemen's Agreement" did not provide for the exclusion of Japanese laborers from Hawaii. The Japanese government did this on its own motion. In 1907, Governor Carter wrote in his Annual Report: "Labor has been fairly plentiful as the present temporary arrangement between our country and Japan exempts Hawaii from an exclusion with which she does not sympathize." In 1908, Governor Frear wrote in his Annual Report: "Japanese immigration has been much reduced through the action of the Japanese Government."

[8] No responsible person thought of competing with continental United States for either Negro or Mexican labor upon which the whole South and a large part of the West had already become dependent.

both nationalities. Porto Rican immigration, stimulated more especially in 1900 and 1901, had been found undesirable, partly because of opposition to the recruiting of Porto Ricans in Porto Rico itself, partly because of the lack of a direct and regular means of transportation. It was also found that those Porto Rican workers who could be secured were not comparable with Oriental labor in physical efficiency and other desirable traits; there was no certainty that the supply could be maintained over any length of time, and the Porto Ricans' Negro blood may also have been a cause of concern. The Filipinos, on the other hand, already had given fair satisfaction at field work, were readily introduced in plantations with a labor force of other Oriental workers, and could be secured in numbers not likely to fall off rapidly through competing labor opportunities. Moreover, direct and relatively inexpensive lines of transportation were already in existence, and large numbers of Filipinos seemed to be anxious to avail themselves of the chance if their transportation were paid for. The Americanization of the Philippine Islands, which, as we shall see, was one of the strongest forces attracting migrants to the mainland of the United States,[9] also exercised a strong pull to Hawaii, partly because of the advantages which the territory offered and partly as a stepping stone to the American continent. Employment of Filipinos had the special advantage, moreover, that it proved of mutual advantage to bring them in considerable numbers for a limited number of years, thus avoiding the accumulation of yet another permanently settled large group of foreigners whose offspring would compete with other native-born for non-agricultural employments. After initial experiments in 1906 and 1907, involving only a few hundred Filipino workers, the movement of their arrival gradually increased, until both in Hawaii and in the Philippine Islands themselves it became a recognized item of importance in the economic system.

2. SELECTION AND TRANSPORTATION

At first, Filipinos were recruited and brought to the Hawaiian Islands with no thought of their return to their homeland. But in 1915, owing to representations of the Philippine government and the passage of laws regulating labor recruiting, the Hawaiian Sugar Planters' Association, a federation of all the more important concerns, worked out a system of individual agreements with Fili-

[9] See p. 218 *et seq.*

pino workers under which the terms of their employment were definitely provided for in advance, and the association undertook to return the laborer, at the expiration of the contract, that is, after three years, to his homeland at the employer's expense. Even before that time, all the expenses of employment, suitable equipment with clothing for the journey, transportation, medical service and final distribution in Hawaii had been borne by the employers, without being refunded by deductions from wages. It is generally admitted that the conscientious adherence of the employers to their part of the contract and the care expended by them on the protection and welfare of these workers has been the main element in the rapidly increasing attractiveness of contract work on the Hawaiian sugar plantations for Filipino laborers, as demonstrated by the ever larger numbers of those who, without solicitation, desired to enter their services. It is impossible here to give a detailed historical account of the sugar planters' developing methods of labor recruiting and management; but it is interesting to note that the reports at home of their experiences by a constant stream of returning contract workers was more effective in creating good will for the industry among potential employees than any amount of advertising could have produced. So strong was the pull to Hawaii thus set into motion that in 1925 it was possible for the association to discontinue altogether aggressive methods of labor recruitment in the Philippine Islands, and to rely almost entirely upon the automatic adjustment of the labor supply to the demand through voluntary application at its offices in Manila and in the provinces, aided only by the occasional use of lectures and movies, describing actual conditions. In 1926 all payment for the transportation of laborers was discontinued. It was possible to count on the strong desire of a sufficient number of laborers to enter the services of the plantations to bear the heavy expenditure of the journey.[10] It is estimated that of the total number of Filipino arrivals in Hawaii—approximately 45,000 between 1925 and 1929—no less than 30,000 (or, to take two full calendar years, nearly 21,000 out of a total number of 21,500 arrivals in 1927 and 1928) have come under this voluntary arrange-

[10] The minimum cost of steerage transportation from Manila to Honolulu is $75. Between October 1, 1924, and September 30, 1929, 29,935 Filipino men, with 194 women and 216 children, paid their own fare under this arrangement. The association pays the transportation for the wife and two children of a laborer who returns for a second contract.

ment. In partial compensation the association, from 1925 on, greatly improved its methods of selection and of medical and social care, so that the immigrant worker more than ever is assured in advance of his ability to "make good" and, with industry and thrift, to accumulate substantial savings. Among these measures is an agreement with the steamship company (the Dollar Line) under which the offices of the H.S.P.A. in the Philippine Islands act as its ticket agents, thus cutting out possibilities of deception and making possible a regulation of the flow of migration, ensuring the absence of both overcrowding and unemployment on arrival. Also the physical requirements were raised and more rigorously enforced; minor physical deficiencies were treated at the employer's expense before departure or on the journey, and welfare workers were employed to supervise the physical well-being of the workers during the journey—more particularly their diet and their protection against changes in temperature and against infectious diseases. The total cost of this careful selection, supervision, protection and distribution of the laborers, which does not include transportation, except from the receiving station in Honolulu to the plantations, is estimated by an informed person as amounting to about $40 per man. The employers can afford this seemingly extravagant expenditure not only because of the returns in increased efficiency and all-around satisfaction but also because, as the largest taxpayers, they are interested in keeping down the rates of sickness and dependency.[11]

Not only methods of control but also methods of selection since 1907 have undergone progressive improvement; and it is to this above all that the Hawaiian planters today ascribe their success with the employment of Filipino labor. In the earlier years, the system did not differ materially from the hit-and-miss methods which other larger employers of common labor use in filling their vacancies. Anyone who presented himself at the company's offices was welcome, provided he could pass a comparatively simple medical examination. As a consequence, many were employed whose mental predisposition was unfavorable to a successful adjustment to the conditions of plantation work. On the mainland of the United States it is often charged that Filipinos coming here after a period of life and labor in Hawaii are "the scum of city slums" or "wharf-rats picked up on the docks of Manila." While this is

[11] A more detailed account of the Hawaiian Sugar Planters' Association's methods of labor selection and management is given in Appendix H, p. 383.

an extreme exaggeration, not borne out by the figures available for the provincial origin of the laborers (see page 167), it is undoubtedly true that among the earlier labor recruits there were many who had had no experience of continuous labor on the land and no special liking for it.[12] There were also many who, though not diseased, were unfit for the strenuous labor expected of them. Many students and others too young or soft to engage successfully in hard work took advantage of the opportunity to take the first step of the way toward an American education and, often without being able to stay out the period requisite for adequate earnings and savings, dropped out to swell the city population of Honolulu[13] or to drift to the mainland of the United States without either resources or experience valuable in securing a paying job. The majority of these laborers were from the Manila region and the Bicol provinces. As the field of recruiting expanded, Visayans were next employed in considerable numbers, until finally in the Ilocos country the association's agents struck a population much richer in available men with a background of rural life, the requisite stature, and the promise of rapid adjustment to the physical and mental needs of plantation work.[14] While in the course of the present study the inquirer has discovered no compelling proof for the many sweeping assertions as to marked differences in the racial characteristics of the different dialect groups that may be heard in Hawaii as well as on the mainland, experience has undeniably proved that, on the whole, the proportion of men fitted for strenuous field labor is larger among the Ilocanos than among any of the other groups. It is not surprising, therefore, that, once this fact had been discovered, the agents of the Hawaiian planters concentrated their efforts on the Ilocos provinces.

The table presented in Appendix C shows the effect of the planters' successive changes in the areas of labor recruiting upon the provincial origins of plantation laborers employed between 1916

[12] In the earlier stages of recruiting, the H.S.P.A. made use of Filipino agents who received from 10 to 15 pesos for each laborer hired. With this inducement, the number of men who could be placed rather than a careful selection for competency was, naturally, a first consideration of those primarily concerned in shipping these laborers off to Honolulu.

[13] The estimated Filipino population of Honolulu for 1928 is 2,865, or 2.6 per cent. Independent estimates indicate a considerably higher figure for 1929, namely 5,000 to 7,000. Again as in the local population estimates on the mainland, a considerable variation in estimates is accounted for by the seasonal exodus of workers.

[14] Restriction of the area of selection has the further advantage of saving in license fees for agencies payable to the provincial authorities and amounting to $250 (in addition to a fee of $3,000 payable to the insular government). See Appendix I, p. 392.

and 1928. In 1916, the Island of Cebu took the lead, but even in 1919 Ilocos Norte sent the largest number of laborers. From 1924, the two Ilocos provinces began to send a majority of them. With La Union, the third province on the northwest coast of Luzon, these provinces contributed in 1916, 21 per cent of the whole, in 1921, 25 per cent, and in 1928, 62 per cent. Incidentally, this table illustrates that the charge against the planters, that they were importing to Hawaii the "riff-raff of the Manila docks" seems unsubstantiated for the period since 1916, during which the combined contribution of Manila with the near-by provinces of Bataan, Batanes, Cavite, Pampanga and Rizal never amounted to more than a very small fraction of the total. Summarized for the last ten years, the numbers and proportions are as follows:

NUMBER AND PROPORTION OF FILIPINO LABORERS MIGRATING FROM THE PHILIPPINE ISLANDS TO HAWAII FROM DIFFERENT PROVINCES, 1919-1928 [15]

Province	*Number of Emigrants*	*Percentage*
Abra	1,476	2.22
Bohol	4,592	6.91
Cebu	9,121	13.73
Ilocos Norte	21,400	32.21
Ilocos Sur	11,307	17.02
La Union	3,031	4.56
Leyte	1,317	1.98
Oriental Negros	2,769	4.17
Pangasinan	6,296	9.48
Tarlac	2,229	3.36
35 other Provinces	2,898	4.36
Total	66,436	100.00

Another charge sometimes made against the planters' recruiting principles is that they have, after earlier unfavorable experiences with intelligent men who became rapidly discontented with plantation conditions, gone to the most ignorant section of the Philippine Islands to recruit labor, in the hope that those unable to read would be less open to the blandishments of the labor organizer. It is true that some years ago, after bad experiences with city men sent by Filipino labor agents, "fountain-pen boys" were looked upon as a liability, and that youths of the school-boy type who wanted work merely as a means to continue their education and men who had

[15] From Annual Reports, Philippine Islands Bureau of Labor.

engaged in other than manual occupations were refused. Today, with a school system extending over the larger part of the Philippine Islands, and a large majority of Filipinos between the ages of ten and twenty literate, it would be difficult for the agents of the H.S.P.A. to discriminate against literates in the age group from which they are recruiting.[16]

Nor can it truthfully be said that the laborers for the Hawaiian plantations are recruited from the Philippine provinces with the lowest wage standards—although, possibly, the withdrawal of a large labor contingent may already have raised the level of wages in the areas with maximum emigration:

AVERAGE DAILY WAGES OF AGRICULTURAL LABORERS (MALE ADULTS) IN THE PHILIPPINE PROVINCES OF MAXIMUM EMIGRATION TO HAWAII, 1927

Province	*Percentage of Migrants to Hawaii, 1919-1928*	*Average Daily Wage Pesos* *
Abra	2.22	.87
Bohol	6.91	1.05
Cebu	13.73	.45
Ilocos Norte	32.31	1.00
Ilocos Sur	17.02	1.00
La Union	4.56	.87
Leyte	1.98	1.13
Oriental Negros	4.17	.88
Pangasinan	9.48	1.19
Tarlac	3.36	.97
35 other Provinces	4.36	—
Philippine Islands	100.00	₱0.98

* Statistical Bulletin of the Philippine Islands, 1928.

3. CONDITIONS OF EMPLOYMENT

What of the actual conditions of employment on the sugar plantations of Hawaii? These also have undergone many changes in the course of years, and what was true of them even as recently as 1925, when the planters had a scientific survey of these conditions made by a distinguished American firm of industrial consultants, has largely been overtaken by the introduction of new wage scales, new forms of contract, and new methods of manage-

[16] While the last available complete statistics of literacy, those of the census of 1918, are clearly out of date, even they do not support the charge that the proportion

ment—not to speak of many improvements in the housing and care of the workers.[17]

a. *Plantation Régime.*

From the first day of my inspection I gave special attention to the behavior of all the persons who exercise some control with the workers, such as the overseers or *lunas,* camp bosses, contract bosses and managers; and of all those whom I have been able to see and to exchange some words with I have noted that the spirit of harmony is in sway in these plantations. A notable fact I have observed in the 33 plantations visited is that I have not seen any manager, camp boss, overseer or *luna* or contract boss carry in his belt a revolver, or have in his hand a cane or whip, something that might distinguish him from the workers. They are only distinguished from the workers in their dress and by the leggings which they wear.[18]

Plantation managers deny that the work is more arduous or monotonous than other agricultural occupations. As a rule, laborers are employed from eight to nine months of the year on the harvesting of cane—including as its major operations cutting, loading and the laying of temporary tracks, with much employment also for teamsters, firemen and extra help in and around the mills—and three or four months in a variety of jobs. The working day is rarely above ten hours and often for long stretches of time only six or eight hours. Nevertheless, it is unquestionably true that American-born and American-bred adults do not readily engage

of illiteracy is abnormally high in the provinces from which a majority of plantation workers have been or are being recruited for Hawaii.

Statistics of the H.S.P.A. which show that nearly all Filipino workers in Hawaii have had some schooling and that the great majority of them can read and write seem more reliable than some rather sensational sample statistics published by the Bureau of Labor Statistics in the Philippines in 1925, to the effect that out of 1,000 emigrants only 60 had attended school but 455 could read. (Bulletin of the Bureau of Labor, vol. VII, No. 25, March, 1926, p. 29.)

[17] It is unfortunate that to the average American the word "plantation" remains associated from the reading of childhood days with conditions of slavery, whether in tropical lands or in our own South. For through this unavoidable mental association the mental picture of those who have no first-hand knowledge of the labor conditions prevailing in Hawaii assumes an ugly coloration. Attention may, perhaps, on this occasion, be drawn to other unfavorable word associations which are apt to prejudice public opinion when questions relating to Filipino immigration are under discussion. When, for example, we are told that Filipinos are "seeping" into this or that occupation, a picture is called up of something underhand and dangerous. In the same way, when resolutions refer to "loathsome" diseases of which Filipinos are alleged to be carriers, one has the sense of a vague menace which is not provoked by the mention of distinct contagious diseases which are known to be controllable.

[18] Report of Hermenegildo Cruz, director of the Philippine Bureau of Labor to the Governor General on an investigation of labor conditions of Filipinos in Hawaii. (Bulletin of the Bureau of Labor, March, 1925, vol. VII, No. 25, p. 16.) This report, made soon after the strike of 1924, was endorsed by the resident Philippine labor commissioner, Cayetano Ligot, and by a committee of workers.

in this type of work. The statement, repeatedly heard in connection with the present inquiry, that native-born workers will not submit to the paternalistic régime of the plantations is considerably weakened if not altogether disproved by the fact that, except for the more basic tasks of agricultural work,—which they are increasingly reluctant to perform on the mainland also—young Americans readily accept plantation jobs. Thousands of American-born and -bred men do the semi-skilled jobs as well as the mechanical and minor supervisory jobs. In the automative force, native-born workers readily accept the conditions of plantation life even though the pay for such preferred jobs often is less than they could earn at long-term cultivating contracts.

The paternal care exercised by the plantation owners and managers over the workers, as often in such cases, is not so galling to those who live and work under it as it is to those on the outside who look upon paternalism in industry as belonging to a form of social order which American public opinion has discarded long ago.

The owners and managers of the industry are deeply concerned in this problem themselves. For, while they share the prevailing ideals, they feel obliged to employ that system of industrial control which best fits the actual circumstances. The large majority of the workers, they argue, are foreigners—often foreigners who, in coming to Hawaii, for the first time are facing our western world with its intense individualism and the right and duty of the individual to look out for himself. If he were unprotected and uncared for, the immigrant plantation worker in his ignorance surely would be the victim of any number of hurtful influences, not always consciously predatory.[19] The early history of immigration to the United States has shown what appalling conditions result when immigrants are left to look out for themselves;[20] and those

[19] Actually some serious abuses which arose when Filipino workers began to arrive in large numbers could only be remedied by vigilant care. The Filipino's love of display, previously noted, led to injudicious instalment purchases of which fraudulent dealers took advantage. Gamblers and prostitutes were attracted to the plantations. With appeals to superstitious fears, fraternal organizations of shady antecedents managed to wheedle enormous initiation fees from ignorant and inexperienced peasants or instilled doctrines of dietary habits that were bound to interfere with physical efficiency. Fleeing from creditors became a serious cause of labor turnover. Even so, efforts made to exclude unauthorized solicitors from the camps do not extend to visitors generally and rarely interfere with the individual laborer's freedom of movement. Out of the 42 plantations of the H.S.P.A. only 5, by reason of location or organization, are able to exercise an effective detailed supervision of visitations to their villages.

[20] See Edith Abbott, Immigration—Select Documents and Case Records. University of Chicago Press, 1925, Part III.

were people with a similar background of culture and civilization, often—as in the case of the Irish—speaking the same tongue. The pragmatic test of results would seem to indicate that, in the case of Orientals and Malaysians, with a long history of exploitation under more or less feudal systems of society in their own countries, special forms of protection are necessary, and this quite independently of the particular form of the labor contract.

b. *Terms of Employment.*

It may be well, at this point, to indicate briefly what the terms of plantation employment are at the present time.[21]

The large majority of Filipino laborers—varying from 80 to 95 per cent on the different plantations—are employed at piece rates and average earnings of about $1.70 a day, with perquisites the value of which it is hard to estimate but which, on the mainland, would be worth at least another dollar a day.[22] The condition of the work, especially cane cutting, is such that productivity depends very largely on individual industry, without the possibility of constant oversight. Hence, in addition to the incentive of piece work wages, two other methods have been introduced to stimulate loyal performance of work: A bonus of 10 per cent of the basic wage for regular attendance, and a profit-sharing bonus of a somewhat complicated nature, described as follows:

> The basis for estimating the "profit sharing bonus" for any month is the average of the New York price of centrifugal sugar for 30 days prior to the 15th of said month.
>
> When the said New York price has averaged 5 cents per pound, the "profit sharing bonus" is 5 per cent. For each increase of one-tenth of a cent per pound in the average price of sugar, the bonus increases 1 per cent.
>
> If, for example, the average New York market price of sugar is 6 cents per pound, this bonus would be 15 per cent. Should the New York price average 7 cents per pound of sugar, the bonus would automatically increase an additional 10 per cent, making a total of 25 per cent.

Even more effective as an incentive has been found the introduction of long-term contracts, so called, under which a group of workers under competent foremanship assume complete responsibility for the production of sugar cane on a given field and are paid by results—that is at the end of the harvest, having in the meantime received an advance on their earnings for living expenses of

[21] A fuller statement is given in Appendix H, page 413.
[22] See p. 386 *et seq.*

one dollar a day. The average earnings of workers on long-term contract are $2.35 per day. This arrangement is frequently misunderstood, and many critics of the plantation system seem to be in the erroneous belief that large numbers of workers earn only one dollar a day and perquisites, not realizing that this is a basic minimum which only few individuals—about 3 per cent of the laborers—receive, usually newcomers as yet without a regular assignment or men temporarily disabled from hard work and employed on some light occupation.

Making allowance for bonuses earned and for the value of perquisites, the average earnings of Hawaiian plantation laborers on short contract are higher—and those of laborers on long contract considerably higher—than average earnings of comparable agricultural labor in the sixteen Southern states of continental United States.[23]

c. *Living Conditions and Welfare Work.*

The increasing use of the long-term agreement is watched with special interest because it seems to many to provide a stepping stone between the old-time slave-driving methods, under which the worker gives as little as possible in return for his assured earnings, and semi-independence of a kind which eventually may attract other classes of workers who under present conditions decline plantation labor because of the constraint associated with it. Certainly, to see a group of young Filipinos return from the fields at two o'clock in the afternoon to have a wash and then engage in vigorous outdoor sports does not give one the impression of forced labor associated of old with the idea of large-scale plantation work. Within a system essentially iron-bound, there are visible here elements of personal choice.

The conditions under which Filipinos work today on Hawaiian plantations, then, are not severe when compared with the régime under which, for example, Chinese coolies were handled on the mainland of the United States in the days of their maximum employment, or, in some aspects, with conditions obtaining in the steel industry as recently as 1910. Having carefully selected their employees to reduce to a minimum the proportion of undesirables, the sugar companies surround them with conditions that make for maximum efficiency. An air of cheerfulness pervades these little settlements, with their gardens, shrubberies and shade trees,

[23] See further below, p. 388.

their recreation halls and playgrounds, schools and churches, company and private stores. Coming often from small inland *barrios* (villages) with primitive living conditions, Filipino men and women here often have their first introduction to American standards of living—proper sanitary arrangements, laundries and shower-baths and a four-room house for every family, individual men usually being housed not more than two to a room. Of course, these living conditions are not equally good on all plantations; in some of them old-fashioned and unsuitable shacks have yet to be supplanted by modern bungalows. In others an air of neglect for appearances is explained by a desire of the management not to provide too much for the laborers in the way of refinement but rather to lead them, by slow educational methods, to provide for themselves those plantings and other decorations they desire. At first, Filipino laborers and their families appreciate congenial neighbors and amusements more than good homes. Care is taken to place newcomers, where they desire it, with or near relatives or friends from their home town.

Experience has shown that the improvement of living conditions cannot be achieved quickly. Enlarged photographs, phonographs and electric lights are more appreciated than good furniture. The women, more particularly, have yet to learn to trust the visiting nurses who show them how to prepare infant food and, sometimes, how to keep house.[24] Even then, many of them revert to the less effective or superstitious practices of their homeland. Assemblies for recreation often are taken advantage of for short lectures on subjects of hygiene; but more generally the teaching is individual; and demonstrations are given with the material at hand in the laborer's home. Classes in English or other general educational subjects are not especially encouraged but are provided when there is a demand for them. The proportion of plantation workers who desire to improve their education by night-school attendance is said to be small.

One criticism heard is that there is too much policing. When a man does not appear at work or a child fails to attend school, someone appears that day at the dwelling to inquire into the reason. This close supervision, perhaps more than any other feature, is branded by outside critics as "un-American," although, as a matter

[24] Filipino nurses are not often employed now. It was found that they used employment in Hawaii only as a stepping stone for the much desired trip to the mainland and continuation of their studies there.

of fact, it first received its fullest development in such American industrial concerns as the Standard Oil Company, the textile industry, and others. Promptness of investigation is defended on the ground that it adds to the effectiveness of nursing, hospitalization, and other welfare services.

Lately, successful experiments have been made in reducing the area of organized welfare activities. A somewhat less rigid supervision of living conditions and habits, less effort to Americanize the immigrant workers in a hurry, have had the effect, on one plantation at any rate, of reducing the labor turnover, although in this case earnings and housing conditions compare unfavorably with those of other plantations.

d. *Industrial Relations.*

Dissatisfaction with labor conditions may express itself in a variety of ways. In 1923 and 1924 the plantations unquestionably faced considerable unrest among the workers, chiefly on account of wages. Although it may be true that the strike which ensued was largely engineered from the outside, the labor organizer and agitator must have something to work upon in the way of actual discontent to succeed. At that time a much larger proportion of the laborers were Visayans, a more volatile and, perhaps, also better educated group than the Ilocanos. The object of the movement was, in the main, a higher minimum day-rate of wages. The contention of the leaders was that the terms of employment should approximate those of other large-scale agricultural operations under the American flag and not be merely a little better than those current in economically backward, tropical countries. It was probably not so apparent then as it is now that a more complicated method of remuneration, by its incentive power more fully insuring the employers of a maximum cooperation of the workers, would eventually benefit the workers more than a high straight wage. The strike was lost, after a disastrous episode in which five policemen and fifteen strikers were killed.

There is now barely the nucleus of a labor organization among plantation workers; and there is not sufficient discontent at the present time to make a recurrence of those unfortunate events likely.[25] One beneficent outcome of that disturbance was the

[25] In this connection it is interesting to know that the principal organizer of the strike of 1924, now resident in California, now is entirely opposed to any but a cooperative attitude toward the Hawaiian employers and acknowledges their humanitarian treatment of Filipino labor.

Photo Bert G. Covell

FILIPINO PLANTATION LABORER EMBARKING WITH WIFE AND DAUGHTER AT HONOLULU FOR MANILA AFTER COMPLETION OF CONTRACT

Bartolome Sales, during three and a half years of work on sugar plantations in Hawaii had a labor record averaging 25 days per month. By taking loading contracts and aided by his wife who helped him load six or seven cars of cane per day, by taking extra cultivating work when the loading season was over, with the aid also of a vegetable garden tended by his wife, he managed to save more than $2,600 during this period. After a vacation in the Philippines during which they intend to place their daughter in a good private school, Mr. and Mrs. Sales expect to return to Hawaii for a second contract period.

FILIPINO LABOR ON HAWAIIAN SUGAR PLANTATIONS

Above, left: Filipinos operating steam plow. *Right:* Planting cane
Below, left: Filipino, Japanese and Chinese planting cane. *Right:* Loading Cane

appointment, by the Philippine government, of a resident labor commissioner in Hawaii, to act as a representative of the workers in any labor dispute and to look after their interest in general.[26] While criticism may occasionally be heard of the way in which this office functions,[27] the prospect which the presence of the commissioner gives that any complaints are promptly brought to the attention of the association—complaints, mostly, concerning nonfulfillment of contractual obligations—has had a re-assuring effect upon the wage-earners. A former provincial governor and holder of other public offices in the Philippines, Cayetano Ligot, holder of this office since its establishment, has extended its activities to other desirable services on behalf of the Filipino immigrant and, in fact, exercises many of the protective functions of a consul. His mature years and experience make it possible for him to interpret mutually between workers and company managers the often intricate differences between them. But there have, in the last few years, been few serious cases affecting considerable numbers, rather a multitude of small difficulties which, unattended to, would cumulatively produce misunderstanding, resentment, and unrest.[28]

Another expression of dissatisfaction is a large labor turnover. On one of the best managed plantations the annual turnover of Filipino labor amounts to from 20 to 30 per cent. Among 1,366 workers who left the services of the H.S.P.A. in the year ended September 30, 1929, without having fulfilled their three years' contract, the average number of plantations worked on was one and a half. These figures show up fairly well when compared with the labor turnover in American industries.[29] In view of the youth of

[26] Section 4 of Act 2486 of the Philippine Legislature, as amended by Act 3148.

[27] An investigation was demanded by Representative Banaga in the Philippine Legislature on August 9, 1929.

[28] A bill was recently before the legislature of the Philippines providing for a similar office of labor commissioner on the Pacific Coast of the United States.

[29] Since there is practically no "lay-off" rate on Hawaiian plantations, comparison should be made with the rate of voluntary resignation in American industry, in so far as this is ascertainable. From reports collected in fifty Rhode Island factories in the first four months of 1927 (*i.e.*, before the industrial depression), the voluntary quit rate ranged from 17.3 in March (on an equivalent annual basis) to 20.2 in April. A report of the Metropolitan Life Insurance Company, presenting data from two hundred plants scattered throughout the United States, shows monthly variations in the voluntary quit rate for the same four months ranging between 21.8 and 31.1 (on an annual basis). (United States Bureau of Labor Statistics *Monthly Labor Review*, June, 1927, p. 41.) These figures probably represent considerable progress in the elimination of labor turnover. According to an intensive study made in Pennsylvania, the total turnover of twenty-four plants studied in the four years 1921-1924 varied from an annual average of 64.1 in 1924 to an average of 114.0 in 1923 (replacements of men employed each month), including a turnover through voluntary resignations ranging from an annual average of 35.1 in 1924 to one of 83.2 in 1923. (*Annals of*

the great majority of Filipino laborers and their well-known desire to see something of the world, it may indeed be said that the absence of a much more pronounced shift from one island to another and from one plantation to another and the relatively small number of cases in which men wander off to try their luck in other occupations, are signs of a high degree of contentment.

4. THE PROBLEM OF THE NATIVE-BORN

Hawaii's problem of a rural exodus of its native-born is in many respects similar to that of the mainland of the United States, of England, Germany, and other countries. It is accentuated by the territory's special difficulties, mainly geographical, in establishing industries that can compete in the world markets. Nevertheless, there have in the last ten or twenty years been many developments that afford employment for those who have crowded into urban communities. Raised standards of living, largely due to the school system, have created not only new occupational and social ambitions but also both major and minor industries to satisfy the new wants. Neither the industrial depression of 1921 nor that of 1929-1930 has resulted in unemployment comparable with that on the mainland. On the whole, the second generation of foreign residents has been able to secure jobs to its liking, at least under pleasanter working conditions than those of field labor. On the plantations themselves there has been a slow but constant increase in the use of machinery, providing employment at skilled and semi-skilled jobs. Moreover, the rapid growth of the two basic industries, while necessitating an ever larger volume of common labor, has brought with it a correspondingly increased demand for skilled and supervisory workers in these industries, and for every type of worker outside of them to meet the needs of the enlarged population.[30]

It is sometimes suggested that the substitution of more machines for hand labor will automatically increase the demand for skilled and semi-skilled workers, providing additional opportunities for

the American Academy of Political and Social Science, vol. CXIX, May, 1925, supplement: Four Years of Labor Mobility.)

A comparison of inclusive net turnover rates shows a much better situation for Hawaii than for American industry, namely 31.0 as against 45.2 for 75 industries employing nearly a million and a half workers for the year ending June 30, 1930. (*Monthly Labor Review* of the U. S. Bureau of Labor Statistics for August, 1930, p. 363.)

[30] Between 1920 and 1930, the sugar crop increased from 556,871 tons tc 930,000 tons, and the pineapple crop from six million to twelve million cases.

the product of Hawaiian schools. Experienced and progressive managers are inclined to doubt the possibility of doing much more in this direction. Costly experiments with cane-cutting machines have been going on for the last ten years and have not been a success. Loading machines are slowly being adopted, though the cost of operation is probably higher than the hand operation covering the same task. Economies in the final costs are secured only in the coupling up of this operation with others. The installation of sprinklers, to take the place of irrigation by hand, has not proved efficient. Experiments are constantly being made in other forms of mechanization with the aim of providing further opportunities for skilled labor.

A general concern over reported unemployment in Honolulu resulted in several inquiries, the latest of which was one conducted by a committee of the Chamber of Commerce, composed of the Secretary of the Territory as chairman, the head of the United Welfare Bureau, and the head of the Bureau of Governmental Research. This committee reported to the Governor on April 15, 1930, after careful investigation, that no condition existed which could be described as a general unemployment situation; that those unable to find work were largely men displaced from construction work which had lessened as a result of the stock market break and general depression; and that many of them were men who had been attracted to Honolulu by unusual building activity in previous years.[31] The committee recommended that, for the present, the urban community should discourage the movement from rural districts to the city.[32]

The school system is sometimes blamed for creating a desire for white-collar jobs and, especially, for not sufficiently encouraging work on the land. On the other hand, the school system is also

[31] For a fuller survey of Unemployment in Honolulu see an article with that title by Peter Entau Chu in the *Honolulu Mercury* for June, 1929, p. 38 *et seq.* A rather sensational account given in the Japanese monthly, *Jitsugyo-No-Hawaii* for June, 1929, dealing particularly with the situation in the pineapple packing plants, is discredited by first-hand accounts kindly secured by a Honolulu correspondent from the principal firms.

[32] About the time this report was made, the sugar plantations expressed a willingness to re-employ those displaced in Honolulu who previously had worked on plantations. After three months of active endeavor to find unemployed workers who desired to return to plantation work, 77 such persons, included in about 30 families or individual units, were sent to plantations. Some of these men were of an age which normally would have made them ineligible for this employment. Only one of the 77 was a Filipino, a man who had recently arrived at Honolulu from one of the other islands with the idea of finding a city job. Most of the men had been displaced by the cessation of building. In October, 1930, only a few of those employed in this experiment still remained on plantations.

blamed by some for "leaning backward," as it were, to make good any defects it may formerly have had in this respect by overstressing the desirability of rural employments, idealizing the plantations and, through an agreement with them, encouraging a form of child labor without educational elements.[33] This last complaint seems in part justified by some of the vocational experiments that are being tried, but in part arises from a misunderstanding of a system under which the plantations make it easy for older groups of boys to work in their spare time and during the summer vacation.[34]

While a substitution of small, independent farms for large plantations seems to many people utopian in these days of increasing farm units the world over, nevertheless, a twofold trend in the direction of larger responsible participation in management has already set in. In the first place, the long-term contract, as we have seen, provides for a degree of responsibility and freedom closely resembling that of independent tenant farming and offers opportunities of earnings higher than even a few years ago could have been dreamed of as within the reach of plantation workers. Second, there is also a movement, fostered by former Governor Wallace R. Farrington, to bring more rapidly into use the territory's area available for homesteads and for general farming.

[33] For example, the following description of a plan of vocational education known as "Type A" is given in the report of the Department of Public Instruction for 1927 and 1928: "Approximately half of their school time is spent in the class room where they receive instruction in English, mathematics, hygiene, geography and agriculture. The other half of their time is spent in the field where, under the direction of the teacher, they do all the work in about 80 acres of irrigated cane. This land is secured from the plantation on a cultivation contract, and the boys receive all the proceeds from their work. Their classroom instruction is very closely related to the field work, and the results are very satisfactory to both the school authorities and the plantation." (P. 117.)

[34] In the summer of 1928, 2,966 boys and 943 girls were employed in sugar-production field work, of these 2,086 boys and 758 girls under fourteen years of age. Six hundred and thirty-one boys and two hundred and five girls worked in pineapple production field work. (Annual Report of the Governor of Hawaii for the Fiscal Year Ended June 30, 1929, p. 74.) These children are employed on light work under special supervision. Many return to school having earned $25, a desirable addition to the family income, and having gained in weight. "Future Farmers' Clubs"—a movement which started on the mainland—have been formed to take advantage of the provision of federal aid under the Smith-Hughes Act. In some cases such clubs undertake the cultivation of sugar fields and are paid at the rate of 30 cents an hour, the work being done on Saturdays and after school hours, with longer workdays during the summer vacation. Whether this type of work really constitutes a training for general farming, as contemplated by the Smith-Hughes Act, is in dispute. Wives and children of plantation workers are also employed at light industrial occupations; the former at sewing bags, the latter at helping in machine, carpentry and painting shops and in garages.

As a result of my study and observation in 33 years residence in Hawaii, I am disposed to take a more optimistic view than that generally held, regarding the probability of our young people turning to the main industries of the territory as a field for their future activities. . . .

There are within the territory today a total of 2,869 homesteads, any one of which might possibly be obtained by a citizen who wishes to cultivate land, own it in fee simple and establish thereon a home. Of this total just given, 1,721 have been patented, that is, paid for and title given to the individual owner. There are 742 now in process of being homesteaded and may be patented when the occupants satisfy the obligation of purchase and residence. Four hundred and seven homesteads are now available to be taken up; with an area of 350 acres of sugar cane land, 181 acres general agricultural lands, and 11,041 acres pasture land. The average area of the lots is 22.4 acres. Sugar cane lots and the areas that might be used for growing pineapples are approximately 20 to 40 acres. . . . The thrifty homesteader may under the law acquire land up to 80 acres. There are opportunities for citizens of this territory, young or old, who wish to go into sugar cane cultivation or pineapple cultivation in the districts where sugar cane and pineapple are the main source of the community revenue. Young men may grow sugar cane and sell that cane to the mill under contracts that are considered as favorable, provided the homesteader is an agriculturist, cultivates his own land and carries on his business on a business basis.[35]

Others take a less hopeful view of homesteading as a means of attracting large numbers of workers to the land. A man close to the sugar industry in Hawaii writes:

Hawaiian experience with homesteading has not been fortunate. It is no opprobrium upon the homesteaders that the general development of the homestead experiments has been that, whichever one of the two major crops—sugar and pineapples—has been undertaken, the financing of the project necessarily falls upon the main industry. In fact, homesteading has usually resulted in the more or less false homesteading activity: The homesteader maintains title to the land which has been handed over to him by the Government and thereafter either does a small amount of work on the land financed by the sugar or pineapple company which buys his product, and is assisted by such company with labor from the company's supply, or he leases or contracts his land to the company to be farmed by the laborers of the company's organized force, sitting by to reap whatever may be the net result of the year's work.

In other instances where more exact homesteading practice has been adopted, individual cases of small moment have been more or less successful; but it would be over-optimistic to use such individual cases as indicating a possibility of any extent affecting large numbers of the people of the Territory.

[35] From an address before the Chamber of Commerce of Honolulu, July 2, 1928.

Mr. Farrington, during his term of office, has facilitated the development of this form of homesteading and small-scale production of sugar cane generally, by securing the sanction of the territorial legislature for the continuation of a sugar expert and, in the face of opposition, expanding the usefulness of this position. The sugar expert advises each applicant, after full inquiry, as to the form of contract with the sugar mill which it is most beneficial for him to sign. Thus, according to a recent report, this officer was able on the island of Hawaii, after a period of discouragement owing to low prices, to negotiate terms of agreement between the local sugar mill and independent growers that were more favorable to these growers, with the result that an area where cane had ceased to be grown was planted anew with sugar cane early in 1929.

> The sugar expert is continuing to publicly voice his belief that, given economic and social independence, enough citizen-born youth living in the non-irrigated sections of the Islands would be willing to take up sugar cane production as a vocation to soon make immigrant agricultural labor unneeded in those sections. The work of the "Future Farmers of America" on the projects in those sections under the Smith-Hughes school vocational training scheme is beginning to demonstrate the soundness of this belief.[36]

Hawaii must needs remain primarily an agricultural country. There is no natural fuel supply, nor are there minerals, nor timber in any quantity. A local fertilizer manufacturing plant supplies, from imported raw materials, practically the whole fertilizer demands of the territory. For two years, the Chamber of Commerce employed an officer to devote all his time to a study of possibilities of starting new industries. In the summer of 1930 a company was formed, with a capital of $2,225,000, to manufacture wall board from sugar-cane bagasse. The principal sugar factors themselves have time and again invested funds in lesser industrial enterprises which, because of the conditions named, have rarely offered opportunities for rapid expansion. It is but natural that in a period during which the major industries were expanding rapidly, any proposals containing elements of risk were most carefully scrutinized before they could be recommended to local investors. To a remarkable extent the financial interest of the whole community is participating in the two major industries; at the same time there is even now considerable diversity in these investments, both large and small.

[36] Annual Report of the Governor of Hawaii for the Fiscal Year Ended June 30, 1929, p. 66.

One of the difficulties which remain is that the American-born children of Oriental immigrants are not always admitted to those opportunities in industry and business for which they are qualified. This discrimination can only give way in time to a greater appreciation on the part of employers for home-grown talents and to a further assimilation of customs, habits and language, without which purely technical qualifications do not always suffice to open the door of opportunity.

Finally, as regards the unfavorable attitude toward plantation work on the part of the older wage-earners, there is every reason to believe that greater familiarity with the conditions that now prevail and the growing up of children of men who have worked under the present, more favorable conditions, will, to some extent, tend to overcome it.

In the circumstances which have been described, it is not surprising that thoughtful citizens in Hawaii do not favor revolutionary changes which might endanger the whole economic basis of the territory's prosperity. It is generally felt that any Congressional action which would suddenly deprive Hawaii of its present immigrant labor supply would be detrimental to the whole population's best interests. This is particularly so because, contrary to the experience of some farming groups on the mainland of the United States, Filipino labor, as at present selected and controlled, has, by general consent, been found to fit admirably the present labor needs of the Islands.

In spite of irrefutable statistical evidence, the charge is still frequently made that the H.S.P.A. is bringing so large a surplus of Filipino laborers to the territory as to create an unemployment problem.[37] A comparison of the average immigration of Filipino laborers for the last five years—about 9,000—with the total number of Filipino employees on the pay roll of the plantations—about 34,000—would indicate that the annual influx amounts to a little less than the number potentially lost annually through completion of the three-year contract. Of course, a constantly increasing proportion of Filipino laborers stay on after the end of three years; but at the same time there must be a considerable annual loss of laborers of other nationalities who can, under present circumstances, be replaced only by Filipinos. Assuming an even demand

[37] For example, in a communication from a graduate of the Central Luzon Agricultural School in the *Manila Free Press* for January 5, 1929.

for plantation labor, these losses would seem to call for an increase in the annual supply of Filipino workers. But, on the other hand, changes in methods and changes in the area under cultivation—owing to the expiration of leases and the lease and irrigation of new lands—make such computations purely theoretical.

5. THE DESIRABILITY OF FILIPINO LABOR

As in California so also in Hawaii it has been found that the desirability of Filipino labor, due to the satisfaction given by its work record and the general adjustment of the group to the demands of the local situation, depends to a large extent on the system of management to which it is subjected. Earlier experiences with the Filipino, though he was found more desirable than the Porto Rican, were not as favorable as later experiences have proved to be. The three outstanding causes of this change have been, first, better mutual understanding [38] and the gradual adjustment of the workers to the tasks required of them; then, a more rigorous selection and, particularly, the increasing return of workers for a second contract period; lastly, a more complete protection against unwholesome influences and the encouragement of thrift.

Like other newcomers to industry, the Filipino was inclined, in the earlier stages of his employment, to lay off frequently for small cause. He is now as regular in attendance as the Japanese or any other of the older groups and more amenable to discipline. In output he equals, and in some operations surpasses, the standard set by any of these groups.

> The Filipinos have proved themselves to be good workers. They adapt themselves well to the tasks in the field, which are the ones in which they are mostly employed. Eighty-five per cent of all Filipinos are engaged in field work, and the volume of work per man turned out by these employees is equal to that of any race we have had experience with. Filipinos, with a very few exceptions, are quiet, orderly, sober and thrifty.[39]

[38] Changes in the attitudes of the employers are no less important in this connection than changes in those of the workers. Professor S. D. Porteus, of the University of Hawaii, distinguishes three distinct attitudes on the part of certain plantation managers to their Filipino laborers since their first employment: (1) "Filipinos are children and must be managed twenty-four hours a day"; (2) (during and immediately after the strike of 1924): "Filipinos are unsatisfactory, but under the existing circumstances are the best obtainable"; (3) Managers with most experience with Filipinos are most favorably disposed toward them.

[39] Address of President Allen W. T. Bottomley at Fiftieth Annual Meeting of the H.S.P.A., November 17, 1930, p. 11.

On one plantation, now employing exclusively Filipinos as cane-cutters, the average daily output increased by almost 50 per cent in four years, with even larger averages in some months of maximum production; and, with the operation of the sliding scale of earnings under the contract system, the earnings of cutters almost doubled. The Filipino's improvidence has given way to a remarkable degree of thrift which, again, acts as the most effective incentive to conscientious work. "Out of every dollar earned the Filipino saves two," is a common saying. A striking characteristic of a few—usually the more mature men, with a background of frugal life on a small farm of Ilocos (the "Scotland" of the archipelago)—lends itself as easily to exaggerated generalization as does the extravagance and instability of a small class of unadjusted Filipinos on the mainland. Many instances of individual savings prove that individual workers can accumulate sums which, through judicious land purchase or other investments at home, will set them up as men of substance in comparison with their fellow townsmen. The returning Filipino who does not carry back with him a considerable sum, measured by his standards, is the exception. During the year ending September 30, 1929, the H.S.P.A. handled nearly $300,000 in voluntary transmittal of individual accounts which ranged from $50 to $1,500 and, in some cases, $2,000. In the calendar year 1928, 3,504 men returning to the Philippines sent and took back with them to that country $1,952,868. More revealing is the fact that, with a total of 33,744 male Filipinos on the sugar plantations in 1929, the savings banks of the territory had 10,041 deposit accounts of Filipinos, averaging deposits of $216.04.

Although both employers and workers seem to take great pride in this remarkable record, criticism is not lacking to the effect that the virtue of saving, in the case of plantation laborers, has been carried to excess and does not altogether contribute to the social welfare. It is a common assumption that a worker with an income of $60 a month can send half of it to maintain a family at home and still live well on what remains. But many with much smaller incomes divide their earnings in the same proportion; and for this reason more than any other, the welfare personnel of the plantations have to exercise, they say, so much supervision over the workers' diet. Occasionally a man may be indisposed or actually fainting in the field for no other reason than continued undernourishment.

It should also be kept in mind that, in a sense, the word "saving" does not apply to all the money sent back to the Philippines, since it contains an unknown proportion for the support of the sender's immediate dependents.[40]

[40] It is known, however, that generally speaking only a small proportion of moneys sent home by emigrant laborers is used up in defraying the family's living expenses; by far the greater proportion is invested in land and capital improvements.

CHAPTER XIII

SOCIAL PROBLEMS

IT is sometimes contended that immigrant labor is costly in comparison with native labor; that it throws additional burdens upon public expenditure. This is not true of the Filipino, as the following illustrative facts will indicate.

1. DESTITUTION

Although inevitably considerable numbers of Filipinos have drifted away from the plantations and others have come to Honolulu on their own account in the expectation of making an easy living there; although, further, many are employed intermittently in the pineapple canneries and on the docks of that city, they rarely become charges of public relief. Statistics of the local Social Service Bureau, which corresponds to the Family Welfare Societies on the mainland, attribute to Filipino families 4.4 per cent of the family cases handled in 1929—in practically all instances in connection with mothers' pensions—and 1.2 of the cases of individuals handled. Among the problems presented, unemployment—or, more often, change of employment—leads with 40 cases; in second place comes tuberculosis with 30 cases; family desertion figures 16 cases, death of breadwinner with 13.

The Humane Society of Honolulu reports, for 1928, a total number of 625 cases of neglect of children. Only 7 of these involved Filipinos.

Owing to the willingness of Filipino workers, in Hawaii as on the mainland of the United States, to take care of their own unemployed, it is difficult to estimate either their number or the effect of their lack of earnings upon the general standards of living of the group. Serafin E. Macaraig, professor of sociology at the University of the Philippines, who made a study of this situation in 1926, estimated the number of Filipino unemployed in Honolulu at that time as 3,000 but includes in this estimate categories of classification which are not usually included in statistics of unemployment:

1. Those who went to Hawaii on a contract basis to work on the plantations but have jumped their contracts in order to get a sinecure in the city.

2. Those who have been weeded out by the different plantations because they have been found to be unfit for agricultural work, or are lazy, shiftless and unmanageable.

3. Some of them were strikers in 1920 and 1924 who cannot be reinstated, or those who do not care to return to the plantation because they feel that they have been maltreated or discriminated against.

4. Those who were formerly employed in the Navy and the Government who, by reason of the ruling that aliens cannot be employed in the United States government, have been discharged. They are now mostly located in cities.

5. There is also among the unemployed a class that lives on the weakness and ignorance of their countrymen. They devote their time trying to get money from the ignorant laborers by doing personal service in securing tickets for transportation or claims against the H.S.P.A. In most cases these people are out of employment.

6. The casual laborers who are employed in the pineapple canneries, those who are doing personal services in the homes of the rich and those who do casual work as stevedores and cutting grass.

7. There are among them also those Filipinos who prefer to work for a few months and then lay off for the rest of the year. These can be found around pineapple canneries and plantations. They work for four months, and for the rest of the year they loaf around to their liking.[1]

The conditions of life, writes the director of the Philippine Islands Bureau of Labor, of the Filipinos living in cities, excepting those who have permanent work, may be said to be difficult and miserable because of their irregular periods of employment. They find hardly enough to sustain themselves, and I can affirm that a great number of them lack the necessities of life. Often they live by securing shelter and aid from their compatriots who are at work and earning their living. These people then become a veritable charge on those who do work and shelter them.[2]

2. HEALTH

The general death rate of Filipinos in Hawaii is relatively low—but perhaps only apparently so because of the low age composition of the group—as will be seen from the following table:

[1] Social Problems. Educational Supply Co., Manila, 1929, p. 223.

[2] Report on Labor Conditions of Filipinos in Hawaii. Bulletin of the Philippine Islands Bureau of Labor, vol. VII, No. 25, March, 1926, p. 4.

DEATH RATES PER 1,000 POPULATION [3]

Race	*Rate per 1,000 population*
American, British, German, Russian	8.00
Chinese	13.10
Filipino	13.18
Hawaiian	33.30
Japanese	9.85
Korean	13.06
Asiatic-Hawaiian	18.61
Caucasian-Hawaiian	17.28
Portuguese	10.13
Porto Rican	15.76
Spanish	3.28
All others	70.08
For Territory	12.69

Filipinos have an exceptionally high death rate from diseases of the respiratory system:

NUMBER OF DEATHS AND DEATH RATES DUE TO TUBERCULOSIS AND DISEASES OF THE RESPIRATORY SYSTEM, 1928-1929 [4]

Due to Tuberculosis	*Number of Deaths*	*Rates per 100,000 Pop.*
Filipinos	76	122
Non-Filipinos	330	113
Total	406	
Due to Diseases of Respiratory System		
Filipinos	187	301
Non-Filipinos	475	
Total	662	

Too much importance must probably not be attached to these figures because registration from the sugar plantations where most of the Filipinos live is likely to be more accurate than registration for the territory as a whole. On the other hand, the death rate is less indicative of the prevalence of disease for plantation work-

[3] Report of Registrar General for the Fiscal Year Ended June 30, 1929, table VII. Unfortunately, data are not available to correct this table for age distribution.
[4] Annual Report of Territorial Board of Health.

ers than for the rest of the population because, where presence of a debilitating disease is definitely diagnosed in Filipino plantation workers, these are usually returned by the H.S.P.A. to their homes in the Philippines. Correction for age and sex composition also would alter the comparison. Some observers believe that working conditions on the plantations are unfavorable and point to the smoke and dust incident to some of the plantation occupations, and to work in rain showers which sometimes are followed by cool breezes. Medical authorities more frequently explain the Filipino laborers' high susceptibility to diseases of the respiratory organs with poor physique due to bad nutrition habits in their home country. The medical officer at one of the largest plantations declares that between 40 and 50 per cent of the Filipino workers are undernourished on arrival, and that newcomers frequently cannot at once be assigned to arduous work. At the same time, he noticed that Filipinos have better teeth than Japanese or Chinese workers; and this he also ascribes to their food habits. In this connection it is interesting to note that the medical and welfare officials at the sugar plantations and Parent-Teacher Associations give special attention to the raising of dietary standards among the Filipinos. It is further stated that the susceptibility of Filipinos to common colds and to pneumonia in Hawaii as much as on the mainland is due to the fact that, coming from a warmer climate, they frequently have still to learn how to protect themselves against undue exposure.

There is relatively little overcrowding of Filipinos in the Hawaiian Islands. Bad living conditions in the cities are sometimes due to under-employment, especially of dock workers. Often, as on the mainland, individual Filipinos and even families crowd together to save rent. Rents for small houses in Honolulu vary from $20 to $30. Sometimes the desire for the company of *paisanos* (countrymen) rather than economic need leads to "doubling up" in a tenement, each family occupying one bedroom and both sharing the living room. Extravagance, as on the mainland, also is a frequent cause of under-expenditure on necessities, including house room.

A high infantile mortality is given by the Board of Health and by physicians at the plantations as further evidence that the Filipino's health hazards are largely due to the ignorance and unadjustment of a newly arrived immigrant group. This seems to be borne out by the gradually lessening rate for Filipinos over a number of years:

INFANT MORTALITY RATES, TERRITORY OF HAWAII (PER THOUSAND CHILDREN BORN) BY RACE, 1924 TO 1929[5]

Race	*1924*	*1925*	*1926*	*1927*	*1928*	*1929* *
Territory of Hawaii .	116.26	103.59	104.21	95.97	83.69	101.76
Hawaiian . . .	291.25	258.50	198.53	237.19	185.71	202.25
Caucasian-Hawaiian .	83.23	76.92	78.75	102.36	85.98	109.70
Asiatic-Hawaiian .	122.97	75.16	103.45	116.17	97.83	132.63
Portuguese . .	87.00	81.03	74.22	78.07	58.47	63.94
Porto Rican . .	124.00	111.11	114.28	122.45	103.45	110.03
†Other Caucasians .	37.95	39.25	75.36	49.69	31.62	——
Chinese . . .	71.25	56.15	61.30	52.76	47.87	64.84
Japanese . . .	87.46	59.81	72.76	55.64	50.31	66.74
Korean . . .	89.15	45.27	42.73	42.91	42.86	69.77
Filipino . . .	262.55	287.38	237.19	226.25	220.30	244.51
All others . . .	40.00	58.82	150.00	200.00	71.43	——

* Report of Registrar General for the Fiscal Year Ended June 30, 1929, p. 32.
† Includes Spanish.

The susceptibility of Filipino infantile mortality to educational influences is illustrated by a comparison of the rate for those under the care of the Palama Settlement in Honolulu—269.50 per thousand births—with those for the city as a whole, excluding those enrolled at the settlement—namely, 430.23.[6]

As on the mainland of the United States, no fault is found with the Filipino's habits of personal cleanliness. Indeed, his frequent ablutions are often remarked upon as a distinct trait.

The Filipino's venereal disease rate is low. Among more than 100,000 men examined in the Philippines by the medical staff of the H.S.P.A., the number of venereal cases was found to be phenomenally small.

The Filipinos in Hawaii have not been a cause of epidemics. Cases of dysentery as well as of other infectious diseases are discovered through the thorough system of medical inspection and the period of medical observation enforced by the H.S.P.A. Typhoid cases have in all instances been traced to local conditions. Malaria

[5] Annual Report of the President of the Board of Health of the Territory of Hawaii for the Fiscal Year Ended June 30, 1928, p. 22.
[6] *Ibid.*, p. 13.

is rare. Meningitis cases are not peculiar to the Filipino but have been introduced also by other travellers from the Orient.

> *Meningococcus meningitis* first showed an undue prevalence following the arrival of the *President McKinley* from the Orient on September 26, 1928, and reached the peak in March, 1929, during which months 68 cases were reported, of which 62 were from arriving vessels from the Orient and 2 from Army transports from San Francisco. For the fiscal year 1928 there were reported 44 cases and 14 deaths, while for 1929 there were 198 cases and 68 deaths. For the year there were 51 cases of local origin, practically all being due to contact with recently arrived Filipino laborers, while 147 cases were removed from arriving vessels.
>
> From information obtainable, it is evident that the disease has prevailed very extensively in China and was the source of infection amongst the personnel on vessels arriving here from the Orient, particularly so as it has recently been authoritatively learned that the crew and steerage passengers of the trans-Pacific steamers have gone regularly ashore at Shanghai, both when outward and inward bound. . . . [Quarantine arrangements made] resulted in absolutely curtailing any danger of the spread of infection. The last trans-Pacific steamer to arrive with Meningitis aboard was the *President Jackson,* May 23, 1929.[7]

Amœba and hookworm, where they have slipped through the medical inspection, are usually cured on the plantation.[8] Beri-beri and trachoma, at one time—with Japanese immigrants—the dread of immigration authorities, are practically excluded under the newer system of examination. Leprosy, relatively rare, likewise, is under complete control.

3. IMMORALITY AND CRIME

One of the reasons for the close interest of the plantation managers in the Filipino's outside relations, as we have seen, is that he is easily influenced and led astray. Like other cosmopolitan cities, and especially those with large garrisons in their vicinity, Honolulu harbors many vicious persons and many who, unadjusted themselves, are forever disgruntled and centers of rebellion around which, in times of unemployment, there gather others. The Filipinos of Hawaii, though the average age is higher than on the mainland, still are, in the main, young men with

[7] Report of the Governor of Hawaii for the Year Ended June 30, 1929, p. 83.

[8] Hookworm is practically non-existent in Hawaii. Although occasionally diagnoses are found in health and hospital reports, further examination usually reveals a confusion of diagnosis between strongyloid and hookworm eggs. See also p. 113.

many other besides economic motives. The married couples of their group as yet are mostly parents of small children and not centers of sociability. So, left to themselves, Filipino laborers join with those of their fellow men in town, who, as on the mainland, have the characteristics of seasonal and casual workers, spend much of their time in pool-rooms and barber shops and, in a city of many races, enter into all sorts of amusements, legitimate and illegitimate.

Gambling among Filipinos in Hawaii assumes serious proportions. It ranges from a mild diversion to gross dishonesty and larceny—nearly always among the Filipinos themselves. Not only in city neighborhoods but also on plantations, in spite of all watchfulness, *panguingi,* a dice game, is surreptitiously played in sheds and odd corners. Women neglect their households and waste their money in these unending games. Such leadership as there is among the Filipinos is well aware of this threat to the welfare and unity of the group. Not only missionaries and officers of organizations but also the Filipino newspapers are in constant battle against it. A single number of the *Hawaii-Philippine News* (November 6, 1929) tells of two serious cases; in one of these, a man in the thirties, after three years' hard work on a Pacific coastwise vessel, was robbed of all his savings, $839, by a crooked dice game while on his way back to the Philippines; in the other case, two young Filipinos were arrested for working a bunco-game among returning plantation workers passing through Honolulu, swindling two of them out of their total savings of $665. An editorial article in the same number berates the countrymen who will thus hazard the reward of years of toil. Another Hawaii Filipino paper, *Ang Kayumanggii,* edited by the Rev. N. C. Dizon, says editorially (November 30, 1929):

> The crookedness of "educated" Filipinos is the root of our helplessness in our desire for unity, so that often we cannot get Filipinos to believe in their fellow-Filipinos so that they would rally around them. The type of leaders we need in Hawaii are those who are honest because of their own volition, and not those who are only "honest" because they are being constantly watched by a "haole" employee or a Japanese foreman.

Disputes over games also are the largest cause of assault among Filipinos. It is out of the passions engendered by illegitimate pleasures, such as gambling and cock fighting, that there arise major delinquencies and crime. Owing to the present régime of the plantations and the stricter selection of laborers, there has been a distinct improvement in Filipino criminality in the course of years, but, as the following table will show, the ratio of Filipino crime is still high in homicide and sex offenses when compared with the rate for the total population.

RATIO OF CONVICTIONS IN THE TERRITORIAL COURTS, 1916-1924, PER 10,000 OF MALE POPULATION 18 YEARS AND OVER [9]

	Assault	*Fraud and Forgery*	*Embezzlement*	*Larceny*	*Robbery*	*Burglary*	*Homicide*	*Sex Offenses*
Hawaiian and Part Hawaiian	298.0	9.9	7.9	97.3	6.0	34.8	4.5	8.4
Portuguese and Other Caucas.	136.5	6.2	9.6	37.3	1.2	8.4	1.4	2.9
Spanish . .	111.9	8.6	—	68.8	4.3	—	—	4.3
Chinese . .	51.3	5.9	4.7	32.4	1.1	4.2	.4	1.1
Japanese . .	29.1	1.3	2.1	10.6	.6	1.8	1.0	.5
Korean . .	207.4	13.9	7.4	118.3	1.8	15.2	2.8	3.7
Porto Rican .	437.4	3.1	1.6	143.9	3.1	37.5	23.4	31.2
Filipino . .	253.2	2.5	7.1	99.8	2.5	17.6	6.8	9.8
Total . .	127.0	3.9	5.2	46.8	1.7	10.4	2.5	3.9

Statistics gathered at the Territorial Jail in 1930 show that, when no allowance is made for the proportion of each racial group in the total population or for its age and sex composition, the Filipino's contribution to crime is decidedly high. An abstract of these statistics made by Professor S. D. Porteus, of the University of Hawaii, shows that about 60 per cent of the murderers incarcerated are Filipinos; of those in jail for rape about one-third. He adds:

For the crime of carnal abuse of females under 12 years of age, 15 per cent of the prisoners are Filipinos; for indecent assault and intercourse with a female under 16 years of age, 53 per cent; for assault and battery, 50 per cent; for burglary, 14 per cent; for robbery, 50 per cent; for larceny and malicious conversion, 18 per cent.

While Filipino crime is, therefore, still serious, the following table shows that it is diminishing:

[9] Data Bearing on Delinquency and Crime. Annual Conference of Social Workers of Hawaii, July, 1929. Table II, p. 9.

RATIO OF CONVICTIONS OF FILIPINOS IN THE TERRITORIAL COURTS IN TWO AND FOUR YEAR PERIODS, 1915-1928, PER 10,000 OF MALE POPULATION 18 YEARS AND OVER [10]

		Assault	*Fraud and Forgery*	*Embezzlement*	*Larceny*	*Robbery*	*Burglary*	*Homicide*	*Sex Offenses*
1915-16	Filipino	517.0	4.4	14.2	253.6	1.1	34.9	14.2	13.1
	Tot. Pop.	201.8	2.3	6.0	82.9	1.0	10.1	3.6	4.6
1917-18	Filipino	272.0	4.7	2.3	158.5	5.5	43.0	19.9	12.5
	Tot. Pop.	138.1	4.5	3.3	64.4	1.5	15.6	2.3	3.7
1919-20	Filipino	196.4	2.0	15.8	137.1	—	10.8	4.1	6.8
	Tot. Pop.	115.2	3.5	4.9	40.1	1.6	9.8	1.8	2.3
1921-24	Filipino	162.1	1.2	4.0	54.2	1.5	6.3	3.8	6.2
	Tot. Pop.	132.2	4.4	6.4	44.2	2.1	8.7	3.0	4.8
1925-28	Filipino	138.5	2.1	3.3	56.0	.3	5.6	5.6	8.2
	Tot. Pop.	119.0	9.9	4.2	43.0	1.7	10.3	2.8	6.1

The two last-named offenses are closely related in a population where the sexes are so disproportionate as in Hawaii. The great majority of these crimes occur in the rural sections of the territory where single males are so largely congregated.[11]

A committee of citizens, recently appointed by the governor, is at the time of writing engaged in a study of the causes of a crime rate for the territory which, it is believed, can be greatly reduced by appropriate measures.

As further throwing light on the nature of the Filipino's offenses against the law, it may be interesting to compare with his ratio of convictions for the more serious crimes his number of convictions for many of the lesser offenses that are handled in the local courts.

FILIPINO CONVICTIONS IN THE DISTRICT COURT OF HONOLULU DURING 1929

Offenses	*Filipino*	*Total*
Adultery	5	11
Affray	1	15
Assault and Battery	45	301
Auto carrying more passengers than allowed by law	2	3
Auto driving carelessly	9	126
Auto driving without due regard for safety	1	59
Auto driving without chauffeur certificate	24	260
Auto driving while intoxicated	1	98

[10] *Ibid.*, Tables I and III, pp. 7 and 11.
[11] *Ibid.*, p. 8.

Offenses	*Filipino*	*Total*
Auto ordinance, other violations	25	521
Auto speeding	41	574
Billiard parlors regulations, violating	2	2
Common nuisances	1	7
Desertion and Non-support of wife	3	48
Drunkenness	21	442
Embezzlement	1	3
Fire arms, non-registration of,	1	1
Fire arms, regulation, violating	1	5
Fishing laws, violating,	11	38
Gambling	4	5
Gambling, present at,	266	446
Larceny, second degree	11	97
Malicious injury	2	16
National Prohibition Act, possession	32	147
" " " sale	2	10
Practicing dentistry without license	1	1
Threats	3	13
Vagrancy	17	115
TOTAL	533	3,364

Particularly revealing is the large proportion of Filipinos convicted in the district court of having been "present at gambling." These men, even when they are found to take part in illegal games, evidently are as much victims as they are perpetrators of an offense. Indeed, many of the gambling houses maintained by Chinese and Caucasian owners depend for their support on Filipino patronage. Occasional special raids and campaigns evidently do not suffice to get rid of this evil or of the institution of commercial vice which flourishes wherever there are large numbers of young men without a normal social life.

According to the best authorities, the crime rate of Filipinos, while regrettable, is not excessive when compared with that of other immigrant groups of a similar age and sex composition in the early years of their arrival. The minor offenses for the most part arise from ignorance of American law and from an excess of youthful spirit, while the more serious offenses, such as larceny and assault, are for the most part committed within the plantation settlements and usually are due to jealousies and rivalries that have not yet learned to express themselves in more civilized ways.[12] The rela-

[12] See Romanzo Adams, The Peoples of Hawaii. Institute of Pacific Relations, 1925, p. 35.

tively large number of sex offenses is explained by court officers and social workers with the fact that in the Philippines girls mature earlier, and that our stringent American laws concerning misconduct with minors are not understood. "Wife-stealing," in popular parlance, is a misnomer; a serious proportion of adultery and remarriage is due to the unusual strains upon a wife's loyalty where her sex is at such a premium and to the difficulty of Filipino women from very simple home environments to adjust themselves to life in a new country. (See above, p. 120.) Intermarriage with women of other racial groups, with widely differing cultural concepts, also enters into the high degree of marital instability.

Among the crimes typical for an emigrant group composed of young men is that of bigamy.[13] Marrying at an early age, they are tempted to leave their wives and children at home when they go out to take advantage of the opportunities which Hawaii offers. Returning laborers report that it is difficult for a man to save if he has a family with him on the Hawaiian plantation, whereas he can send one-half or more of his earnings home, sufficient to maintain his family in the Philippines, and still have a fairly good time. The temptation to marry again arises when he has been away from his wife and children for some time, not only because of the physical comfort but also because, with the scarcity of marriageable women among his friends and acquaintances, the possession of a wife on the plantation confers a special prestige.

> I have two relatives, said a public official in Abra Province, who went to Hawaii ten years ago and have never come back. For the first three years they sent money regularly, since then they have sent none. But they write that they have automobiles and are doing well. They were married here and left their families. Now they have married in Hawaii. Many do that. Few take their wives with them from here. Hawaii is not considered safe for women.

Perhaps one reason for this unfortunate development is an increasing insistence on the part of parents in the Philippine Islands, disturbed by the reports of the "wild life" of the emigrant young men abroad, that their sons marry before they leave. According to an official of one of the steamship companies, about one in every five of those who go to the mainland of the United States are married but leave their wives behind. Many of them get married just

[13] Kate Holladay Claghorn, The Immigrant's Day in Court. Harper & Brothers, 1923, p. 82.

before leaving, he says, to bind them more closely to their home and to prevent them from getting into trouble abroad.

Of the general charge against Filipinos on the mainland, that they are too aggressive in their pursuit of women, echoes may also be heard in Hawaii. But only echoes, not corroboration. On the plantations, there is no evidence that social evils are even as prevalent among the Filipinos as might be considered normal for a group of men of any race. In the towns it is only among non-Caucasian women that the young Filipino follows his romantic bent. In spite of the marked exclusiveness of some of the other racial groups, especially the Japanese, the Filipino does not find himself altogether barred from social intercourse; a strict taboo against him is enforced only in circles which, because of his low social and economic status as the most recent immigrant, he would not be likely to reach anyhow.

4. INTERMARRIAGE

In view of the opinion which so largely prevails on the mainland of the United States that the Filipino is only interested in white women, it is interesting to note the exceedingly small proportion of marriages between Filipinos and Caucasians in Hawaii. The following figures show that marriages with Filipino women far outnumber all others:

FILIPINO MARRIAGES FOR FIVE YEARS ENDED JUNE 30, 1929 [14]

Race of Bride	*Number of Grooms*
Hawaiian	144
Caucasian-Hawaiian	39
Asiatic-Hawaiian *	36
Portuguese	84
Porto Rican	85
Spanish	8
Other Caucasian	7
Chinese	6
Japanese	36
Korean	—
Filipino	1,257
Total	1,702

* Mostly Chinese-Hawaiian, including also Filipino-Hawaiian.

[14] From annual reports of Registrar General.

Of course, not absolute preferences but the actual contacts between young Filipinos and the women of other races, more often outside than on the plantations, determine these selections. The great majority of these marriages are between immigrant Filipinos and second-generation immigrants, that is either girls that have been brought to Hawaii by their parents in childhood or were born in Hawaii of foreign parentage. More Filipinos marry Hawaiian women, however, than do either Japanese or Chinese.

There is conflicting evidence concerning the success of these mixed marriages. Hawaiian, Portuguese and Chinese wives of Filipinos frequently state that Filipinos make better husbands than men of their own kind because their attitude toward women is similar to the American one; that is, primarily, they do not demand that their wives work. They are generous in providing their wives with good clothes and with living conditions and amusements that are satisfactory in comparison with those enjoyed by other women of their class. On the other hand, the divorce rate among Filipinos is relatively heavy. As has been explained elsewhere, this is mainly due to the absence of an older and more established married group and to the high valuation placed upon the society of Filipino women, because of their scarcity, which makes for infidelity and transfers of affections.[15] This tendency is observed, however, more in the urban communities than in the plantation villages.

5. RACE RELATIONS

Concerning race relations generally, it should be borne in mind that the behavior and fortunes of a new immigrant group in the first ten years of its residence furnish no forecast as to their more permanent character in the new setting. At first, there are many false adjustments, and other adjustments are slow. Just because they consider themselves closer to American civilization than other Oriental groups, the Filipinos in Hawaii have much to unlearn; and many of the first contacts which are unfortunate have to be supplanted by others, as they acquire a better understanding of language and customs, before real assimilation can take place.

While the Filipinos have had no outstanding difficulties in their associations with other racial groups, nevertheless they are not entirely exempt from the dislike of the newcomer. Teachers, public officials, business men, no less than foremen and fellow workers

[15] See page 195.

of other races, have to learn to understand the newcomer's ways and the reasons for them. Many Filipinos come to Hawaii without knowing any English. Restless and emotional, they easily take offense.[16] Some, having been taught to be cautious in contacts with their countrymen, extend that suspicion to all who would befriend them. Others, caught up by enthusiasm for Philippine independence, the one spiritual bond of the different dialect groups, incline to interpret whatever misfortunes or hardships befall them as part of a situation in which their countrymen are oppressed by the dominant power. Sensitiveness to insult occasionally leads to fights. But this sensitiveness and other attitudes unfavorable to a rapid adjustment are more pronounced among those who have drifted away from the plantations than they are there. "They behave like brothers," said one plantation manager, referring to Filipino and Japanese fellow workers. "It seems to make no difference to them whether the *luna* (foreman) is of their own race or of another, so long as they feel assured of his fairness and he does not cuss at them," says another. "At first," says a social worker among women, "we thought it would take years to get the Filipinas to mix with the other women; but they did in an astonishingly short time."

On the plantations Filipinos can often be seen playing on mixed baseball and volley ball teams.[17]

In spite of this general openness to new associations and of the strict watch kept by the plantation managers over outside influences unfavorable to the Filipinos' welfare, as they see it, there are many flourishing organizations of their own. Three Filipino newspapers and periodicals are published in Hawaii, and there is considerable circulation also for others coming from Manila and from Los Angeles. The Filipino Federation of America has a membership of thousands among plantation workers although its officers are not admitted to the plantations. Other societies and lodges have made less progress. On the plantations, some managers try to keep all social organizations much in their own hands; others have successfully experimented with letting the workers themselves organize

[16] Professor S. D. Porteus, of the University of Hawaii, points out that those first to take part in a movement of migration to a new country are apt to contain an unusual proportion of "firebrands," of men abnormally sensitive and therefore also likely to be most vocal in the statement of grievances. The earlier wave of Filipino migrants to Hawaii and the mainland of the United States contained many whose main motive was a desire to get away from their families. (See further below, p. 264.)

[17] Boxing contests are discouraged, not for the reason that they might arouse undue passion in race rivalry, but because it develops professionalism and loses the plantations good workers!

and run their social activities. In these latter cases, there is usually cooperation with outside organizations. The annual Rizal Day anniversary, as in the Philippines and on the mainland, is celebrated everywhere in Hawaii by Filipinos with much pomp and circumstance.

In short, the absorption of the Filipinos into the life of the Hawaiian Islands is taking a normal course—and better than normal, if the kind and degree of their adjustment is compared with that of earlier immigrant groups. It cannot be said that they are a menace to the social peace of the territory or that they themselves fail to any large extent to benefit from their residence there.

PART IV

CAUSES OF FILIPINO EMIGRATION

PART IV. CAUSES OF FILIPINO EMIGRATION

CHAPTER XIV

ARTIFICIAL STIMULI

THROUGHOUT the discussion of Filipino immigration since first it attracted public attention runs the question: Why did this movement start just when it did? Is it merely a coincidence that it began to assume large proportions in 1923, immediately after the first quota immigration law, designed to shut off a large proportion of European immigration, came into effect?[1] It is obvious that there are special advantages for peoples not under the ban in such a situation. Especially, in the lower ranks of resident labor there will be new opportunities, as the labor supply dwindles, comparable with those of a period of unusual industrial activity. These opportunities will first reach those previously on the margin of the permanently employed, giving them more regular work; and to the lowest paid they will give a chance to rise. Thus it was observed in many communities that, with the diminution in the number of immigrant "greenhorns," many of the minor occupations previously performed by them have gradually been filled with Negroes, while immigrant groups previously limited to unskilled and menial tasks have filtered into higher types of work.[2] As unemployment diminishes and wage standards rise, the unfilled demand for labor will eventually make itself felt beyond the national boundaries. But how? The attractions of a foreign country exercise no direct pull. After all, human labor is not a fluid which may be relied upon to fill of its own weight the vacant spaces, as water flows down-hill. There must be special media by which

[1] Facts About Filipino Immigration into California, p. 16. Curtailment of European immigration began, of course, soon after the beginning of the World War. But while the channels were already prepared for Mexican immigration and a large influx of labor from Mexico was encouraged, there was no such immediate incentive and opportunity for an influx of an as yet untried labor supply from the Philippines.

[2] Niles Carpenter, Nationality, Color and Economic Opportunity in the City of Buffalo. The Inquiry, 1927. Charles S. Johnson, The Negro in American Civilization. Henry Holt & Co., 1930, chapter III.

the need of a country for labor becomes an effective drawing power. And in our modern civilization, with its complex organization and manifold wants, these media tend to be diverse and intricate.

It is not surprising that public opinion, especially that part of it which is hostile to immigration, should look for active generators of the movement in groups with a special interest in it. Thus, whenever there is an unpopular influx of labor, its cause is seen in recruiting on the part of employers desirous to keep down their labor costs and in efforts of transportation companies to increase their volume of traffic. In the case of Filipino immigration, labor and traffic recruiting have been held responsible for the movement as a whole by many speakers and writers. We shall therefore do well to commence our survey of the effective causes by examining the part played by these two interests.

1. LABOR RECRUITING

The Hawaiian sugar planters no longer need to recruit actively. Their labor supplies from the Philippines, as we have seen (p. 164), have become sufficiently assured for them to be able to discard all aggressive methods of recruiting. Indeed, the officials of the H.S.P.A. resent the use of the term "recruitment" for the activities which the association is now carrying on through its Philippine agencies to direct the voluntary flow of labor to Hawaii. Nevertheless, it cannot be denied that methods used in the past and now discarded still are effective in the minds of the people.

> The Hawaiian Sugar Planters' Association, said a high government official in the Philippines, is entirely responsible for starting the emigration movement. It advertised the glorious adventure and the beautiful opportunities that would be offered. Consequently, in those parts where pressure of population was intense, many left the islands for Hawaii.
>
> The steamship companies do not persuade the laborers to emigrate, says a provincial school officer, but rather the H.S.P.A. In . . . , in addition to the man in charge of general recruiting, there is one who goes from town to town, showing a movie of life in Hawaii. One scene shows the handing out of checks. The movie is free and is usually shown in the town plaza, so that everyone has a chance to see it. This and ordinary conversation, rather than advertising, are the most important agents of propaganda.

The association admits that it is making use of lectures and moving pictures to stimulate interest and to explain the advantages offered by its terms of employment. The moving pictures are taken with a view to showing without exaggeration the most favorable aspects of plantation life. Thus, several reels were recently taken on one of the plantations of an annual Harvest Home festival in such a way as to show a maximum number of Filipinos, both in the parade and among the spectators, close enough to make their recognition possible—and at a moment of natural exhilaration and pleasure over the spectacle. This can only mean that the association still is anxious to make the most favorable possible impression, to have as many inhabitants as possible of the provinces from which labor is secured visualize their relatives in Hawaii dressed in their best and in a mood of contentment. The certificate of contract fulfilment (see further below, p. 386), likewise has for part of its purpose to dignify the plantation worker's status with the effect of inducing others to try and attain to it. These methods conform to general usage.[3]

The agents and sub-agents of the H.S.P.A. are instructed not to exaggerate conditions in Hawaii or to falsify facts. But the higher officials speak no Ilocano and sometimes little Spanish. They do not know exactly what these sub-agents do or say in the outlying districts. These native sub-agents have no strong financial motive to lie;[4] but in most cases not having themselves been abroad, some of them may not be over-careful of the accuracy of the information they impart. Officers of the H.S.P.A. feel certain, nevertheless, that their system of supervision, built up as a result of more than twenty years of experience, guards against misstatements. For, these men are checked up at every step, and in practically every community, by the direct knowledge of men who have been in Hawaii. A further check is exercised by the political officers of the various provinces—Presidentes, Fiscals, and Governors —who are ever watchful, and often suspicious, of the activities of the H.S.P.A. It is probable, then, that sub-agents are neither over-careful nor extremely careless in their representations. Without falling into either of these extremes, they may so picture conditions

[3] The principal aim is to secure more applications from men who already have served one contract period and may be encouraged to go again (see page 386, Appendix H), and from relatives of workers now on the plantations. A not unimportant secondary motive is a desire to contribute to the contentment of families left behind and of securing the good will of the community that has provided many desirable workers in the past.

[4] These agents are paid only ₱3.50 for each laborer finally accepted and shipped from Manila. This system is favorably contrasted by Philippine critics with the efforts of their own Bureau of Labor to stimulate inter-island migration through the services of salaried agents. (The Philippine peso—₱—equals about 50 cents.)

as to leave on the prospective emigrant a very favorable impression.

And indirectly, as the Hawaiian planters recognize, their labor system does affect migration to the mainland as well. This, of course, is entirely involuntary and against their own desire. For, obviously, the Hawaiian employers have no interest in either diminishing their source of labor supply or expending large sums on bringing laborers to their plantations only to lose them again through further migration to the mainland. And they have sought to diminish these risks to the extent of their influence and resourcefulness.

Their problem in this respect is not a new one. At one time or another, Spaniards, Porto Ricans, Portuguese and Filipinos who have come to Hawaii for labor have moved on from there to the Pacific Coast. In the case of the Filipinos, the planters' own concern to retain the workers whose adjustment to the local conditions of life and labor has been the purpose of so much care and expenditure, is reinforced by the concern of the Philippine government. In 1922, because of a business depression on the mainland, Filipinos who were the last comers and, consequently, the first to be cut adrift, were out of work in considerable numbers. This led Philippine officials to ask the H.S.P.A. to induce these men to come to Hawaii. This was done over a period of several months; and the result was not satisfactory. It was found that unemployment in California was almost entirely confined to part-time students who preferred to stay and endure the hardship rather than go to Hawaii and engage in work of a kind they had never done before and for which they were largely unfitted. From that time, influential Filipino officials have collaborated with the sugar planters in discouraging a movement of Filipino laborers from Hawaii to the mainland. Today, the planters, through the H.S.P.A., do all they can to keep steerage traffic between Hawaii and the mainland at a minimum.

The H.S.P.A. is practically the only concern that recruits labor in the Philippine Islands. Partly due to the general advertising which Hawaii had received as a land of opportunity, other agencies have attempted, in the past, often successfully, to persuade Filipinos to go to the territory without a contract and without promises of employment that have legal validity. The H.S.P.A. and the Dollar Line are doing everything within their power to stop this business, both by word of mouth and by posting notices to the effect that only laborers recruited through the H.S.

P.A. offices are guaranteed a job on arrival in Hawaii. But the Filipino (as we have seen in so many other connections in the course of this report) is remarkably credulous. He was continually falling into the snares of men who had no other interest than quick returns and who could evade the consequences of their action by repeated changes of residence and, sometimes, of name.

The independent agents and brokers have undoubtedly been more responsible than any other party for the exaggerated impressions that Filipinos have received of opportunities, both in Hawaii and on the mainland. This has been so thoroughly recognized in the Philippine Islands themselves that the government is constantly increasing the sharpness of the supervision extended to and restrictions imposed upon these people. The government does not, of course, intervene directly in the recruiting of laborers in such a way as to favor one set of employers as against others. But it favors indirectly the more responsible agencies, first by a system of licensing adopted in 1915, when recruiting first was recognized as a serious menace, and second, through the activities of supervision exercised by the Section of Emigrant Laborers to Foreign Countries under the Bureau of Labor.

The licensing law provides that any person or firm enlisting and shipping labor must pay annually five hundred pesos to the provincial treasurer of each of the provinces where laborers are recruited; that free return passage at the end of the contract or in case of physical incapacity must be provided; and that an annual license must be taken out at a cost of six thousand pesos. The act further permits the Governor-General to appoint commissioners outside of the Philippine Islands to insure the compliance of employers with the terms of the contracts made with Filipino laborers, and places the supervision of all contracts into the hands of the Director of Labor.[5]

The Bureau of Labor, through the special section organized under this law, exercises a pretty full control over the contracts signed between Filipino laborers and the H.S.P.A., involving a careful filing of these contracts and an analysis of the destinations, provinces and towns of origin, and the like, and also supervision over the execution of the employers' contractual obligations, such as the free return of laborers on the completion of their contract. It is

[5] The text of this important law, which also contains interesting minor provisions, is given in Appendix I, p. 392.

also charged with the location of relatives of laborers who die in Hawaii and with mediation of differences of interpretation that may arise between the parties to the contract.[6]

It will be seen that the law of 1915 was drawn up to meet the particular needs of a situation in which a group of responsible employers desired the assistance and protection of the Philippine government in carrying on a systematic activity of recruiting. But it did not contain any provisions or even indicate methods by which less responsible corporations or individuals might be held to a similarly exacting code of obligations. Indeed, by raising the license fees required of those desiring to recruit labor for work abroad to so high a figure, the law virtually invited evasions and clandestine operations. The subject has repeatedly come up in the legislature. In several recent reports, the Bureau of Labor has discussed these difficulties:

With the increasing number of emigrants, reports relative to the activities of private recruiting agents were received at the Bureau of Labor. These agents were recruiting, enlisting and shipping laborers to Hawaii without the necessary license required by Act No. 2486. These activities of unlicensed recruiters did not only deprive the Government of the revenues due to it, but they also subjected the unwary country folks to unjust exactions through misrepresentations, besides exposing them to unnecessary risk and hardship upon their arrival in Honolulu. . . .

The independent recruiting agents carry on their campaign of recruitment personally and through sub-agents who go and call at each and every house of the laborers in the different towns of Ilocos Norte, Ilocos Sur, La Union and Pangasinan. Sometimes they carry the campaign with the help of the Municipal President of the locality. The agents in coming in contact with the Municipal Officials necessarily make friends, and these friends are the ones who bring them in contact with the agricultural laborers. At times the laborers are being induced, and occasionally other laborers go personally, to see these recruiting agents. The laborers, after making up their mind to emigrate to Hawaii, usually dispose of the only lot, house, or work animals they may happen to possess in order to raise the amount necessary for the trip from Laoag or Vigan to Manila and from Manila to Hawaii. The money raised by these laborers ranges from ₱150 to ₱180 each, the usual amounts charged by the respective agents for the whole trip referred to, including food and lodging during their stay in Manila. These amounts are deposited by the laborers with the agents either in their home towns or upon their arrival in Manila.[7]

[6] Bulletin of the Bureau of Labor No. 25, March, 1926.
[7] Nineteenth Annual Report of the Bureau of Labor, 1927, p. 106.

The report proceeds to compare the relative advantages of recruitment undertaken by the H.S.P.A. and by those independent recruiting agents who had chartered the S.S. *Consuelo* of the Madrigal Company of Honolulu. Since the reader is already familiar with the former, we shall here only quote the latter:

1. The emigrant laborers are given the opportunity of a direct voyage from Manila to Honolulu, in which case the laborers are not exposed to unnecessary expenditures at the ports of call in China and Japan, and to sickness detrimental to their health.

2. They have all things Filipino with respect to treatment and food. The steamer is provided with rice sufficient to last for 35 days, condiments for food, such as vegetables, *bagoong,* dried fish, beef and pork.

3. The laborers can stay on the main deck during the whole day and sleep throughout the whole night; 800 cots were purposely bought to be spread and placed on the main deck and below. The boat has all the necessary facilities being used in making trips across the Pacific, as it was one of the U. S. Army transports. The laborers may have their daily sea baths on the open deck near the stern.

4. Clothing necessary to protect them during winter can be dispensed with as the steamer will sail eastward toward Guam direct to Hawaii, and it will not follow the direction of steamers that call at Chinese and Japanese ports bound for Honolulu.

The conclusions arrived at by this comparison are interesting:

1. The emigrant laborers depend very much upon the good faith of the independent agents in the performance of the latter's part of the agreement. The laborers have suffered much in the hands of the independent recruiting agents who, due to unfavorable circumstances, had on several occasions failed to ship the emigrant laborers to Hawaii.

2. The laborers are not given any guarantee at all for the faithful performance, on the part of the recruiting agents, of their part of the contract, aside from the fact that they are not assured of any work in the plantations upon their arrival in Honolulu.

3. No measure has been adopted on the part of the independent recruiters to send only those who are physically fitted for work.[8]

A year later, the Bureau of Labor returns to this subject. After repeating the previous statements concerning the activities of unlicensed recruiters and their effects, the report continues:

Cases arising out of the anomalous relations between these private recruiting agents or brokers and laborers have been brought to the courts of justice, but

[8] *Ibid.*

the former were acquitted. For this reason, an amendment to Act No. 2486 was submitted.

This practice of sending laborers recruited by private agents to Hawaii without the intervention of the Hawaiian Sugar Planters' Association has reached such a point as to compel the Bureau to take action on the matter in order to protect the interests of the laborers. . . .[9]

On this situation one of the newspapers comments:

An official of the Bureau of Labor puts the blame for the rush of emigration on free-lance labor agents who claim to represent the big plantation companies and thus be in a position to give jobs to the laborers when they arrive in Hawaii. Spurred on by the agents' stories of gold and easy riches awaiting eager hands, the uninformed laborers are easily duped into mortgaging their properties or borrowing from their relatives and thus getting sufficient funds to pay their passage. Many of the labor recruiters receive this money and then disappear, or say that the money has been misappropriated by someone to whom it was entrusted. Several prosecutions have been initiated by the government, but they were conducted lifelessly and so far have failed to stop the practice complained of.[10]

Definitely fraudulent practices attracted the attention of the government. Certain unscrupulous individuals attempted to take advantage of the irksome restrictions placed by the Hawaiian planters upon the recruitment of labor by presenting, especially to men who had been excluded by the rigorous system of medical inspection, opportunities of getting to Hawaii independently. They travelled in the provinces and secured cash deposits from laborers, varying in amount from a legitimate charge for steamer passage to two or three times such charge. Hundreds of laborers came into the city of Manila to find that they could not proceed to Hawaii and that their money was lost.

Discussion came to a focus in the summer of 1928 when, contrary to the advices of the Philippine labor commissioner in Honolulu and of the governor of Hawaii to the effect that there was no work for men other than those already contracted for by the H.S.P.A., certain ship agents in Manila chartered a Norwegian steamer to transport six hundred Filipino laborers to Honolulu. Public opinion in the Philippines at the time, as represented by the newspapers, resented any governmental interference with the free movement of Filipino citizens but at the same time demanded sharp measures of punishment for labor agents who deliberately

[9] Twentieth Annual Report of the Bureau of Labor, 1928.
[10] *Philippine Free Press,* November 24, 1928.

entice emigrants by false promises and deception. The ship was allowed to sail, and a large proportion of its human cargo found themselves unemployed in Honolulu. Unfortunately, the incident closed with recriminations against public officials who, to judge from the record, had done everything they could to prevent the catastrophe, but did not lead to the establishment of a system of control that would have made illegal recruiting in the provinces impossible—if, indeed, such a system can be found. It is one thing to state, as one senator did, that "in the recruiting of laborers . . . deception and fraud are used in many cases, the recruiting agents retaining in their pay certain persons to pose as having made money working in the Hawaiian plantations, and using them as tools to induce others to go there." It is quite another to apprehend such offenders in a country of the size of the Philippine Islands, or to prevent new illegal agencies from springing into existence when those found operating have been removed. Nevertheless, recruiting by independent brokers may now be said to have completely broken down due to the spread of information on work opportunities in Hawaii.

In the spring of 1930, an application by the H.S.P.A. for a renewal of its license provided the occasion for the Philippine Bureau of Labor to review the whole situation. It found that in practice the association was enjoying a monopoly. It considered methods by which the terms of the license might be made instruments for ensuring more fully the return of contract workers and for preventing their further migration to the mainland. With reports of shortage of labor from different sections of the Philippine Islands, and aware of the rising tide of antagonism to Filipino immigration on the Pacific Coast, the director of the bureau was disposed to insist on new terms—more especially on a bonus for contract fulfillment payable by the employer after the worker's return to the Philippine Islands. In the end, the license was renewed—except for recruiting in the province of Tarlac—without new conditions but on the understanding that the H.S.P.A. will carefully consider a new bonus system on the lines advocated by the director of labor.

2. TRAFFIC RECRUITING

As we have seen, the financial interests involved in labor recruiting and in selling steerage passenger transportation to the mainland of the United States cannot neatly be separated in all cases. There is no question that the largest element of profit in such transactions is in the transportation charges. Often the employment agent is primarily interested, not in the jobs he can fill but in the passages he can sell, whether it be by stage to another city or by ocean liner to a country thousands of miles away.

But the charge against the big steamship lines that they deliberately misrepresent conditions in order to swell their receipts from steerage passages sold is so frequent, so sharply worded in resolutions of responsible organizations and in public speeches, that it deserves separate discussion. The charge has a historical basis.[11] It was the cause of rigorous federal legislation which makes it illegal not only to make misleading statements but to do any advertising at all other than of sailing dates and rates of transportation.[12] Yet, advertising by the steamship companies takes first place among the causes named by many individuals and organizations on the Pacific Coast for the rapid increase of Filipino immigration in recent years:

Steamship agents go from house to house in Hawaii, advertising the advantages to be found on the mainland and offering low rates of transportation, says a California state official.

The first large movement of Filipinos to the United States, said another state official of California in a position to know, came through the Los Angeles Steamship Company, which was not then controlled by the sugar growers.

Exaggerated advertising of the advantages offered by life in the United States, chiefly by agents of the Dollar Line, is as frantic as any advertising of particular localities here by runners who meet the boats, states a Filipino business man in California.

The Filipino secretary of a national religious organization says: The main cause of Filipino immigration is the propaganda of the steamship lines. They misrepresent conditions here both in text and picture. One of their highest officials in San Francisco has given out the statement that there is no unemployment in the United States.

A public health officer of the Federal Government, posted at one of the Pacific ports, says: Attraction of Filipinos to the United States is largely the

[11] Henry Pratt Fairchild, Immigration. Macmillan Co., revised edition, 1925, p. 151 *et seq.*

Edith Abbott, Historical Aspects of the Immigration Problem. Chicago University Press, 1926, p. 314; Immigration—Selected Documents and Case Records. University of Chicago Press, 1924, Part I.

[12] Section 7 of the Immigration Act of February 5, 1917, 39 Stat. 874, prohibits common carriers from soliciting alien traffic whether by advertising letters or circulars, both within and without the United States. The penalty is $4 for each violation.

work of steamship companies who placard the villages with exaggerated statements as to the high wages that can be earned here. This policy was adopted after the Japanese exclusion, when they found that Filipinos were the only group available to fill their steerage.

In December, 1929, James A. Taylor, president of the Washington State Federation, sent a telegram to William Green, president of the A. F. of L., demanding on behalf of the state body that something be done immediately to stop Filipino immigration. Among other things he said: Vessels plying between our coast and Manila are bringing in steerage loads of Filipinos among whom Spinal Meningitis is raging. . . . Throughout the Philippines placards advise the Filipinos to come here and share in extraordinary prosperity. . . .

Steamship advertising, said a minister in the state of Washington, formerly a missionary in the Philippines, has been a big influence.

A Filipino minister who for many years occupied a pulpit in his own country: The steamship companies in every province unquestionably are making exaggerated promises. Leaflets of the companies, while they do not misrepresent, advertise cheap fares (at $75) and make it seem a great advantage to take this trip. Their agents verbally state that work here can easily be found at $5 an hour or some such fantastic sum. I have heard them say so.

A Filipino graduate student in the same state commented: Propaganda is carried on systematically in the Philippine Islands by shipping companies, chiefly through the employment of agents in every town, who, paid by results, exaggerate American opportunities. . . . The activity of these companies, more than anything else, has caused the large influx of Filipinos here in the last three years.

Another Filipino student, in a class paper, writes: For the past few years the steamship lines had been rather encouraged by the increasing number of passengers. And to keep up that increasing business, boosters were sent to all parts of the Islands. Their agents were everywhere, telling and convincing young people of the bright aspects of life here. They told stories of "streets strewn with gold," that innocent and a bit ignorant folks often believe. . . . These agents, of course, are working on a percentage basis, and the more they can induce, the better are their incomes. Their [reward] runs from two to three per cent of the prospective passenger's fare.

There were many witnesses on this point in the Philippine Islands, too:

A man exceptionally qualified for social observation said: Last November I made a trip myself into the Ilocos region to learn more about emigration. . . . I managed to secure a copy of part of a letter which is given to recruiting agents. This letter described the possibilities of work on the West Coast, giving the wages and some of the conditions of work and of ways of obtaining employment in ten or fifteen occupations. In two or three cases, Filipinos were advised that expensive equipment was needed and advised not to plan to go into them. Accompanying this list were instructions to the managers of local offices regarding recruiting, which I did not see.

The principal of a rural school in Ilocos Sur said: The steamship agents greatly exaggerate the conditions to be found in America and convince the people that if they go they will be sure to find jobs and make a great deal of money.

A university teacher of history: The steamship lines are much to blame for persuading Filipinos to leave. They advertise in the vernacular press that jobs can easily be obtained in the United States.

The activities of well-paid agents of local steamship companies, writes Professor Macaraig, fire the imagination and the adventurous spirit of rural folk by ambiguous and alluring advertisements of conditions in Hawaii which do not really exist.[13]

What is the truth of the matter?

The Matson Line, plying between San Francisco and Honolulu and other island ports, does not engage in steerage business. This is but natural, for at no time during its history would this company, which depends so largely upon the sugar industry for its business and in which many of the large sugar agencies are financially interested, have wanted to deprive Hawaii of a labor supply that was badly needed. From the standpoint of steamship economics alone, the steerage business in this case is probably not attractive.

The activities of the independent American steamship companies in bringing Filipino laborers to the Pacific Coast must be seen, likewise, in relation to their major traffic concerns. As we have noted, the control of steerage passage to and from Honolulu, under present conditions of voluntary labor recruitment and the undesirability of an immigrant labor surplus, has become a problem of major importance for the Hawaiian planters. The H.S.P.A. some years ago attempted to secure this control by becoming the exclusive steerage passenger agent of the steamship company which then alone was serving the movement between Manila and Honolulu. By using the right to engage sufficient space for the numbers required in Hawaii and no more, leaving the steamship company free to assign the remaining space to other ports, it became possible for the planters to limit the numbers coming to Hawaii to those who were actually needed. This is actually the case today: The variation from month to month, and indeed from boat to boat, is very con-

[13] Social Problems. Educational Supply Co., Manila, 1929, p. 202.

siderable, and the number of arrivals never exceeds the actual needs of the plantations. This arrangement makes possible that careful system of selection which has already been described: Those ineligible for plantation work, on medical or other grounds, are discouraged not only by word of mouth but actually find it all but impossible to secure passage to the Hawaiian Islands. And, with work assured all Filipino steerage passengers landing in Honolulu, there can be no large drift to the mainland.

But, of course, this arrangement does not cover the total movement of Filipinos to the mainland of the United States. The Los Angeles Steamship Company undeniably does bring large numbers of Filipinos to Los Angeles from Hawaii. The Dollar Line unquestionably is the principal carrier of Filipino laborers from Manila to Seattle and to a lesser extent in recent years, to San Francisco. But they are not advertising the advantages of this travel in contravention of the law of 1917. In spite of diligent search, those who have taken part in the present study have not been able to lay their hands on any pamphlets or posters that contain misstatements of fact. The Dollar Line distributes literature in the Philippine Islands, both in the Ilocano language and in English, advertising its own facilities: the comfortable berths, good food, size and steadiness of its liners, ventilation, medical attendance, deck sports, in short, "a healthful, happy and comfortable voyage." The illustrations are of the ships' accommodations, not of the splendor of the sights to be seen. It lays stress in this literature on the advantage of having a contract before setting out for Honolulu, of the danger to entrust strangers with money, of the desirability to have spending money when arriving in the United States, of the necessity to observe simple rules of hygiene. It also advertises the railroad fares to the principal cities—ignorance of which, according to all accounts, is widespread and one of the main causes of congestion in the coast cities of America. The company may directly or indirectly be responsible for published statements giving information on wages and work opportunities; but such statements have not been discovered. Until recently the proportion of steerage passengers from Manila to San Francisco paid by friends of the traveller in this country was 5 per cent.

The Dollar Line has six branch offices besides its headquarters in Manila.[14] These offices employ numerous sub-agents who are

[14] These offices are in Laog, Ilocos Norte; Vigan, Ilocos Sur; San Fernando, La Union; Dagupan, Pangasinan; Cebu, Cebu; and Iloilo, Iloilo.

paid on a commission basis. The steerage space for the trip from Honolulu to San Francisco has lately been almost entirely converted into traffic space for the transportation of Hawaiian products.

Several officers of the Dollar Steamship Company were interviewed in the Philippines. From these it appears that both that company and the H.S.P.A. have gone to considerable trouble to rid the country of independent brokers. These brokers have undoubtedly been more responsible than anyone for exaggerated impressions which Filipinos have received. At present, the activities of these brokers are very much restricted, and the number of emigrants leaving under their auspices is constantly decreasing.

I appointed twelve sub-agents in three provinces, said one of the agents; but only two or three of them have been active this year. They go from house to house soliciting. Last winter I often left this office and went out to solicit, but I received instructions to stay in the office and sign up passengers as the sub-agents bring them in. There do not seem to be any independent agents here.

You have found my office closed, said another, because I have been out in the province recruiting passengers. It is difficult for the recruits to come here, and so I must go to them and sign them up and get their money. The people around here have had bad experiences with sub-agents. These have frequently cheated them. And so the prospective emigrants will no longer give their money to anyone except the agent. . . . I have as many sub-agents as there are towns. We tell the people what a fine place the United States is, and that if they are going they must go on an American ship.

In another province, the Dollar Line agent said: The office is kept open throughout the year, partly as an advertising measure. (He had previously explained the seasonal nature of the traffic. See p. 243.) Our advertising takes the form of posters, but not circulars. There are about twelve agents in our district. These operate in nearly every town, following up by house-to-house canvas any rumors or possibilities of emigrants. These agents are all natives of their district and consequently know the inhabitants well. We warn them not to persuade by colorful promises, because if these fail to come true it is bad for business. We tell them simply to say that wages are higher, and so on. We do not watch these agents all the time; of course, some of them may exaggerate. Preference is always given to the authorized agents. There are independent solicitors, but I have not done business with a single one in the past year.

A higher official of the company said: We put out a lot of literature and maintain agencies in the provinces, not in order to persuade Filipinos to emigrate, but in order to compete with the other steamship lines in getting our share of the business. We feel that these people are going to America, and that a large share of the business should come to us. If we did not have to compete with the Canadians and the Japanese we should not have to maintain these agencies. . . .

Our agents are instructed not to recruit business outside of their offices. But if a ship-broker comes in with some men, our agents must accept them. That's business. Many of the ship-brokers are crooks; they misrepresent facts; they overcharge emigrants; and often they are pimps. There happen to be three of them in this office now (pointing them out). We call them body-snatchers.

We have to deal with these brokers. There is nothing else we can do. It is up to the government to control the issuance of licenses and to supervise the brokers' activities. Here is what we are up against: That fellow over there came in this morning with fifteen recruits. He asked me to sell them passages. I knew him and told him I would not deal with him but directly with the men. He told me he had twenty-five hundred pesos in his pocket, and that they had none. With that he walked out and booked the men on another line. We lost that much business. We can't do that; we have to take business when it comes.

Another officer of the company explained: We have three offices in the North now. . . . We have about forty ship-brokers in the northern provinces recruiting for our boats. They get 5 per cent on each passage they sell. You will find these agents in nearly all the towns of any size.

All the steerage space on our San Francisco boats is taken up by the H.S.P.A.[15] If a man comes in here and wants an independent passage to America we have to send him to Seattle because we haven't any free space on the Honolulu–San Francisco boats.

In spite of conflicting testimony, then, it is possible to state with some sense of assurance that the steamship companies are not openly advertising the advantages of emigration, and that oral influences in that direction exercised by their agents or brokers are increasingly becoming a minor factor in the total situation. Although the agents and sub-agents continue their activities to solicit steerage passage, they have come to depend more and more on those who have already migrated to create the demand for travel to Hawaii and the continent from the Philippines. In several ways, as we have seen, the migration movement furnishes its own publicity.

[15] *I.e.,* from Manila to Honolulu. From Honolulu to San Francisco the space is given to cargo. See above.

CHAPTER XV

INFLUENCES OF AMERICANIZATION

BEFORE interested groups can effectively stimulate emigration, there must already exist a predisposition in that direction. The importance of the artificial stimuli lies in the fact that they tend to exaggerate a movement and to encrust it with unnecessary problems and difficulties. An immigration which, extended over a long period, might have been absorbed without difficulty, has several times in our national history been forced into a hectic rush which produced congestion, friction between natives and newcomers, and sometimes intolerable living conditions. The immigration of Filipinos has not assumed dangerous proportions, but it was unexpected and unprepared for. We have seen that the part played by active propaganda has probably been much smaller than public opinion has believed it to be. On the other hand, there has been a much more effective ferment which public opinion has not recognized as such at all; and this is worth special attention because it also operates in other territories under the American flag and is likely to play an even larger part in our population problems as foreign immigration is increasingly restricted.[1]

How rapidly the new influences brought to the Philippine Islands with the American participation in government are impressing themselves, is a debatable question. Obviously the public mind is more preoccupied with the new than with that which is familiar, and prone to exaggerate the changes that are taking place. At any given moment there may be said to be an existing order of things, reinforced by habits and traditions, and many forces working for change in different directions. There are also certain recognizable factors by which a close student of events might measure the tempo at which the older give way to newer forces. In the Philippines it would seem that direct influences from America and the rest of the world affect social change more rapidly than economic change. The minimum essentials of life are relatively easily se-

[1] Migration from Porto Rico to the mainland of the United States is probably three times as large as migration from the Philippines, and equally concentrated.

cured, and the spontaneous struggle for a higher standard of living is consequently less than in other Oriental countries which are over-populated and where failure to adopt new methods of economic improvement might mean actual starvation. But in cultural re-adjustments impelled by other than immediate economic urges, probably a longer time must elapse before the generations brought up under the old order relinquish their place of influence to the younger people educated according to the newer standards. Hence a marked difference between the rate of progress in the adoption of western ways in the Philippines and in Japan. For example, we are told that the local government in the Islands today is in the hands of two classes of educated men: an older generation whose education was purely Spanish, and a younger generation whose early training was Spanish but who have completed their education during the American régime. The younger members of a family are checked and influenced by the older ones who have not gone to American schools.

Within the last thirty years, however, many new instruments have been created for the interchange of knowledge and ideas. The great majority of Filipinos between eight and twenty years of age have been to school and know some English.[2] Mail, telegraph, roads, railroads, and boats link the Islands with each other and with other parts of the world. Foreigners come to do business, demand one product and reject another, establish modern sugar and coconut plantations in the midst of those being run on antiquated plans. Within the last quarter of a century, well over one hundred and fifty thousand Filipinos have left from all parts of the Philippines for Hawaii and the United States, and forty-five thousand have returned. They write or tell about "new worlds"; they acquire new tastes and possessions—ranging all the way from woollen suits to sewing machines.[3]

In the past, one of the most inflexible and resistant institutions in the Philippines has been the Catholic Church which, bound up with the Spanish culture pattern, has played a significant rôle in Philippine history and development. It is variously represented as the great teacher and friend of the Filipinos and as their greatest oppressor and tyrant. For our purpose it is sufficient to say that the Church, which at one time rigidly controlled the political, educa-

[2] The influence of the school system is further discussed below, p. 221 *et seq.*

[3] The press (see p. 226), American moving picture films (p. 229) and other special influences are further considered below.

tional, even economic, as well as religious fields of Filipino life, today exerts its influence almost entirely in the religious and ethical fields. For example, this influence has so far prevented a liberalization of the divorce laws. The number of Protestants in the Islands is not large, but the Protestant Church seems by its competition to have to some extent modernized and liberalized the Catholic attitude.

It is not possible within the scope of the present report even to sketch adequately what government under American direction has contributed to the general change of point of view, or how, owing to the circumstances which have been named, its achievements in the economic field are bound to lag behind those in the cultural. The public school system and the government's activities in the field of public health illustrate the impact of a unified endeavor, directed by the central government, upon an established civilization. But it is just in this field that one may also observe its conspicuous limitations. The government can enforce the keeping of health records, vaccination against smallpox, quarantine regulations, and the like; it cannot force mothers to nourish themselves and their babies properly, or make people go to hospitals when in need of medical treatment, or dispose by law of superstition and prejudice. Thus, two of the mission hospitals in Ilocos Sur and Ilocos Norte, well equipped and well run, staffed with Filipino as well as American doctors, were forced to close their nursing schools for lack of patients. Public education has not reached the point where hospitals are understood, except perhaps in Manila and in such special cases as the leper hospitals.

The government does not touch the lives of many except indirectly or rarely. Not long ago, officials of Mountain Province reported that their tax collections were far behind because they could not make the inhabitants (non-Christian tribes) understand the function and operation of taxation. Other difficulties are encountered when modern laws are contrary to the common law of the people. It is generally known that the Moros have their own customary law, decidedly different from that adopted by the other Filipinos; and adjustments have always been made accordingly in the application of Philippine law; but few people realize that in province after province the civil statutory law is fundamentally different from the prevailing common law and from the law as it is practised in all but criminal cases. The *caciques* and *illustrados* and the gradually increasing numbers of fairly well-to-do farmers, have little direct contact with the government and still go for advice or help to some influential individual rather than seek it directly from the appropriate government official or by vote.[4]

In all this the potential influence of the government is retarded largely by the preoccupation of the more politically minded public opinion with the status of the Islands. The politicians often have little direct knowledge of the actual problems of the people and do not function as effective intermediaries between local and national desires and policies.

1. THE SCHOOL SYSTEM

Because it is the main channel of Americanizing influences, the school system of the Philippine Islands deserves special attention as a predisposing cause of emigration. Indeed, many observers place it foremost among the factors that have made successful the more specific recruiting activities of American employers and shipping companies.[5] For those unfamiliar with colonial sentiment in other parts of the world, it may be difficult to realize the extraordinary desire of the Filipinos, after a quarter of a century of American occupation, to get into closer touch with the great country of which they were taught to consider themselves a part. It was as though thousands but waited for the opportunity to realize a long cherished hope.

The first great impetus to emigration was given by American teachers and by the use of American history textbooks, with their insistence upon the greatness of the United States. Their influence upon a naturally emotional people can hardly be over-estimated. The teaching of patriotism in the Philippine schools took the form of extolling everything making for the progress of the country's civilization—on the American model. English is being taught from the first grade and in the early days was considered essential as a means to use American materials and textbooks throughout. Many of the Filipinos now in the United States went to school when special textbooks had not yet been introduced in the Philippine Islands, when George Washington and Abraham Lincoln were made

[4] See further Appendix K, p. 425.

[5] For an analysis of Americanizing influences in the Philippines, showing a more rapid acceptance of the English language and of the American school system than of American standards of material and social values, see Albert Ernest Jenks, Assimilation in the Philippines. Publications of the American Sociological Society, vol. VIII, 1914, p. 140 *et seq.*

childhood's heroes and even the less interesting events of American history and its succession of Presidents were taught with the same insistence as in Kalamazoo or Podunk. Now this system has considerably changed; the reading books for the lower grades are composed in large part of Philippine folk tales; Philippine history is taught in a way to engender love for the home country, and with the same view the national patriots are placed before the children as models to imitate.[6]

Apart from this somewhat misleading orientation of the civic teaching of the schools, now happily greatly improved, there are many complaints that the school system of the Philippines predisposes the pupils for vocational tastes and interests that cannot be gratified within the economic opportunities of their country and of their class.

The public schools in a way have helped to elevate the standards of living of the people. And while socially the people have advanced, the country's economics has not kept pace with social progress. Thus, we find here a disequilibrium, social progress outweighing economic progress. And consequently we find a considerable portion of the people migrating to other lands where better opportunities are offered for them to live within the standards denied them by the country's economic backwardness.[7]

But in this respect there also has been considerable improvement:

Within the last few years, said a high school official in one of the Ilocos provinces, not only the authorities but also the public have come to put great emphasis on the vocational training in schools. In the primary grades every child has what is called pre-vocational training which consists in handcraft, basketry, carpentry, sewing, cooking—, and always gardening (begun in the first grade for children who are big enough). A girl may bring to school whatever sewing or mending her family needs to have done. When the girls are old enough, they are taught certain native recipes and are then asked to go home and cook these same dishes at least once for their families. Every effort is made to have this training directly practical, not for production or earning, but for better homes.

[6] Practically all newer textbooks especially written for use in the Philippine school system have come into use in the last ten years. They include among other items a delightful series of readers by Camilo Osias, the present Philippine Commissioner in the United States and at one time President of the National University and also first Filipino Division Superintendent of Schools; Miller and Polley's Intermediate Geography (1918); Conrado Benitez's History of the Philippines for High Schools (1926); Hugo H. Miller's Economic Conditions in the Philippines, a particularly helpful textbook from the point of view of focusing interest on national events and problems and taking the place of the usual physical geography (1920).

[7] Manila *Herald,* November 27, 1929.

While the general tendency of the school system is considered by many as making still too largely for urges which cannot be gratified by the vocational opportunities at hand, and thereby indirectly as making for an accentuated desire to go abroad, either for more education, fitting the student for a government position, or simply for better economic chances, it is not generally held that the public school teachers directly and deliberately encourage emigration. On the contrary, district school superintendents testify to the fact that the teachers often stand out in the community as propagandists for the economic opportunities of the area where they find themselves and as informants concerning the less promising aspects of life in Hawaii and on the continent.

If nevertheless the one topic of conversation, especially among high-school students, often is the prospect of going abroad, the cause must be sought in other sources of inspiration, chief among them the direct communication of students with others who have gone before them and the general talk of the town.

But it is not enough to look at the school system from the point of view only of its direct bearing upon attitudes toward emigration. By its very existence, by the models upon which it is formed, and by the methods which it employs, it may have a potent effect on popular opinion which indirectly encourages and even inspires the search for new values, not to be found within the confines of the homeland. What, then, is this system, and what its general influences?

There are, first, the public schools, established since the American occupation—primary schools, high schools in the larger provincial towns that give both academic and vocational courses, farm schools throughout the Islands, the University of the Philippines in Manila and its proposed branches in Cebu and Vigan, and finally the agricultural college at Los Baños. There are also many private and many Church schools which, regardless of the date of their founding and of their auspices, are helping to fulfill the promises of "education for everyone" and which are required to conform to government standards.

Many observers attach great importance to the influence of the schools. They see in the younger generation a new alertness and independence and self-reliance.

The "cacique" . . . is an extinct species. The public school has driven him to cover. He can no longer rule the town as he did of yore. The generation educated in the public schools has given him no quarter, and he is discredited and despised. The "tao" no longer depends on him. The "tao" depends on his boy or girl who has gone through the intermediate and high school. If it is not his boy or girl, it may be his nephew or his niece or the neighbor's son. He can no longer be exploited. He knows his rights and he fights for them.[8]

However, the influence of education is far slower in changing economic than in changing social standards. We see crowded academic schools and unemployment for their graduates on the one hand and farm schools with too small an enrollment—in one case without a graduating class—on the other.[9] During the Spanish period the greatest prestige fell to the rich and to those in professional positions—the educated. The Americans entered with an entirely different point of view, but circumstances have forced the carrying on of the old standards: The government needed primarily officials to do its work and teachers for its schools. The very Americans who most stressed the dignity and importance of labor themselves occupied governmental or teaching positions.

The cultivation of the dignity of labor was an outstanding policy. But the Filipinos are good imitators. Because of the fact that the Americans who came to the Islands did not themselves practice what they preached, the preaching did not do the natives any good.[10]

One hears it frequently said that the high schools prepare students for "white collar" jobs rather than for a life on the agricultural lands of the Islands. Up to the present, the government and commercial offices have absorbed thousands of high-school graduates. The Bureau of Education has been able to assign teaching positions to many thousand graduates of the normal schools. Now there are fewer and fewer of these positions to be had. The government has nearly reached its limit as a potential source of employment. In a letter to Governor General Leonard Wood of April 6, 1927, President Coolidge said:

In the Islands the officials of the municipalities are exclusively Filipinos, as are the officials of the fully organized Provinces. In the central government

[8] Manila *Tribune*, December 28, 1929. For a definition of the two classes named, see pp. 416 and 417.

[9] The farm schools are under the Bureau of Education, not as usually in the United States, under the Department of Agriculture. This is perhaps one reason for their orientation toward agronomy and farm management rather than practical farming. The graduates for the most part do not come from small farms and so do not return to a life where trained intelligence is most needed at the present time. Some go into teaching. Some have taken up homesteads and made good.

[10] Serafin E. Macaraig, Social Problems. Educational Supply Co., Manila, 1929, p. 50.

the legislature is made up entirely of Filipinos. . . . The lower judicial officials are all Filipinos. The judges of first instance, with but two exceptions, are Filipinos, and of the justices of the supreme court four of the nine are Filipinos. The chief justice is a Filipino. Of the heads of the executive departments, six in number, five are Filipinos. The attorney general is a Filipino. Prosecuting attorneys throughout the Islands are Filipinos. The personnel of the bureaus of civil service, treasury, and commerce and industry is entirely Filipino, and the bureau of customs and bureau of posts is more than 99½ per cent Filipino. The American officials are but 1½ per cent of the total in the government.[11]

This means that while new office holders of all kinds, including teachers, are constantly required, openings for them cannot be found at anything like the rate at which they were needed during the earlier stages of development. And this also is true, to some extent, of the personnel of business houses. Yet the curricula of the high schools and normal schools have not been changed to suit different conditions; and the enrollment in them, rather than falling off, increases. What, then, happens to graduates who have been fitted for a life they cannot live, and who have acquired desires which the economic conditions of the country cannot fulfill? Some of them undoubtedly go to the United States in search of further education or in search of whatever they can find.[12]

Emigration will go on, say many persons well acquainted with these conditions, until there are more inducements for Filipinos to stay at home. This might be interpreted as meaning: Emigration will go on until the social desires of the Filipinos and the economic conditions of the Philippines are in some way correlated.

Many people believe that, owing to the influence of the schools, there has already started a shift in social standards, and that labor and business no longer suffer as degraded a status as in the past. Hugo H. Miller, former chief of the Industrial Division of the Philippine Bureau of Education, attributes this change to the following influences: Democratic examples and the teaching of democratic principles; change from a medieval to the American point of view; change in the aims of education; industrial work; inflow of capital—giving greater opportunity for employment in various kinds of industrial labor; greater protection afforded to the laborer; increase and diversification of wants.[13] Teachers and the

[11] Annual Report of the Chief of the Bureau of Insular Affairs, 1927, p. 19.

[12] Yet, it should be remembered that the total number of students migrating to the United States is small compared with the 18,000 to 25,000 students enrolled in the degree-giving institutions of Manila alone.

[13] Economic Conditions in the Philippines. Revised edition, Ginn & Co., 1920.

government are doing everything possible to deflect students from purely academic training to that which is practical. Many Filipinos, women as well as men, are entering business and production. A few of the farm schools report that their students are going on with farming and taking up homesteads and doing very well.

But still the old tradition of class difference cannot easily be overcome. Some believe that the very separation of the agricultural from the academic high schools has accentuated it:

> Students of the academic schools often call their brothers in the agricultural schools farmers, while those in the trade schools are dubbed as blacksmiths or carpenters. Probably a different idea would have been roused towards going into the trade schools and farm schools if these were organized as parts of regular high schools or colleges within the provincial grounds or university campus.[14]

It is evident, therefore, that the educational system of the Islands cannot be judged in its general effects upon attitudes merely from what it has achieved thus far; one must take into consideration also the general impetus that it has given to activities along many other lines. And so, with a generous inclusiveness of currents set flowing, those observers may not be altogether wrong who declare that the schools, more than any other influence, must be regarded as the window opened in the house of the Filipino people to a new world, and also as the impetus to that exploration of the new world which has taken so many of its sons overseas.

2. PRESS AND MOVING PICTURE

Two other influences of Americanization must be considered in their bearing upon emigration, the press and the moving picture. Although their predisposing effect is unintentional, they have a peculiar strength.

The vernacular press of the Philippines is strictly localized, and its total circulation probably no more than the combined circulation of the papers printed in English. None of these has a large circulation either. Since 1924, the number of daily papers has jumped from 131 to 172 (47 in English, 25 in Spanish, 100 in dialects or more than one language), and the total circulation from 108,161 to 164,787. They reach only a small minority and

[14] Serafin E. Macaraig, Social Problems. Educational Supply Co., Manila, 1929, p. 51.

are often extremely local in their news. The papers printed in English reach the better educated people in Manila and to a less extent in Cebu, with few outside subscribers. The American-owned *Bulletin* is the most reliable and the most successful of the papers. The *Herald* is the public voice of Senate-President Quezon. The *Times,* after having been sold by its American owners to Filipino interests, has recently discontinued. The *Free Press,* known as the "student's philosopher," has a circulation of approximately 25,000 and is particularly active in displaying the lure of America and the successes and temptations of Filipinos in America. It combines many unique features which make it very influential among educated Filipinos, in the provinces as well as in the capital. A section of it, largely relating to traditional romantic and cultural interests, is printed in Spanish, so that the older generation may read it as well as the younger generation to which primarily it addresses itself.

The influence of the press on attitudes toward emigration may be illustrated by an article which appeared in the *Free Press* on February 25, 1928, just after the country had been saddened by the news of the death of a number of Filipino emigrants on the *President Cleveland.* It was accompanied by pictures illustrating the joys of the voyage from Manila to Hawaii, a Filipino orchestra on the ship, deck games, daily exercises to keep in good shape, packing the warm clothes provided by the H.S.P.A.. "At the risk of being thought a propagandist," the writer gives a glowing account of "The Bright Side of Hawaii," describing more particularly a group of "several hundred men, fresh from the fields of Ilocos, being prepared to board today's boat for Honolulu":

> These happy men, looking forward to adventure and golden dreams, gave a new impression from that caused by reading the cabled story of the unfortunate nineteen who died last week. There were no gloomy ones among these men. Hope for the future had placed a new light on faces that are usually impassive. Almost all of them are relatives or friends of laborers who had gone to Hawaii, had found work and made money, and had sent back to the crowded, unfertile fields of Northern Luzon the story of opportunity awaiting. . . .
>
> The stay of about two hours was continually interrupted by bursts of song and laughter and joking from the assembled men. A Visayan member of the *Free Press* staff says it was probably the Visayans who were doing the singing. Though having just left their familiar *barrio* homes, and the friends whom they had known all their lives thus far, homesickness was already behind them, and they were seeking a future of hope.

The article proceeds to tell of the protection of these emigrants against swindlers, the physical examination, the food, the warm clothing provided, the kindliness of the care given them; and then of the conditions awaiting them on the Hawaiian plantations. It ends with the rhetorical question: "That doesn't present such a gloomy picture, does it?"

Nor are the other papers free from such free advertising of the advantages of emigration. Arrivals of important visitors from Hawaii are nearly always featured with interviews that stress the cordial reception awaiting Filipino laborers in the territory. Editorials on race riots in California endeavor to lay the blame on a limited "low class," and examples are given of similar flare-ups that have occurred in the Philippine Islands. There was a little tiff between different papers over the appropriate manner in which public opinion should express itself over the killing of the youthful Filipino farm laborer at Watsonville; but the predominant note seemed to be that such demonstrations should be of a dignified character, of sorrow over a great misfortune but not of anger against the American people. Even in the discussion of the exclusion bill, there is, in all these papers, discernible an effort to understand the point of view of its proponents; and their protests are not unmixed with appreciation for the rich opportunities which emigration to America has in the past afforded the Islands' citizens.[15]

While it is not one of the strongest stimuli, since it reaches only a minority of the population, the press of the Philippine Islands may be said, therefore, to be in the stream of the current thought and feeling about the advantages to be gained from emigration.

Mention must also be made of the influence of newspapers and magazines imported from America. Their distribution is, of course, even smaller. The New Year's editions of Los Angeles papers—bulky encyclopedias of the advantages of Southern California, richly illustrated—and among the popular periodicals more particularly the moving picture magazines are said by Filipino students in America to have exercised a lure, in their own case, unlike any other. For this is not propaganda aimed at Filipinos, to be treated with scepticism. One remembers how, immediately after the war, the book-stores and news-stands of Europe were bulging with American literature. The undefined demand was there for

[15] The part played by the press in reporting on the fortunes of Filipino emigrants will be further considered below. (P. 247 *et seq.*)

literature describing a brighter side of life than that immediately experienced, and the trade was not slow to supply it. So the provincial school teacher and business man in the Philippines, likewise, avidly consumes the stories of a world, not too inaccessibly distant, in which happiness and progress and success are glowingly portrayed. And even those who cannot read English are impressed with pictures of sky-scrapers, social and sporting events, homes, beaches, parades. Everyone in the United States seems to be having a good time.

To this influence of the printed word there must be added that of the moving picture. Even in our own country it has contributed to mutual misunderstanding between different classes and different sections. The moving picture exaggerates whatever it touches of the actualities of life. The manufacturer's home becomes a palace, the ranch a romantic park, the small town the scene of exciting adventures. But to the unsophisticated mind the photograph still is a likeness of reality; and the less there is of first-hand acquaintance with the conditions depicted, the more credulous is the average man prone to be. Thus the America of Hollywood is too largely the America which the home-staying Filipino sees before his eyes. American films are shown in Manila and the larger provincial towns; and their subjects range without discretion from "Broadway" to "College Love." To these must be added the special educational and propagandist films, like those on Hawaii which the H.S.P.A. is exhibiting in many towns of the Ilocos provinces. (See p. 204 *et seq.*)

Eyewitnesses describe the influence of American moving pictures on public opinion as much stronger than their relatively limited diffusion among the rural population might suggest. College students are said to be completely under their spell. Their lure leads hundreds of emigrants straight to Hollywood—or as soon as they can get there. This town, said the secretary of a large Filipino organization, is their *Eldorado:*

> They try to get close to screen stars and so attract more to come there when they succeed. The ambition of every boy in the Philippine Islands seems to be to come to this wonderful place where their screen heroes live. And many of them get jobs there in domestic service.

CHAPTER XVI

PREDISPOSING ECONOMIC FACTORS

IT will have become evident to the reader that an accurate picture of the causes of emigration requires something more than the selection of one or two outstanding factors and attribution to them of responsibility for the whole movement. Except in the cases of a very few of the emigrants it cannot be said that there is a single sharply defined cause. Immediate motives must be seen in the light of larger, predisposing factors. Inducements held out by interested groups or individuals largely owe whatever degree of effectiveness they have to the actual economic situation. While differences in economic opportunity do not automatically produce a movement of population from one country to another, they do, to some extent, determine the effectiveness of the inducements held out to footloose individuals. And not only actual differences in conditions are important in this connection, but the way in which they reflect themselves in public opinion. Thus, to understand why Filipinos emigrate, we must understand their impressions of the unfavorable environment which they leave and the favorable one to which they go.

I. ECONOMIC PRESSURE

A discussion of the dissatisfactions with present conditions of economic life in the Philippines necessarily involves a review of that life in its totality which would take us far outside the scope of the present report.[1] For our immediate purpose, we must confine ourselves to some of those negative sides of economic progress in the Philippines which most directly bear on our topic. Many emigrants leave the Islands in order to find elsewhere opportunities they cannot find at home. Often the impression of unfavorable conditions in the homeland is more vivid and more definite than the impression of favorable conditions in Hawaii and on the mainland of the United States, received at second hand.

[1] For some of the major facts see Appendix K, p. 415.

a. *Backward Economic Development.*

Living conditions along the Ilocos coast and in certain sections of the Visayan Islands are extremely difficult. Landholdings are small, in the Ilocos averaging only one half of one hectare (1.24 acres). Capital is hard to obtain. *Caciquism* (the abuse of power derived from land ownership) and usury are found in every part of the Islands. Wages are low. There is a lack of steady employment. From harvest time to June many people are idle and, lacking industrial opportunities, can find no way whereby to supplement their farm incomes.

Whether conditions in these respects are improving or not cannot be stated with authority. The political leaders at times make it part of their tactics in the campaign for the Islands' political independence, to belittle or deny all economic progress made under the American régime,[2] while others attribute marked improvements in the condition of the people to the protective tariff. Again others, perhaps more realistically, point out that its benefits are distributed very unevenly, that is, that the advantages of the American market, undeniable for middlemen, millers of copra and other special classes, have not so far reached the broad masses of producers.

One of the greatest blunders of the American administration, says Dr. Serafin E. Macaraig, professor of sociology in the University of the Philippines, is the raising of the Filipino standard of living without any solid economic foundation upon which to sustain it.[3]

And again:

In the Philippines, the *tao* [rural laborer] belongs to the class of the insufficiently fed, clad and sheltered. According to Dr. José Fabella, there are many families and individuals whose means of support are not even sufficient to meet the necessities of life. This condition has been manifested by the great number of babies and children that are underfed and are found under an insanitary environment. It is also true that the great majority of our laborers and tenants have been so exploited that they are never in a position to meet the necessaries of life, so that except in the wealthier homes, the details of household belongings in the ordinary *barrio* home are rather simple and limited. Their diet is very meager, and usually consists of rice, vegetables,

[2] For example, the Speaker of the House of Representatives, Manuel Roxas, in an address delivered at the University of the Philippines, November 19, 1929, and quoted by the Philippine Islands Bureau of Labor in a special report, "The Problem of Filipino Emigration Abroad," December 6, 1929.

[3] Social Problems. Educational Supply Co., Manila, 1929, p. 272.

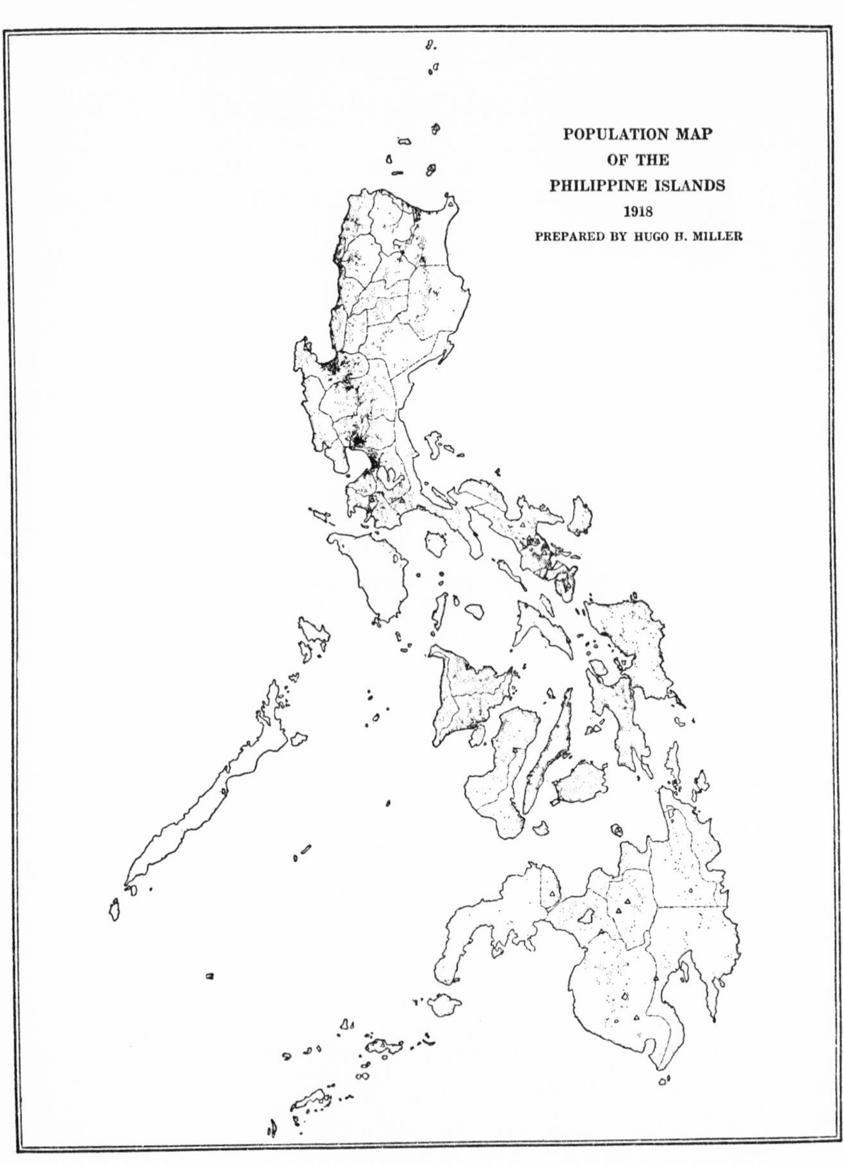

DISTRIBUTION OF POPULATION IN THE PHILIPPINE ISLANDS

Each Dot Represents 1000 People

Through the courtesy of Ginn & Co., from Intermediate Geography by Hugo H. Miller and Mary E. Polley

camotes, corn, beans and grains, which may be varied by fish caught during the wet months and an occasional piece of meat.[4]

The Manila *Times,* in an editorial article attempting to sift the causes of emigration, says:

The migrating Filipino sees no opportunity for him in the Philippines. . . . Advertise in a Manila paper and offer a job at ₱25 a month, not a living wage in Manila, and you will get a thousand applicants. Make the same offer in any provincial town, and the response will be twice as great, comparatively. Is it any wonder, then, that the lure of pay four to ten times as great, in Hawaii or the United States, draws the Filipino like a magnet? Plus the certainty he feels that he will get a job?

Any plan to stop Filipino emigration, unless it is absolutely prohibited, either by Filipino or American authorities, must strike deep at the fundamental weakness of the Filipino economic system. There must be a quickening of Filipino economic life, a steady forward progress of Filipino industry, and a raising of the wage scale before we can stop emigration. In other words, we must provide jobs at living wages. . . .[5]

In more measured words, the Governor-General (Henry L. Stimson), in his annual report for 1928, stated:

The annual exodus of Filipino labor continues as previously. This arises from the fact that, although the Islands as a whole are under-populated, in certain provinces, particularly Northern Luzon and in the island of Cebu, the population has become congested, and there is an insufficient opportunity for employment. This situation emphasized the importance of a wise and comprehensive attempt to develop the economic resources of the archipelago as a whole, with the aid of foreign capital if necessary. If this were done, abundant opportunities would be offered for all the existing Filipino labor and much more.[6]

More recently, a report of the Philippine Islands Bureau of Labor, on "The Problem of Filipino Emigration Abroad" summarizes as follows: "the most important causes of the exodus of Filipino labor":

[4] Social Problems. Educational Supply Co., Manila, 1929, p. 375. Several correspondents consider this description an exaggerated one. Thus W. Cameron Forbes, former Governor General of the Philippines, writes: "I think Dr. Fabella paints an unduly black picture of the condition of the majority of the laborers in the Philippine Islands. It all depends on what is meant by the 'necessities of life.' The diet he describes is not so meagre when amplified by the inclusion of fruits which are abundant and nourishing, especially bananas, mangoes, breadfruit, plantains. The diet is further improved by more or less cacao grown in the yards."

[5] November 26, 1929.

[6] Mimeographed copy, p. 34.

1. The unevenness of the distribution of population.

2. The unemployment in large urban centers, such as Manila and other large cities.

3. Due to lack of opportunities farm laborers can only eke out a hand-to-mouth existence.

4. The waste of man-power due to forced idleness during off-season.

5. The small farmers and tenants barely earn enough to support and maintain their families from their share of their products.

6. The lack of incentives for agricultural workers in the Philippine Islands.

7. Letters to relatives at home relating the labor conditions in Hawaii, such as high wages, good working conditions, abundance of work, and the thousands of *pesos* in money orders exchanged in the post offices of the Ilocos provinces serve as potent promoters of the present exodus.[7]

While the rich valley of the Cagayan River in the northeastern part of Luzon remains largely undeveloped, overcrowding on the Ilocos coast is intensified by the inflow of new capital from the savings of Ilocano laborers in Hawaii (see further below, p. 252). Instead of developing the hinterland, this new investment has had the effect, rather, of shooting land values on the western coast sky-high.

In spite of this phenomenon, it must not be thought that on account of desperate conditions of life and labor there is a universal urge among the poorer people of the Philippine Islands to be up and going. Whether a man is moved to so serious a step will depend somewhat on whether, in comparing his conditions of life with those of others, he is looking forward or backward, eastward or westward. Thus, the Bureau of Labor itself, in many of its reports, takes the view that the common laborer's lot has undoubtedly improved since Spanish days. For instance:

. . . Little can be said of the wages paid prior to the American occupation, because that period was almost patriarchal, and, under a semi-paternal régime, some wages were paid but were so low that, compared with those given today, they appear to be negligible. This was due to the few needs which the mass of the people in general had to satisfy, the low cost of living then prevailing and the relatively low prices of secondary articles, as well as those for luxury. . . . The common laborer started to take part in the struggle for existence with wages which were deemed commensurate to their class, as determined by custom and the locality. At most, one could receive only \$.25 or \$.30 daily. Skilled laborers began with daily wages from \$.375 to \$.60, while foremen received from \$.75 to \$1 daily. Just before the American occupation, the foreign trade of the country received a great impetus, and,

[7] Mimeographed report, December, 1929.

for causes which were not clearly known, the prices of the articles of first necessity all rose, making the life of the laborer unbearable. Skilled laborers began to receive better wages than in previous years, while the common laborer received $.375, all in Philippine currency, during the Spanish régime.[8]

The Filipino head of a mission hospital who received his medical education in the United States, in an interview emphatically expressed the opinion that conditions had been improving considerably:

The standard of living is rising. The homes are better, many of them are built of re-inforced concrete with iron roofs. Food is more varied.

Similar statements are common; and Governor-General Leonard Wood himself, as recently as 1926 said:

Labor in the Philippine Islands is in general well paid, prosperous and contented. There are comparatively few strikes.[9]

Independent American observers who have visited the country from time to time in the last ten or twenty years nearly always take an optimistic view of its economic improvement. Such visible proofs of growing prosperity as the substitution of metal for thatched roofs, and houses more strongly built to withstand typhoon and fire hazards, the larger purchasing power shown in the increased distribution of imported merchandise, the greater number and variety of locally capitalized enterprises of many kinds—seem to them convincing enough without need of argument.

b. *Asiatic Immigration.*

Economic conditions do not remain stationary. In many parts of the Philippine Islands population pressure has increased, not only through the natural growth of population but also through immigration. The Filipino experiences in his own land that competition of "Oriental labor" of which he is at present charged with being the chief cause in the United States—but in a different form.

Only gradually emerging from a feudal social organization in which a small land-owning class alone carried on the larger commercial operations, the Philippines are entering upon an era demanding the services of a middle class. This function, as in other parts of Malaysia, the Chinese are fulfilling admirably; but at the same time, the experience and efficiency of these immigrants do not per-

[8] Bulletin of the Bureau of Labor, March, 1927, p. 54.
[9] Annual Report, 1926, p. 22.

mit the Filipinos themselves to build up a large middle class of their own whose success would enrich their own countrymen. Still in transition from an economy of local self-sufficiency to one of participation in world trade, the Filipinos are handicapped by the presence of these foreigners in building up a strong middle class such as has naturally arisen in other countries that have passed through a similar stage. Though it cannot be said to affect directly the volume of Filipino emigration, the presence of Chinese in the Islands is therefore an important item in the general economic situation.

CHINESE ARRIVALS AND DEPARTURES TO AND FROM THE PHILIPPINE ISLANDS, 1914-1928 [10]

Five-Year Period	*Arrivals*	*Departures*	*Excess of Arrivals Over Departures*
1914-1918	45,266	37,713	7,553
1919-1923	71,026	60,530	10,496
1924-1928	78,961	65,710	13,251
Total	195,253	163,953	31,300

Japanese immigration is less important, but still a factor not without significance.

JAPANESE ARRIVALS AND DEPARTURES TO AND FROM THE PHILIPPINE ISLANDS, 1914-1928 [11]

Five-Year Period	*Arrivals*	*Departures*	*Excess of Arrivals Over Departures*
1914-1918	11,530	4,499	7,031
1919-1923	4,831	6,711	1,880
1924-1928	12,181	5,530	6,651
Total	28,542	16,740	11,802

No attempt has been made in these summary tables to distinguish between immigrants and non-immigrants, that is, between those who come for the first time to settle and those who return to residence in the Islands, having a previous legal right thereto. The com-

[10] Bulletin of the Bureau of Labor, March, 1927, and Annual Reports of the Bureau of Customs, 1926-1928.

[11] *Ibid.*

plaint is that, in addition to much fraud concerning the admission of Chinese and Japanese entitled to residence, there is also a great deal of smuggling in of Chinese and Japanese immigrants. The figures given, therefore, are likely to be incomplete.

The economic function fulfilled by these Orientals is a large part of the wholesale business and an ever-increasing encroachment upon Filipino retail trade. In some of the provincial cities, both classes of business are almost entirely in the hands of the Chinese. As middlemen in almost every area of the country's economic life, they thus have a direct effect upon both the cost of living and upon the natives' ability to rise out of the class of manual labor. What holds back the Filipinos in competition with the Chinese is largely the formers' lack of business experience and of cooperation within their own group. As a keen observer states it:

> A bunch of them will work in a foreign cooperative enterprise. They will get their supplies from a cooperative venture. They will be surrounded by organizations depending on cooperation. Yet when they return home they will not adopt cooperation, in the smallest things. They will cart their agricultural produce individually. They will not combine on cultivation.

On the other hand, since a large proportion of Filipinos already have Chinese blood, there is no racial antagonism and, there being no bar to intermarriage in the mutual attitudes of the two groups, it is held by some that the Chinese on the whole tend to energize and heighten the economic life of the Islands and thus have the general effect of raising rather than lowering standards of living.

> The Chinese in Cebu, said Senator Sergio Osmeña, former Governor of that province, operate the retail stores. They do not compete with the Filipino laborers. It is a difficult thing to guard our coasts so as to keep the Chinese out. As a matter of fact, there is plenty of room for those who do get in. The immigration of Chinese has no effect on Filipino emigration.

c. *Lack of Homestead Facilities.*

An unfavorable distribution of the population has already been mentioned as among the causes of economic hardship. (See p. 234.) It is a contributing factor to that poverty which inevitably springs from congestion and a lack of outlets for surplus population within the archipelago itself. Although there has always been a natural, unaided migration to the less from the more populated sections and islands, this movement has not, in recent times, been able to keep pace with an ever-increasing scarcity of cultivable land, particularly on the Ilocos coast and in the Visayas. Nor have modern improvements in irrigation and cultivation sufficiently increased the yield of these areas to support a larger population. A degree of impoverishment has taken place in some sections which no longer permits the application of any remedies to the local situation that require even small sums for capital investment; and the energies of the poorest of small farmers are so absorbed by the struggle for existence that they cannot readily enter into new schemes of individual or cooperative improvement.

This situation has been slightly relieved, over varying periods and with varying degrees of success, by seasonal migration, by the settlement of public lands, and, of course, by migration to Hawaii and the mainland of the United States, the subject of our present report. It is pointed out that both the natural and the government-aided forms of migration had long been in operation when the Hawaiian sugar planters first started to recruit labor in these congested provinces; so that often the new emigration was little more than a change in direction for those who would have left anyhow. Of course, it can hardly be said that the migration of a few thousand individuals each year in a population of about twelve million really represents a "relief" of population pressure. But where such pressure is strictly localized even a relatively small exodus may sufficiently lessen the competition for labor to make conditions more tolerable for those who stay behind.[12] But it is not possible to bring the number of homeseekers aided from year to year by the Philippine government to reach some other part of the Philippine Islands into any revealing relation with the figures of emigration to Hawaii. Not only are the numbers too small for any such comparison, but a sharp decrease of aided inter-island migration in and from 1922 was directly due to a change in government policy.

During a period of eight years, from 1918 to 1925, 13,983 homeseekers and 8,708 contracted laborers were shipped from the densely populated regions to those that are sparsely populated, particularly Mindanao. It is to be noted that 10,337 homeseekers (including family members) and 8,708 contracted laborers were shipped during the first four years, but during the last four years, that is from 1921 to 1925, only 3,646 homeseekers were shipped. The number of contracted laborers greatly decreased during this latter period by reason of

[12] Political and social reforms no less than economic betterment in European countries often have followed emigration movements whose psychological effect was far stronger than the material effect of their relatively small withdrawals of labor power would seem to have warranted. See also Manuel Gamio, Mexican Immigration to the United States. University of Chicago Press, 1930, p. 160.

the small demand for workers in the plantations and industries from 1921 to 1923 when production decreased due to the great economic crisis following the World War.

Other causes of this disproportion between the number of homeseekers and laborers sent during the first four years, 1918 to 1921, and the number of homeseekers sent during the last four years, 1922 to 1925, were: More funds were available during the first four years, a better understanding and cooperation existed among the officials in charge of the activities of intermigration, also better means of transportation; whereas during the latter four years funds were limited and the means of transportation were rather expensive.[13]

The following table shows that the greater part of this movement has been from the crowded provinces nearest to those most under-populated:

HOMESTEADERS TRANSPORTED BY THE GOVERNMENT, 1918-1925

Origin and Destination	*Number of Homeseekers*	*Number of Dependents*	*Total*
Visayas to Mindanao	2,400	7,086	9,486
Luzon to Mindanao	587	1,747	2,334
Luzon to other Provinces . .	492	1,671	2,163
Total	3,479	10,504	13,983

From 1926 on, there has been a gradual increase in the number of homeseekers aided by the government. But the total number transported in the four-year period, 1925-1928, did not reach that of the first four-year period, 1918-1921: 5,887 as against 13,983 (and an additional 8,708 contract laborers).

Several circumstances combine to retard the relief of local and provincial population pressure by re-settlement within the limits of the archipelago:

The character of those willing to move is thought by some to stand most in the way of success. Many of the first colonists to leave the Philippines were social and political outcasts or exiles. On the other hand, many of those who went later, and especially in recent years when migration to Hawaii and to the United States offered so attractive an alternative, were men who chose the nearer goal precisely because they were somewhat lacking in a spirit of adventure and unwilling to undergo hardship for an uncertain end. Many of them were persons of little ability. The

[13] Bulletin of the Bureau of Labor, March, 1927, p. 48. Government expenditures on transportation and subsistence expenses of homeseekers decreased from ₱76,000 in 1918 to ₱15,000 in 1925.

motive of the intra- or inter-island migrant is that of permanent settlement, to realize less ambitious but more immediate and seemingly more certain advantages. But close observers believe that migration to Mindanao and the establishment of permanent homesteads there requires more of the hardihood and capacity which today ensures success elsewhere.

Settlement in certain localities has been too rapid. Many migrants lost their lives by a homesteading of ground that had, after clearing, been insufficiently drained. In other ways also, there was a regrettable lag between colonization and improvements that would make life secure and labor profitable. And this failure is not limited to those enterprises that require large capitalization. Lack of adequate credit facilities has been a serious deterrent of agricultural development both in old areas of settlement and in new. There is need, throughout the Philippine Islands, for two types of credit more particularly, according to Professor Carl L. Alsberg, of Stanford University: a system which will help to finance the acquisition of land by thrifty and enterprising small farmers, and a system of financing crops which too often are mortgaged at high rates of interest or which the growers are forced to throw upon the market at times of low prices. He draws attention to the methods adopted in Java, under the Dutch régime, to assist native planters in these two important ways. The Bureau of Agriculture in the Philippine Islands has a rural credit division which has assisted in the organization of credit associations of the Raiffeisen type, but which has no power to finance rural credits. The National Bank, originally intended to fulfill that function, has failed the small man who often needs a small loan to tide him over an illness, or help him buy a *carabao* (water-buffalo), rebuild his house or do any of a hundred things which a small cash advance can help accomplish, with equal benefit to the individual and to the community. A somewhat paternalistic effort to establish rural credit associations from the top down, inevitable as it was, has not tended to give these institutions the soundness and intimate relation to local needs which they have in other countries, nor has it protected the associations against domination and, sometimes, maladministration, by acquisitive large landowners and money lenders.

Behind all these causes of economic backwardness, and involved in all of them, there is a deep-seated difficulty which need only be mentioned to be appreciated: the constant preoccupation of the country's leaders with a political concern that overshadows in importance every other. In the midst of their campaign for independence, the Filipinos can hardly be expected to exhibit those characteristics of conservative management which foreign investors would recognize as promises of future security, such as would warrant participation in long-term enterprises. And in such a time of stress it is the characteristic qualities of the politician rather than those of the statesmanlike administrator that are most apt to guide the country's destinies.[14]

It is not possible, within the scope of the present report, to enter fully into these and other alleged causes of failure. But it may properly be assumed that experience of it by friends and neighbors has greatly added to the lure of more distant lands. Moreover, it is known that the Dollar Line, when it started out on a systematic development of steerage passenger traffic between the Islands and the United States, reckoned with frustrated desire on the part of many in the congested sections.

d. *Special and Seasonal Causes of Poverty.*

Some of the largest of European migration movements to the United States have started with catastrophic changes in the condition of peoples: Such were some of the earlier Scotch and Irish emigrations of evicted crofters and the waves of Jewish migration to America following pogroms in Russia, Poland and Rumania.[15] Nothing of this sort has happened in the Philippines. But there have in recent years been accentuations of misery in certain parts of the Islands which probably gave further force to other predisposing causes. The collapse of the rice market (November, 1929—January, 1930) is said to have been such a factor.

Temporary local disturbances of the economic equilibrium do not much affect emigration, however. The family organization of the Filipinos absorbs those who in the Occident would become public charges. If a crop fails in one locality, the persons involved turn to their relatives for support until the next crop matures. Where the whole family suffers, recourse is traditionally had to the money lender who, in the Philippine Islands, is an institution at once necessary under present conditions and historically one of the greatest obstacles to general prosperity.[16] Yet, in the course of the present inquiry, many cases were heard of exceptional agri-

[14] See G. T. Garratt, An Indian Commentary. Jonathan Cape, 1929, p. 321.

[15] For the effect on migration of local and periodical famines, see Charles E. Woodruff, Expansion of Races. Rebman Co., New York, 1909, p. 139.

[16] See Appendix K, p. 413.

cultural catastrophes affecting a large number of people, which have directly resulted in a greater demand for means of emigration. Typhoons and violent storms which sweep portions of the Islands each year destroy crops and create conditions of real need. The economic effect of these tropical storms is much accentuated by the lack of diversification of crops. The members of a *barrio* in Abra are reported to have sold their houses and livestock upon the complete failure of the rice crop; and all of them arrived at the office of the Hawaiian Sugar Planters' Association, asking to be taken to Hawaii.

In a previous section (see p. 54), a correlation between the seasonal flow of Filipino emigration to the mainland of the United States has been attempted with the season of maximum demand for Filipino labor in the Alaska salmon canneries. But the seasonal variation of Filipino emigration may also, to some extent, be connected with seasonal periods of unemployment in the Islands.

In recent years, with the introduction of modern methods of farming, the tenant system is being replaced in big *haciendas* by what is known as the *obrero* system. Briefly, it is a method which does away with the relation of tenant and landlord. Laborers are employed on the wage system and are dismissed after the grinding or planting season, as the case may be. This unsteady employment drives many laborers during the off-season to go to the cities to supplement their earnings on the farm. This system is in vogue in the sugar plantations of Negros, Capiz, Iloilo, and Pampanga. There are also regions where there is an off-season for tenants because of the lack of rainfall, and only one crop is raised. These tenants usually go to the neighboring towns to work. Agricultural laborers from the Ilocos regions spread out to the central plains of Luzon after their harvest is done. Portions of Tayabas and other coast regions are dry for half of the year, and the farmers usually migrate to neighboring towns for different kinds of odd occupations.[17]

The major places of origin and destination of seasonal labor within the Philippine Islands have been summarized as follows:

1. Ilocos provinces to the tobacco region, composing the provinces of Cagayan and Isabela.

2. Ilocos provinces and La Union to the rice region in central Luzon, consisting of the provinces of Pangasinan, Nueva Ecija, Tarlac and Bulacan, and the sugar *haciendas* in Pampanga and Laguna.

3. Iloilo, Antique and Cebu to the sugar district of Occidental Negros.

4. Cebu, Bohol and the sub-province of Siquijor to Mindanao.

[17] Serafin E. Macaraig, Social Problems. Educational Supply Co., Manila, 1929, p. 348.

5. Capiz to Mindoro, Batangas to Mindoro, Laguna to Tayabas, and Pampanga to Mindoro.[18]

Especially after a poor harvest, laborers flock to the cities and wherever opportunities for work may possibly be found. This tendency cannot, of course, affect the volume of migration to Hawaii, which is almost entirely regulated by the demands of the sugar plantations; but the rapidly rising monthly quotas of emigrants to the mainland from January on may, perhaps, be explained in part by their coincidence with the seasons of least remunerative labor at home. This flow is somewhat accentuated in March by the close of the academic year, propelling the heaviest emigration of students to the United States in that and the following month.

Our heaviest bookings, says a Philippine official of the Dollar Line, come in January, February, March, April and May. In December the rice is being cut in Panganisan, and the workers are pretty busy all over the north. But in a month they will begin to come down here in great numbers to go to Hawaii and the mainland of America. Then in March, when the laborers begin to slack off a bit, the schools end, and the students will begin to come in. The students, however, form a very small percentage of the total number.

In another province the Dollar Line agent said: At the present time (end of December), business is slack since it is still harvesting time. January is the heaviest month for laborers and March for students. There are about 50 per cent of each sent to the United States.[19]

2. ECONOMIC PULL

People do not leave their homes because things are bad, unless they see something better elsewhere. As we have seen, all sorts of inducements beckon from the United States. But it cannot be said that there is a definite relation between the attractive force of these inducements and the actual economic opportunities. It would seem, for example, from the figures collected by the California Department of Industrial Relations[20] that there has been an increase in the number of Filipinos admitted to that state in 1929 over the number admitted in 1928, in spite of a condition

[18] Bulletin of the Bureau of Labor, March, 1927, p. 31.

[19] The contradiction in these two statements concerning the proportion of students is chiefly one of interpretation of the term, the former informant having explicitly limited its use to those actually intending to go to school immediately upon their arrival in the United States.

[20] Facts About Filipino Immigration into California, p. 18.

of economic depression throughout this country.[21] But the Filipino laborer or small farmer has no reliable way open to him to find out whether conditions are good or bad when he contemplates the venture of seeking his fortunes in the United States. Nor is the student and educated man much better off. He may, through reading the papers, be somewhat better informed on the relative prosperity of the United States; but he has no way of knowing whether there is an opening that he can fill under conditions which he is willing to accept. Even when he is in direct correspondence with Filipinos in the United States, their information often is vague and influenced by their personal interest in an enlarged or a restricted immigration, or by their desire for the company of particular persons. Even the printed information which the would-be emigrant finds in the newspapers and official reports of his own country is colored by the attitude, at the time being, of editors and public officials toward migration to the United States. Only in this way is it possible to explain the sharp lights and shadows of these reports, the often almost incredible exaggerations to be found in them.[22] Not even simple factual information on data necessary for persons seeking a specific vocational or other opportunity in the United States is available.[23]

a. *Reports of Opportunity.*

The most important source of news on opportunities abroad is the written message.[24] Successful emigrants almost invariably write

[21] Notwithstanding the figures quoted by the California Department of Industrial Relations, the general impression on the Pacific Coast is that the stream of Filipino immigration has lessened since 1928. Historically, variations in the current of immigration to the United States usually have followed changing economic conditions here rather than in the countries of origin: The economic pull is stronger than the economic push. (Harry Jerome, Migration and Business Cycle. National Bureau of Economic Research, New York, 1926, p. 208.)

[22] See, for example, a section describing the condition of "Filipino Laborers in the United States" in the Annual Report of the Bureau of Labor, 1928, which is explainable only by a strong desire to discourage emigration to the mainland.

[23] A group of students interviewed at the University of the Philippines, in reply to a question, stated that neither at the university nor anywhere else in Manila, to their knowledge, was there a collection of American college catalogues from which to make an intelligent choice of courses according to their individual needs or desires. Nor did they know where they could go for information on the cost of living and opportunities for employment in different cities. "A student hears one thing from one person and another from someone else, and in the end does not know what to expect in the United States."

[24] Reports of Consular officers in Russia, Austria, and Germany before the war emphasized the strength of the pull toward the United States of alluring letters from relatives here, often accompanied by money orders and bank drafts. See Frank Julian Warne, The Tide of Immigration. D. Appleton & Co., 1916, chap. V. Henry Pratt Fairchild, Immigration. Macmillan Co., Revised Edition, 1925, p. 158 *et seq.*

home. The emigrant's family, proud of the son's success, passes the letter around to relatives and friends. Soon everyone in the *barrio* knows of the wonderful time this emigrant is having. The letter tells of ideal working conditions to be found in Hawaii, or of the large wages earned in America. His accounts of personal experiences become exaggerated as they are passed on by word of mouth. Hawaii and the United States become lands where one can earn high wages, where jobs are plentiful, where everyone has a good time and gets rich.[25] Fernandez, who left town a year ago, now owns an automobile. Juan, a cousin whom the writer sought out, is president of the local Rizal Club. Pedro works for a rich merchant, taking care of his garden. Ignacio has gone to Hollywood and has been promised a part in a moving picture. (He was registered, with thousands of others, as a possible super for pictures with an Oriental setting, but really is washing dishes in a small Los Angeles coffee shop and has never been inside a studio.) With repeated telling, Fernandez becomes a successful business man, Juan a coming politician, Pedro a head gardener on an important estate, and Ignacio an embryo movie star.

Describing "The Beginning of Emigration in Great Numbers," a report of the Bureau of Labor says:

> The greatest factor was the economic boom which swept the United States during and just after the Great World War when Europe was still staggering and the industries which sprung like mushrooms all over the country enjoyed undisputed supremacy in the world's commerce. The wages were sky-high, employment was abundant, while labor was scarce. News and letters from countrymen already over there glowed with promises of better opportunities of living and a happier life. Stories of young men who successfully graduated in different colleges of the United States as self-supporting students aroused hopes in the hearts of Filipino youths. . . .
>
> The first great contingent of Filipinos met with great success. Their letters home contained happy news together with practical results in the form of presents and money orders in more or less big amounts. Stories of their successes grew in volume and became a by-word in their home towns where others wait for opportunities and means to simulate the successful emigrants.
>
> This brief period of prosperity developed into a widespread propaganda for the advantages to be derived from going to the United States, and its effect is still felt in every nook and corner of these Islands.[26]

[25] Appendix G, p. 376 *et seq.*, gives the results of a sample study made of the effect produced by letters received from emigrant Filipinos upon their friends.

[26] The Problem of Filipino Emigration Abroad. Mimeographed report, Bureau of Labor, 1929, p. 23.

Exaggeration, said a school superintendent interviewed in Abra province, is found in the letters sent back from Hawaii and given publicity. These letters tell of the group life, of the opportunity of living with relatives, of the comfortable hospital, of the mutual relations, of high wages. About one-third of the letters give discouraging news, but no one hears about them.

A Philippine sociologist has made a collection of about a thousand letters sent by men in Hawaii and on the mainland to friends and relatives at home. He says:

A look at the condition of them, worn and often folded, shows how they are passed around from one to another. It is obviously the outstanding way in which reports about conditions abroad are gained. Those who make failures just don't write, and their failure to do so is not talked about and probably forgotten. . . . There are many reports of a "good time," stories, much exaggerated, of men who have married women of good families—often girls from the streets.

Among the young men another type of letter is passed around: It describes the sex freedom in the American city. There are stories of beach parties and dances, of dates made with girls, of shows seen.

Gossip was spread that life in this country was not a bit difficult—which, I later found out, was not altogether true. It was said that much could be earned with little work. It was proved from letters of intimates how easily one can earn and go to school at the same time. Such news carried me off entirely, so I brought the matter before my parents. They were not a bit in favor of the idea, but after much pleading and promises to go to work and to go to school, I finally got their consent. Just after the close of the school year I embarked. . . .[27]

Reports about the success of Filipinos in the United States are the chief cause of emigration, said another Filipino student in an interview. Failures don't write home. And all are apt to write exaggerated accounts of their fortunes. I myself wrote to three cousins advising them to come here. I sent my sister $15 and encouraged her to go to high school. I have been criticized by fellow students for encouraging others to come. They say that if anyone writes home of difficulties encountered here, no one will believe him.

The cumulative effect of such news in letters is described by another Filipino student:

Those hearsay news date back as far as my early recollections can take me. The earliest news were probably from those who had enlisted in the Navy and who stayed on in the States after they were honorably discharged. They had

[27] From a class paper of a Filipino student.

been telling of the easy and wonderful time they were having, stories that may attract any youth that has never had the fling of life. These conditions, when they became known, spread to relatives, friends, and later to the entire village. It was not taken seriously then, for there were no proofs of their truth. Then somebody had nerve enough to try and find out for himself. This was about 1918 and 1919. From the bunch of boys that came about that time was heard again of the ease to obtain work at a rather high rate of compensation as compared with the wages one earns there. This was, without doubt, due to the World War. By these luring news the young men seemed to be finally convinced of the realness of the news that formerly had caused a lot of comment. These recent news corresponded with those that were previously spread by those who were here first. From then on, here and there, bunches of boys started to come. . . . No one can positively predict when this is going to stop.

One element that must not be overlooked is the effect produced by pictures among simple people. Filipinos are notoriously fond of having their photographs taken; and the photographic studio is one of the few remunerative forms of business in which a considerable number of Filipinos in the United States engage. So the worn and oft-folded letter that passes from hand to hand in the *barrio* often is accompanied by a group portrait in which the delighted relatives and friends recognize not only the sender but other boys of the town as well—all dressed like leisured gentlemen, pants neatly pressed, and a fountain pen sticking out, with the inevitable silk handkerchief, from every breast pocket. The group may be posed before a shining automobile on an elegant avenue; or to the unsophisticated, the photographer's much worn back-drop and rug seem proof of palatial surroundings.

After the written word and the photograph come the printed sheet and the photogravure. As these two media belong more into the category of artificial stimuli, they have been discussed under that heading above. (Page 226 *et seq.*) Suffice it to say here that, so far as the actual reporting of opportunities for Filipino emigrants is concerned, their principal function, within the limits of their circulation, is that of corroborating the verbal reports of those who return and those contained in letters written home. Thus, a Filipino newspaperman in Chicago contributes to the Manila *Tribune* a stream of news about the academic successes of Filipino graduates in the United States, of athletic and debating victories won by Filipino teams, of banquets, celebrations, and the foundation of new societies.

Sometimes, the very stories which ostensibly deal with the pitfalls for Filipinos in the American city paint vice so attractively as to produce the effect of a lure for adventurous youth. Such, for example, are the articles in the *Philippine Free Press* about the life of Filipino students in the United States, the temptations of Main Street, Los Angeles, of a "pajama party," and of the gambling dens of Stockton.

The student in Manila and in the provinces reads of an Ilocano who has just won a scholarship of a famous hotel which entitles him to study hotel management at an American university; of a Cebuan who has made good in Hollywood; of the Filipino Postal Club in Chicago and the high earnings of its members; of a picnic in Van Cortlandt Park, New York; of the fortunes of a single family of seven boys, all of whom made good in successive stages of migration and who are now living with their mother in Los Angeles. And nearly always these articles are well illustrated.

For every ten such stories at most one will tell of the unemployment among Filipinos in California, of the numerous tragedies that befall emigrants, of the antagonism and prejudice which they must meet in a foreign land.

Several references have been made (p. 246) to the fact that, apparently, only those letters from emigrants which produce a favorable impression are given wide currency and credence. This point is too important to mention only in passing. Indeed, it is one of the most frequent complaints of thoughtful Filipinos in the United States that letters which discourage further emigration to the mainland are not believed or have little influence. As early as 1925, an organized effort was made under the auspices of the Philippine Press Bureau at Washington, D. C., to set going an organized stream of correspondence from Filipinos in the United States to their friends at home to enlighten them on actual conditions in this country.

One Filipino club, in the northwest, recently scheduled a discussion of the question how the actual facts of life in that region could effectively be brought to the attention of people at home. No conclusions were reached; the general thought was that, no matter how unfavorable reports *now* coming from the United States, the after-effects of past propaganda would outweigh them, and young men, hungry for new experiences, would come just the same. These students were especially concerned over the large proportion of failures among those coming at a very early age and among those, usually over 30 or 35 years of age, who had difficulty in learning English and in adjusting themselves to new conditions. Students at the University of California mentioned complaints about bad treatment and difficulty in finding work as "major themes of letters written home." One of them had just received a letter from a friend who, directly in consequence of his own letters, had decided not to come to the United States. A mixed group of boys, in different wage-earning occupations in San Francisco, stated that many of them had written letters home discouraging friends from coming over. They were confident that these letters, going out in large numbers, would be effective, when taken in conjunction with the raised fare of transportation on the Dollar Line.

Still more effective, in the opinion of some, is the gradually increasing number of those who are actually returning because they find life too difficult in the United States. Their influence, so far, seems to be felt in Hawaii rather than in the Philippine Islands themselves. For, often, they only have money enough for the first stage of the return trip and hope to acquire some savings on the sugar or pineapple plantations before they go back and face their families. A former teacher in the Philippines who has met about a hundred of such men in Hawaii, felt that they were still restless and not likely to do particularly well in Hawaii; he did not have the impression that they had learned much.

A number of coincident circumstances are mentioned by the president of a Filipino organization in San Francisco as likely to produce a discouraging effect on emigration: first, the fact that officials of the Philippine government itself had made inquiries on the mainland which must have informed them of the truth of the situation. He also mentioned an official of a Philippine labor organization, José C. Hilario, who recently had come over to study labor conditions and had placed his findings before the Philippine legislature. Second, the increase in the number of returning emigrants in proportion to the arrivals. Third, reports of a trade depression in the United States through the press. He did not expect that returning trade prosperity would immediately reverse this influence because it helped to lay the myth that there is always work for everyone in America.

Most important among the less direct forms of discouragement that affect public opinion in the Philippine Islands are the efforts of government agencies, and especially of school officials, to help people realize the truth. Reference has already been made to the evidently intentionally propagandist report of the Bureau of Labor [28] from which we quote the following sentences:

> According to reliable reports, the Filipino laborers in the United States are actually facing serious difficulties. . . . Those who are working in agricultural occupations and in the salmon canneries are employed only at certain periods of the year, as both industries are seasonal. The others work the whole year round. However, such occupations are not easy to find and are growing less and the pay lower day by day, due to the rapid increase of Filipino immigrants and the keen competition between them and the laborers of other nationalities. . . . As a consequence, a great majority, it is said, four out of every five, of the Filipinos in the United States are actually unemployed, undergoing all the hardships and miseries resulting from such a situation. Among these unfortunates, some who have graduated as doctors of medicine, bachelors of arts and of science, etc., are to be found.

Newspapers also increasingly play their part in discouraging the flow toward the United States, in so far as it results from false expectations. There is a definite policy among the newspapers in Manila to do so, according to one authority. "But," complains a school superintendent, "apart from the teachers—and only few of these—and the principal government officials, very few see a newspaper up here [in the Ilocos]." "A Risky Adventure, This Going to America" is the title of an article in the *Philippine Free Press* which has done so much to encourage it. Quoting at length from a communication received from a correspondent in Seattle, it says:

> No, the United States is not a place where honey and milk flow, nor are its streets paved with gold. An idea of how hard life is getting to be for the Filipino laborer may be obtained from the Yakima incident where the lives of Filipinos have been threatened. . . . Instances have been cited where Filipino laborers were deposited in county jails by the ranchers employing them, to prevent injury to the Orientals, as they call Filipinos here. These parts of America are not safe places to stay in. . . .

Under the sub-title, "A Sharp Contrast," this correspondent continues:

> When I was employed in the Wenatchee Packing Corporation, I was surprised on the first pay-day because the cashier of the company would not let

[28] Annual Report, Bureau of Labor, 1928, section on Filipino Laborers in the United States.

out any cash to be placed in the laborers' envelopes until a policeman came to stay with us in the room while we were counting the money. Here is where the contrast comes, as on one side we see that in an American city the handling of a little over three thousand dollars necessitates the presence of an officer of the law while on the other hand we have the Mindanao country (considered there as dangerous) wherein travelling deputy provincial treasurers journey for days carrying from twenty to fifty thousand pesos without the attendance of anybody but a *cargador* and a revolver.

b. *Demonstrations of Opportunity.*

Stronger than all reports, whether verbal or pictorial, are the practical demonstrations of prosperity that arrive in the form of objects which can be handled and used.

Reference has already been made to the remarkable evidences of well-being in America, and especially in Hawaii, that come to many Filipino homes in the form of money orders. (See p. 183.) Of course, not all the amounts that are quoted represent savings, much less free-will gifts to relatives and friends. A certain proportion of the payments made by Filipinos in Hawaii and on the Pacific Coast to persons in the Philippine Islands probably represents purchase of merchandise—either directly or through some Filipino or Chinese tradesman. A larger proportion represents re-payment of debts incurred to defray travelling expenses. Considerable must be the payments which constitute maintenance of dependents and which merely represent expenditures which, unless the dependents (usually wife and children) stayed at home, would have to be made where the emigrant resides. It is a mistake, therefore, to quote the whole of the money order transactions as though they represented actual savings of emigrant laborers. At the same time, as evidences that the emigrants are in large number employed and able to earn more than must be spent on their immediate personal needs, these payments undoubtedly have an effect upon attitudes toward emigration. And this effect is the more impressive when we consider the large number of individual accounts of which their total is composed—the fact that silver and gold coin and bills are brought into thousands of homes where the sight of money in fairly large denominations is rare. It is for this reason that the following figures are significant:

MONEY ORDERS ISSUED IN CONTINENTAL UNITED STATES AND IN HAWAII DURING THE YEARS 1927-1929 FOR PAYMENT IN THE PHILIPPINE ISLANDS [29]

Place of Issue	*Number of Money Orders*	*Amount Dollars*	*Average per Month Dollars*
		1927	
Continent . .	45,276	1,798,937.61	149,911.47
Hawaii . . .	36,339	2,205,474.61	183,789.55
Total . . .	81,615	4,004,412.22	333,801.02
		1928	
Continent . .	55,720	2,468,020.02	205,668.34
Hawaii . . .	54,950	3,207,195.42	267,266.29
Total . . .	110,670	5,675,215.44	472,934.63
		1929	
Continent . .	73,602	2,987,896.99	248,991.41
Hawaii . . .	55,155	3,317,049.93	276,420.82
Total . . .	128,757	6,304,946.92	525,412.23

The report of the Bureau of Posts shows a continually increasing amount of business of all kinds handled. . . . It is interesting to note that money orders sent out of the Islands totaled less than two million pesos while orders coming into the Islands amounted to over eleven and one-half million. Of this amount more than six and one-half million pesos was sent from the Territory of Hawaii alone where large numbers of Filipinos have emigrated and are evidently prospering.[30]

Impressive is not only the actual amount of money often handled by families with one or more members in the United States but the visual evidence of what it will buy. The effect of these payments is evidenced in land ownership, better homes, and improved living conditions. In the Ilocos country, more particularly, there has been a decided change of ownership as tenant after tenant managed to scrape together enough money to buy a little freehold.[31]

Every month, said a local agent of the H.S.P.A., about 100,000 pesos is sent back to Ilocos Sur from Hawaii and about 200,000 pesos to Ilocos Norte. These amounts, added to the drafts which I cash for the returning laborers, bring into these two provinces approximately four million pesos a year. This

[29] Money Order Division, Bureau of Posts, Philippine Islands.
[30] Annual Report of the Governor-General, 1928. Mimeographed copy, p. 33.
[31] Whether this has been an altogether beneficial tendency is doubtful. See p. 264.

money has naturally had a tremendous effect on the country. You can see the results in the improvement of houses and in the increased number of landowners.

On one hectare, he proceeded, a Filipino family can live fairly decently. One hectare produces on an average twenty-four *cavans* of rice a year, and the average consumption for a family of three or four is about one *cavan* per month. So, with what he saves in three years' work in Hawaii, a Filipino can come back and buy enough land, even at the high rates prevailing, to keep himself and his family.

Of interest to us here is the effect which the inflow of cash payments has on communities which often were previously on the edge of destitution. Consider the position in which a small Ilocano landowner finds himself: He owns three-quarters of a hectare on which he and his wife and their three children barely make a living when the rice crop is good. Many neighbors, some of them his relatives, have gone over into the Cagayan Valley. He knows that the land is better there, that the soil is more fertile, and property either free to the homesteader or very inexpensive to the buyer. But so many Ilocanos who have settled there have worked four or five years to clear the land and get a good crop only to find that a stranger has come with papers and dispossessed them.[32] This Ilocano is unwilling to take the chance. The risk of wasting four or five years of his life is too great. Yet he cannot go on with his small piece of land; life on it is too hard. He has heard that in Hawaii laborers are paid a minimum of two pesos a day. His friend in the same *barrio* the other day received one thousand pesos from her husband in Hawaii, and he heard that with the money came instructions that it was to be spent only on new property. He knows vaguely of several other cases of the same sort. Moreover, has he not frequently read letters from Filipinos in Hawaii that told of the free medical attention, free passage home, the house—with plenty of water—given the laborers, and the weekly entertainments—all furnished by the employers? He can borrow enough money to pay his passage to Manila and then to Hawaii. His wife can pay the debt with money which he will send back in five or six months. He will probably be away three or four years, but at the end of that time he will have saved up enough money to buy two or three more hectares, right in his own town. With a total of four hectares of land he will no longer be a poor peasant. He will be a

[32] See p. 402.

large landowner in his *barrio;* he will have influence and social prestige.

In short, his neighbor's money receipts were one of several influences, not the only one, that point out the course to follow. Take away the influence of the letters he has read about conditions in Hawaii; or the impression he has of the land-holding situation in the Cagayan Valley; or his desire to own more land, so that he and his family can not only live better but also gain a better social position—take away any of these, and perhaps the sight of those money orders would not have persuaded this man to emigrate. Why did he finally decide to go to Hawaii? Not for any one of these reasons, but for all of them. And it is not necessarily the size of the remittances that is the determining factor.

One influence not yet mentioned is the returned emigrant himself. Here is Jacinto, but a few years ago as poor as anyone in the community. Last week he arrived in a new suit and a silk shirt, carrying a shining yellow suitcase from which his delighted family extracted all sorts of lovely presents. Jacinto never was exceptionally bright, nor exceptionally robust either. But here he is, healthy, cheerful, with a golden front tooth and a fine watch-chain, looking like a salesman of automobiles or a government official. And how he talks! The mayor himself has been sitting there listening to him for a whole afternoon. The things he has seen! It is true, then, that in Hawaii they have even an orchestra on the plantation; that they had a big procession on Rizal Day in that strange land, with the Americans and the Japanese and all the other strangers looking on; that the doctor gives you medicine without your having to pay for it; that one can get extra jobs and be paid for them; that the big boss comes around every once in a while, with a new joke and a slap on your back, just as though you were his nephew. And here is Jacinto's certificate; it is in English, but one of the boys can spell it out: "This is to Certify that Jacinto Urbano has fulfilled contract of employment with the Hawaiian Sugar Planters' Association by working continuously, satisfactorily and well. . . ."[33]

Jacinto has looked over his father's new farm. But, he says, it needs a new house, three, four steps above the ground, with a porch and a railing, painted white. He is going to have an en-

[33] Those certificates, said an official of the H.S.P.A., have become diplomas of distinction. I have heard of cases in which they were used to impress the police in the Philippines when the holders got into trouble.

largement of that picture of himself with the automobile which, of course, he could not bring along. And a player-piano—he has always wanted one. He seems to want a lot of things. Will the money go around to do all this? Well, maybe not. But he can go back and earn some more: They have told him he could come back. (And eventually Jacinto finds that even with two pesos to every dollar a lot of his dreams remain unrealized, and so he applies for another contract, having saved just enough to pay his fare. This time he will take Domingo along with him. Domingo is his younger brother, a promising lad. He chuckles as he anticipates the eyes the boy will make when he sees the big ship, and all those queer people with wreaths on their hats and so many other things one cannot altogether describe.) [34]

I do not know why so many of them want to come back, says an experienced plantation manager in Hawaii. I believe many of them go home after their contract is up just to show off a bit in their home town and to lord it over their fellow townsmen. They already know when they leave that they want to come back.

Then there is Hilario. He also has made good and has come back, well groomed, with money in his pocket. But Hilario is not going back to work on a plantation, not he: There are other ways of making money, and one need not work so hard. That week he spent with his cousin in Honolulu he has seen and heard about them. Yes, he is going back to Hawaii—next year maybe. But he is going to stay in Honolulu. He smiles enigmatically. How to get a job? No difficulty at all, he has been told, that is, if you know the ropes. He'll get there somehow. But maybe he'll go to Los Angeles instead and see something more of the world. There's nothing to this business of travel, really, once you have found out how. And there in California, they say—he knows several fellows who have been there—you can get six pesos a day, and at clean work, too. And as Hilario's plan ripens, he too infects others with his dream; and four tickets, not one, are bought eventually from the broker in the nearest town. As a rule, only those emigrants who have done well return at all. And of the failures who return, most make a show of success by travelling with a new steamer trunk, a suitcase, and a victrola. It is a social disgrace to return as poor as one left.

[34] Next to "repeaters," the H.S.P.A. favors relatives of others already working on the plantations because they can be expected to be under some sort of control and adapt themselves more quickly to new ways.

> The most important advertisement . . . . is the outward appearance of those who come from Hawaii. . . . When these people return to the Islands dressed in woollen suits, expensive hats, sport shoes and silk shirts, the rustic and thrifty Ilocano's imagination is fired with ambition to such an extent that in the rural districts of the Ilocano regions there is what is commonly known as the "Hawaiian fever." [35]

The present investigators have also seen them as they arrived at the Manila dock. These men told amazing stories of the conditions they had found. Many of them had large money orders, or several hundred dollars of cash in a money belt. One morning, at the Dollar Line offices in Manila, one could see five one-hundred dollar bills handed over the counter by Filipinos buying passages to the United States. They said that the money had been given to them by emigrants who had just returned.

There is divided opinion on the question whether the influence of returned immigrants on the popular attitudes is a lasting one or whether it disappears when the new clothes are worn out and the story of adventure has been told many times. Probably conditions in this respect vary in different localities. The thrifty Ilocano who, by means of his savings, is making himself independent of wage labor by acquiring enough land to live upon with his family, will continue to stand out as a shining example. In other parts, the returned emigrants are less thrifty, and their money soon goes. A school superintendent in Pangasinan said:

> When they come back they usually have a good deal of money; but in this province they are likely to spend most of it. Some is invested in land and houses, but as a rule the people here are not so thrifty as the Ilocanos. They take life easily here. You will often find sharks hanging around the post offices when money orders are coming in. The people receiving the money often cannot write and have no experience in handling money. So when the shark offers to help them in this way or that and protect them they readily sign whatever he gives them or attach their finger prints. As a result, the sharks swindle a good deal of money that comes back. In any case, even the people who return from abroad do not live very differently from those who have not gone. They very soon fall back into the easy way of living, they settle back into the ways of their community.

[35] Serafin E. Macaraig, Social Problems. Educational Supply Co., Manila, 1929, p. 202.

Photo Philippine Bureau of Science

Photo Philippine Bureau of Science

Above: PLOWING A RICE FIELD IN THE PHILIPPINES—AN OLD CRAFT
Below: PLOWING ON A SUGAR ESTATE, LAGUNA PROVINCE, PHILIPPINES —A NEW INDUSTRY

Photo Philippine Bureau of Science

Photo Philippine Bureau of Science

Above: HIGH SCHOOL GIRLS AT AN AGRICULTURAL FAIR IN THE PHILIPPINES DEMONSTRATING MODERN METHODS OF PRESERVING VEGETABLES

Below: ILOCANO "MASCOTA" DANCE-GAME, ONE OF MANY FOLK CUSTOMS SURVIVING IN THE MIDST OF CHANGE

CHAPTER XVII

PREDISPOSING CULTURAL FACTORS

LIKE other Orientals, Filipinos as a rule have a great love of home. Home ownership is quite general, even in the cities. Family ties are very strong, and the mutual dependence of parents and children an essential feature of the established folkways.[1] The ability to control and spend money is not, however, to the same degree as it is with us the key to recognition of personal worth. In Hawaii, plantation managers say that a slightly better house offers no attraction to the Filipino worker comparable in force with the attraction of neighborly friendship. Like the Chinese and the Japanese before him,[2] the Filipino is charged with excessive clannishness. On the other hand, concerning all three nationalities, group organization and discipline have also been mentioned as among the chief assets to their employers.[3]

It is not contended, of course, that an entirely different set of values motivates the Oriental laborer from those with which we are familiar among Occidentals. But there is a noticeable difference in the degree to which enjoyments are sought that can be tasted individually and those that necessitate social status and a social setting.

The Filipino's desire for status manifests itself, as we have seen, in many ways which are now sometimes considered characteristic of this group, although some of them have also been observed earlier as distinctive of other immigrant newcomers: the large number who describe themselves as students and try to dress the part;[4] the love of honors which breaks up as many clubs and societies as it builds; the flair for oratory; the effort to associate

[1] Serafin E. Macaraig, *op. cit.*, p. 103. See also Appendix K, p. 419 *et seq.*

[2] Mary Roberts Coolidge, *op. cit.*, p. 441, H. A. Millis, *op. cit.*, p. 248.

[3] Eliot Grinnell Mears, *op. cit.*, p. 252.

[4] The Filipino's craving for good clothes, says an American employer in the Philippines, is not limited to emigrants or to those belonging to any one class. In Manila, a boy coming out of the forest, barefooted, with only a shirt and trousers, if given employment as a houseboy, will immediately borrow money from his employer for a pair of shoes; and soon he will look as well dressed as his compatriots in Los Angeles.

with members of a superior class or of the dominant race; the exaggeration of small distinctions won in scholarship or athletics or business success; the intense sensitiveness to slights and, reversely, the exaggerated attachment to a superior who shows ordinary human interest; the love of diplomas and ceremonial; above all the unparalleled search for college degrees and for official positions.

1. SOCIAL STATUS AND EDUCATION

An education gives a much higher prestige in the Philippine Islands than it does in the United States. The profession of teaching itself carries with it a place of honor in the community which has been all but lost in our own country where once it existed too, though perhaps to a lesser degree. A school superintendent in Ilocos Sur cited several cases, which he considers typical, in which teachers were willing to hold their positions at salaries less than they could live on rather than make more money in some other vocation for which they were qualified. The important point, for our purpose, is that a teacher trained in the United States carries a much higher prestige and can command a higher salary than a graduate from either the Philippine Normal School or from the University of the Philippines, and this irrespective of the prominence or obscurity of the American college that has granted the diploma.

The Filipino's desire for an education is by no means limited to emigrants. Thus, the *Free Press,* while it capitalizes the general interest of students in America, does not neglect educational affairs in the Islands. The Manila *Tribune* recently discussed in a long article the cost of a college education in the Philippine Islands and illustrated it with large pictures of commencement exercises at the University of the Philippines. But the chances of securing a higher education in the Philippines are poor precisely for the reason we are here considering: In the tradition of the people the class separation of the old Spanish régime survives; it is not possible for a scholar to soil his hands with manual work. Thus it is significant that in the article just named, though it elaborates all necessary costs, including tuxedos and midnight refreshments after parties, there is not even a hint that a student might contribute toward some of these expenses by remunerative employment; but in the concluding paragraphs the whole thing is put up to parents who, it is recognized, "oftentimes work their fingers to the bone at their jobs in order to send Juan or Juana to college."

A group of students interviewed at the University of the Philippines had two main motives for going to the United States: first, to take up studies which were not given at home, or which they considered given there inadequately, including medicine, advanced business administration, and engineering; second, to help pay their expenses. They said that it was almost impossible for a student to get work in Manila, and that such jobs as could be had paid almost nothing.[5] All these boys were Ilocanos. They expected to leave the Philippines with from ₱300 to ₱500 each. This would leave them with from ₱100 to ₱300 when they arrived in the United States. They thought this would keep them until they got a job. None of them knew how much it costs to get to Chicago—the Mecca of Filipino students.

> The people feel, said a school superintendent, that the exodus of men from the community is affecting the country. Yet parents are ambitious to have their sons go. Others know that with an American degree they can get better jobs here. Some parents who themselves really do not know what education means urge their children to attend an American university.

Now the point to remember in this connection is that parents do not necessarily expect financial gain from sending the sons to school. For there are examples enough in the community of men with high-school diplomas who have had to go back to laboring on the farms because there is no other work for them and, the school superintendent significantly adds, "receive the treatment people are accustomed to give persons in such occupations." In other words, if despite all difficulties the search of such a large number for a college education continues, it is because of the honor which the resulting status of the graduate confers upon the whole family. One is reminded of the sacrifices which poor and oppressed Jewish families in Eastern Europe have made, generation after generation, to preserve the prestige that comes from having a doctor or a lawyer, if not a rabbi, in the family circle. The title was everything; the size of his earnings did not matter.

There is, apart from the reports that come back from emigrants who have gone before, a great deal of mutual stimulation among the high-school and college students. At one of the high schools of Manila "there was last March but one question under discus-

[5] One of the professors explains this situation with the fact that the students are not really looking for the kind of remunerative work which they later will gladly do in the United States because there "everybody does it," while in Manila it carries with it a social stigma.

sion, whether or not to go to the United States." Many of the boys, according to their own testimony, were persuaded to go "just because everyone else was talking about it and making plans."

Nor is the prestige conferred by a college diploma limited to men. In a theological seminary, the investigators met with a class in which there were six girls; so their plans also were discussed. They said that if they married they would probably stop teaching; in certain provinces it was required by law. But whether she was working or not, an educated woman had great influence in the community. This influence, they said, was not exerted by political activities or by *any* very definite form of activity but rather by the example of her way of doing things. "If she is living in a *barrio* where a number of people are sick and no member of her family is, people will ask her why, and she will say that it must be because she boils all the water they drink."

2. SOCIAL STATUS AND OFFICIAL POSITION

We have seen how closely, in the educational field, the desire for an education is linked up with a desire for a position in the public school system. Both motives are part of the inclusive motive of prestige which is here under discussion. The educated woman, in the Philippines as in America, need not have a paid position to have her superior ability recognized and to play, accordingly, the part of a community leader. But in the case of men, the popular attitude in the two countries is dissimilar. There is a rising complaint that in the United States we pay homage to those, even among our professional men, who can show the largest evidence of material success, and that the highly paid business executive is more influential than the college professor. In the Philippines, due to the slow growth of a middle class, the value estimates of an older type of social organization have more largely been retained in the places accorded to different types of men in the scale of social distinction. Next to the large landowner, it is the government official whose prestige stands highest.

In time [under Spanish rule] there developed among the more educated Filipinos a feeling that to direct and to serve the government was more honorable than to till the soil.

The aristocratic spirit of the Spanish administrators, which was also copied by the natives, influenced a great deal the latter's attitude toward the dignity of labor; while the educational system, which emphasized the professions more than the use of the hands, helped to cultivate both in the old and the young man, the idea that labor is degrading.

There was a great deal of intermarriage between the intellectual and rich classes because of the high social positions of the professions.[6]

Thus education is very largely the means of acquiring status through appointment to office. Not the salary check but the standing of the individual in the hierarchy of public service is the thing that counts for most.

Therein lies the tragedy of American-Filipino failure in the Philippines: Leaders of both races have over-emphasized political progress and have accentuated the natural Filipino disinclination to economic pioneering. We have created a great public schools system whose chief aim seems to be to prepare its graduates for government work. The civil service rosters are filled with thousands of applicants for notoriously easy government jobs. A paternal system of government has encouraged this. A scale of pay, out of proportion to that in force in other countries of equally limited tax-collecting powers, encourages men in government office to seek political jobs. We make politics our god, and they fill our life. Every agency of life in the Islands, almost, encourages the growth of this system.[7]

For many years the government put up normal schools and took every possible candidate for a teaching position. Today, the requirements are steadily being raised and with them the expense of training; and still there are far more applicants than positions.

And this applies to all public positions. A conversation with two intelligent Filipino students at the University of California threw light on the prevailing attitude. Both had chosen political science for their major course of study. Both felt sure that their services would be needed by their government; but neither of them was able to visualize with any definiteness the nature of his career, other than that it was to be in the government service. Similarly, two Filipino students interviewed at the University of Oregon were bent on graduating from the law school with no intention of practicing law on their return to the Philippines, but with the expectation of either entering the government service or of going in for a political career. In both cases, the question was raised whether students who had the opportunity of visiting an American University could not be of even greater service to their country by choosing a more technical or at least a less crowded profession. But these

[6] Serafin E. Macaraig, Social Problems, Educational Supply Co., Manila, 1929, p. 48 and p. 19.

[7] Manila *Times*, November 26, 1929.

boys did not seem able to visualize any possible disparity between their ideas of personal success and of service to their country; both objectives in their minds were too firmly attached to the traditional ideal to be entertained as possible separate considerations. The Philippine Islands abound with men in good public positions who have taken their degrees in the United States and some of whom started on their return home from a high place on the ladder of promotion with almost no further effort. But today, there is much more of an element of competition in the desire for the better positions. It is no longer a case of a government anxiously scanning the horizon for trained officials but a case of large numbers of students seeking those qualifications—whether actual or only in popular estimation—that win the higher honors. And increasingly they realize the variety of paths that may lead to this end.[8]

3. ADVENTUROUSNESS AS A TRADITION

Migration is nothing new in the life of the Filipinos—especially the Ilocanos. Their racial history, their climate, the topography and natural resources of their archipelago, and those culture traditions that arise from the conjunction of these major influences, have kept the people mobile, courageous in the face of danger and hardship, always looking beyond the horizon of their immediate environment for fresh opportunities.[9]

We cannot here pursue this theme through the whole of Philippine history but must content ourselves with relatively recent evidence:

> The Ilocanos, said H. Otley Beyer, professor of anthropology at the University of the Philippines, in an interview, have been migrating for a hundred years. Only during the last fifty years has their annual migration become a problem. Conditions in the Ilocos are such that 25,000 must leave each year. The territory from which they come is not one which can be developed much economically. The land is not good, and there are no new resources to be tapped. Emigration seems to be the only method of relief.
>
> In the old days the Ilocanos would send out two or three scouts who would explore a distant piece of land. When word was received that the new land was favorable for settlement, the Ilocanos would migrate and settle upon it. This would happen year after year.

[8] See Appendix F, II, p. 374 and Appendix G, p. 382.

[9] For the effects of island environments upon the cultural history of peoples see Ellen Churchill Semple, Influence of Geographic Environments. Henry Holt & Co., 1911, chapters IV and XIII.

The traditions and customs of this migration which had for so many years relieved the congested areas of surplus people was upset by legislation in 1916. Game laws were enacted which seriously restricted the wanderings of the migrants. Once the Ilocanos became aware of this change in their circumstances, they looked for new fields; later amendments of the game laws did not break off the new channels of relief that had been established.

The Hawaiian sugar planters did not create a demand for emigration. They found a long established spontaneous migration and directed it to another locality.

The Philippine government's effort to guide it so as to open up new territories for colonization did not succeed because it did not have the facilities for supervising a colonizing movement. . . .

The Ilocanos have always been able to work out their own emigration problems.

A number of informants warned against the danger of overemphasizing economic pressure as a cause of emigration by pointing to a series of reasons why the Filipino may, at the present stage of his history, feel impelled to seek fresh adventures.

Our vast areas of unsettled land throughout the archipelago furnish . . . testimony that the nation is more than equipped to care for its inhabitants. It's the lure of the distant land that draws them away from their homeland, especially when transportation is furnished and employment assured. It may be mentioned in passing that some forty thousand Americans emigrated to Canada this past year, to say nothing of the ten thousand who reside in China, and the thousands in other parts of the globe. Are conditions in the United States so terrible, then, that these people had to leave? The steady stream of immigrants to America from practically every country known should likewise indicate that there is something the matter with the rest of the world. No, we fear that these critics are somewhat hasty in their conclusions and neglect the greatest factor when they neglect the lure of the unknown.[10]

Opinions are divided on the question whether Filipino emigrants have the true pioneer spirit—that is, the desire not only to explore but also to perform the hard labor necessary to clear new ground.

A conservative estimate of the agricultural public lands in the Philippines puts them at about eight million hectares which are now available for settlement. . . . Those regions remain unsettled because Filipino laborers will not take the risk and uncertainty of unknown regions without good inducement and proper facilities for settlement. . . . The lack of initiative and the fear of the Filipino *tao* to go out into the open and support a family have been overcome in Hawaii by the paternalistic system of welfare capitalism.[11]

[10] The *Philippine Free Press,* June 4, 1927.
[11] Serafin E. Macaraig, *op. cit.,* chapter XV.

It is clear, then, that we must distinguish between a footloose group that is willing to risk everything in a wild dash to places that hold the appeal of unusual advantages, and a much more conservative group, composed of typical peasants, that is more likely to follow when the first contacts have produced tangible results and when conditions are such as to assure at least a modicum of security.

This, indeed, has been the typical experience with new migrations. With notable exceptions—such as the Puritan Pilgrims—the earliest comers were not primarily colonizers in purpose, but came from a variety of motives in which negative elements—to get away from the restrictions of the home community—played as strong a part as the search for a new home.[12] Sometimes, in spite of a bad reputation, such men of adventure have become mainstays of flourishing colonies.[13]

A school officer in Abra Province distinguishes three motives: economic pressure, the pioneer spirit, and a desire of young men to get away from their families. A medical missionary, graduate of an American university, denies the possession of a pioneer spirit to the majority of those who go to Hawaii. For, he says, when these laborers return, they do not go to Cagayan. All they do with the money they have saved is to increase it by loaning or to raise land values, already high, by buying land in their home community. He entirely distinguishes from this type those who want to "see America" about which they have heard so much.

A Filipino minister points out that a large proportion of his compatriots in Greater New York have at one time or other been in the Navy:

> These men were recruited in Manila and, many of them, trained in the Navy station there. Many of them were young fellows out for adventure. The long seafaring tradition of the Filipinos, caused by the topography and livelihood opportunities of the Islands, has made them more adventurous than other Oriental peoples. They naturally adopt every opportunity to travel. When the war ended, before many of these recruits had had a chance to get into it, many tried to get into the Navy just the same under the usual three-year contract, and others entered such employment as they could get in the

[12] Edith Abbott, Historical Aspects of the Immigration Problem. University of Chicago Press, 1926, Section I. Jeremiah W. Jenks and W. Jett Lauck, The Immigration Problem. Funk & Wagnalls Co., Sixth Revised Edition, 1926, Part II. Henry Pratt Fairchild, Immigration. Macmillan Co., 1925, p. 158. John S. Lindberg, The Background of Swedish Emigrants to the United States. University of Minnesota Press, 1930, chapter II.

[13] Edith Abbott, *op. cit.,* Section III.

Navy yards—always in the hope of eventually coming to the United States, or simply of seeing the world.

Those who come from Hawaii, said a Filipino university graduate and social worker in Chicago, almost without exception are here for higher earnings or for adventure, not for an education. Those who have come by way of Navy discharge or as stowaways are exceptional and largely of the adventurous type. Much the largest number in Chicago came to study.

Wanderlust, the desire for new experiences, not coercion or direct encouragement by any organized group, are mentioned in a paper by a Filipino graduate student as primary motives of emigration. The implication is that those who stay at home are lacking in capacity to succeed. Contrary advices received at home are regarded as a restriction on personal liberty.

In another such class paper we read: A number of them come because everybody else is coming. From one town almost one half of the entire number of young men have left to come to this country. When a young man has nothing to do or is not doing well in his particular type of work and has heard of the progress of his mates who have gone away, what next, do you think, is he going to do?

Certainly, one of the causes of the population movement here, said the principal of an agricultural high school, is the desire of many to wander and see new lands. When the United States needed soldiers to fight in the Philippines, she had no difficulty in getting as many as she wanted to come out here. It is the same with our people. There is another element which frequently causes people to move, that is, among the lower classes, a desire to move to a new locality in order to start out all over again with no lack of social status as a handicap.

A Philippine government official denies that political oppression or persecution of any sort plays a part among the non-economic motives of emigration. He further does not believe that escape from local ties, including those of the family, are an important element. On the other hand, several other informants mentioned the absence of a liberal divorce law in the Philippines as a distinct cause, though they admit that for the vast majority of the emigrants the strength of the family organization must be regarded as a deterrent rather than a motive. Among Filipinos interviewed in the United States, there were several who had come away from home because they did not wish to marry the girls selected for them, and several who did not wish to live with their wives.

Many men come here, said the president of a Filipino organization in Detroit, because they seek freedom from hampering home life and conventions. They feel too much under parental restraint.

"Adventurousness," then, may be a euphemism for less positive qualities, and indeed seems to have become a somewhat stereotyped explanation for a Filipino's desire to emigrate when no very definite motive can be ascribed to it.[14] It often appears in retrospect as a possible cause when an individual has acquired a roving spirit after leaving home. It is a common observation that:

> . . . Migration produces a changed type of personality. . . . Energies that were formerly controlled by custom and tradition are released. The individual is free for new adventures, but he is more or less without direction and control. . . . The stranger stays, but he is not settled. He is a potential wanderer. That means that he is not bound as others are by the local proprieties and conventions.[15]

But this general tendency is magnified when—as in the Philippines under the long era of Spanish, and later under a generation of American occupation—old social traditions have already begun to disintegrate under the impact of a foreign culture, so that the more advanced in outlook tend to become footloose and cosmopolitan.[16]

A Filipino contractor in the State of Washington testifies:

> Just as soon as they see that others are moving and packing up their things, they will pack their things too. All you need to do is to get a car to load them. You do not need to make any contract when it comes to their minds to follow you. But their minds may change in a minute; so get them off quickly.

S. D. Porteus quotes a Filipino student at the University of Hawaii as saying: "The fields on the other side of the river look always greenest, and so we damned fools spend most of our time in the river." [17] "They would go to hell," said the manager of an agricultural labor bureau in California, "if free transportation were offered."

4. PATRIOTISM

The paradox that citizens may leave their country for love of it is not a new one. The United States owes some of its most illustrious sons to such migrations; and whole national groups

[14] See Appendix G, p. 377 *et seq.*

[15] Robert E. Park, Human Migration and the Marginal Man. *American Journal of Sociology*, May, 1928, vol. XXXIII, No. 6, pp. 887-888.

[16] *Ibid.*, p. 882.

[17] S. D. Porteus and Marjorie E. Babcock, Temperament and Race. Richard S. Badger, 1926, p. 68.

have been brought to our continent for patriotic reasons.[18] But in all these cases the motive was one of resentment against an oppressive régime, and the country that received these emigrants was showing its tolerance of political heterodoxy if not of the particular cause advanced by a particular set of revolutionaries. The case of the idealistic Filipino emigrant obviously is entirely different; it is even more paradoxical; for he turns to the only country from which, in the minds of some of his compatriots, there is to be expected any danger of oppression. To hasten on the emancipation of his republic from a "foreign yoke" he is seeking to acquire the resources of modern science and organization, and of education generally, from the great power that is occupying his home land.

This situation, while it may play a minor part in the whole causation of Filipino emigration, nevertheless is one that must not be neglected.

The motive of both sons and parents, says the president of a Filipino organization in America previously quoted, often is distinctly patriotic when they make every effort to get the son over here to go to college. They want to do something to help bring their backward country to the state of civilization to be found in the United States. Particularly do they wish to learn constructive skills for the upbuilding of the home land; hence so much emphasis in recent years also on engineering as a career.

Called in from sweeping a floor, a Filipino in a Christian institution in Chicago said: We have learned at school the history of the United States and want to find out more of western civilization. We know that the progress of civilization in our own country depends on us young people.

Again and again, Filipinos of mature years in the United States, men successful in business or in one of the professions, declared in the course of an interview—sometimes not without astonishment that such a question should be raised at all—that certainly they intended to return to their own country, as soon as they considered conditions ripe, to exercise their skills on behalf of their countrymen. Among them, the reporter recalls three engineers: a general inventor who has had a number of his inventions patented; a man who was studying the technical side of the fruit canning industry with a view to starting something along that line in his native province; and one hopeful of introducing into the dairy and farming industry of his native country more and better machinery. Filipino doctors and editors also spoke in similar terms.

[18] For various examples see Edith Abbott, Historical Aspects of the Immigration Problem. Chicago University Press, 1926.

Reference has already been made (p. 147) to the inability of many Filipino students to distinguish between the aims of personal success and of service to their country. Still another instance may be interesting: A Filipino law student at one of the western state universities misquoted Governor-General Stimson to the effect that what the Philippine Islands most needed was political reforms. He then proceeded to argue that Filipino graduates from American law schools have done more for their country than any others who have obtained an education in the United States. Even when they could not obtain government positions, these men, by their knowledge of corporation law, had substantially helped in promoting business.

There is also another expression of patriotism which at times is remarkable in its intensity: Graduates from religious seminaries in the Philippines may be found in Hawaii and on the mainland for the express purpose, not of permanently establishing themselves in positions of authority, but of exercising a helpful influence on the young emigrants of the laboring class. While much has been heard of the exploitation of simple-minded Filipino emigrants by their countrymen, due recognition is not always given to the organizational leaders who, instead of returning to their country to take up positions of importance, often stay on, with very small financial reward, to continue the rôle of shepherd or counsellor which they played in student years.

Among the rank and file of Filipino emigrants, the remembrance of their duty to the mother land is probably a larger incentive to worthy behavior today than any formal religious attachments are.[19] While this bears only indirectly on our present topic, the frequent reports of great patriotic celebrations on the part of the young emigrants cannot but contribute to the consciousness of the idealistic youth at home that migration to the United States or to Hawaii, so far from meaning expatriation, may provide him with new opportunities of expressing and exemplifying his love of country.[20]

The Filipino patriot often is a nuisance by the too aggressive earnestness of his pleading for his country's rights. But among the immigrants there are also many whose sense of loyalty is not

[19] See p. 122 *et seq.*

[20] Among disillusioned Filipinos in the United States, especially of the student class, there is sometimes bitter complaint that the teaching of patriotism through the schools in the Philippine Islands is so little connected up with the opportunities for its practical expression in the local community. Local patriotism, say some, is not taught at all.

narrowly limited to a particular political cause; among them we find many who have come here because they wish to understand better how their own island country may help to play that part which America has historically played in the substitution of democratic for outworn autocratic forms of government.[21] And then there are those who consciously identify themselves with the cause of all poor and oppressed peoples, whose patriotism has merged into an all-inclusive humanism. To hear a group of Filipino students discuss the larger purpose of their stay in the United States often is an uplifting experience.

[21] See p. 221.

PART V

POLICIES AND PROGRAMS

PART V. POLICIES AND PROGRAMS

CHAPTER XVIII

IN THE PHILIPPINE ISLANDS

THERE is an obvious difference in the nature of the considerations that apply to the attitudes of the receiving and those of the sending countries in the study of a migration movement. The receiving country primarily has to make up its mind on the desirability of the *particular* group which is under discussion and only as a secondary consideration needs to take account of possible alternatives—that is, other possible sources of population increase, unless such is deemed altogether undesirable. The sending country, on the other hand, is primarily interested in the *outflow of population as such,* that is in the broadest aspect of the subject, and only as a secondary consideration in the particular destination of its emigrants. Therefore, we must start our survey of attitudes in the Philippines toward exclusion of their emigrants from the United States by taking note of what people there think generally of emigration, irrespective of its goal.

1. FAVORABLE TO EMIGRATION

Almost all the causes which have been enumerated in the preceding chapters as making for emigration (p. 203 *et seq.*) are still operative. The discouragement produced by news concerning experiences of unemployment or hostility in the United States may be balanced by a desire to go while the going is still good.

The members of a small nationality, especially, stand to gain from a world citizenship which enlarges their opportunities. In the confraternity of nations, these opportunities play a part which may be significant far beyond the strength of its population. A country forced to admit its backwardness in economic and cultural development, in comparison with the leading nations of the world, has more to gain by an exchange of population than a country which, within itself, contains all the resources of further progress.

The people of the Philippine Islands, broadly speaking, therefore, have actually and psychologically much to lose by any restriction of their freedom to tread the paths of the world's highways and to mingle their fortunes and their lives with those of other races and nations. And this loss is felt by many of them, even when immediate considerations of the national welfare forces them to the conclusion that a concentration of their efforts upon the upbuilding of their home country might have its advantages. The first reports of a proposed amendment of the American immigration law which would, by classing them as aliens, shut the doors of the United States to their citizens, were received with gloom. It was only when the reaction of this proposal on the prospect of national independence was realized that a more hopeful note entered into the discussion of that proposal.

> Of all the measures now pending in Congress, said Senate President Manuel L. Quezon in an address occasioned by the conferment of a degree upon him by the University of the Philippines, on March 26, 1929, none is causing more bitter feeling than this one. . . .
>
> I see a great injustice in the move to prohibit our laborers from entering the United States as long as America retains the islands.

The right of their countrymen to emigrate wherever they wish to go is a primary desire, in the Philippines as elsewhere; and while some governments have attempted to restrict the free movement of their subjects, such restriction has never been the object of a popular demand. In the Philippines there are many practical and political reasons for wishing the present outflow of laborers to slow down; but more fundamental is the desire for freedom of movement.

2. UNFAVORABLE TO EMIGRATION

a. *The Attitudes of Emigrants.*

The great body of emigrants from any country may be expected, off-hand, to favor a continuation of emigration—to draw after them their relatives and friends and to surround themselves with a congenial group of compatriots. But in the case of the Filipinos this statement would not be true without qualification. As we have already seen, a considerable number of the more thoughtful Filipinos in the United States desire to stem the flow at least to the extent of disabusing false expectations (see p. 248). Looking back upon the causes which induced them to go to the United States, many of the emigrants interviewed discovered that some of these had been of a deceptive nature and that others are no longer operative. Not only this, but many considerations impress themselves on the intelligent emigrant which were not effectively represented in the arguments for and against of his own choice.

One Filipino, writing from the United States, says in the *Free Press:* It is a poor investment for our nation to let so many laborers come to America instead of sending them to Mindanao in order to have that place tilled by our own people. For the few dollars that the Filipino laborers can earn here they pay highly in terms of moral well-being.

Another emigrant writes in the same newspaper: The immigration of Filipinos to the United States must be discouraged except to those who are planning to study in American colleges. Even these should have enough funds to carry them on, and plenty of backbone to resist temptations. The present tide of Filipino immigration in such great numbers is a detriment to Philippine prestige. . . . Many of those coming here are not assets but liabilities to our country.

The failure of so many of their friends in the United States has served as a warning. Yet this warning has not been heard by the masses from which the emigrants emanate. Unaware of the hazards of emigration, these people are eager either to go themselves or to enable their sons to go.

b. *The Attitudes of National Leaders.*

The economic, social, and political leaders of the country, though hostile to the exclusion bill, often express opposition to unrestricted emigration. Much of this sentiment antedates the agitation against Filipino immigration in the United States, but that agitation has given a wider diffusion to a point of view that has steadly gained in force.

There are a number of reasons for this attitude: Most pronounced is the feeling that the Philippines needs all her own people. Leaders in every department of life realize that the economic development of the Islands is slower than it should be. Those interviewed were united in feeling that one of the essentials of this necessary development is man power. With many thousands of energetic young men annually leaving the country and proportionately few returning, fear has grown that lack of this essential may become a real difficulty in the future.

Another reason is the feeling, expressed by some, that those emigrants who return after a few years in the United States or Hawaii are of less value to the economic upbuilding of the country than those who have stayed behind. It is recognized that they bring back money, that they buy land, that they build houses of stronger materials; but the net gain to the progressive development of the country is not proportionate to these evidences of prosperity. The returned emigrants, said some of the leaders, are more disposed to settle back into the easy life made possible by their better houses and increased land holdings than to go out into the undeveloped regions of the Islands and to cultivate new lands. They do not even introduce improved methods commensurate with their improved capacity to invest.

Still another reason is the sense of uncertain benefit to the emigrants themselves. Moreover, every Filipino in the United States who is a poor representative of his people brings discredit on his country. Although, as we have seen, the proportion of Filipino crime is not excessive, considering the age composition of the group and the social status of a majority of its members, Filipino leaders are very sensitive in their reaction toward the hostile attitude generated among Americans toward Filipinos by reports of their many failings. What Americans think of Filipinos is a matter of primary importance to the leaders of Philippine public opinion.

All these elements in an attitude unfavorable to emigration have become overshadowed by the impact of a revived hope for an early attainment of the Islands' political independence. In speech after speech and article after article, we find the view expressed that the cessation of Filipino emigration to the United States is a cheap price to pay for national freedom. This sentiment also tends to color somewhat the considerations previously stated. Never before was there such keen appreciation for the home-staying laborer as a participant in the economic development of the country.[1]

Most of the pronouncements in criticism of unrestricted emigration apply to laborers rather than to students. It is felt that Filipino students in the United States have not fared so badly as have laborers. Yet, so little is popularly known in the Philippine

[1] While the general effect of the exclusion proposals on the Pacific Coast on public opinion in the Philippine Islands has been to stimulate a desire for restriction, they have also given rise to a movement in the opposite direction: Under the leadership of Antonio de las Alas, acting speaker of the Philippine House of Representatives, a small group of radical autonomists, in the spring of 1930, urged a heavy movement of Filipinos to the mainland of the United States in order to foment anti-Philippine sentiment and to strengthen the case for independence. It cannot be said that these

Islands about emigrating students and laborers, their numbers, occupations, the provisions for their welfare, or anything else, that a distinction between the two types is not always clearly made. The most fantastic calumnies of anti-Filipino propagandists are sometimes re-echoed in the Philippine press without any proper investigation whatsoever, at the same time that glowing accounts of emigrant success, likewise from the most miscellaneous sources, are featured as trustworthy news. The natural desire to speak well of their emigrant countrymen and to press the case for restricted emigration as a part of a policy of separation from the United States thus set going contradictory generalizations from which the politician may choose what best happens to fit the immediate occasion of his public deliverances.

It is natural, however, that the situation of the emigrant students, who are closer to the makers of public opinion, is somewhat better understood and more realistically presented. A number of well informed people believe that, although that situation has recently shown signs of improvement, the students have left at too early an age. During the last year or two, a tendency has set in for older students only to emigrate. But one still hears the opinion expressed that something should be done to prevent the younger ones from leaving the country. These immature boys, it is believed,—not without a warrant of actuality, as we have seen (p. 146)—land in the United States without the experience necessary to overcome the dangers of the new environment. No objections are made to the emigration of students who are properly prepared academically and of sufficient maturity of years and outlook.

The attitudes here stated are largely shared by Filipinos and by Americans resident in the Philippines who are able to visualize the problem from their point of view. Other Americans in the Philippines, of course, look on the matter entirely from the point of view of the United States. They are conscious of the fact that Filipino labor underbids American labor and undermines American standards of living. Since their attitudes are shaped largely by what they hear from the United States, and particularly from the

tactics have commended themselves to any large section of public opinion, and it is improbable that their advocacy will tangibly affect the volume of emigration. It is interesting to note, however, that under the influence of an agricultural depression in 1930 which has thrown thousands of laborers out of work, a number of national leaders—including the director of the Bureau of Labor, Hermenegildo Cruz—have reversed a previously hostile attitude toward large-scale emigration and are holding up to their countrymen the prosperity of the emigrant colonies in Hawaii and on the Pacific Coast.

Pacific Coast, they enlarge on these two conditions and also reiterate criticisms concerning the relations of Filipino emigrants with white women in America. But, in addition, their unfavorable attitude to a continuation of Filipino emigration is influenced also by what they hear of the difficulties of those Filipinos who return to the Islands with American wives.

3. REACTIONS TO THE SPECIFIC PROPOSAL FOR FILIPINO EXCLUSION FROM THE UNITED STATES

A distinction must be made between attitudes toward emigration generally and the attitudes which have developed around a specific proposal to limit it as regards the United States, and the form in which that limitation is to be applied.

Outside of Manila, the investigators did not run into any marked agitation over the question of exclusion. Those interviewed in the provinces either were not fully aware of the proposals which have been made in the Congress of the United States or did not realize their implications as fully as their more sophisticated compatriots in the capital realize them.

a. *In Opposition.*

The political leaders of the country, the newspapers, and Filipino business men see in the exclusion bill an attempted insult to the national dignity of the Philippines. At the same time, as we have seen, they realize that one consequence of that act might be to put their country one step nearer political independence. Between resentment of insult and being pushed on the road to independence, the Filipinos would be likely to choose the latter; but it is not a choice which sensitive men or statesmen with an eye to the future of their relations with other nations would make unless forced. Thus, Senate President Quezon, in the speech previously quoted (p. 274), also said:

> The movement to bar Filipino laborers from the United States shows conclusively that the racial differences between the two countries constitute an obstacle to the permanent political union of the two countries that is insurmountable. . . .
>
> We have every reason to tell Americans that if they will not permit us to enter that country they have no right to keep us. And those fair-minded Americans will say: "It is evident that we are not meant to be married. Let us be divorced."

The Manila *Times* in editorial comment says: It is unthinkable that the American flag should fly over the Philippines while the citizens who look to it for defense and support are barred from entering the United States.[2]

On another day, the same paper pointed out that restriction of Filipino immigration on the part of the United States can lead to but one thing, the overthrow of the United States' entire ethical and political responsibility for the Philippines—in a word, independence. Exclusion by the United States, besides being considered an indignity and an insult, is generally regarded among these leaders as unfair, a game of "heads I win, tails you lose." All the traditions of equity in the peaceful affairs between nations, they hold, should make it impossible for the United States to take such a step.

Filipino admiration for America in the earlier days was due to the fact that Filipinos were freely admitted into the United States. The attempt to exclude Filipinos now in the United States is alienating many of our people from their admiration for the American people, and many are bitter because the gesture savors of race prejudice.[3]

Manuel Roxas, Speaker of the Philippine House of Representatives, and leader of a commission appointed to represent the Islands' legislature before Congress, at a hearing of the House Committee on Immigration and Naturalization, on April 12, 1930, voiced the unanimous protest of both political parties in the Philippines and of all racial and religious groups in the Islands against the proposal to exclude the Filipinos from the United States under the provisions of the Welsh bill. He pointed out that the total number of Filipinos in the United States (approximately 55,000) was less than the *annual* immigration of Mexicans and only a fraction of the annual immigration of European aliens. The proposal to prevent the migration of nationals to the motherland had no precedent in the law of any other country. (Great Britain does not exclude Indians and Japan does not exclude Koreans, nor Holland the Javanese.) The Filipinos had not been excluded from Spain when under Spanish rule.

There was no menace to the homogeneity of the American people because the Filipinos, though technically immigrants, do not come to stay but for temporary residence only. Exclusion would inflict a serious moral injury upon the Filipino people, especially since the practical objective of the measure could better be secured by other means. He pointed to the unwisdom of dealing piecemeal with various difficulties that were arising from the present relation between the Philippines and the United States. The general effect produced by the discussion of such measures was to create an attitude in the Philippines of receding faith in the good will of the great nation to which the country

[2] January 28, 1930.
[3] Serafin E. Macaraig, Social Problems. Educational Supply Co., Manila, 1929, p. 288.

had voluntarily (not by cession on the part of Spain) surrendered its sovereign powers—on the understanding that this was a temporary arrangement, an understanding repeatedly encouraged by clear pronouncements of the intentions of the United States Government.[4]

It is argued by some that every government has the right to impose restrictions upon the movement of its subjects if such measures are deemed necessary to insure their protection; and in the United States it has been argued that sovereignty carries with it the right to exercise such protective function. The peculiarity of the situation, in the present case, however, is that it is proposed to exercise it partially, for one class of subjects—vaguely classed as "nationals,"—while at the same time actually or virtually declaring them "aliens." In the Philippines, the right of the United States government to exercise such a function, even in a protective sense, is not recognized. The opinion was several times expressed that the Filipino, in wanting to go to the mainland of the United States or to Hawaii, need not justify his ambition with a desire to improve his condition, but that he has a perfect right to make the trip for no other reason than to "see the world." Any legislation which would make the fulfillment of this desire impossible would be unjust.[5]

There is division of opinion regarding the probable economic consequences of exclusion. Some people believe that it would produce a very serious situation in the Philippines by cheapening labor, causing excessive unemployment, and obstructing the largest present source of relief for population congestion. The Manila *Times* says:

> There must be a quickening to Filipino economic life, a steady progress of Filipino industry, and a raising of the wage scale before we can stop emigration.

The exclusion of Filipinos unable to pay for their tuition fees by working their way through college, it is feared by educated Filipinos, would tend to revive the old class distinctions in the Philippines, since only the sons of wealthy parents in that case could enjoy the advantage of an American education and would get all

[4] Hearings on H.R. 8708, April 12, 1930, p. 101 *et seq.*

[5] A recent student of this subject comes to the conclusion that the Philippine Government does not, either under general constitutional provisions or in exercise of the police power of the State, have the right to interfere with the free movements of Philippine citizens. He refers to a bill introduced in the Philippine legislature which would impose a tax of 100 pesos for each person recruited to discourage the activities of emigration brokers, but finds that the present provisions for discouraging labor recruitment are sufficient. Juan N. Gerardo, *Philippine Law Journal,* October, 1930, X, No. 4, p. 153.

the best government positions. On the other hand, they believe, students in the United States generally would suffer by the stigma imposed upon their nationality under a law practically declaring their non-student compatriots to be "undesirable."

A more optimistic view is taken by others who consider the number of those Filipinos who come to the United States to seek an education excessive, anyhow, in relation to the country's needs. Deprived of this opportunity, a large proportion of them, who are of farming stock, would use their energies in helping to develop the country's resources by taking up homesteads. Thus, we are led back to the outlook for the farming and laboring population generally:

A division school superintendent in the Ilocos country expressed the opinion that the laborers' earnings would fall to the level of mere subsistence, and that consequently a few large land owners and employers would profit enormously at the expense of the masses.

An American scientist who has lived in the Philippine Islands for many years writes on this point: The *illustrados* have for years tried to prevent, not only emigration to Hawaii, but free movement of the laboring class within the Philippines. In the provinces of Tarlac, Pampanga, Negros Occidental, and Negros Oriental, the landed aristocracy is much opposed to allowing emigration and state that if laborers were kept at home they would work for 40 centavos a day instead of a peso a day.

The most influential support for the exclusion bill, said an American business man with extensive operations in the Philippine Islands, comes from wealthy land owners, mostly Filipinos, whose estates in the past had been thought of little value except for growing coconuts and sugar cane, which they could not market in competition with producers in other countries. Now, that a larger market for coconut oils, copra and sugar seems assured, these men want to restrict emigration to secure a larger labor supply.

Other business men in the Islands strongly dissent from this view. The relative chances of large-scale coconut and sugar production, in their opinion, are determined in the main by tariff considerations, and differences in wage-scales between the Philippine Islands and other producing countries have nothing to do with them or, at any rate, are much less important. While the subject does not, strictly speaking, belong within the scope of the present report and cannot be further developed here, mention of the desire of many Filipinos to have exclusion brought about through a declaration of Philippine independence necessitates the brief statement that other opinions, in this respect, are very gloomy. Many believe, though they hesitate to say so in public statements, that the immediate passage of an independence act would produce a coincidence of regional population pressure with a most dangerous situation for Philippine production, unprotected by the American tariff, in its sudden thrust into world competition.

b. *In Favor.*

These pessimistic forecasts as regards the economic consequences of exclusion are by no means generally shared. The governor of one of the congested provinces thought that exclusion would work for the betterment of conditions in that it would force Filipinos to work for the development of their own country. Other leading men interviewed in the provinces expressed the same belief. The Philippines are potentially rich, they said; they only await manpower to be developed. So long as Filipinos can go elsewhere for the improvement of their personal fortunes, they will not pioneer in their own country. Likewise, many feel that until the government is forced by strong public opinion, it will not take the necessary steps to facilitate inter-island migration, homesteading, and the settlement of public lands. In other words, even if there were some immediate hardship in increased competition for available employment, that very pressure would have a beneficial effect.

It would not take long, say those on this side of the argument, for Filipinos to adjust themselves to the new situation. They would soon learn to go out into their own country. They would learn that even in the congested districts improved irrigation systems, better methods of farming, a more wholesome diet and a general raising of standards would permit a still larger population to live in comfort.

In the United States the feeling was frequently expressed that it would be much better if, in place of an exclusion law passed by Congress, the Philippine government were to prevent emigration by suitable legislation. This view is less often heard in the Islands. In commenting on the adoption of a resolution in favor of Filipino exclusion by the American Federation of Labor at its annual convention, in Toronto, October 16, 1929, the Manila *Tribune* stated:

> Any step taken by the federal government to restrict the number of Filipinos going to the United States has always been considered unfair by the local labor leaders. But inasmuch as American labor does not favor the influx of Filipino laborers to their country because they compete with the

American workers, local labor leaders would prefer that measures intended to solve that question should be considered by the Philippine government.

The Philippines are short of labor in carrying out the national program of economic development, local labor leaders claim. The shortage of labor should be solved locally, it is urged, not by permitting the immigration of Chinese or Javanese laborers—which has been strongly objected to by all Filipino labor organizations—but by preventing Filipino laborers from leaving the country.

The movement to restrict the emigration of Filipinos to foreign countries, like the United States, as advocated by local labor leaders, is provided for in the resolutions adopted by leading local labor organizations which have urged the authorities to take steps with a view to preventing the Filipino laborers from leaving the country, and to attracting them to settle on agricultural lands.

Recent arrivals from the United States, including President Hausermann of the Bolatoc Mining Company and Supervising Architect Arelano of the Bureau of Public Works, have urged that the local authorities should take measures to curb Filipino emigration to the United States before the Federal government or the American Congress can take action to the same effect.[6]

More widespread is the opinion that it would be impossible for the Philippine government to prevent emigration. A number of Filipinos, therefore, look to the United States to do for them what they cannot do for themselves. But nearly always there is implicit in this opinion one indicated before but not always openly expressed, namely, that exclusion would bring the Islands one step nearer independence. One difficulty encountered in this quest for an understanding of prevailing attitudes is that frequently the public pronouncements—not only of political leaders but also of other educated and influential Filipinos—differ considerably from private statements of their views. To many of them it seems impossible to admit any advantages as possibly deriving from exclusion without a simultaneous declaration of Philippine independence; but privately they may feel that the advantages of stopping emigration would be considerable even if there were no immediate change in the Islands' political status.

4. IN FAVOR OF EMIGRATION CONTROL

While few Filipinos believe that their own government could effectively *prevent* emigration, many believe that the common interest of the United States and of the Philippines could be served by the introduction of measures of restriction. Between the conflict-

[6] October 18, 1929.

ing attitudes of those leaders who oppose emigration and of those who oppose exclusion, one way out of the difficulty is recognized by many: to control emigration without going to the extreme of prohibiting it. But in this matter, although there are a number of specific suggestions, much talk so far has resulted in little action. There is no organized movement to restrict emigration.

Some who have looked into the present difficulty of the would-be emigrant to secure accurate information on conditions in the United States believe that such information, widely spread, would have a sufficiently discouraging effect. A laborer would think twice were he to learn before he bought his steamship ticket that there are no jobs for Filipinos in San Francisco, that the fare from Seattle to Chicago is so much, that living costs are very high, that the thermometer sometimes registers seventy-five degrees lower than in the Philippines. No exaggeration would be necessary, they say,—just plain statements of fact.

In a majority of cases, proposals for the control of emigration are linked up with proposals for speeding up the internal development of the Philippine Islands.

> There is a solution. The key to the solution is in the Philippines. But the key will not be found in politically worded prayers and politically designed demonstrations. Neither will it be found in legislative resolutions and public addresses. It must be a more practical solution than is to be expected through this class of things.
>
> Industrial or vocational education recently has been much discussed along with proposals for the economic development of the Islands. Employers called into these conferences have complained of difficulties in getting skilled laborers. The employers, Filipino and non-Filipino, grasped at the chance that the school system might help to relieve the situation.[7]

Another suggestion stressing the educational rather than regulatory side of possible solutions was made by a former government official:

> Production can be increased if the employers here learn how to manage their workers and how to cultivate their crops. In the Philippines, the amount of sugar cane raised per acre is about one-fourth the amount raised per acre in Java or Cuba. The Filipino employer has no idea how to feed his worker, how to regulate his hours, what entertainment to give him. A worker will not be efficient on dried fish and rice, nor will he do a dollar's worth of work for

[7] Manila *Bulletin,* January 29, 1930.

sixty or seventy centavos. I have found that by paying them a good wage I could increase their efficiency, that by giving them a movie show once in a while, I could increase their contentment. All these things increase production.

The government's attempts at promoting colonization have failed largely because the settlers do not know scientific clearing and cultivation methods, and there is no one to show them.

It is no part of the present study to inquire whether, and to what extent, a more rapid development of the country's natural resources could, either by itself or in association with restrictive emigration measures, be relied upon to relieve population pressure. It may here be stated, however, that in the most enlightened circles there exists some scepticism as regards the possible speed with which such measures could be accomplished. One of the provincial governors is strongly opposed to a continuation of the present emigration trend which deprives the country of its best young men, or sometimes sends them back with tastes that cannot be gratified at home and so makes for unrest or later re-emigration. He believes that a more speedy execution of road building programs in certain regions would have the effect of providing both work and new opportunities for opening up undeveloped areas of good land. He desires more liberal homestead laws and favors industrial developments, especially sugar centers. A government official, in the course of a lengthy interview, gave many reasons why such developments, and others that have been suggested, cannot be very much accelerated without grave danger. Among other things, he said:

Through economic development of the Islands we can, of course, eventually persuade our people to stay here; but that is a slow process. We are, for instance, building irrigation works as rapidly as possible. We are very much handicapped, however, by lack of funds. We cannot go ahead with tremendous schemes as you can in the United States. Furthermore, we have several times been in error by hastening too much. Several of the irrigation projects were put in too rapidly and, because technically imperfect, have proved failures.

Lines of communication are the most important thing in opening up new country. You will find that as soon as the Cagayan and Mindanao are properly equipped with roads people will settle in them. There has been considerable experience of this in the past. . . .

All of us in the government are very conscious of this problem of emigration, and we are all determined to do what we can to prevent it.

A provincial governor (not previously quoted) likewise pointed to the natural limits of any plan to accelerate programs of development:

> We have already taken what steps we can in this province, but we cannot offer such wages as those which emigrants find in the United States, nor do we have factories in which to employ our people. Irrigation would help a good deal. But we have had to suspend one irrigation project partly because of its cost.

The following are some of the specific suggestions that have been made to control emigration by more direct means: A bill was introduced in the legislature in 1928, providing that recruiting agents, whether individuals or organizations, pay a tax of ₱5 per laborer recruited. The director of labor, in his report for 1928, states:

> This office recommended the approval of a bill providing, among other things, that no Filipino emigrant can leave this port for the United States or for any other country unless the Philippine Government has assurances from the corresponding authorities of the countries to which he intends to emigrate that in said countries he could obtain employment under satisfactory conditions.

Some feel that only those should be allowed to go who have sufficient money with them to subsist in the United States until such time as they can reasonably be expected to find a job. Sometimes the suggestion is made that the Philippine Government might require a deposit of money sufficient for the return trip from the port of destination, so as to insure that lack of funds shall not become the cause of permanent loss of an emigrant. It is realized, however, that—the legality of such a procedure apart—this measure would not deter those possessed of a little capital or of sufficient energy to save money, that is, precisely those persons whose retention is most needed for developments at home.

It is also often suggested that the activities of independent recruiters of labor be stopped altogether, or at least strictly controlled, so that, for one thing, emigrants would not land in Honolulu without jobs, and, in the second place, opportunities in foreign lands would not be falsely represented to would-be emigrants.

Filipinos who have lived on the Pacific Coast have repeatedly urged the appointment of a Filipino labor commissioner in California, with functions similar to those exercised by the commissioner in Hawaii.[8] On the last occasion, this proposal was linked with

[8] See p. 175.

one for the establishment of a government-supported Filipino community house in San Francisco or Los Angeles, to accommodate new Filipino arrivals and furnish them with reliable information.

Related to suggestions of this sort is the demand for an official survey of the Filipino labor situation in the United States by a representative of the Bureau of Labor, which took the form of a definite recommendation by the Director of that Bureau in a communication to the Secretary of Commerce and Communications, in March, 1930.

The suggestion has also been made by influential persons that the Philippine Government charter several boats to bring back from the west coast of the United States the thousands of Filipinos who are unsuccessful. Others, especially Filipinos who have resided or now reside in the United States, feel that a declaration of Philippine independence would be a sure, and the only, effective method of inducing a large proportion of the emigrants to return home, and this irrespective of their personal success or failure in the United States.[9]

With regard to student emigration, the suggestion has already been mentioned (p. 277) that only the older, better prepared ones, perhaps only graduate students, be allowed to leave the country.

None of these proposals has so far found sufficient favor to be widely demanded. Many would regard any legal form of control or restriction as unconstitutional. This in itself weakens any attempt at legislation. The more indirect methods of control require a considerable degree of understanding for the whole problem which is not general. Indeed, there is, as we have seen, confused opinion rather than consensus regarding the fate of emigrants. Another complication is that, many Filipinos feel, a strong movement for the restriction of emigration in the Philippines now would be interpreted by the outside world as an admission of their non-desirability as immigrants in the United States. Exceedingly sensitive to public opinion on this point, they would prefer to see a gradual reduction in the number of emigrants, as the homeland, through judicious and well planned programs of development, could create opportunities at home so favorable as to set a natural bar to the flow of emigration, without putting up any artificial bars or seeming to overhasten, in compliance with American demands, methods of diverting that flow.

Fairly general among Filipino leaders was found the opinion that

[9] See p. 267.

a great improvement in the type of emigrant permitted to leave for the mainland of the United States could be effected by an informal exercise of the powers of control vested in the government. More specifically, it was pointed out that the Governor-General, in consultation with the party leaders, could introduce a passport system which in effect would limit emigration to persons able to read and write. As soon as a proposal of this sort is made a matter of public discussion, a political sensitiveness makes itself felt which might frustrate decisive changes. On the other hand, administrative action tending in one way or another to raise the standard of qualifications for emigration would have very general support.

Perhaps the situation could be summed up, if a summary may be risked, by saying that there are many pronounced opinions on isolated aspects of the emigration problem but none on all the many aspects of the problem considered together.

CHAPTER XIX

POLICIES AND PROGRAMS IN HAWAII

1. REACTIONS TO THE EXCLUSION PROPOSAL

a. *In Opposition.*

THE prevailing sentiment on Filipino immigration has already been described throughout the section on Hawaii's part in the situation. With two exceptions, all groups in the territory favor the present arrangement which so exactly fits the labor requirements of its two major industries. This arrangement has been termed "ideal" because it avoids all those larger social, economic and political complications which result from a large increase in the permanent population. The Filipinos at present help to keep going those primary economic operations which, directly or indirectly, provide a large proportion of Hawaiians with their means of livelihood. Earlier immigrant groups have to a considerable extent become emancipated from the hard grind of cutting cane because the newcomers from the western archipelago have lifted them to higher positions on the vocational scale. As consumers, this new labor contingent forms a home market that profits general farmers, truck gardeners, builders, artizans, and middlemen of every kind. It also enhances the promotional opportunities of civil servants and teachers, of the lower ranks of officials on the plantations themselves, and of native-born workers in offices, hotels, stores and restaurants. While indirect contributors to taxable values, the Filipinos take no part in the control of public expenditures. Owing to the fact that the right of citizenship is denied to Orientals, the political power of the territory remains in the hands of the Caucasian and Hawaiian minority who have thus been able to maintain a system of steady, progressive improvement, undisturbed by the less responsible vote of large masses of recently enfranchised newcomers. For the same reason—the temporary nature of the Filipinos' stay—the number of their marriages is small, and the birth-rate low. Because of the sex and age composition of the group, it throws no undue burden upon public expenditures for education, hospitalization or poor relief. Amenable to discipline, it has created no new problems for the preservation of order; and, since it is assimilable to other groups present in the Islands, no serious race antagonism has been produced by its presence. New demands upon public services incident to the presence of these foreigners, especially public health facilities, schools, and courts, are amply balanced by their contribution to the Islands' prosperity. A sudden decrease in the production of the basic crops, which must be expected to follow a reduction of their labor supplies, would throw thousands of people out of work by upsetting the present occupational balance.

Officially, Hawaii has taken notice of the exclusion proposal in a radiogram sent the territory's delegate to Congress, Victor S. K. Houston, by Governor Lawrence M. Judd, on January 27, 1930, instructing him to oppose the Welsh bill. The governor, voicing the opinion of the large majority of Hawaiian citizens, declared that to bar Filipino immigration would be detrimental to the interests of the territory. In giving evidence before the House Committee on Immigration and Naturalization on May 8, 1930, Mr. Houston produced both official and unofficial testimony to the all but unanimous opinion in Hawaii on this matter. He opposed the Welsh bill in its present form:

> First, because it is unfair to the Philippine Islands in view of our relations to those islands, and, further, because of the industrial and labor situation in Hawaii, where Philippine labor has been used since 1906 upon the assumption that it would be available until independence should be granted to the Philippine Islands. Before suddenly cutting off such a source of labor, there should be provided a period of readjustment during which such laborers as wanted to come in should be allowed to do so.[1]

b. *In Favor of Exclusion.*

The two groups which are hostile to continued Filipino immigration, are, first, those who deplore every influence which prevents the Hawaiian workers from rapidly attaining to those standards of living which obtain on the mainland,[2] and, second, those native-born of all races who fear that the present situation will in the years to come give way to one in which increasing numbers

[1] Hearings on Exclusion of Immigration from the Philippine Islands, p. 238.

[2] It is not contended here that living standards in Hawaii today actually are lower than on the mainland. Owing to climatic differences, an actual comparison would be difficult. As has already been seen, total earnings on the plantations compare favorably with those in sixteen southern states. Casual observation would lead the present writer to conclude that in housing, clothing and recreations any direct comparison would be misleading, but that there are few slums or other evidences of primary poverty.

of Filipinos will make their permanent residence in Hawaii and become active competitors for the better forms of occupation.

And not only exponents of the interests of organized labor and those of groups seeing themselves confronted with a menace of economic competition, but many disinterested persons belonging to neither of these classes are beginning to wonder whether the present system of supplying the plantations with labor is really so satisfacory and so promising for the future as at first glance it may appear to be. The question they raise, more particularly, is whether the present arrangement under which the great majority of Filipino workers return at the expiration of their three years' contract will, in the long run, really work out that way. Three years is a long time for any young man to stay away from home and to sacrifice the comforts of a normal social life. If large numbers of Filipino laborers stay on, they contend, the rate of intermarriage with other racial groups in Hawaii will undoubtedly increase, there will slowly but surely occur an increase in the immigration of Filipino women, and the schools of the territory will be flooded with Hawaii-born children of Filipino parentage, entitled to American citizenship.

Although the agreement between the Filipino workers and the H.S.P.A. contains no clause providing for compulsory return after three years (which could not be legally enforced), there is no visible tendency to stay on indefinitely. Of those who had fulfilled their three-year contract in the year ending September 30, 1929, the average stay in the territory was 54 months, and the average stay on plantations of the H.S.P.A. 53½ months (the difference being explained largely by the time taken up in distribution). In the same year only 1,366 men returned at their own expense to the Philippines, not having fulfilled their three-year agreement. But even these had been an average of 36 months in the territory and an average of 27 months on the plantations of the H.S.P.A. These figures are a remarkable testimony to the holding power of the plantations—especially when compared with the large mobility shown by Filipinos on the mainland. But they show no tendency to settle. It is chiefly because of his newness that the Filipino is as yet excluded from most of the better industrial opportunities outside the plantations; but already, it is pointed out, he increasingly competes with the members of other racial groups in the less skilled occupations of the building trades—and is more and more getting a footing also in the personal service and the culinary trades. On the plantations themselves, Filipinos are finding their way into mill work. The navy yards, until 1924, when under a special order they discharged 306 Filipino workers as non-citizens, turned out a number of Filipinos who, through taking special courses or otherwise, had prepared themselves for semi-skilled and skilled work as mechanics, machine operators, painters, electricians. There are on the plantations many Filipino firemen some of whom will eventually become locomotive drivers. And some are even now in the carpentry shops.

While theoretically there may be cause for these apprehensions, actually thus far there is little ground for them. Even after marriage with women of other races in Hawaii, contract laborers almost invariably return to the Philippines where Hawaiian, Chinese and Portuguese wives of returned laborers are no longer a novelty. It is true that the motives of second-period contract laborers in returning to their home town are often different from those who have completed their first period. A correspondent describes the difference as follows:

> The laborer returning to Hawaii for a second time is no longer the emissary of the family group. In the first instance, he has returned home to "show off" or to help in selecting the land that is purchased with his savings. Or he may have gone home to assure himself that his money has been properly invested. If he returns to Hawaii it is to complete the project from surplus earnings. Even though on this second trip he may outstay the normal period of four or five years he will eventually return under the operation of the policy of the H.S.P.A. to pay his return passage, whether he has been working lately on a plantation or not. Even before completion of his contract he is returned free if he has become incapacitated for general work in the territory.

Nevertheless, it is pointed out that precisely those Filipinos who have proved themselves least satisfactory or have become somewhat demoralized by city life and irregular employment are those who are most likely to continue their residence in Hawaii and to add to its permanent population. The typical Filipino casual worker in Honolulu does not earn enough (or save enough, which comes to the same thing) to buy his fare to Manila; nor has he the same incentive as the successful worker to return to his family. Another type is the ambitious Tagalog or Visayan who, although he originally came to work on a plantation, has taken advantage of the larger opportunities which Hawaii affords an intelligent and industrious young man. These men are successful in their competition with Chinese and Japanese for those of the more remunerative employments to which public opinion allows non-Caucasians to be admitted. They engage in small businesses or contrive to make a living in semi-professional occupations. While normally Hawaii is but a stepping stone to the mainland for men of this type, many of them become settled, having, at least for the time being, found enough opportunity in Hawaii or enough *joie de vivre* to satisfy them.

In short, two conditions, apart from the almost universal desire of the laborer to return to his family, have held down a large increase in the permanent Filipino population of the territory: the attraction of the mainland and the lack of opportunity in the Philippines themselves.

The optimum situation, from a selfish Hawaiian point of view, it is conceded, would be one in which migration to the mainland is effectively discouraged and in which a steadily progressing development of the Philippine Islands draws back to the homeland those of their young citizens who have undergone the training in agricultural labor and in good citizenship which a period of life and labor on Hawaiian plantations provides. It thus would seem that the Hawaiian stake in Filipino migration, so far from clashing with that of the mainland and that of the Philippine Islands themselves, really coincides with these.

But there are many who do not accept so optimistic a conclusion. They invite attention to the general objections that are raised, in Hawaii as well as on the mainland, to the whole system of plantation labor as at present administered. (See p. 170 *et seq.*) Can we permit, ask those, more particularly, who are influenced by the philosophy of the American labor movement, to keep our whole economic security based upon so precarious a foundation as the constantly renewing stream of imported labor? Has everything possible really been done to make labor conditions on the plantations good enough to attract native-born workers of all races?

The danger for the sugar industry, say those who doubt the "ideal" nature of its present labor policy, and therewith for the welfare of the territory as a whole, lies not in the demands of a new situation but in the possibility of changes too rapid to permit of considered adjustments: A sudden interference with its sources of labor might, indeed, be catastrophic. But new claims upon the resourcefulness of the leaders, upon the flexibility of methods, upon the willingness to face reasonable risks, they expect, will have the same invigorating effect that such claims have always had in the past. And the general tendency which they favor is a gradual transition from plantation methods to those of independent farming, such as has been discussed in an earlier chapter (see p. 178 *et seq.*).

2. POSSIBLE SUBSTITUTES FOR FILIPINO LABOR

Of course, the alternative to a continuation of Filipino immigration is not always stated with such finality. There are those among the sugar and pineapple growers who believe that the immediate and most obvious substitution for Filipino labor, if it were cut off by an exclusion bill or by a declaration of Philippine independence, would be resort to large-scale Porto Rican immigration. This possibility, however, is not anticipated with any enthusiasm. In the first place, Porto Rican labor has not proved very satisfactory in the past. Moreover, being American citizens, the Porto Ricans would exercise the franchise and if coming in large numbers might upset the present balance of political power.[3] Their transportation would be more expensive. Both the Porto Rican and the United States governments would be hostile to such a policy, and all the problems incident to permanent residence of a large immigrant group would be aggravated. In other words, only a sudden, catastrophic interference with Hawaii's present labor supply would, it is generally thought, justify this step—that is a transference of the recruiting machinery of the H.S.P.A. to Porto Rico and re-commencement of methods of aggressive propaganda which have become unnecessary in the Philippines. As one of the largest growers said:

> We should again have to go through the same procedure: The first crowd to come probably would be very poor, then we should learn how to make a better selection. We should still be accused of introducing "cheap labor"; new social problems would be created; and there would be even greater criticism that the system decreases the per capita wealth of the territory.

Others are more optimistic:

[3] Not immediately, for over 80 per cent of Porto Rican emigrants are illiterate and as such denied the ballot in Hawaii.

The Porto Ricans have done fairly well in Hawaii. Their food habits, climatic experience and general habits fit them well for life in the Hawaiian territory. Some of them have prospered here and others have drifted out; but the recruiting has been haphazard, chiefly on the sea board. With a proper system of selection, the Porto Ricans would make good workers.

A Hawaiian sociologist, in contrast, points out that those Porto Ricans who have come to Hawaii and been there for some time have shown little evidence of "picking up":

There are few Porto Rican foremen on the plantations; almost none hold responsible positions in the city of Honolulu; and they have contributed no quota of students to the racially mixed student body of the university. And this is not due to race prejudice. No matter how dark his color, when a man is known as a Porto Rican he can go and be served in the finest barber shop that has a good tourist trade, while a fair mulatto from Alabama would be sent on his way.

3. TEMPORARY ADJUSTMENT

Some who like to look upon the bright side of things express either the firm conviction that the Welsh bill cannot be passed, or if passed held constitutional by the Supreme Court of the United States. The passage of one of the independence bills now before Congress would not necessarily impair Filipino immigration to Hawaii, say others. The view was frequently expressed in the discussion of this topic that the Philippine Islands have so much to gain from the present arrangement of contract labor in Hawaii that they would surely stipulate in any treaty regulating their relations to the United States a continuation of the system. "The Philippines would still need the money their laborers earn and save here," was an expression repeatedly heard. "Development of the waste lands of the Philippine Islands requires just that training which their young men can get here on our plantations," was another.

If any of these bills were passed, said one of the leading planters, the Filipinos now in Hawaii probably would be less eager to return to the Philippine Islands, though of course our contractual obligation as to free return passage must stand. They would realize that they can neither go to the mainland nor return here once they have left. They would know, further, that a rapid return of tens of thousands of Filipino laborers from Hawaii and the mainland would create a surplus of labor in the Philippine Islands of which the planters there would take immediate advantage to lower wages. If, then, a considerable proportion of our present Filipino force decided to stay on, we should perhaps have to devise new means to keep them, but we should not be thrown out of business.

Even with an independence law which would at once make operative the exclusion of Filipinos as "aliens," said a former government official, it is not impossible that future Congresses would be favorable to legislation permitting the introduction of contract labor to Hawaii for limited periods, and with guarantees for their return.

Another proposal to tide over a period of re-adjustment is one made by Vicente Villamin, well known Filipino lawyer and economist in New York, who in July, 1929, suggested that the sugar planters might actively recruit laborers on the Pacific Coast, thus at the same time freeing the mainland from a proportion of its undesired Filipino population and insuring themselves of a new if limited source of labor.[4] He pointed out that many of the Filipinos now on the Pacific Coast already have passed through the experience of plantation labor in Hawaii, and that others have received on the mainland a preliminary training in continuous, disciplined work on the land making for competency and physical fitness.[5] In opposition to this proposal it is stated that probably a large proportion of the Filipinos on the mainland would not be satisfied with the terms of employment and conditions of life which the sugar plantations of Hawaii are able to offer;[6] that many have gone to the mainland precisely because they were dissatisfied with those conditions; and that in the event of passage of the exclusion law, there would be no longer a justification for the present interest of Hawaii to aid in the reduction of the Filipino population on the mainland.

Opinion in Hawaii is divided on the question whether the major objections to the Welsh bill also apply to a substitute bill proposed for the exclusion bill introduced by Senator Samuel M. Shortridge, of California (see p. 307), which exempts Hawaii from the provisions of the exclusion law. A further substitute proposal endeavors to overcome the traditional objection of Hawaii (not shared by many of the larger business concerns) to the attachment of an exemption clause for the territory to Congressional legisla-

[4] This proposal was later embodied by Mr. Villamin in an article published in the *Washington Post* for April 14, 1930. See also editorial comment upon it in the *New York Times* for April 17, 1930.

[5] In an address before the Commonwealth Club of California, on October 2, 1930, Mr. Villamin added: "I made it a point to find out if this can be carried out. I found that if the term of contract of employment is reduced from three to, say, one and a half years for this purpose many will go to Hawaii. For many of them re-employment in Hawaii is the only means of ever returning home."

[6] This was the result of an earlier experiment. See above, p. 206.

tion by making it optional for any state or territory to claim exemption from the operation of the exclusion law.[7]

Quite apart from the doubtful constitutionality of its reference to the eventuality of Philippine independence, this bill is objected to in Hawaii on the ground of its impracticability. It is thought that, no matter how modified to meet its immediate need of Filipino labor, any exclusion law would at best be a sort of suspended sentence for Hawaii, and that eventually the territory would be forced to face a complete change of policy as regards the recruitment of labor for its major industries. The conditions surrounding a special "proclamation" of the territorial need for Filipino labor and its ratification by the President and the appointed official (who *may* grant the demand but is not required to do so) are too precarious to form a safe basis for Hawaii's economic structure.[8]

The same major objection also applies to the Reed bill of December 2, 1930,[9] which exempts Hawaii from the operation of a temporary suspension of Filipino immigration as part of a general measure of immigration suspension for a period of two years.[10]

In summary, then, Hawaiian opinion with few dissenting voices is hostile to any measure which would have the effect of altering the *status quo* as regards Filipino immigration. But at the same time, many minds are already busy planning possible new ways of meeting the territory's need for common labor and possible expedients for safely passing through a, perhaps, prolonged period of re-adjustment. The people generally have full confidence in a political and economic leadership that has proved its ability to weather every storm.[11]

[7] For the issuance of permits to travel to the United States an official shall be designated as provided in paragraph (f) of section 28 of the immigration act of 1924, as amended, *Provided:* That when a governor of a State or Territory by proclamation declares that there is work within his State or Territory for laborers and with the approval of the President, the official designated may also issue permits to travel to laborers not to exceed the number stated in the proclamation, and only to proceed to the State or Territory concerned.

[8] Evidence submitted by Hon. Victor K. Houston, delegate in Congress from the Territory of Hawaii, at the hearing of the House Committee on Immigration and Naturalization on Exclusion of Immigration from the Philippine Islands, May 8, 1930, pp. 240, 243.

[9] S. J. Resolution 207. See p. 37.

[10] Less objectionable, from a Hawaiian point of view, is the proposal adopted by the House Committee on Immigration, on the motion of Congressman Arthur M. Freer, of California, on February 16, 1931, to limit Filipino migration to the mainland for two years to 500 annually. However, by drawing administrative distinctions as between different parts of the United States, this bill faces the same questions of constitutionality as other similar proposals.

[11] For a history of this adaptation of policy to changing conditions see Katharine Coman, The History of Contract Labor in the Hawaiian Islands. Publications of the American Economic Association, vol. IV, No. 3, August, 1903.

CHAPTER XX

ON THE MAINLAND OF THE UNITED STATES

1. THE DEMAND FOR FILIPINO EXCLUSION

As we have seen, a majority of Americans are as yet only vaguely aware of the fact that a large and increasing number of Philippine Islanders have found their way to the mainland of the United States, and that their presence has given rise to apprehension in those western states where most of these newcomers have concentrated. This concentration is, in fact, the main cause of the "problems" which this migration has brought with it. It not only occurs in a region exceptionally sensitive to Oriental immigration but also prevents the rest of the country from having intimate knowledge of the facts. News on any Oriental race problem coming from the Pacific Coast is not accepted at its face value by the country at large; and proposals emanating from that region for dealing with such a problem are suspected to have their source in sectional interests. But in the present instance, the plea for the exclusion of an immigrant group has too wide a basis of support to permit its explanation with the narrow interests of a small group of people. The active campaign in support of this measure is prompted by concern for an American standard of living and for "race purity"—both of them exceedingly vague and unsatisfactory terms, but roughly indicating feelings and desires that are shared by many millions of Americans in every part of the country.[1]

As regards the uses of the press as an instrument of propaganda, experience in connection with Filipino immigration tends to confirm the findings of a study made by Professor Charles N. Reynolds, of Stanford University, of the history of newspaper publicity concerning the Chinese and the Japanese, to the effect that on the whole the treatment of news and the editorial discussion reflect rather than create public opinion.[2]

[1] See p. 35 *et seq.*

[2] Newspaper Treatment of Oriental-White Race Relations. Publications of the American Sociological Society, vol. XXIV, No. 2, May, 1930, p. 152.

The California State Federation of Labor and the California Joint Immigration Committee were instrumental in focusing upon a particular legislative proposal, the Welsh bill for declaring Filipinos "aliens" for purposes of our immigration law, a widely diffused feeling that something should be done.[3] With the aid of the American Coalition,[4] national support was secured for this proposal, taking advantage of the widely prevalent opinion that it is desirable, by successive legislative steps, to restrict immigration to potential citizens and to groups readily assimilable to the country's ethnic make-up and traditions. It has since the war become an axiom accepted by a majority of Americans that the national security lies in the maintenance of the inherited culture complex, subject to gradual modification from within rather than its rapid assimilation to that of other parts of the world. At the same time, organized labor also is deeply interested in the maintenance of this culture complex because it provides security against the encroachment upon its hard-won standards of life and labor from outside groups with much lower standards. It is this sharing of a common interest in the *status quo* of the nation's racial composition—since past intrusions upon it cannot be undone—that is giving the Coalition a strength which few popular movements in America have had in recent times. Thus, without having to count on any special knowledge of the matter on the part of the masses, the Coalition can count on a popular sentiment, in the greater part of the country, entirely favorable to the exclusion especially of those foreign nationalities which are obviously distinct in racial make-up and accustomed to lower standards of living. In addition, it has the support of those economists who believe that the future prosperity of our country depends on a rapid increase in the home market for our products—that is, not only an increased consuming power in the sense of a wider diffusion of the national income, but also an increased volume and variety of needs on the part of the citizenry. The introduction of large numbers of immigrants with low standards of consumption, they hold, instead of adding to the relative importance of the home market, on the contrary adds to the present disparity between consumption and production by depressing the consuming power of those with whom they compete for employment.[5]

[3] See p. 34.

[4] See p. 34.

[5] Considerations of this sort are, of course, largely theoretical or concerned with future possibilities so far as Filipino immigration is concerned. The differential in

The economic motive is also associated, as we have seen, with a growing, though often pseudo-scientific, appreciation for eugenic factors in national well-being. While this view is not accepted without important reservations by biologists and anthropologists, the popular view today is that the failures and strains of assimilation outweigh the advantages of diversity in the racial make-up of the population.[6] It is increasingly realized that relative racial values of superiority and inferiority cannot be established in the abstract but only in relation to actual tasks of adjustment to environment. It is argued, therefore, that while our state of culture and of civilization may not be superior to others, it requires for its perpetuation and development the qualities most likely to be possessed by the descendants of those who have created that state. And this line of thought naturally leads to the further conclusion that, next to those born on American soil with American parentage, those groups will best fit into the general composition that have in the past most substantially contributed toward it. Hence, a strenuous opposition to immigration from sources that have not figured largely in the past.

It would be difficult to say whether the totality of the impetus derived from non-economic motives equals the force of simple resentment against a new source of labor competition. Referring to the question of the Filipino's alleged inability to assimilate (p. 36), the chief spokesman of organized labor in California writes:

> So far as the organized workers are concerned, it does not make the slightest difference whether biology or culture is involved,—we are against the Filipinos and want them excluded. If there are to be any experiments we trust they will be in some other countries.

Nevertheless, even the motives of organized labor in favor of Filipino exclusion are not purely economic. Time and again, its published statements deal with the social consequences of the influx of Filipinos in white communities; and declarations are made to the effect that white workers will quit the job if forced to associate with Filipinos, even though these may receive equal pay.

These are some of the larger underlying attitudes that have reacted favorably toward the proposal for Filipino exclusion, once it was made. With a vague notion that a new Oriental invasion

the consuming power of Filipino workers now on the mainland of the United States is insignificant in comparison, for example, with the millions spent by American tourists in Europe.

[6] See p. 35.

must be stopped, the specific proposal arose ostensibly from considerations of those material problems created by the Filipino's presence in large number which have been discussed in the second section of this report. Two subjects of primary concern, more particularly, may be said to have inspired it, competition for work and disapproval of the Filipinos' social pretensions. It so happened that two events—the epidemic of spinal meningitis in the spring of 1929 (p. 100 *et seq.*), and the series of clashes between Filipinos and native Americans in the early months of 1930 (p. 13 *et seq.*)—provided further effective campaign material and, indeed, as handled by the press, became occasions for pressing the proposal.

The economic argument is particularly strong, of course, in favor of including immigration from the Philippine Islands in any emergency measure designed to suspend immigration during the severe industrial depression through which the country is passing at the time of writing. There is felt to be a particular danger of a large increase of immigration from countries not subject to the quota restrictions of the general immigration law if the quotas are temporarily suspended. Hence the inclusion of a section expressly declaring as aliens for the purposes of such suspension act the citizens of islands under the jurisdiction of the United States who are not citizens of the United States.[7]

The major lines of argument, then, are realistic and deal with actual experience, however much embellished by exaggeration. But behind them there are theoretical arguments which, perhaps, express even more fully the strength of the existing feeling. Most powerful among these is the appeal to historical memory. Almost every important speech or paper in the exclusion campaign contains references to earlier phases of America's effort to keep out the "teeming hordes" of Orientals, anxious to improve their fortunes by coming over to the American continent. Not only that, but memories are revived of interests in our own country which are entirely favorable to such an influx. The curious thing is that, while it is not possible to quote a single important pronouncement of either American capital or of American shipping in favor of a large Filipino immigration, the memory of their past influence in this direction survives. Unquestionably, some groups of American employers would benefit from the introduction of Filipino labor in even larger volume than has taken place hitherto; but so

[7] S. J. Resolution 207, 71st Congress, third session, December 2, 1930. See p. 297.

far they have been very quiet. More doubtful, in view of the enormous expansion of traffic on the Pacific Ocean in recent years, is the question whether American shipping companies have a strong interest in filling with Filipino emigrants steerage quarters which often can be converted to other uses. A statement made on their behalf in opposition to the exclusion bill based the case entirely on their need for Filipino seamen and did not mention passenger traffic.[8]

In addition to the attitudes and arguments that have briefly been indicated, there are two other sources of opinion favorable to exclusion which have only developed since the campaign began. One is the willingness of certain employers of agricultural and common labor who are unable to make an effective direct case for a liberal immigration policy, to jettison some of the cargo of their unpopular barge of cheap labor to save the rest: Thus we find no more forceful advocacy of Filipino exclusion than that of the Agricultural Department of the California State Chamber of Commerce which is fighting for the retention of Mexican immigration, now menaced by legislative proposals before Congress. Not the vegetable ranchers and fruit growers who actually employ Filipinos in considerable numbers, but those corporations, including the railroads, which feel themselves primarily in need of Mexican labor are dictating this strategy.

The *Detroit Free Press* in an editorial article (February 1, 1930) comments:

> The *Los Angeles Times* insists that the influx of Filipino laborers into the state was caused by economic pressure. "They came in to fill the vacuum resulting from decreased Mexican immigration." . . . The *Fresno Republican* takes a little different view. It remarks acidly, "If we find men in large numbers attacking the Filipino residents, we cannot acquit the protagonists of Mexican labor from a share in this responsibility. For, during the last two or three years at least, the Filipino has been made the whipping boy for the Mexicans." And, elaborating, the *Republican* continues: "Whenever some political or labor leader would propose to enact laws to restrict Mexican immigration, at once there has arisen the shout, 'Filipinos are worse.' "
>
> The comments indicate rather conclusively that there is a scarcity of a necessary sort of labor in southern California and, we presume, in other border states also; and that for some reason or another, the native inhabitants of

[8] Hearings before the House Committee on Immigration and Naturalization on H.R. 8708, statement of James H. Mac Lafferty, vice-president of the Pacific American Steamship Association and Shipowners Association of the Pacific Coast, May 7, 1930, p. 171.

those parts prefer to have Mexicans rather than Filipinos meet the want. Probably there are a number of causes for this preference [which the article proceeds to enumerate along familiar lines].

Another large secondary support for Filipino exclusion comes, as we have seen, from circles favorable to the political independence of the Philippine Islands. They are convinced that the passage of that measure would greatly strengthen the case for severance of the political tie that binds the island nation to the United States. We only note in passing this political issue in so far as it bears upon our immediate subject of immigration.

Reversely, some independent voices in the all but unanimous sentiment on Filipino exclusion on the Pacific Coast are expressing alarm over this, largely unforeseen, consequence of the campaign. They feel that the political issue is too large to be decided as a by-product of domestic policy in the matter of immigration. They wish to see the Filipino excluded; but since the campaign got under way, owing to this change in the situation, have shown a strong inclination to desire it to occur, not as a drastic measure of separate legislation, but rather as the automatic outcome of a considered method of establishing self-government in the Philippines.[9] It is to be noted that this point of view, while the campaign for the exclusion bill proceeds with undiminished vigor, also has somewhat changed the emphasis of Labor's case. In earlier resolutions, expressions of sympathy for the national aspirations of the Filipinos were tacked on to strong declarations in favor of exclusion, sincere enough, no doubt, but primarily, it would seem, to sweeten the pill, with no expectation that so fundamental a change in the political status of the Islands could soon be materialized. More lately, a demand for Philippine independence has moved into the foreground of Labor's case.

Lastly, no large political movement ever achieves success except in so far as it carries with it a public opinion built up on sentiments that have little relation to the actual case. A single experience which shows a Filipino in an unfavorable light, or no experience at all but merely the residue of much rumor, suffices to induce the average citizen to endorse measures of vast consequence. A trusted leader, an appeal to patriotism, a general xenophobia suffice to secure thousands of adherents to a cause the full consequences of which they do not realize. This is an inevitable by-product of

[9] See, for example, the report of a special Committee of Five of the Commonwealth Club of California, October 14, 1930.

any legislative campaign even when the leaders conscientiously endeavor to promote an intelligent interest in what they conceive to be its rational basis.

2. AGAINST EXCLUSION

The negative side in a national controversy is usually not so strong as the positive one. In the present case, opinion hostile to the proposed exclusion law is diffuse, unorganized, largely unvocal. It may briefly be divided into three categories: the feeling that the object of the proposal is against the national interest, the feeling that it can better be attained by other means, and opposition to it on grounds of personal or group interest. But larger and more influential than any of these three motivating factors is doubt whether the proposal does not go too far. While convinced that some control and restriction of Filipino immigration may be desirable, some—especially among those schooled in political action—believe that the proposal to eliminate it altogether is too extreme to be statesmanlike in an age of compromise and mutual accommodation between opposing interests.

The main political argument against exclusion was presented by Brig.-General F. LeJ. Parker, Chief of the Bureau of Insular Affairs, at a hearing held in Washington on April 11, 1930. He emphasized that 25,000 Filipinos had during the World War volunteered to serve in the armed forces of the United States, thus giving evidence of their wholehearted loyalty. To spurn this allegiance, after it had been nurtured for thirty years, for the sake of a minor domestic difficulty in one part of the United States, he represented as a matter requiring the most careful consideration. The proposal to exclude the Filipinos after they had been advised during this long period to come here to study our institutions was a complete reversal of policy which could be justified only by the gravest emergency.[10]

At the same hearing it came out that, as subjects of the United States, the Filipinos travel to other countries with American passports. A law declaring them "aliens" (if held constitutional), therefore, might have the effect of depriving them of that privilege and make them practically a people without a country in their personal contacts with the rest of the world.

[10] Hearings on the Exclusion of Immigration from the Philippine Islands before the House Committee on Immigration and Naturalization, 1930, pp. 88-89.

We have not fulfilled our national obligation to the Philippines by helping them establish a stable and progressive government, says a California employer of Filipinos. One of the largest contributions we are making to that end is the opportunity we are giving them of coming here and learning American methods. Permitting college students alone to come here would not do this. The training these boys are getting on our ranches is exactly what their country needs to develop its own resources.

Similarly, an industrial employer of Filipinos considers their continued immigration—upon which he looks as temporary, not for permanent settlement—as an important item in their education. Young Filipinos, he said, should have an opportunity of seeing the world, especially of observing American conditions of life.

A California scientist who has lived for many years in the Philippine Islands is strongly opposed to exclusion on the same grounds. Moreover, he considers the Filipinos more assimilable than other groups that have come in large numbers to the Pacific Coast, and a desirable addition to the stock.

Another California scholar who has lived for long in the Philippine Islands is opposed to exclusion mainly on the ground of the effect of such a measure on the social and political attitudes in the Philippine Islands themselves. He believes that an agreement on measures to be taken by the Philippine government itself could be reached which would have almost the effect of exclusion without the very undesirable by-product of a national affront.

A Catholic official, close to Filipinos in this country, is emphatically opposed to exclusion: the Filipinos, he says, have not proven a detriment; they would be a benefit to our labor situation if they were trained instead of being neglected. We need them, he says, and they need us.

Generally speaking, one may say that the strength of the sentiment for exclusion decreases in proportion to the degree of personal knowledge of Filipinos possessed by informants. Personal sympathies are liable to outbalance impersonal considerations for the more distant demands of the social welfare. This does not mean that all those who know the Filipino well are opposed to his exclusion. But they are less certain about the matter. It seemed significant, for example, that local labor officials interviewed had a somewhat different attitude from that of two state officials seen. While they were entirely favorable to the resolutions in favor of the Welsh bill adopted at local, state and national conventions, they were less bitter in their denunciations of the Filipino as a worker and as a man and, in several cases, deplored the tone of enmity that had developed in the course of the campaign. They are perturbed by the gradual encroachment of the Filipino upon the preserves of organized labor, but they are also conscious of an injustice done to him by the harassing experiences to which he is subjected and by the uncertainty of his status as a "national" who yet cannot be treated like a citizen or a man eligible to citizenship. As has already been explained, one element in this situation is the frequently expressed willingness of Filipino workers in the culinary trades and in industry to join the union if they were permitted to do so.

The same relation of degree of personal acquaintance to attitudes toward exclusion was observed among religious and social workers. Those most emphatic in their denunciation of the Filipino's social menace usually were men and women who had had almost no personal contacts with him. Others were more doubtful, and more inclined to advocate measures of restriction rather than of complete exclusion.

Of course, the largest single group of opponents to exclusion are employers whose experience with Filipino workers has not been unsatisfactory; but, as has been stated, they are not organized to make their attitude known. They are conscious of the weakness of their case in that it is necessarily selfish. Among these employers one may, perhaps, make a further distinction between those who prefer Filipinos to other immigrant workers—that is, usually, Mexicans—and those who have become afraid that passage of the Harris Bill (formerly the Box Bill) now before Congress will deprive them of Mexican labor so that they must turn to another racial group for common labor. In either case, employers state emphatically that cheapness of labor is not the underlying motive. Rather they take it for granted that American workers will not do the type of labor now performed by foreigners. As this matter has been previously discussed, we need not here examine the justification for that view, but merely state it as an important cause of opposition to Filipino exclusion.

There are further those who oppose the Welsh bill because they feel convinced that it will be held unconstitutional by the Supreme Court of the United States. They fear that its passage will have an unsettling effect upon labor conditions and upon the relations of the United States with the Philippines, and with the Orient generally, without accomplishing any practical result. This attitude is not widespread but was found among some who had closely studied the whole situation and who, on other grounds, were equally divided in their views as to the desirability or undesirability of Filipino immigration.[11]

In summary, then, it will be seen that, on the Pacific Coast at any rate, attitudes opposed to Filipino exclusion are neither so widely diffused nor so deeply centered in a larger social outlook as are the attitudes in favor of it. Movements of aggressive hostility develop and organize themselves more quickly than movements of protection and defense on behalf of the group under attack.[12] This is also reflected in the fact that the California state legislature has adopted a resolution favoring the passage of the Welsh bill, and that there was no organized opposition to that action. In the country generally, the trend in recent years has been entirely in the direction of restriction. The argument that weighs most heavily with those who have no intimate knowledge of the part played by Filipinos in economic and social affairs is that the country has definitely set itself against an unlimited influx of immigrants from Europe, and that therefore it is illogical to permit Mexicans and Filipinos to come to the United States in unlimited numbers. Only a very small minority today are opposed to the restrictive policy inaugurated with the quota law. The more liberal groups familiar with all the aspects of the subject stand behind various proposals for amending the existing law with a view to the avoidance of hardships which it has created—more particularly the disruption of families—but there is little demand for a repeal of our restrictive law.

Perhaps one ought to mention also as a separate attitude one which has been growing since the war and which exists both among those who do and those who do not favor further restrictions of immigration: namely, that all changes in legislation affecting foreign migration should be regarded as in the realm of foreign rather than of domestic policy. They feel that often unnecessary friction develops around such legislation which could be avoided if all inter-

[11] Partly owing to the doubtful constitutionality of the Welsh bill (sponsored in the Senate by Senator Hiram W. Johnson, of California), Senator S. M. Shortridge, of California, on April 14, 1930, introduced a new bill, S. 4183, to the effect "that from and after July 1, 1930, migration of citizens of the Philippine Islands to continental United States shall be limited to students, visitors for business or pleasure, merchants, government officials, their families, attendants, servants and employees." It further stipulates that "this Act shall be in force and effect for five years from and after the date of its approval, and if within that time the independence of the Philippines shall have been granted or by Act of Congress definitely provided for, then this Act shall continue in force indefinitely thereafter." The constitutionality of this proposal likewise is open to question.

[12] R. D. McKenzie, Oriental Exclusion; University of Chicago Press, 1928, pp. 177-178.

ested parties were consulted in advance and if an effort were made so far as possible to combine the separate interests in the matter of the countries concerned in a joint program—whether realized through treaty or through separate national legislation.[13] This point of view is gaining ground more especially among those who realize that often not only the sending and the receiving country have an interest in interferences with the flow of population between them but other countries also. In the present case, for example, not only the Philippines and the United States are concerned but also those Asiatic countries with considerable population pressure which look upon the Philippine Islands as a possible future outlet for their own population surplus. Moreover, Great Britain and the Netherlands are vitally interested in the status of the Philippines in its political relations with the United States as affecting movements for independence among their own subject peoples in the western Pacific. However, it cannot be said that attitudes and points of view such as these play as yet a very important part in the popular opinion of the United States as it expresses itself in the press and on the platform.

More prevalent is a negative attitude toward the exclusion proposal simply on the grounds that it emanates from the Pacific Coast. Many people in other parts of the country feel that in the matter of Japanese exclusion Congress was stampeded into a form of action which was not the most desirable, all things considered, no matter how strong the case for restricting immigration from Japan may have been. They have become afraid that hasty action might repeat that mistake. Not in principle opposed to the restriction of Mexican and Filipino immigration, they are alarmed that once more such a purpose may be accomplished with a maximum of international friction by a choice of means offensive to the dignity of friendly nations. They are asking for more time so that possible counter-proposals may have a chance to mature.

3. IN FAVOR OF RESTRICTION

None of the counter-proposals heard in connection with the present inquiry had behind them the earnestness of conviction,

[13] Thus a high government official in an interview suggested that the countries in the Western Hemisphere if consulted on the probable effects of the quota law on the migration of their citizens to the United States—inimical to their own interests—probably would have requested inclusion under the provisions of that law whereas efforts now made to extend the quota law to include them are resented as an unfavorable reflection upon the racial qualities of their citizens.

the vigor of statement or the volume of argument found in the movement for exclusion. And that is but natural; for they were espoused by individuals rather than by groups, and were made without that passion which arises from the recognition of a menace. They represent rather the reactions of people accustomed to discriminate between different degrees of urgency and to anticipate possible undesired by-products of measures which may be plausible enough as effective answers to the primary problem. In such circles—both on the Pacific Coast and in the East—an inclination was found to consider possible methods of restriction and control less sweeping than total exclusion, such as is contemplated under the terms of the Welsh bill; an inclination also to consider the relative effectiveness of action by the United States Congress and of such action as the Philippine legislature might perhaps be persuaded to take. It is not the purpose of the reporter here to set forth in systematic arrangement a set of proposals which possibly might be mistaken for recommendations of his own, but rather to present some of the opinions he found to exist among persons who recognize the problems created by Filipino immigration but hesitate to support the demand for its complete suppression.

a. *New Forms of Student Exemption.*

First, there are those who, as already intimated, consider a continuation of Filipino student migration to the mainland of the United States as entirely desirable and to be encouraged. While, with the Welsh bill, declaring Filipinos aliens, students would still be permitted to come to this country, the present legislative provisions that exempt students from the operations of the quota law are such that in practice the great majority of Filipino students would be eliminated.[14] For, as we have seen, the possibility of self-support is precisely what draws a majority of them here instead of attending the colleges and universities in their own country. Moreover, as we have seen, the proportion of time required to earn enough money for self-support during college attendance in the United States is much greater in their case than in that of American students because of their greater difficulty in securing remunerative jobs. On the other hand, even the present provisions for student exemption are regarded as too liberal by many, especially

[14] Sections 4 (e) and 15 of the Immigration Law of 1924 provide for a rigorous system of reporting to insure that aliens admitted for study are actually in attendance at an accredited school, college, academy, seminary, or university. The Secretary of Labor is obliged to deport those admitted as students who fail to maintain this status.

those watchful for the interests of organized labor, who fear that college attendance too easily becomes a mere excuse for a wage-earning activity on the part of foreigners. This difficulty might be overcome, it has been suggested, by the issue of a special student passport with a definite if generous time limit, placing persons in possession of it under rigid control as regards their wage-earning activities by making these directly subject to supervision by a board composed in part of educational counsellors and in part of representatives of the United States Department of Labor. Another suggestion made was to the effect that persons with a student passport shall be liable to deportation unless during the whole of their residence they are enrolled in a recognized educational institution; that is, that all their wage-earning activities must be subject to the control and under the supervision of the institution. It has also been suggested that the Philippine government might appoint a student counsellor, with considerable powers as regards revocation of the passport, to work in cooperation with such a board.

Another suggestion, made independently by some of those interviewed, both Americans and Filipinos, is that there should be a minimum age requirement in order to assure a more responsible attitude of the immigrant student-worker and a larger prospect for his success, as well as the probability of better educational preparation before coming here. Some would make graduation from a high school in the Philippine Islands a prerequisite of obtaining a student passport.

Differences of opinion arise when the time required for the most advantageous period of study in the United States comes up for discussion. Not only on financial grounds but also on those of a rounded practical experience of American life and labor, some feel that the permissible period for work should equal that required for a college course of four years. It is also thought by some that, even with a high-school certificate, many Filipino students require more time than American students to complete the regular studies; and furthermore, there are those who stress the values of graduate-studies. On the other hand, it is believed that a definite limitation of the total period permitted for study would act as a special stimulus, would keep out or eliminate those who are not serious students, and thereby make the standing of the Filipino student a much higher one than if an additional temptation were provided for all and sundry to enroll in educational institutions because other opportunities of coming to this country are taken away. There would probably be a consensus of opinion among those educators and Filipinos who have given thought to the matter that there must be a definite limitation of the number of years covered by a student passport but that some board or bureau should have power to authorize an extension of time in individual cases where a premature closing of the career of study might be held undesirable or productive of particular hardship (as in the case of illness, for example).

More influential than any of these suggestions is one sponsored by the Institute of International Education to the effect that all undergraduate study by Filipinos at American colleges should so far as possible be eliminated. In a recent letter to college presidents, previously quoted, Dr. Stephen P. Duggan explains this proposal as follows:

> My suggestion is that Filipino students be treated like foreign students from all over the world. Under our immigration laws a foreign student will not be admitted to an American institution until he has forwarded his credentials to that institution and received, under its seal, a statement to the effect that he will be matriculated if he comes to the United States. Because the Philippines are under the sovereignty of the United States, the Immigration authorities cannot apply this law to Filipino students; but there is no reason why the colleges and universities themselves should not apply such a regulation. If it were to become known throughout the Philippines that the best colleges and universities of the United States would receive Filipino students only under these conditions, I am confident that, while the large flow of students would not cease, it would be materially diminished.

Individual western universities are known to be favorable to such action which, however, must be taken jointly, at least by the more important of them, to become effective. The report of the Educational Survey Commission [15] confirms them in the belief that there are adequate facilities in the Philippine Islands for undergraduate study, or at least that such facilities could shortly be so improved as to give a sufficient grounding for every kind of professional training.

In contrast with these various suggestions, there are also current proposals for widening rather than restricting the basis upon which the status of students may be recognized among immigrants.

[15] Philippine Islands Department of Public Instruction, 1925.

It is felt in some circles that the concept of student exemption in our immigration law should be so liberalized as to make possible a more varied educational experience of foreigners in the United States. More specifically in relation to the possible passage of a Filipino exclusion law, it is urged that such practical training in agricultural and mechanical trades as a period of residence in the United States affords is more needful to the development of the Philippine Islands than graduate studies in law and education. Thus it was suggested by an American employer of Filipino rural labor and approved in discussion by a group of Filipino contractors that the educational opportunities provided by American ranch labor might be systematized and enhanced. With the present tendency in the San Joaquin and Salinas Valleys to concentrate the housing of Filipino workers in larger camps from where they can be sent out to work within a considerable area from their home, it would be possible, they thought, to provide educational and recreational features of a kind not provided in the past. The employer just named expressed the hope that the State of California would eventually provide a type of short course in agriculture particularly designed to meet the needs of these young Filipinos whose desire to learn is undisputed. He suggested that Filipino workers in agriculture also might be admitted under some kind of student passport providing, not for college attendance, but for attendance of farm courses given by a recognized institution—presumably a state institution—in direct conjunction with the practical remunerative work in those regions where Filipinos have won the favor of agricultural employers. The difficulty with this proposal, said other employers with whom it was discussed, is that the work on the ranches is strictly seasonal for the great majority of those employed. The school would have to be itinerant, and a method of long-time advance planning for the employment of each group would be required, which is contrary to the present practice of employers. However, if the Pacific Coast were really faced with a shortage of labor, some of them thought, it might not be impossible that some agricultural employers' association might be willing to enter into an arrangement under which permanent employment for the greater part of the year, at least, might be insured in advance; that is, if eight or nine months of work were planned for in advance, the remaining four or three months could be given exclusively to study—thus still making possible earnings sufficient to pay for the round trip from and to the Philippines.

b. *Selective Measures.*

Opposition to exclusion in many cases was accompanied by suggestions for forms of restriction which would reduce the proportion of "undesirables" and of those likely to create difficulty. Usually, it is true, these suggestions are very vague. There was considerable feeling, for example, that wholesale exclusion was too extreme a step to take if the aim was to prevent the introduction of infectious diseases. In one way or another, it was held, the regulations now enforced by the federal government could be strengthened; a period of quarantine might even be insisted upon if this were held to be necessary; and the Philippine government itself might, by insisting upon a more rigid health examination before issuance of a passport, insure a first elimination of the unfit. In this connection the system operating in connection with the migration of Filipino workers to Hawaii was frequently mentioned as a model which it might be possible to follow, at least in its less costly features. It was thought that some system, throwing the cost of such a close medical inspection upon the immigrant, would have an effect also on the reduction of numbers.

Re-introduction of a passport system was widely held to be essential to any regulation of Filipino migration, as much in the interest of the Philippines themselves as of the receiving country. A passport fee, of course, would further have a deterrent effect and reduce numbers.

Some Filipinos in the United States thought there ought to be an upper as well as a lower age limit, because the older Filipino emigrant finds it more difficult to adapt himself to new conditions. The general feeling, both among Filipinos and Americans, seemed to be that students should not be admitted under the age of eighteen, and others—if such a separation were possible—preferably not under the age of twenty, chiefly because the strain of the type of work obtained by Filipinos here is too heavy for those who have had no or little previous experience of hard work. There was, however, also some testimony to the contrary on this point, namely, that between the ages of eighteen and thirty the employer has no special preference.

Another suggestion repeatedly heard was for the introduction of a literacy requirement for emigrants on the part of the Philippine government—chiefly because of the greater difficulty of entirely unlettered immigrants to adapt themselves to the conditions they find and their greater liability to become the dupes of all sorts of exploiters.

4. OTHER FORMS OF CONTROL

a. *Information and Advice.*

The lack of any system of accurate information on conditions in the United States, work opportunities, wages, costs of living and of travel, and the like, frequently was mentioned as a cause of much evil. Both interested Americans and Filipino leaders hoped for the eventual establishment of a strong, inclusive organization which would effectively pursue activities in this direction which are now too limited in scope and operation. More widely prevalent is a desire for the establishment of official channels of information and advice. This takes the form, on the one hand, of the suggestion for the establishment of an American bureau of information in Manila, to which all desirous of coming to this country could be referred for every type of useful information, and, on the other, the appointment of a Philippine labor commissioner for the Pacific Coast, with functions similar to those exercised by the labor commissioner in Honolulu. (See p. 286.) The Filipino emigrant to the United States does not even at the main ports of arrival have a representative of his country to turn to when in difficulty and, especially with the vagueness of his status under federal and state laws—in the matter of marriage, for example—is liable to get into trouble that is avoidable if he can have recourse to a trusted counsellor.[16]

b. *Organization of Employment.*

One attitude frequently found was that American employers on the mainland themselves are to be blamed if they find Filipino

[16] It is sometimes pointed out that, with Filipino Resident Commissioners in Washington, D. C., who in the past have maintained very close and sympathetic relations with the Bureau of Insular Affairs, a citizen of the Philippine Islands on the mainland of the United States is no worse off than the citizen of any state who resides in another state. This argument would seem to disregard the special difficulties of persons speaking a foreign language, and with a cultural and social background very different from that of their new environment. On the other hand, those who urge the appointment of a Filipino labor commissioner on the Pacific Coast may not be aware of the large extent to which the Bureau of Insular Affairs aids in adjusting the affairs of individual resident Filipinos or of the effectiveness of its friendly efforts, due to its prestige as a Federal Bureau, compared with the results of intervention by the agencies of foreign governments. The further difficulty has been mentioned that a special officer of the Philippine government on the Pacific Coast, by becoming a focus of attention in pending political issues, may not be best able to secure for the resident Filipinos a more sympathetic interest on the part of employers, public authorities, and American citizens generally.

workers undesirable because of their failure to use even elementary methods of selection and control. Their lack of system in the employment and management of immigrant workers is held up against the system established by the Hawaiian sugar planters; and the view is expressed that, with more cooperation, not only the employers in a given industry or branch of agriculture or of a given region, but the employers of seasonal labor for the whole of the Southwest or for the whole of the Pacific Coast could secure for themselves a much more satisfactory and reliable labor supply, at the same time discouraging those who, because of incapacity or unwillingness to apply themselves, can manage to eke out a living only in an unorganized scramble for work. Others point to the difficulties which any large-scale cooperation with the aim of stabilizing labor would involve with the actual climatic conditions that obtain and consider these difficulties practically insuperable. There is, therefore, a demand for state regulation of a kind which would exercise a stronger control over the movements of itinerant workers, native and immigrant. No very definite proposals of this kind have come to the attention of the present investigator; and those most forcible in the denunciation of the present state of disorder, as regards the market for seasonal labor, usually were unable to formulate any possible method of overcoming it.

c. *Discouragement of Migration.*

Many of the informants held that not legislative restriction but effective counter-methods of information are needed to reduce the influx of Filipinos to more "natural" dimensions. In addition to those methods of spreading knowledge of actual conditions as have already been named, they suggested a stricter control of steamship advertising and of recruiting by contractors—though both, as we have seen, do not at present play the important parts they once played as causative factors.

A new suggestion came up early in the investigation and was subsequently often discussed with others: In so far as the largest impetus to migration to the United States was given by the return of emigrants who have been successful, either financially or in winning coveted college degrees, why not balance the too favorable picture of conditions in the United States thus disseminated by accelerating the return of emigrants who have been less successful? As individuals, many of these migrants find it difficult to confess their failure to "make good," and, at the price of much unhappiness, refuse to face the criticism of their families and friends. But if a general movement were instituted in which the individual return were part of a concerted plan, many of them, perhaps many thousands, would be willing not only to go but to save money for their return passage. It was suggested, therefore, that simultaneously with the operation of a new and more effective plan of land development, including attractive features of free transportation, credit facilities, etc., the Philippine government should issue a call to Filipino emigrants in the United States to come home and help carry out the project—at the same time offering as a special inducement a contribution toward the return passage to which—with a large-scale passenger movement in months during which it is most convenient to handle it—it is believed the steamship company would willingly add a further reduction of fare, thus making possible a really substantial saving.[17] Suggestions of this sort are particularly favored by those who are opposed to the exclusion bill because of the political effects expected from its passage. They believe that some such process as has been indicated would practically rid the United States of that part of its Filipino population which most gives substance to the demand for exclusion. Not only that, but it would demonstrate the good faith of the many declarations of Filipino immigrants generally that they are here temporarily and not to settle and fuse with the native population.

5. ADJUSTMENT AND AID

There are those who consider the chief cause of Filipino maladjustment, and the chief cause of the agitation against his presence, to lie in the failure of American institutions to facilitate his adaptation to American conditions. They prefer administrative and voluntary methods to legislative ones, and feel that the judgment of the value of Filipino immigration is premature until steps have been taken to protect it against avoidable causes of becoming a

[17] It is computed that at a cost of about $200,000 the Philippine government could thus secure the return of 10,000 nationals now on the mainland of the United States under conditions favorable to the inception of a new colonization scheme. Assuming willingness of the steamship company, with a minimum guarantee of fares by the government, to reduce its fare from San Francisco to Manila from $87.50 to $62.50, and willingness of the government to subsidize the movement to the extent of 10,000 contributions of $20 each, the remaining fare for the returning emigrant, of $42.50, would be less than one-half of the regular fare—a reduction so substantial as to produce an effective stimulus. Almost every Filipino emigrant, it is argued, can, without aid from home, save that amount in a few weeks' or a few months' time if he is willing to make the effort.

source of social and economic difficulty. They look to the educational institutions themselves, and to religious and social agencies, as primarily possessed of the resources for making the Filipino's adjustment more complete and satisfactory. In addition to many minor measures which were advanced by educators, religious and social workers, and public officials as locally desirable, the feeling was repeatedly expressed that a more deliberate study of the Filipino's needs in the fields of health, of recreation, of vocational and educational guidance, and of housing would overcome most of the unfortunate conditions that have arisen. Some of these informants also believe that, in time, a better understanding of the Filipino by his American neighbors, which can be fostered with appropriate educational means, would overcome much of the present adverse attitude toward him.[18] In any case, even with the passage of the exclusion law, they argued, there would probably remain in this country for some time to come several tens of thousands of Filipinos; and it was necessary to inaugurate immediately those services and forms of friendly interest which would help to make the continuing contacts between Filipinos and Americans conducive to a happier relationship while, at the same time, preventing maladjustment and failure on the part of the immigrants.[19]

6. IN FAVOR OF FURTHER CONSIDERATION

Frequently, opposition to the exclusion bill is, as we have seen, inspired by a desire to have that proposed measure studied in all its aspects and relationships to different fields of policy before approving it. This attitude is finding a more positive expression in various proposals for further study, or for more inclusive considerations, with due recognition of all the interests at stake.

An expression of this viewpoint is the resolution introduced in Congress by Senator Hiram Bingham of Connecticut on January

[18] In this connection, special attention may be drawn to the efforts of the Junior Red Cross and of the Federal Council of Churches' Commission on International Goodwill to promote friendship between American and Filipino children through the exchange of letters and gifts, and to the educational work of mission societies which increasingly stresses commendable qualities rather than need. As illustrations of this newer approach in missionary education see two books sponsored by the Missionary Education Movement: Frank C. Laubach, Seven Thousand Emeralds, and Jean Moore Cavell, Filipino Playmates. Friendship Press, 1929.

[19] There has recently been formed, with offices in San Francisco, a Pacific Coast Philippine Commission, for the purpose of reinforcing other institutions and organizations in watching over the welfare of Filipinos on the mainland of the United States, and, more particularly, to "encourage Filipinos in America to be law-abiding, honest, trustworthy, industrious and frugal."

6, 1930 (S. J. Resolution 113), primarily aiming at a delay of action upon either of the two Philippine independence proposals before Congress: a resolution introduced by Senator William H. King of Utah, providing for complete independence of the Philippines (S. 3108, January 13, 1930[20]), and the bill introduced by Senator A. H. Vandenburg of Michigan, looking toward a more gradual accomplishment of that purpose.[21] This resolution provides for a joint commission of Americans and Filipinos to meet in Manila to consider the Philippine problem—that is, primarily the problem of the Islands' political relations to the United States —in all its bearings. This resolution received considerable support in the public press, as providing an opportunity to review all the possible consequences that would arise from the passage of either of the independence bills. It is also occasionally quoted as a desirable preliminary to exclusion legislation.

A less elaborate procedure, bearing more directly upon the subject of Filipino immigration, proposed in an article by Professor Emory S. Bogardus, of the University of Southern California, was repeatedly mentioned in connection with the present study as worth following up:

> The present situation represents two extreme positions. On one hand the Filipino is admitted freely to our country; on the other hand, his opponents would exclude him entirely. Both positions are subject to serious criticism. Unlimited immigration needs definite modification, but it is unnecessary to go to the opposite pole. . . .
>
> To work out a just procedure includes the consideration of our labor standards and at the same time the feelings and good will of a rapidly developing people living under our own jurisdiction. The establishment of a special Federal Commission with adequate representation given to the Filipinos, is a natural first step. Careful inquiry, under the direction of a duly accredited body, into the immigration situation could give the data which are needed as a basis for solving the problem. In the meantime, there is need that temporary

[20] Substitute for S. 2500, introduced December 9, 1929, and S. 204, introduced April 18, 1929. Similar bills were introduced in the House by Congressmen Dyer and Knutson—H.R. 5652 and 5182.

[21] S. 3379, January 31, 1930. The bill provides for independence at the end of ten years, a period to be used for a gradual shifting of responsibility to the Philippine government and the adjustment of the economic situation to the American tariff. A similar bill was introduced on March 5, 1930, by Senators Hawes of Michigan and Cutting of New Mexico—S. 3822—authorizing a Philippine constitutional convention to draft a constitution for an independent government and giving the United States government the right of interference for a transitional period of five years. For fuller information on these various proposals and a survey of the problems of Philippine independence, see a special number of the Foreign Policy Association *Information Service,* April 30, 1930, vol. VI, Nos. 3-4.

limitations be instituted by the Governor-General of the Philippines which will be satisfactory to both Filipinos and Americans. Admission of Filipinos under definite control with reference to their personal standing and racial status, and to our social and economic situations, would seem to be a reasonable standard to adopt until a better procedure could be developed.[22]

Still others would prefer to see immediately brought into operation unofficial conferences, free from hampering associations, for a simultaneous study in the United States and in the Philippines of all the points of difficulty involved in exclusion or in any other proposals for restriction that may commend themselves to the attention of serious students of the subject—that is, a procedure not unlike that adopted by the Institute of Pacific Relations in regard to other controversial issues of the Pacific. It is not a part of this proposal to take the problem out of the realm of domestic policy and place it into the arena of international discussion; but it was pointed out that independently in the United States and in the Philippines preliminary conferences might take place which would ensure that no reasonable interest is overlooked in the formulation of a practical measure of exclusion or restriction.

[22] *Sociology and Social Research,* May-June, 1929, p. 479.

PART VI

SUMMARY AND CONCLUSIONS

PART VI. SUMMARY AND CONCLUSIONS

THE present report had its origin in a desire to lay a factual basis for an impassionate and unprejudiced discussion of the proposal to exclude Filipinos from the mainland of the United States. This task precluded both too academic a treatment of the subject and one limited to the problems occasioned by Filipino immigration in that part of the United States where at present they are most felt. Three areas under the jurisdiction of the United States, apart from the interests of the country as a whole, require sympathetic consideration for their particular stake in this matter: the Pacific Coast which has suffered the major impact of this migration and of its accompanying problems on the mainland, the territory of Hawaii which has economically become dependent upon Filipino contract labor, and the Philippine Islands themselves. Moreover, while many features of the subject run parallel to those experienced in the past with other immigration movements, the influx of Filipinos particularly invites some of those larger considerations of national policy which in the past have not always sufficiently figured in the shaping of public opinion and of legislation on similar issues: The Filipinos are subjects of the United States, and every change in their status in continental United States reacts upon the political relationship between this country and the Philippines. Again, they are at present the sole representatives of Oriental peoples that seek to come to this country in large numbers. For this reason, their treatment is watched by other peoples of the Far East, and of the world, as indicative of American attitudes and policies toward the yellow races generally. For the same reason also, they constitute the only outstanding menace of an infiltration of Mongolian blood into the racial composition of the American people (at least in popular opinion, since American Indians are not officially so classed). One other special element in the situation is that, by successive legislative steps, the United States have reduced the volume of emigration from Europe: This, of course, by lessening competition, adds to the country's attractions for peoples not included in the newer restrictions; and the danger that the purpose of these restrictions may be nullified by their influx is evident.

1. MAIN FACTS

Filipino migration to the mainland of the United States in noticeable volume began several years after the end of the World War. A considerable migration to Hawaii had started a decade earlier, chiefly as a result of the need of the sugar plantations to make good the loss to their labor supply from the voluntary restriction of Japanese migration to Hawaii by the Japanese government. There are today (beginning of 1931) about 75,000 Filipinos in Hawaii and about 60,000 on the mainland of the United States. The great majority of these immigrants (nine-tenths on the mainland) are male, and most of them (four-fifths on the mainland) under thirty years of age. Practically all the migrants to Hawaii are on a three years' contract at (or soon after) the end of which they return to their home country. Only a very small proportion of those who come to the mainland intend to stay permanently; yet so far only one out of every fifteen Filipino immigrants has returned. Probably about four-fifths of those who have come to continental United States have remained in the Pacific Coast states.

2. CAUSES OF EMIGRATION

Because of its recentness, it is possible with some accuracy to ascertain the main causes of this migration movement. Most of them are still operative; but as the movement continues, secondary factors—among them the relative success of the earlier migrants—increasingly take the place of the original stimuli. The effectiveness of the various pressures and pulls that make up the totality of motivation depends not only on their respective strength but also on the ways in which, in given circumstances, they interact. Hardly one of them ever appears as the only decisive element. Moreover, some are constant and others only appear with a given combination of circumstances; some are relatively rare, others widely diffused; some act with explosive force, others mature slowly; and in normal life all are so intermingled that it would be futile in any given instance to try completely to disentangle them.[1]

[1] See Carl Bücher, Industrial Evolution. Henry Holt & Co., 1901, chapter X. Also The Migration of Races. *The Round Table,* London, March, 1921, No. 42, p. 241 *et seq.*

Unfortunately an effort, in connection with the present study, to secure a quantitative picture of the relative importance of the diverse motives for emigration named, did not succeed. In the first place, there is the danger of slightly changing the emphasis of a motive named in an interview or in responses to an attitude test by endeavoring to combine that response with others in categories. Second, it became evident that to present numerically, as though equivalent, opinions expressed by persons with very different degrees of knowledge or of closeness to the minds of emigrants was misleading. Third, there are also different degrees of ability to express oneself accurately, according to the occasion. Fourth, owing to the circumstances of an investigation which had to be conducted in English—that is either with English speaking Filipinos or through interpreters—the point of view of the educated classes would, in any statistical presentation, far outweigh that of the laborers. Correctly to interpret these facts requires that one give the right degrees of prominence to motives advanced, according to the degrees of emphasis and frankness with which they are stated, and the speakers' degrees of width and intimacy of knowledge. It may be permitted, therefore, to substitute for any such statistical attempt a brief summary:

In the totality of motivations found for Filipino emigration at the present time, economic causes outweigh social ones. Two trends have contributed to their rapidly accumulating force: the re-direction of an existing migration movement from intra-island and inter-island to foreign destinations, and the acceleration of a movement to Hawaii and the mainland of the United States by the reports of success and by propaganda. At first indefinite as to aim and limited to the more adventurous groups and types, the movement has assumed more definite objectives and affected increasing numbers of staid and conservative groups. There is no uniform population pressure; as in other migration movements in the past,[2] local and seasonal pressures suffice to impel a fairly large exodus.

In other ways also, the causation of Filipino emigration shares many elements with that of other emigration movements that have helped to populate the American continent and Hawaii: the desire for larger earnings and a higher standard of living; the attractions of countries with a more developed form of civiliza-

[2] Edith Abbott, Historical Aspects of Immigration. University of Chicago Press, 1926, documents No. 16, 17, 18, 24, 25, 39, 46. Manuel Gamio, Mexican Immigration to the United States. University of Chicago Press, 1930, p. 23. Robert F. Foerster, The Italian Emigration of Our Times. Harvard University Press, 1919, p. 37 *et seq.*

tion; escape from hampering social restrictions; on the other hand, the strength of family ties which induces men to undergo hardship to assist the family fortunes. But it has some features which are unique: the efficiency with which the movement to Hawaii has been guided and controlled; the sense of a right to take part in all the advantages afforded by American sovereignty; the prestige conferred by higher education in the social scale of values.

Among the stimuli which have further developed this movement we can also distinguish features common to previous waves of migration to the United States from those which are particular to this instance. Among the former: the rôle played by steamship companies in working up traffic; the diffusion of exaggerated information on existing opportunities; the success stories of early pioneer-migrants and of returned travellers; the actual evidence of money orders and savings brought back. Among the latter: the total impact of a generation of American influences on the government of the Islands; more particularly the Americanizing effect of the public schools. Among predisposing cultural factors we can distinguish the relative conservatism of social institutions still largely under the influence of centuries of Spanish rule, compared with the reported liberalism of social relations in America.

Thus a picture unfolds of large and small causes which not only throws light on the special subject of our study but also affords an insight into the forces which, independent of specific local conditions, have also impelled other migration movements in the past.

3. PROBLEMS ON THE MAINLAND

Normally, a new movement of immigration produces a sequence of reactions which may briefly be charted as follows:

First phase. Growing awareness to symptoms of disharmony and conflicts of interest:

1. in popular attention—
   a. aroused self-interest,
   b. aroused group interest,
   c. aroused national interest

(each category of "awakening" brought about through a progressive number of experiences).

2. in specialist attention—
   a. social engineer—

social worker,
public official,
politician;

b. opinion maker—
press,
pulpit,
school,
interest group;

c. social student.

Second phase. Action:

1. Specialist—
   a. on public opinion—
      press,
      preachment,
      education;
   b. on specific situations—
      social programs,
      administrative rulings,
      court decisions;
   c. on knowledge—
      sponsored research.
2. Popular
   a. Antagonistic behavior—
      taboos,
      segregations,
      agitation and lynching;
   b. counter-reactions—
      individual defense,
      counter agitation.

Third phase. Organization:

1. Popular—
   a. Campaigns for segregation,
   b. for restriction or exclusion,
   c. Counter-campaigns against a. and b. and for group defense.
2. Specialist—
   a. Demands on public authorities and institutions,
   b. Legislative proposals,
   c. Conference and concerted research,
   d. Movements for appreciation and cooperation.

There is a fourth phase which, however, has not been reached in the case of Filipino immigration, the phase of stabilization in relations, gradually leading from accommodation to assimilation.

The general pattern does not, however, preclude wide variations with the impact of each new immigration movement—variations due not only to the strength and characteristics of the particular influx but also to the previous history and present condition of the region that receives its major impact. Thus Filipino immigration was favored by a demand for labor for certain classes of field work; it was disfavored by the previous experience of the Pacific Coast with Oriental immigration. It fell heir to the attitudes developed by two conflicting American traditions: reliance upon immigrant hands for the least pleasant and least remunerated labor tasks, and hostility to the encroachment of alien peoples upon the ethnic and social homogeneity of the population. These conditions, important as they are, only form the background, however, for concrete conflict situations that arise from actual contacts and specific clashes of interest—situations which, in spite of their repetitive character, have for those who participate in them all the elements of novelty and annoyance.

There is competition, both actual and potential, for the daily bread. The Filipino, unaware of our tastes and customs, transgresses the sense of native-born people of what is fit and proper in his social conduct. He is suspected of immoral attitudes and of criminal tendencies. He is said to be a menace to the health of the community. In short, the prevalent attitudes toward him are as much the typical reactions of a public opinion prejudiced by previous experiences of immigration as they are the results of experience, observation and calm inquiry. Thus, the most serious "problem" of Filipino immigration is the state of feeling which it has aroused. Irritation over the stranger's presence develops a sense of uneasiness, gradually of antagonism and of fear; it produces a suspicious temper in the community. Charges are made and answered. One group is accused of deliberately introducing foreigners in order to lower wage standards; another of disregarding the amenities of social life by forcing citizens to associate with their inferiors. The accusation of prejudice is made. The immigrant group itself becomes resentful under a constant and frequently unjust stream of criticism. Some section of it allies itself with other dissatisfied elements in the community. Societies spring up, the purpose of which is not perfectly clear and which are suspected, therefore, of sinister aims. A foreign language is spoken at street corners by dark-skinned foreigners who have no inherited interest in the welfare of the community, and conspiracies are hinted at.

Soon the community is in conflict within and against itself as much as against the stranger. We thus have the growth of antagonisms that introduce an imminent danger of violence, such as was recently experienced in several districts of the West.

Perhaps even more dangerous is the growth of a permanent undercurrent of prejudice and hostility in the relations between different groups that are obliged to live together. For, these animosities do not exhaust themselves in the immediate clashes but live on.

The more specific causes of difficulty in this matter of Filipino immigration may, then, be summarized as follows:

Economic competition of Filipinos with white Americans is limited almost entirely to wage-earning occupations of the lowest paid kinds. It does not expand over the whole range of common labor, either in town or country, but by its concentration—both geographically and occupationally—it often produces unemployment for those of the native population who already are economically weakest, such as elderly persons in domestic and hotel service, or laborers and small ranchers and their families dependent on occasional extra earnings in seasonal agriculture. Women and the members of other immigrant groups, also Negroes in certain urban employments, are more hard hit than American-born white men.

While this competition is not, except in limited areas, of dimensions inviting national attention, it forebodes a much more serious difficulty if Filipinos were to come in larger numbers and if those now in this country were to remain and settle. For, as they acquire experience and become more fluent in the use of the English language, the Filipinos would drift into other occupations and might even be employed on purpose to hold down and reduce established wage standards.

At least as serious as the economic problems are the social problems introduced by Filipino immigration, if in that term we include the friction occasioned by prejudiced attitudes. The actual liabilities to the community, as we have seen, are relatively small. Indeed, where a preference is expressed in favor of Filipino as compared with Mexican labor, the explanation is often made that the latter bring too many social problems into the community to be a worth-while addition to the population. It is largely a question of choice between different difficulties when the problems produced by one immigrant group are held up against those produced by another. The Mexican has been the costlier of the two nationalities, from the point of view of direct expenditure: Not only has his unwillingness to separate from his family increased the school budgets of the Southwest and local expenditures on public relief and public health; but owing to the ease with which relief can be obtained by deserted families in the United States, the occasional burdening of the community with the support of his family has become a frequent expedient of the itinerant Mexican worker. The Japanese have aroused antagonism, on the other hand, because they are too successful. Popular feeling always tends to suspect newcomers who rapidly advance economically, and does not discriminate between those who do so at the expense of the rest of the community and those who do so by tapping new resources open to all. Thus, in the East, there have at different times been waves of apprehension over new burdens upon society introduced by destitute immigrant groups—such as the Porto Ricans in New York today [3]—but also over the unequal competition, as it seemed, of groups which rapidly forged ahead—such as the Russian Jews a generation ago.[4]

The Filipino introduces moral problems which many people regard as much more serious than the economic problems produced by the Mexicans.

One difficulty is that, brought up in an American school, the Filipino considers himself a social equal to the groups with which he happens to come in contact, whether old-stock American, immigrant Caucasian, Japanese or Mexican. But in fact his living standards are often actually lower than those of the surrounding community, so that his one extravagance, the care for personal appearance, stands in striking contrast with his expenditures on food and housing. In this respect, the situation is identical with that experienced with the Japanese in the earlier years of their immigration.[5]

On the moot subject of sex relations, the consensus of opinion among those best informed seems to be that in their attitude toward members of the other sex the Filipinos do not differ much from any other group of young men finding itself in a foreign country,

[3] According to a report of the State Department of Social Welfare, there are about 150,000 Porto Ricans in New York—nearly all of recent arrival. They represent, in the neighborhoods where they reside, from 4 to 20 per cent of cases handled by the charitable agencies and a large proportion of the out-patients of local hospitals.

[4] "Whatever the enemies of Jews may say against them, they recognize an intense intellectual keenness and a desire to learn. Some antagonists sometimes turn to this very ability as a factor which makes it difficult for the rest of the population to compete with them." Charles S. Bernheimer, The Russian Jew in the United States. John C. Winston Co., 1905, p. 408.

[5] See H. A. Millis, *op. cit.*, p. 254.

far from the control of family life or of older persons of its own nationality. In fact, there is no evidence that they differ in this respect from those of their own age in the American communities where they live. But there is the fact that in Latin countries the personal prestige of a young man is to some degree measured by his success with women. Hence, the Filipino immigrant is not content with the rôle of lonely bachelor which some communities wish to see him assume. In the long run, especially with longer residence here and the gradual upbuilding of Filipino colonies composed in part of families, this cause of apprehension would naturally disappear—only to raise an even larger problem, of course.

The Filipino's mobility, since he is not burdened with family responsibilities, and the attitude of almost the entire group toward American residence as only temporary, make for a slow rate of fusion into the community life of America. But these factors also counteract a strong organization of Filipinos because of the instability of local residence on the part of organization members and officers. In public resolutions, the Filipino is often described as unassimilable; but what is meant evidently is that his assimilation is considered undesirable. For, speaking the English language, predisposed by his schooling in the Philippine Islands for a love of America and all its traditions and customs, anxious to acquire the skills and knowledge which America has to offer and to mix socially with Americans, the more educated Filipino is, if anything, *too* assimilable to accept the limitations imposed upon him by public opinion; and the problem which he creates is not that of the stranger who cannot be Americanized, but rather that of the would-be American who refuses to remain a stranger.[6]

Two other problems said to be introduced by Filipino immigration seem to be shown by the evidence to be less serious than at first they appeared to be:

The Filipino is not a health menace in the sense that he exposes the community to new or dreaded infections. But he does to some extent carry infections to which he has become immune. The age composition of the Filipino immigrant group and the healthy outdoor occupations of the great majority of its members are making for a high degree of physical efficiency. If in one instance he has been the carrier of a serious contagious disease to these shores, the

[6] Emory S. Bogardus, The Filipino Immigrant Situation. Pamphlet, Council of International Relations, Los Angeles, 1929.

Filipino has been the victim rather than the villain—having been exposed to it as a traveller passing through other countries.

The alleged criminality of the Filipino is largely a fiction, as is his liability to become a public charge. Irresponsibility and lack of a strong adult group back of the young men and boys who compose the typical Filipino colony inevitably expose it to temptations which exist to a smaller extent in a more organized community group. Poverty, helplessness and exploitation are circumstances predisposing to anti-social sentiments and actions. Yet, the Filipino delinquency rate is not large, in so far as it can be measured by court convictions. Exposed to prejudice as well as strangeness, Filipino immigrants tend to congregate and, in an informal and unorganized way, to see each other through every kind of trouble. Hence their demands on outside charity are rare, and public expenditures for their relief almost non-existent.

To sum up, there is no overwhelming evidence that the Filipino as an immigrant is either a great asset or a great liability to the United States. On the one hand, no major industry particularly needs him, even when it considers imperative *some* labor supply additional to available sources of native American labor; he has introduced no new skills to enrich the land. On the other, he is no disturber of the public peace, charge upon taxes, or menace to health or morals. But he does produce difficulties and problems that cannot be ignored. Biological questions apart, the Filipino, suddenly coming in large numbers, does upset the social equilibrium by settling in a relatively limited area, by competing within a relatively limited choice of occupations, and by causing hostility through his unwillingness to look upon himself as racially inferior to the white man, or indeed as anything other than a white man. He does not fit into our idea of what a well-behaved immigrant should be like, particularly when he insists on interpreting American democracy as giving him the right to leave the kitchen and come into the drawing room. His moral standards are those of a different civilization. But the problem lies more especially in the uncertainty of his intentions; his coming seems once more to open the door to an almost unlimited Oriental invasion. If the number of departures kept up with that of the arrivals, popular attitudes toward him, even on the Pacific Coast, probably would be quite different. The popular objection is to Oriental settlement and race fusion, not to a temporary sojourn of students and tourists.

4. PROBLEMS FOR THE IMMIGRANTS THEMSELVES

With the special purpose of this book, it was incumbent upon the writer to pay special (though not disproportionate) attention to the problems which the Filipino immigrants themselves encounter on the American continent. For, however much we may wish to discuss the subject from a purely American point of view, we cannot disregard the fact that at the present time the Philippine Islands are an American possession, and that we are not dealing with a foreign people when we make laws to regulate the movement of our own "nationals." Of course, the problems which have already been named are those of the Filipinos quite as much as those of continental Americans. In so far as they share the fortunes of the United States, the immigrant group and their compatriots should be as concerned over the welfare of our Pacific Coast states as are the people of Iowa and Vermont. But obviously, the relative seriousness of common problems for the receiving and the sending regions depend on whose shoe it is that pinches. The primary concern of the Filipinos is the fortunes of the immigrants themselves.

No attempt has been made in the preceding pages to depict those problems which all immigrant groups, in their first phase of contact with the special conditions of a new country, have to meet. Whether due to the lack of facilities in virgin territory or to the necessity of adjustment to a fully developed civilization, these problems are inherent in the circumstances and readily recognized by those who have studied the history of migrations. But there are several novelties in this latest large-scale influx. One of them is precisely that it is the latest, that it inherits all the defenses which a people has built up in its institutions and in its attitudes after a period of enormous population mixture from which it is only just emerging into an era of difficult assimilation. As the latest comer, the Filipino encounters checks in national and state laws, in the precedents of discriminatory treatment set by custom, in the prejudices built up by previous race contacts of the dominant group. Thus, a comparison of the Filipino influx with the earlier Japanese wave of immigration is misleading unless one remembers that while the earlier Japanese immigrants, welcomed to this country, were able by their competency to establish a high degree of prosperity which later became an important factor in fortifying the position of the larger group, the Filipinos were not privileged to establish such a pioneer colony that might later take up the advancement and protection of the national group as a whole. The result is a lack of responsible, economically anchored leadership, which constitutes one of the greatest concrete obstacles to the success of the Filipino group in America as a whole.

The Filipino immigrant is further handicapped by the distance of his homeland, which necessitates considerable sacrifice, on his own part or that of his family, before he can make the expensive trip, and usually lands him at his goal without further resources. This distance also makes impossible a rapid adaptation of the current of emigration to the employment conditions in the receiving country and prevents the return of those who, either for personal reasons or because of a choked labor market, find it difficult to make a living.

The limitations of the Filipino are partly physical and partly cultural. His smallness of stature makes him unsuitable in the eyes of employers for work requiring hard muscular exertion. Bad dietary habits often render him much weaker than organically he need be. Overcrowding, the frequenting of smoke-filled poolrooms and insufficient sleep also impair his physical efficiency. Mentally, the Filipino worker is alert enough to take his place beside other national groups; but his vocabulary usually is limited, and, unless a Filipino foremanship should grow up from among the more experienced workers, employers have difficulty in handling this class of foreigners.

Against the Filipino's chances in competition for work are further his temperament (sometimes) and his reputation. While as an individual the Filipino is considered docile, he often finds himself barred from employment because of the assumption that, as a group, Filipinos are temperamental, prone to take offense easily and to walk out on an employer at small provocation, quarrelsome among themselves and revengeful when considering themselves injured. Moreover, employers, especially in small and rural communities, are influenced more largely by non-economic motivations than in large cities and industrial plants: It is sometimes considered unwise to employ Filipinos where there are women around or where their work may be regarded as in competition with that of white Americans, even when there are no complaints on either score. Again, in the hotel and restaurant trades and retail business, employers are obliged to consider the prejudices of their patrons; and Filipinos find themselves debarred from promotion to positions as waiters or salesmen even when their own employer would consider them qualified and desirable.

Like other newcomers, Filipinos find themselves the victims of many forms of exploitation—by labor agents and contractors, by foremen and straw bosses, by venders of goods and of transportation, by gamblers and racketeers. Ignorance of work opportunities, of their rights when employed, of means to gain legal redress, of prices and charges, of the functions and duties of officials, of American customs; often a childlike faith in the printed word or misplaced confidence in a countryman, romantic hero-worship, inability to resist argument when couched in flamboyant terms—all these handicaps make it difficult for the Filipino immigrant worker to prosper and to realize his economic ambitions on coming to the American mainland. Moreover, he does not know how to avail himself of such protection as American community organization and state legislation afford.

But there are other difficulties not shared by earlier immigrant groups. The permanent settlement of the Filipinos is feared; and this fear reacts against them. In vain do they point out that they have not come here to stay and settle. Just because they are ever conscious of the temporary nature of their stay, they find it harder than those who come for permanent residence to make those adjustments of habits and tastes that would ensure a rapid assimilation.

This statement may seem contradicted by the actual ease with which Filipinos seem to adopt American ideas; but observation here is often at fault: The tastes and notions which the Filipino immigrant endeavors to express through his mode of living are those of his own country with its long history of Spanish cultural domination, modified, to be sure, by an aggressive North American impact during the last thirty years. A bird of passage, the Filipino in his attitude to American life is comparable with other transients rather than with those who come here to settle and throw in their fortunes with native Americans. This makes for a certain aloofness which is only partially disguised by the Filipino's desire for social recognition and the company of American men and women. He wishes to learn from these contacts, not to become one of us.

Closely linked with these conditions, there is the Filipino's youthfulness—or, if you will, immaturity. This is not merely a matter of age composition of the Filipino group, which is lower than that of any other wave of immigration this country has ever had. Employers, college deans, social workers and public officials frequently comment upon the seeming inability of Filipinos, well in the higher twenties and in the thirties, to take a responsible attitude toward their obligations to others. More specifically we have found, in the preceding pages, as militating against the Filipino's success as an immigrant the absence of a normal home life, the excessive mobility that prevents the formation of close ties within a community, even within his own national group.

Bad housing conditions, limitation of vocational opportunities, exposure to unscrupulous profiteers, especially of their own nationality, ignorance of their legal rights and obligations, the general neglect of the community—these are evils which every newly arriving group of immigrants has had to face. In the case of the Filipinos they are aggravated by lack of experience and the absence of those checks which a normal age- and sex-composition place upon individual recklessness. The very adventurousness which makes it possible to suffer temporary misfortune, in the case of the Filipinos, is producing an unusual crop of evils; it encourages an instability which stands in the way of those opportunities which only the growth of a reputation for sustained effort opens to newcomers. Thus criticism by employers and by teachers helps to give substance to the inevitable popular verdict that the newcomers are "undesirable."

We shall not attempt, in these summarising paragraphs, to attach the correct weight to the Filipino's reputation for immorality—perhaps the heaviest of adverse judgments which he has to combat. That he considers himself a member of the white race is his privilege, but in a sense also his misfortune; for it introduces a vagueness into his recognized status which places him socially beyond the pale. Without the steadying influence of women of his own nationality or of compensating recreational outlets, and unable to understand the finer distinctions which westerners draw between permissible and non-permissible freedom in the relations between the sexes, he often sustains by his conduct a popular judgment which, more than anything else, excludes him from social, and also from many occupational, opportunities. The home life of Filipinos in their own country does not support the conclusion that as a race they are over-sexed. They happen to behave exactly as other groups of young men behave when released from the normal restraints of home. But we have to look also among them for a specific social inheritance which may in part explain the romantic predisposition of the Filipino immigrant. This we find in the social class division of both the East and of the Mediterranean, which allots to the privileged members of the community a life of luxury and *amour propre* made possibly by the hard work and frugality of the lower classes. Although but a fraction of the Filipino group in America belong to this class of *illustrados,* the example set for so many generations by the leading circles in their country has permeated all classes for whom the newer dreams of freedom and economic advance too largely contain visions of that ease which has hitherto been denied them. How to overcome traditional handicaps, such as this, to a fuller sharing of what western democracy has to offer in the larger satisfactions of life is a matter of self-education for the Filipinos.

All in all, the present position of the Filipino immigrants on the mainland of the United States has been rendered difficult by the presence among them of too many failures. Even though the proportionate number of these may not be excessive, considering all the circumstances, the more thoughtful Filipinos are conscious of a dead weight to be carried along. No economic dependency of old and young, of sick and temporarily unemployed, produces enervating doubt as much as a belief that too many members of the group are drifting and too few are realizing their hopes. It is impossible at this stage to undo the past, to help to success those who in their own minds already have fallen from the way toward attainable success; but it has repeatedly been suggested in the course of the present inquiry, both by Filipinos with more than ordinary insight and by American friends of the Filipinos, that the elimination of these failures by some general movement that would take them home to their own country, would have a most invigorating effect upon the chances of those remaining.

It is difficult, in a summary statement primarily concerned with "problems" to avoid the impression that the whole movement has failed, and that its immediate and complete stoppage would be in the interest of the Filipinos as much as in that of Americans. But such an interpretation is not justified by the facts surveyed in their totality. After all, the great majority of Filipino immigrants are well treated and do realize their ambitions: They earn and save money which they could not have earned or saved at home; or they gain college degrees that raise not only their own social status but often that of their whole family. Their contact with American life at many points gives them (and through them transmits to their home country) a knowledge of the modern world which could not be gained in the Islands. They often receive new vistas of western culture and acquire skills that have been developed in Europe and America through centuries of slow development. Our ethics and social traditions, seen in their native habitat, acquire for them new meaning. Superficial acquaintance with western tastes is deepened. Thus, and to this extent, they become interpreters of Occident to Orient and help an understanding of America that no political connection and no school system thousands of miles remote from its prototype can give.

It may be that these advantages are too dearly bought. But against the difficulties and problems that have been described in detail we must set those achievements and successful adjustments that require no detailed account because we have learned to expect them in all immigrant groups as the normal lot of the majority.

5. THE SPECIAL INTERESTS OF HAWAII

Only about one-tenth of the population of Hawaii is made up of North Europeans, Americans, and their descendants of white blood. The great majority of the not quite 400,000 inhabitants of the territory are the descendants of other immigrants brought there to develop its natural resources. The Filipinos today, although largely single, make up 18 per cent of the total population and 69 per cent of the employees on the sugar plantations. They more than any other group perform the basic functions of the Islands' economic system, and this to the entire satisfaction of their employers who compare their capacity favorably with that of other racial groups. These laborers are hired and transported to Hawaii in numbers corresponding to the actual needs of the sugar and pineapple plantations and returned, at the employers' expense, after completion of a three years' contract.

With a system of selection and management adapted to the circumstances and improved through half a century of experience with immigrant plantation labor, the number of misfits is exceedingly small; so that the great majority of immigrant laborers are enabled to make earnings satisfactory to them, and often substantial savings. The desire for contract work in Hawaii under present conditions is such in the Philippine Islands that active recruiting is no longer necessary to secure an adequate labor supply, and a constantly growing proportion of the contract workers are repeaters. Working conditions and wages earned on the plantations compare favorably with those in many sections of the American South. Since these concerns carry the largest share of the local taxes, it is to their interest that, during his stay in the territory, the immigrant laborer shall be in complete physical and mental efficiency.

Although, owing to the age and sex composition of the group, Filipino crime is higher than that of the other groups, and although, often coming from somewhat primitive rural surroundings, these immigrants do not always quickly adapt themselves to the new living conditions and customs, the social problems created for the territory by the Filipinos are not great. This is due in part, of course, to the fact that the population already is a very mixed one, with a preponderance of Asiatics, so that social distances between different racial groups are graded and undisturbed by humiliating taboos.

There is no demand in Hawaii for an immediate change in the present immigration law, especially not for complete exclusion of the Filipinos which, it is generally realized, might be catastrophic to the territory's prosperity. But as those native-born of all races who have passed through American schools desire something better for themselves and their children than the hard work of cutting cane or other unpleasant field work, the question is much discussed in Hawaii whether gradually the economic system of the Islands cannot be changed so as to provide a wider range of opportunity in industries and mixed farming and, correspondingly, a lessening dependence upon common labor. Owing to the distance of the territory from possible markets and sources of supply, and to its limited resources of industrial raw products, there is little likelihood of an early and considerable industrialization. While movements are under way to increase non-agricultural production and to encourage farming, the best chances of meeting the rising desire for more lucrative labor seem to lie within the basic agricultural industries: Already mechanization has greatly increased opportunities for skilled and semi-skilled labor on the plantations; and the labor contract itself, for many of the purely agricultural operations, is undergoing progressive changes in the direction of increased participation of the workers in responsibility and profits.

Hawaii, then, has no immediate problems connected with Filipino immigration that could be solved by the substitution of other available sources of labor or could be other than seriously aggravated by any sudden interference with the established system of hiring and management. With an eye to the future, however, Hawaii is sharing the concern of continental United States for the gradual abolition of forms of labor that native Americans are reluctant to perform and, reversely, a modification of popular attitudes toward field labor so that an ever increasing part of essential labor may be performed by native Americans under conditions permitting a dignified and relatively satisfactory standard of life.

As on the mainland of the United States, the problems of the Filipino laborers themselves ought to be separately considered. Although it has not been possible in the present study to investigate closely the attitudes of Filipino contract workers in Hawaii, there is sufficient evidence that satisfaction far outweighs whatever hardships may be experienced by them. Some of their troubles, as in continental United States, are due to faulty adaptation and, especially, to the lack of an experienced and trusted leadership. They are subject to exploitation by crafty fellow countrymen to the extent to which they prosper. Sometimes the change from the freedom of the paternal small farm to the rigorous discipline of the plantations is so great as to produce homesickness and suffering. But on the whole, a carefree social life prevails in the plantation villages. So long as earnings and the possibility of saving in Hawaii outdistance similar opportunities in the home country as much as they do today, there will be no dearth of Filipinos willing to engage themselves for plantation work over a span of years.

6. THE CASE FOR AND AGAINST EXCLUSION

Large classes of people, especially on the Pacific Coast, are determined to stop Filipino immigration before it has reached damaging proportions. This demand, increasingly expressed through disorderly demonstrations of resentment over the presence of Filipinos in the community, however much it may have been fostered by propaganda, arises out of actual experience—partly recent, with the Filipinos themselves, and partly in the past, with other Oriental immigrants. Perhaps most striking among the positive arguments advanced for the exclusion of this group from the American mainland is the fact, already referred to, that no considerable industry in continental America considers itself dependent upon Filipino labor, though in a few industries it is favorably received as a substitute for European immigrant labor. While employers claim that Filipino labor is not cheap labor, others point out that nevertheless its availability does hold back the rise of wage standards. It postpones, they say, possible forms of mechanization which would reduce the necessity of common labor and, on the other hand, the natural death of parasite industries that cannot maintain themselves in competition if forced to provide for their workers American standards of living. This argument is based on the assumption that, with the aid of tariffs, the United States can indefinitely maintain for its own population higher standards than those obtained in the rest of the world.

There is no large public opinion today that challenges this assumption. The era of progressive industrialization with the aid of immigrant labor may be looked upon as definitely closed. Those who oppose a Filipino exclusion law are influenced in the main by considerations not directly related to domestic economic requirements. They point to the delicate nature of our relations with the Philippine Islands which we have undertaken temporarily to govern for their own good—a good which might be held to involve a right of the islanders to participate in the advantages afforded by the higher standards prevailing on the continent and the opportunities for training in all the arts of modern civilization which it offers. They also point to the unfavorable reaction to the proposal on the part of other Oriental peoples with whom we desire to be on terms of friendly understanding and who interpret every exclusion law directed toward the East as evidence of race prejudice. Furthermore, they do not consider either the present volume of Filipino migration or its probable growth as serious enough to warrant so exceptional a measure.

All these arguments against Filipino exclusion are accentuated in the case of Hawaii which has become economically dependent upon immigrant labor and finds the present arrangement of Filipino contract labor the most advantageous it has ever had. While the territory in all probability would desire exemption from an exclusion measure if such commended itself to Congress, such a step would be taken regretfully in view of its possible unfavorable effects on the future relation of Hawaii itself to the United States—particularly its eventual claim to statehood.

The exclusion proposal, both on the mainland and in Hawaii, has given rise to a number of counter-proposals which have been reviewed and which have in common an effort to secure a drastic reduction of Filipino migration to continental United States by other means. Since the exclusion proposal was first made, there has developed simultaneously a growth of popular support for it and a growth of interest in the larger political problems involved in the issue. Its complication with the issue of Philippine independence and the tariff has produced a more favorable attention to the interests and claims of the Philippine Islands themselves. It is increasingly felt that these claims and interests are not essentially irreconcilable with those of the areas and groups that suffer most from the present status of Filipino immigration.

Yet for the time being the campaign for exclusion has helped to spread and intensify an antagonism toward Filipino immigrants which otherwise would have remained more largely latent. Thus it has created a precarious situation, vocationally and socially, for the Filipinos in our midst. It has made it more difficult for them to secure jobs and has transplanted to other parts of the country the specific social attitudes of the Pacific Coast toward Orientals. As a not negligible compensation, in the eyes of many Filipinos; the agitation has given them new opportunities of getting a hearing for the political aspirations of their country.

Diverse as it may seem in its various manifestations, public opinion in the United States on Filipino immigration has one feature which distinguishes it from public opinion on previous problems of a similar nature: There appears to be a larger capacity to take a long view. The proposal for exclusion itself derives its strength not so much from demonstrations of great present evils as from forecasts, based upon past experience with other Orientals, of what this immigration movement would mean if it were permitted to continue. On the other hand, those opposed to an exclusion law and the proponents of alternative restrictive measures also stress contingent eventualities rather than the needs of the moment. This insistence on the lessons of the past and on the tasks of the future is an element in the discussion that distinguishes it from other historic debates on immigration which much more largely represented clashes between clearly marked immediate interests.[7]

The question, then, which our survey of the whole situation raises is one to which there can be no obvious answer but which must be seriously considered, not only by Congress but also by all interested groups of citizens: Can the movement of Filipinos to the

[7] See Edith Abbott, Historical Aspects of the Immigration Problem. University of Chicago Press, 1926, pp. 697-701.

mainland of the United States be stopped in the immediate future without injury to American foreign relations in the Far East, without precipitating an unwise and dangerous change in our political relations with the Philippine Islands, without upsetting the labor situation in Hawaii, without prejudice to the legitimate ambitions of the Filipino people themselves? It is hoped that the present report may provide the most important requisite information to invite a calm discussion of this question and to further its wise solution.

APPENDICES

APPENDICES

APPENDIX A

AN ESTIMATE OF FILIPINO POPULATION ON THE MAINLAND OF THE UNITED STATES

IN the absence of recent census statistics, the most reliable basis for arriving at the number of Filipinos on the mainland of the United States is the excess of arrivals over departures, taken from the manifests of incoming and outgoing passenger steamers. The following table has been prepared by the statistical office of the Immigration Bureau in the United States Department of Labor. Using as the most reliable sources of information the reports annually published by the Bureau of Insular Affairs on the number of persons migrating between the Philippine Islands and the United States, and those published by the United States Immigration Service in Hawaii concerning the number of Filipino steerage voyages to and from the Philippines and the mainland of the United States, this computation arrives at 48,480 as the net increase from immigration of the Filipino population on the mainland in the calendar years 1920-1929.

FILIPINO MIGRATION TO THE UNITED STATES

January, 1920–December, 1929

From Reports of the Bureau of Insular Affairs and the United States Immigration Service in Hawaii.*

1.	Departed from Philippines for mainland and Hawaii . . .	113,144	
2.	Arrived in Philippines from mainland and Hawaii . . .	31,995	
3.	Net increase for entire United States		81,149

* The Hawaiian figures for 1920 to 1921 are partly based on estimate. The figures for July to December, 1929, are estimated, on the basis of previous returns for half-years, as somewhat less than one-half for the first part of 1929.

4.	Arrived in Hawaii from Philippines	75,464		
5.	Arrived in Hawaii from mainland .	760		
6.	Total arrivals in Hawaii . .		76,224	
7.	Departed from Hawaii for Philippines	29,360		
8.	Departed from Hawaii for mainland	14,195		
9.	Total departures from Hawaii .		43,555	
10.	Net increase for Hawaii . .			32,669 *
11.	Arrivals at mainland from Hawaii .	14,195		
12.	Arrivals at mainland from Philippines	37,680		
13.	Total arrivals at mainland . .		51,875	
14.	Departures from mainland for Hawaii	760		
15.	Departures from mainland for Philippines	2,635		
16.	Total departures from mainland .		3,395	
17.	Net increase for mainland . .			48,480 *
18.	Net increase for entire United States			81,149 *

* These estimates do not allow for changes in Filipino population through birth and death.

To arrive at the total Filipino population in continental United States at the beginning of 1930, three other sources of increase or decrease must be considered, as well as the number of Filipino residents enumerated in the census of 1920.

1. The number of Filipinos arriving other than by steerage, concerning which no definite information is available, is generally considered by immigration and shipping officials to be negligibly small. The number of arrivals by second class is likely to be almost if not entirely balanced by second-class departures. The Filipino immigrant practically always travels steerage.

There is some division of opinion as to the influx of Filipino immigrants over the land borders of continental United States. Again, while no statistics are available, it is not believed that the net increase from this source is likely to amount to substantial figures. Inquiries made in Canada do not reveal the arrival at its ports of considerable numbers of Filipinos in transit to the United

States or the presence of Filipino colonies large enough to warrant the assumption of a migration movement across the border.

2. There is some doubt concerning the volume of Filipino steerage travel to the mainland of the United States from ports other than Manila and Honolulu. That there is such a movement is indicated by the figures collected by the State of California Department of Industrial Relations concerning the arrival at Californian ports of Filipinos embarking at foreign ports, giving a total of 2,785 such arrivals for the ten-year period 1920-1929.[1] These immigrants came chiefly from Hongkong and Shanghai in China and from Kobe and Yokohama in Japan.[2] Unfortunately we do not know how many Filipinos departed to these foreign ports in the same period. It is improbable that there has been a similar influx of Filipinos from the Far East to other than Californian ports. A net increase of the Filipino population on the mainland from this source of about 2,000 is probably a fair estimate.

3. Lastly, no accurate basis is available for computing the probable effect on the total number of Filipinos on the mainland from the ratio between births and deaths in the ten-year period since the last census. Considering the age and marital composition of the group[3] it is certain that both birth and death rates are exceptionally low. The possible excess of one over the other cannot be estimated by analogies with other groups because of considerable differences in modes of life and may, therefore, for our purpose, best be neglected.[4]

We thus arrive at the following estimate of the total number of Filipinos on the mainland of the United States:

Resident Filipinos enumerated in 1920	5,603
Excess of arrivals over departures of steerage passengers from and to the Philippines and Hawaii, 1920-1929	48,480
Excess of arrivals over departures from and to other ports, 1920-1929	2,000
Total	56,083

[1] Facts About Filipino Immigration into California, p. 24. See also Appendix B, p. 353.

[2] The Philippine Islands Bureau of Labor estimates that there are 60,000 Filipinos in China, 20,000 in Indo-China and Siam, 15,000 in Japan, 12,000 in Dutch West Indies, and 6,000 in the Malay Peninsula. (Bulletin of the Bureau of Labor, vol. VIII, No. 26, March, 1927, p. 20.)

[3] See p. 23 *et seq.*

[4] With a small immigration of women, a low marriage rate, and a relatively high death rate (in so far as this can be assumed from fragmentary data), it is probable that there is a small excess of deaths over births, possibly amounting to a total of between 1,000 and 2,000 for the whole immigration period.

APPENDIX B

THE MOVEMENT OF FILIPINO POPULATION TO AND FROM HAWAII

By PROFESSOR ROMANZO ADAMS, University of Hawaii

I. MOVEMENT OF FILIPINO POPULATION BETWEEN THE PHILIPPINES AND HAWAII

FIRST PERIOD: 1907-1919 [1]

	From the Philippines to Hawaii				From Hawaii to the Philippines			
	Men	*Women*	*Children*	*Total*	*Men*	*Women*	*Children*	*Total*
1907 [2]	188	20	2	210	2	—	—	2
1908-1909 [2]	697	70	52	819	—	—	—	—
1910 [2]	3,009	227	113	3,349	35	9	3	47
1911 [3]	677	93	31	801	165	33	23	221
1912 [4]	2,573	275	190	3,038	100	7	8	115
1913 [4]	4,518	766	462	5,746	180	19	12	211
1914 [4]	2,548	412	224	3,184	427	54	36	517
1915 [4]	834	232	166	1,232	325	52	41	418
1916 [4]	1,527	118	99	1,744	329	53	49	421
1917 [4]	2,515	250	165	2,930	520	42	62	624
1918 [4]	2,077	278	314	2,669	857	62	95	1,014
1919 [4]	2,255	268	204	2,727	543	79	114	736
Total	23,418	3,009	2,022	28,449	3,483	410	443	4,336

[1] Steerage passengers only.
[2] 1907-1910. Calendar years.
[3] First half of calendar year.
[4] Fiscal years ending June 30.

SECOND PERIOD: 1920-1924 [5]

	Men	*Women*	*Children*	*Total*	*Men*	*Women*	*Children*	*Total*
1920	3,029	291	184	3,504	906	110	135	1,151
1921	2,823	327	144	3,294	1,782	221	279	2,282
1922	7,550	791	334	8,675	1,517	234	323	2,074

[5] Steerage passengers only.

	From the Philippines to Hawaii				From Hawaii to the Philippines			
	Men	Women	Children	Total	Men	Women	Children	Total
1923	5,838	1,008	490	7,336	878	80	90	1,048
1924	3,947	1,761	709	6,417	1,274	194	154	1,622
Total	23,187	4,178	1,861	29,226	6,357	839	981	8,177

THIRD PERIOD: 1925-1929 [6]

	Men	Women	Children	Total	Men	Women	Children	Total
1925	9,414	631	324	10,369	2,122	259	388	2,769
1926	4,794	129	72	4,995	2,208	265	242	2,715
1927	6,404	385	86	6,875	2,585	425	661	3,671
1928	12,254	180	138	12,572	2,742	473	793	4,008
1929	9,320	143	130	9,593	3,788	346	675	4,809
Total	42,186	1,468	750	44,404	13,445	1,768	2,759	17,972

[6] Passengers of all classes.

II. MOVEMENT OF FILIPINOS BETWEEN HAWAII AND CONTINENTAL UNITED STATES [7]

FIRST PERIOD: 1907-1919

	From Cont. U.S.A. to Hawaii				From Hawaii to Cont. U.S.A.			
	Men	Women	Children	Total	Men	Women	Children	Total
1907 [8]					2			2
1908, 1909 [8]					44			44
1910 [8]					39			39
1911 [9]					201			201
1912 [10]					41			41
1913 [10]	2	1		3	120	5	8	133
1914 [10]	15			15	170	3	3	176
1915 [10]	10		2	12	258	1	1	260
1916 [10]	8			8	257	7	2	266
1917 [10]	2			2	489	11	6	506
1918 [10]	2	4	1	7	441	4	11	456
1919 [10]					247	6	5	258
Total	39	5	3	47	2,309	37	36	2,382

[7] Steerage passengers only.
[8] Calendar years.
[9] First half of calendar year.
[10] Fiscal years ending June 30.

SECOND PERIOD: 1920-1924 [11]

	From Cont. U. S. A. to Hawaii				*From Hawaii to Cont. U. S. A.*			
	Men	*Women*	*Children*	*Total*	*Men*	*Women*	*Children*	*Total*
1920					152	3	3	158
1921	7	2	1	10	152			152
1922	35	3		38	90	3	5	98
1923	11	1		12	1,042	26	30	1,098
1924	19	3	1	23	2,002	93	53	2,148
Total	72	9	2	83	3,438	125	91	3,654

[11] Steerage passengers only; fiscal years ending June 30.

THIRD PERIOD: 1925-1929 [12]

	Men	*Women*	*Children*	*Total*	*Men*	*Women*	*Children*	*Total*
1925	97	29	10	136	751	37	43	831
1926	136	27		163	2,436	317	135	2,888
1927	75	2	1	78	2,023	80	151	2,254
1928	117	6	9	132	1,405	47	63	1,515
1929	135	22	23	180	2,192	48	58	2,298
Total	560	86	43	689	8,807	529	450	9,786

[12] All classes of passengers; fiscal years ending June 30.

III. SUMMARY

	From Philippines to Hawaii				*From Hawaii to the Philippines*			
	Men	*Women*	*Children*	*Total*	*Men*	*Women*	*Children*	*Total*
1907-19 .. 12½ yrs.	23,418	3,009	2,022	28,449	3,483	410	443	4,336
1920-24 .. 5 yrs.	23,187	4,178	1,861	29,226	6,357	839	981	8,177
1925-29 .. 5 yrs.	42,186	1,468	750	44,404	13,445	1,768	2,759	17,972
Total 22½ yrs.	88,791	8,655	4,633	102,069	23,285	3,017	4,183	30,485

	Men	*Women*	*Children*	*Total*
Net gain by excess of arrivals over departures	65,506	5,638	450	71,584

	From Cont. U.S.A. to Hawaii				*From Hawaii to Cont. U.S.A.*			
	Men	*Women*	*Children*	*Total*	*Men*	*Women*	*Children*	*Total*
1907-19 .. 12½ yrs.	39	5	3	47	2,309	37	36	2,382
1920-24 .. 5 yrs.	72	9	2	83	3,438	125	91	3,654
1925-29 .. 5 yrs.	560	86	43	689	8,807	529	450	9,786
Total	671	100	48	819	14,554	691	577	15,822

	Men	*Women*	*Children*	*Total*
Net loss by excess of departures over arrivals	13,883	591	529	15,003
Net gains to Hawaii from both movements, 1907-1929	51,623	5,047	−79	56,581

NOTE

THE data for all years before 1925 are taken from the annual reports of the Governors of Hawaii to whom they were furnished by the Hawaiian Sugar Planters' Association. They are for steerage passengers only; but it is believed that there were very few passengers other than steerage, and that the arrivals and departures of such non-steerage passengers nearly balanced. The data for 1907-1910 are for calendar years, those for 1911 are for six months, and those for 1912-1924 are for fiscal years ending June 30. The data for the five years 1925-1929 are from a dependable source which I am not permitted to quote. They are for the fiscal years ending June 30 and include all classes of passengers. The use of two sorts of data, the one for steerage only and the other for all passengers, is subject to some criticism, but one must use the available data as best he can. The error due to the inclusion of first- and second-class passengers in the later years, or due to their exclusion in the earlier, cannot exceed a few hundred in the final balance.

In the ten years ending June 30, 1929, Hawaii gained 47,481 by excess of arrivals from the Orient, including some who sailed from Hongkong, over departures to the Orient. But during the same period Hawaii lost 12,668 by excess of departures to Continental United States over arrivals from there, so that the net gain was 34,813.

Due to a considerable immigration of Filipino women in the years 1920-1924, the birth rate has increased, so that the total Filipino population in Hawaii has increased by several thousand through excess of births over deaths in the last decade. Among those who departed from Hawaii were several thousand Hawaiian-born children of Filipinos, and to this extent the figures for departures should be reduced if one desires to determine the number of immigrants who have left the Islands.

APPENDIX C

PROVINCES OF ORIGIN OF FILIPINO LABORERS MIGRATING FROM THE PHILIPPINE ISLANDS TO HAWAII, 1916-1928[1]

Province	*1916*	*1917*	*1918*	*1919*	*1920*	*1921*	*1922*	*1923*	*1924*	*1925*	*1926*	*1927*	*1928*	*Total*
Abra	..	7	10	10	24	20	110	214	294	203	88	242	271	1,493
Agusan	..	2	..	..	3	5	14	3	3	..	..	1	..	32
Albay	18	7	4	9	..	6	5	..	..	..	3	2	..	54
Antigue	13	15	2	9	4	24	19	6	..	1	2	..	..	95
Bataan	6	..	..	..	7	1	2	..	.	..	..	2	2	20
Batanes	39	53	9	6	17	27	23	6	76	12	6	1	..	275
Batangas	9	11	4	4	5	13	2	2	4	..	..	1	2	57
Bohol	137	113	135	463	330	987	1,063	691	496	352	77	40	93	4,977
Bulacan	38	2	2	8	1	15	9	6	1	1	..	3	..	86
Cagayan	4	3	5	5	16	23	42	25	29	45	4	94	118	413
Camarines Sur *	10	9	2	3	6	12	3	..	1	..	..	..	..	46
Capiz	56	74	11	51	30	66	32	22	14	20	1	2	5	384
Cavite	7	1	..	2	1	6	4	..	1	..	..	5	4	31
Cebu	669	952	1,049	808	813	1,825	1,994	1,339	1,218	717	209	60	138	11,791
Davao	..	..	..	..	..	4	2	..	..	1	..	..	..	7
Ilocos Norte	348	612	844	949	1,072	1,072	2,159	2,738	3,997	2,009	915	3,701	2,833	23,204
Ilocos Sur	79	147	163	412	371	572	705	1,014	2,100	1,220	349	2,519	2,045	11,696
Iloilo	53	32	20	20	33	42	43	6	12	10	6	7	6	290
Isabela	1	1	1	..	..	2	5	1	5	3	1	42	35	97
Laguna	15	5	..	8	3	2	11	4	..	1	..	1	6	56
Lanao	..	..	..	1	..	2	8	..	..	..	..	..	..	11
La Union	32	18	13	11	76	30	107	302	407	395	24	807	872	3,094
Leyte	73	48	32	69	87	290	327	164	226	92	48	10	4	1,470

Manila	9	20	2	1	..	7	3	1	5	1	1	68	11	129
Marinduque	..	..	..	..	..	2	..	..	..	..	..	..	..	2
Masbate	..	..	..	..	1	..	5	1	..	4	..	..	..	11
Mindoro	9	2	..	1	..	6	3	1	..	..	..	..	..	22
Misamis	23	18	1	51	42	81	114	83	21	13	13	1	1	462
Mountain Prov.	6	2	..	..	..	5	1	..	..	..	..	1	..	15
Nueva Ecija	19	15	..	1	13	11	50	6	18	25	3	17	29	207
Nueva Vizcaya	1	2	2	..	1	1	5	3	1	2	..	9	5	32
Occ. Negros	24	8	17	15	13	35	24	17	10	6	10	1	..	180
Or. Negros	221	134	306	710	284	646	555	379	83	38	12	16	46	3,430
Palawan	6	1	1	..	1	..	..	..	.	..	..	..	..	91
Pamganga	31	18	3	9	10	11	12	13	3	6	6	1	17	140
Pangasinan	151	122	50	59	138	611	474	68	598	711	59	1,352	2,226	6,619
Rizal	19	13	2	15	2	6	3	..	1	2	..	4	3	70
Romblon	..	..	3	5	2	18	8	3	8	2	..	..	..	49
Samar	20	7	3	3	9	16	12	4	7	5	..	..	..	86
Sorsogon	11	3	2	12	8	8	8	1	..	2	..	..	..	55
Surigao	12	3	4	3	6	31	14	9	9	3	3	1	..	98
Tarlac	24	96	47	47	47	245	145	117	200	578	94	237	519	2,396
Tayabas	13	16	4	13	1	2	15	1	..	1	..	1	1	68
Zambales	4	5	4	2	12	4	13	..	15	37	1	22	25	144
Zamboanga	4	1	4	9	10	22	30	11	6	1	1	3	5	107
TOTAL	2,214	2,598	2,761	3,804	3,454	6,814	8,183	7,261	9,869	6,519	1,936 †	9,274 †	9,322	74,009

* Camarine Norte included.

† Number of laborers contracted only by the Hawaiian Sugar Planters' Association, while the true number of emigrants including those who went voluntarily are 3,356 and 10,074 respectively.

[1] From Bulletin of the Philippine Islands Bureau of Labor, March, 1927, and Annual Reports of the Bureau of Labor, 1927 and 1928.

APPENDIX D

THE RACIAL COMPOSITION OF PERSONNEL EMPLOYED IN THE ALASKAN SALMON CANNING INDUSTRY

Compiled from the Annual Reports of the United States Bureau of Fisheries

	1928	*1927*	*1926*	*1925*	*1924*	*1923*	*1922*	*1921*	*Total*
Fishermen									
Whites	4,501	4,443	4,360	4,728	4,052	4,281	4,289	3,444	34,098
Natives	2,189	1,860	1,723	1,725	1,764	1,633	1,511	903	13,408
Chinese	1	...	...	...	2	...	...	...	3
Japanese	4	1	1	...	4	...	1	...	11
Filipinos	16	7	16	11	15	...	...	...	65
Mexicans	6	1	6	1	...	...	...	...	14
Kanakas	5	2	4	...	...	...	...	...	11
Miscellaneous	...	...	1 [2]	6 [3]	2 [4]	28 [5]	26 [5]	5 [5]	68
Total	6,722	6,314	6,111	6,471	5,839	5,942	5,827	4,352	47,678
Shoresmen									
Whites	5,971	5,370	5,548	5,287	4,955	4,410	3,655	2,577	37,773
Natives	2,027	1,850	2,300	1,987	2,203	2,302	2,118	1,556	16,343
Chinese	1,065	1,089	1,112	1,242	1,325	1,311	1,219	887	9,250
Japanese	1,445	1,299	1,481	1,518	1,371	1,056	885	611	9,666
Filipinos	3,916	2,857	2,584	2,213	1,659	1,431	1,520	957	17,137
Mexicans	1,269	1,366	1,046	1,502	1,320	1,749	1,362	1,357	10,971
Kanakas	61	42	60	...	...	...	...	...	163
Porto Ricans	44	16	20	150	129	...	...	...	359
Negroes	195	252	255	252	175	160	147	108	1,544
Koreans	...	17	...	...	...	...	...	...	17
Miscellaneous	24 [1]	...	43 [2]	88 [3]	74 [4]	63 [5]	101 [5]	51 [5]	444
Total	16,017	14,158	14,449	14,239	13,211	12,482	11,007	8,104	103,667
Transporters									
Whites	1,567	1,566	1,210	1,023	983	917	800	489	8,555
Natives	82	51	75	46	47	64	42	38	445
Chinese	8	12	5	6	8	...	...	...	39
Japanese	13	23	43	12	11	...	...	...	112
Mexicans	...	...	...	1	1	...	...	...	2
Filipinos	7	5	6	6	6	...	...	...	30
Koreans	...	1	...	...	...	...	...	...	1
Porto Ricans	...	1	...	...	...	...	...	...	1
Negroes	11	...	6	...	...	...	5	...	22
Miscellaneous	1 [1]	...	1 [2]	1 [3]	1 [4]	34 [5]	16 [5]	3 [5]	57
Total	1,689	1,659	1,346	1,095	1,057	1,015	863	530	9,264

	1928	1927	1926	1925	1924	1923	1922	1921	Total
Total									
Whites	12,039	11,379	11,118	11,038	9,990	9,608	8,744	6,510	80,426
Natives	4,298	3,761	4,098	3,758	4,014	3,999	3,671	2,497	30,096
Chinese	1,074	1,101	1,117	1,248	1,335	1,311	1,219	887	9,292
Japanese	1,462	1,323	1,525	1,530	1,386	1,056	886	611	9,779
Filipinos	3,939	2,869	2,606	2,230	1,680	1,431	1,520	957	17,232
Mexicans	1,275	1,367	1,052	1,504	1,321	1,749	1,362	1,357	10,987
Kanakas	66	44	64	...	...	...	...	...	174
Koreans	...	18	...	...	...	...	...	...	18
Porto Ricans	44	17	20	150	129	...	...	...	370
Negroes	206	252	261	252	175	160	152	108	1,566
Miscellaneous	25 [1]	...	45 [2]	95 [3]	77 [4]	125 [5]	143 [5]	59 [5]	519
Total	24,428	22,131	21,906	21,805	20,107	19,439	17,697	12,986	160,459

[1] Koreans, Arabians, etc.
[2] Hawaiians, Koreans, etc.
[3] Hawaiians, Koreans, Kanakas, etc.
[4] Kanakas, Koreans, etc.
[5] Koreans, Porto Ricans, Kanakas, etc.

APPENDIX E

TWO ILLUSTRATIVE CASES OF ACUTE ANTAGONISM TO FILIPINO IMMIGRANTS

I. IN WATSONVILLE, CAL., JANUARY, 1930

WATSONVILLE is a progressive country town in Santa Cruz County, California, with a population of about 10,000, the center of the Pajaro Valley, famous for its Newtown pippins and other apples of which nearly eight million boxes are shipped to all parts of the country every year. It also is a shipping center for apricots, cherries, pears, plums, strawberries, blackberries and other fruit. The loganberry originated in its vicinity. In recent years, another large crop was added to the local industries: Changes in the dietary habits of Americans have elevated the lowly lettuce from a bit of pleasant garnish to an important food product. The Pajaro Valley was not slow in converting many thousands of acres previously under root crops, vegetables, hay, and old apple orchards to this profitable crop.

This agricultural innovation brought with it important economic and social changes, of which indirectly the recent rioting was an unfortunate and unanticipated outcome. It brought into the valley outside capital and outside companies, which leased large acreages from the local land owners and, without the same direct interest that local growers have in the consequences of their operations, introduced methods which, while of unquestionable economic benefit to the community as a whole, nevertheless also introduced new problems.

For, it was found that the local American farm population did not wish to perform the arduous labor of lettuce cultivation, thinning, weeding and cutting. Mexican laborers were tried but—statements of the Agricultural Committee of the California Chamber of Commerce to the contrary notwithstanding—were not found satisfactory. Of Chinese and Japanese laborers, accustomed to high-speed stoop-labor for long hours, not enough could be found to meet the demand. But it so happened that a large influx of Filipino labor to California coincided with the rapidly increasing demand of the market. (Even in 1924 the quantities of lettuce shipped from the Pajaro Valley were more or less insignificant; in 1928 nearly 20,000 car loads were iced and sent East, 5,000 of them the strictly local output.) Without the availability of Filipino labor at this time, the expansion of this local industry, according to all informed witnesses, would have been impossible.

As in the larger lettuce area of the Salinas Valley, only part of the operations are carried on under direct employment by the grower. During the period of harvesting, which runs from about April 1 to about December 1, additional labor needs are met by hiring Filipino contractors who in turn accept responsibility for keeping a given number of men on the job. These workers may be housed in a camp on the ranch but in the Pajaro Valley more frequently, because of the relatively small acreage of individual holdings, are living in the contractor's own camp, either in the town or near some cross-roads whence a considerable number of potential employers can easily be reached by truck or auto-bus. The contractor usually is paid a fixed price per acre for whatever operation he is engaged for, and the workers are paid from 30 to 45 cents per hour. This great diversity of wages is explained, in part, by variations in the local labor supply and the ease with which new contractors can come into the business by undercutting those longer established; in part, by the provision or non-provision of housing facilities on the part of the employer. Probably 40 cents is the wage most widely received by workers providing their own board and room.

As elsewhere, there are divided opinions about the satisfaction given by Filipino workers. These are not in this industry in competition with white workers, since the local growers, benefiting from earlier unpleasant experiences in Salinas, have scrupulously avoided employing Filipinos in the packing sheds or on trucks, tractors and cultivating machines. Nevertheless, the lettuce growers, by attracting Filipinos to the valley, have made it possible for a few local fruit growers occasionally to employ Filipinos at fruit picking, peeling and coring in competition with white American workers—mostly, at the latter occupations, women and girls. Also, at least a few hundred acres now under lettuce must previously have offered seasonally or even all-year-around employment to local white workers. While all these different forms of competition do not in the aggregate amount to very much, nevertheless the few individual instances of worklessness or destitution which came to the reporter's attention seem to point to the probability that for large numbers of local families, occupying exceedingly small holdings of their own—so small, in fact, as barely to deserve the name of farm or ranch—opportunities of occasional labor, whether for a few days or for a few weeks at a time, are essential to eke out a precarious livelihood. And it is precisely these odd jobs and short seasonal employments of all sorts which the Filipino, easily found available in sufficient numbers, is likely to get.

Contrary to some of the newspaper reports, migrant American labor had nothing to do with the recent disturbance around Watsonville; for the time of their annual pilgrimage to the apple orchards and to the packing sheds had not arrived.

But it is very doubtful whether competition for jobs, apart from supplying a background of ill-will on the part of the economically weakest section of the population, can be named as the cause of the outbreak of violence. This outbreak had been preceded by much occasional unpleasantness on the streets and wherever American youths and Filipinos met. The local Filipinos showed their relative prosperity in ways offensive to their white American neighbors when they spent a large part of their income on clothes and automobiles. Worse than that, with money in their pockets, the Filipino youths were seen to be lavish in entertainments and gifts to members of the other sex and sometimes went too far for local traditions in bringing themselves to the favorable attention of the fair.

The denunciation of the Filipinos as a race by Justice of the Peace D. W. Rohrback of Pajaro township, which took the form of a resolution proposed to and adopted by the Chamber of Commerce of Northern Monterey County (not to be confused with the important Chamber of Commerce of the Pajaro Valley, which has its seat in the neighboring city of Watsonville) on January 7, 1930, and which was the unintentional immediate cause of the troubles in January, was the outcome of many observations and experiences of this kind. The judge, a conscientious and public-spirited elderly man whose carriage and attitudes recall the old-time magistrate of a village in Baden or Württemberg, had for long been worried by the things he could see from his little shack of a courthouse of the Filipino settlement across the way and around the corner. Complaints were continually being brought to his attention by neighbors and clients. Filipino boys were frequently seen accosting American girls. One of them, standing on the bridge connecting the somewhat gloomy looking town of Pajaro with its more prosperous neighbor, Watsonville, was patting a little girl, not yet fourteen, as she passed him, asking her what was the hurry. Two girls, thirteen and fourteen years of age, of American stock, drove up to their house at 12.30 A.M., accompanied by a Filipino. The children of an American neighbor are going wrong: the father cannot keep them in decent clothes because the Filipinos—so he says—take his jobs away; and "these foreigners, with their gambling and wicked ways, show a bad example." Then there was the case of the Filipino boy who in near-by Salinas was found occupying a room with two little girls of German stock, aged sixteen and eleven, in a Filipino rooming house (though the case, on later examination, did not appear nearly as bad as it had seemed at first, for the boy considered himself, and was considered by the parents, engaged to the older girl and had harmed neither of them).[1] Men come from the camp grounds, and women too, asking for help; and everywhere as he drives through the country, Filipinos—he counted fifty-two of them in one field alone—are hoeing their rows of lettuce.

The good judge was deeply perturbed. He had been pondering the matter for weeks (maybe had read some thundering editorials on the subject of the Filipino in the California press); and so one day he drafted his resolution demanding that the Filipinos be sent upon their way and followed it up with a lengthy interview in the *Evening Pajaronian,* setting forth his views. The world took little notice of either resolution or article; the *Watsonville Register* did not even find them worth mentioning; but a Filipino organization in Stockton took hold of it with a vengeance and flooded the valley with leaflets denouncing the judge and the organized campaign of slander of which, somehow, he was declared to be the mouthpiece.

Probably the situation would have simmered on in this fashion, had it not been for the unfortunate fact that the local Filipinos chose this particular time for a new experiment in merrymaking. In view of the resentment shown to their association with local girls, they rented a house on the beach and there opened a club to be

[1] It is sometimes difficult, because of discrepancies in the reports, to decide whether two accounts are of the same incident or of separate occurrences. V. S. McClatchy has told the House Committee on Immigration "of a young girl, seventeen or eighteen years of age, who associated with a Filipino. Her parents endeavored to stop it but without avail. She was missing for two or three days, and they started to hunt for her, and she was found hidden in a Filipino hotel. She made complaint that she had been mistreated, and she was taken to the detention home. That was only one of the incidents which inflamed the public." Hearings on Exclusion of Immigration from the Philippine Islands, Seventy-first Congress, Second Session, April 10, 1930, p. 35.

used as a center for healthful recreation. Or rather, as usual in such cases, an enterprising individual started the venture, had the club incorporated and registered with the local authorities, made the rules of membership and then, in order to start off with the biggest possible attraction, engaged a dozen or so white American girls from the town of Guadalupe, Santa Barbara County, to entertain the boys as professional dancing partners. He afterwards contended that all the female staff of the establishment were the wives of either Filipino members or of members of the orchestra; but the very strict rules concerning the conduct to be observed by the taxi dancers, which he permitted to be published, rather belie this picture of a family party.

Now the fat was in the fire. What was more natural than that local rowdies wanted to horn in on the festivities! For a week or more the show outside the premises, for of course non-members were refused admission and only Filipinos were admitted to membership, was more exciting than that within. Nightly the crowd increased: eighty, two hundred, five hundred, eight hundred. The proprietor of the house leased to the Filipinos fastened a heavy chain across the street and, with his brother and some hired men, warded off the shouting assembly. He also wrote to the district attorney asking for protection. In fact, the authorities took no notice whatever of these disturbances, except for three deputy sheriffs who watched the dance itself, presumably with a view to finding cause for closing it. (The Filipinos, by foolish rather than by vicious behavior, certainly had given ample grounds for watchfulness.) Nor did any organization of American citizens indicate displeasure even long after the tone of the mob had become menacing, when windows had been broken, private dwellings been entered and searched, Filipinos been attacked with bludgeons, and shots been fired into passing automobiles. Only the accident of a fatal bullet, almost a week after these occurrences had started, produced action by the authorities and resolutions by the civic organizations. Public opinion permitted the young rowdies to hector the Filipinos without interference wherever they found them, to throw a group into the river mud here, to belabor and tear the clothes of another group, to break up their club on the beach. Even after a group of Filipino boys had been brought to the police station for protection and were cowering there afraid for their lives, the police permitted a crowd of hoodlums to stay outside as though ready to lynch the Filipinos as soon as they might come out. Filipinos who by their previous behavior had at least contributed toward their widespread criticism now felt themselves martyrs in the cause of public order and decency.

The offenders were not transient fruit pickers or other strangers; the eight boys who later were arraigned on a charge of entering a Filipino camp and forcing the inmates to dress and leave the house were local residents. Many of the others who took part in the rioting were at first impelled, no doubt, by nothing more than a desire to watch the fun. The assemblage grew as verbal repartee changed into that of rocks and rifle shots; for now, the owners, considering themselves unprotected by the guardians of the law, resorted to the defence of their premises with rice shots—among which, they later confessed, a few regular bullets may "inadvertently" have slipped.

It did not take long for this localized battle to develop into a widespread disturbance. If the police only arrested some of those who took part in a single raid, the reason is not that witnesses could not have been found to identify the perpetrators of other raids. But it was left to the Filipinos, afraid for their lives and uncertain of the attitude of the police and courts, to prefer charges; and in the one case in which they did so, their testimony that firearms had been used and that small articles were stolen during the raid was not accepted by the court. Automobiles crowded with youths toured the district and shot stones or bullets into passing automobiles when these were supposed to contain Filipinos—in one case nearly killing a farmer and his wife—and into farm buildings supposed to house Filipinos.

It was during one such raid, on January 22, that Fermin Tobera, twenty-two years old, a wholesome, bright-eyed youth against whom none had a grudge, was killed. As a carload of men reached the ranch where Tobera worked, and began firing into the camp building, the Filipino workers, including Tobera's brother, hid in a cupboard, fearing that the house would be raided and they be subjected to physical violence. When the noise ceased, Tobera was still in bed, and his companions thought he had slept through it all. Next morning he was found to have been shot through the heart; and it was too late for the police to apprehend the killer or to learn the identity of the raiding party.

This fatality sobered the community. The authorities at once showed some vigor in prosecuting the boys who had been arrested for rioting and endeavored, unsuccessfully, to secure evidence against others. Members of the American Legion patrolled the approaches to the city of Watsonville, "to prevent the entrance of suspicious characters." The Rotary, Kiwanis and 20-30 Clubs, with the American Legion, the Spanish War Veterans and the Merchants' Association, met and passed an appropriate resolution.

At this point in the passage of events, various interests began to search in the Watsonville affair for useful propaganda material. Supporters of the movement for Filipino exclusion took care that the world heard about this affair; and no part of the country could help reading of it as an illustration of America's most recent race problem. Filipino organizations, both regional and national, apt students of propaganda methods as of other American inventions, were not slow to point the political moral: "Give the Philippine Islands their promised independence; and we shall go home and prevent the recurrence of such events as these." The Agricultural Committee of the Chamber of Commerce of California used the occasion for a strong repetition of its plea for Mexican labor and against its further restriction. A Communist organization, the Agricultural Workers' Industrial League, circulated a leaflet asking American and Filipino workers to combine against the farm owners' conspiracy to prevent a united front of the wage earners.

The body of Tobera was shipped to the Philippine Islands with much pomp and circumstance; but while he is described in the Philippine press as a martyr of American intolerance, it does not seem that large numbers of his compatriots have followed him to the homeland to escape persecution. As an indication of the differences in group attitude that follow differences of treatment, it is worth observing that attempts of American Filipino organizations to stage a demonstration at the bier of Tobera in Honolulu as it passed through that port failed to materialize because the Filipino organizations in that city found that they had nothing to gain and much to lose by magnifying the killing of Tobera into a major issue between themselves and their Caucasian fellow citizens. Instead of holding a mass meeting, the various organizations combined in a dignified church service after which delegates from each went to the ship and laid wreaths on the dead boy's coffin.

Eight young Americans were convicted of rioting in Judge Rohrback's court and were eventually given a suspended sentence of two years in the county jail by the Superior Court of Monterey County. Four of them were minors; these already had served about 30 days in jail. The four who were of age were sentenced to serve one month in jail before being permitted on probation. All of them were first offenders; and the district attorney joined the probation officer who had carried on the investigation in recommending the utmost leniency. To the present writer only one of the older men and one of the minors looked what might be called "tough." Leniency was indicated as a desirable element in the court's decision not only by the youth and previous good behavior of the defendants but also by a letter making a plea for it which the court received from the regional Filipino organization, and especially, by the sense of the community at large.

One of the immediate effects of the Watsonville affair was a movement of Filipino workers to other cities. Another was a decided change in the recreational habits of those who remained; it was no longer safe, as one of the local Filipinos reported to a paper in the Islands, to stroll alone in the streets at night.

But the excitement in Watsonville soon died down. At the Superior Court hearing in the neighboring city of Salinas, which passed sentence upon the eight rioters, barely a score of persons were present. The streets of Watsonville, at the end of February, were quiet. Across the bridge in Pajaro, Filipinos, between jobs, were playing pool as usual. On the ranches there was no shortage of Filipino labor.

2. IN THE YAKIMA VALLEY OF WASHINGTON, SEPTEMBER, 1928

On September 19, 1928, a "committee of citizens" met two bus loads of Filipino laborers at Dryden, four miles west of Cashmere and escorted them back over the Blewett Pass. The Filipinos had been engaged by a reputable fruit-buying concern in Seattle to pick and pack apples for them near Cashmere; there were forty or fifty of them. The so-called citizens' committee consisted of about 150 local men, fruit workers, orchard owners, and others. Accompanying the two buses to the summit of the pass some thirty-five miles from Cashmere, this "committee" instructed the drivers to "keep going" and threatened violence if they should attempt to unload their passengers on the eastern side of the mountain.

At Sunnyside, in the Yakima Valley, about the same time, a number of Filipinos asked to be locked up in the local jail for safety. They had been threatened with violence in a town near by called Toppenish, which is located on the Yakima Indian Reservation.

The Filipinos left the neighborhood soon afterwards, and nothing more was heard of the affair.

On September 21, 1928, two hundred white laborers at Wenatchee appeared at a camp occupied by twenty-two Filipinos, who were working in the local cannery and warned them to leave town. The mob was dispersed by the local police. No damage was done to property, and no physical violence was used. The Filipino laborers afterwards placed themselves under the protection of the local police and were no longer molested.

These three incidents, and one or two others concerning which not even such meager particulars as those given above could be secured, became the subject of much investigation by state and federal authorities. The press had made them appear more serious than they actually were, and interpellations, both in Congress and in the Philippine legislature, aroused widespread interest.

The following explanations seem to satisfy those who have most closely looked into this situation: First, the Sunnyside incident has little to do with the general situation in the valley, as a quarrel concerning a white woman was the main cause, not economic competition. The two other incidents both arose from the use of Filipinos in occupations which local and itinerant white American and immigrant workers had filled in the past and wished to retain. These workers, to some extent, had the sympathy of other local folk because they spend their money in the valley whereas the Filipinos live cheaply and take the bulk of their earnings away with them.

In Cashmere, the Filipino workers arriving in the latter part of September were not needed, according to local information, to harvest the apple crop; enough local and seasonal labor was available at that time, and the employment of more Filipinos from the outside meant that the employment of white workers present in the community, who had been looking forward to that job, was curtailed to that extent. The Filipinos were to have been employed at the regular price for picking apples, namely, five cents per box; but American workers—according to one disinterested local informant—had hoped to be able to boost this price to six or seven cents. In Wenatchee, both night and day work in the cannery had previously been done by women; but when it was unable to secure enough women to make up the night shift, the concern sent for Filipinos. After the trouble was over, until late in November, about 75 Filipinos continued to work in the orchards and in the cannery under the special protection of sheriff and police. In the first instance, though informed of the plan to stop those buses, the police had appeared on the stage too late to intervene.

In both cases, the more responsible citizens expressed themselves as on the side of the Filipinos and their right to work unmolested at the jobs they were filling to their employers' satisfaction. The aggressors at Wenatchee, in the local opinion, were migratory workers who, under the leadership of professional labor agitators, were attempting to force up wages beyond a reasonable figure. The presence of other persons in the mob at Cashmere, including a few local orchardists, were explained as due to curiosity.

Whether the prices for apple picking were reasonable or not, is of course a matter of dispute which can only be answered by the relation between offer and demand. According to one large-scale apple grower, five cents per box—with an extra penny on varieties that bruise easily and must be treated with care—had been the price paid for the last ten years. This, in view of the general rise in the cost of living, would suggest that the American laborers had a just cause for grievance. But according to the witness mentioned, most of the crew averaged earnings of over $5 a day, over a season, in his orchard, of 35 days, while a few expert pickers could make as much as $10 a day.

The Filipinos employed in the cannery were on night work, for which they received the straight time-wage of $3, the same amount as that paid to the women making up the day shift. No women were employed at night and no Filipinos in the day time. These boys had been contracted for by a Filipino employment agency in Seattle at the same time that some three hundred white men in Wenatchee were looking for work, because the apple season that year was unusually late. Among these seasonal workers there are always some who do not really desire continuous employment during the season even when it can be had but manage, somehow, to lead a more or less parasitic life.

The fact is stressed that, although there was much ill-feeling, no violence was used and no property damaged and that, in fact, Filipinos continued to work in the district the rest of that season and again the following year. There is no doubt that, but for the presence of these foreign workers, more Americans would have been employed; and considering the fee paid the Filipino employment agency and the general state of the market, the white migrant workers were not altogether unreasonable in surmising that the market might afford a slightly higher rate of payment. These incidents, then, are a clear illustration of a purely economic rivalry in which the Filipinos' lower standard of living merely served as ocular evidence of "unfair" competition.

APPENDIX F

FILIPINO STUDENTS IN THE UNITED STATES, 1929-1930

Compiled by the Committee on Friendly Relations Among Foreign Students

I. DISTRIBUTION

	Women	*Men*	*Total*
ARIZONA			
University of Arizona (Tucson)	..	10	10
CALIFORNIA			
Citrus Junior College (Agusa)	..	6	6
College of Medical Evangelists (Loma Linda)	..	1	1
Fresno State College (Fresno)	..	5	5
Pacific Union College (Angwin)	..	1	1
Pasadena Junior College (Pasadena)	..	8	8
San Jose State College (San Jose)	1	38	39
St. Ignatius College (San Francisco)	..	9	9
St. Mary's College (Oakland)	..	2	2
Stanford University	..	4	4
State Teachers College (San Diego)	..	4	4
University of California (Berkeley)	1	58	59
University of California at Los Angeles	..	16	16
University of Santa Clara (Santa Clara)	..	1	1
University of Southern California (Los Angeles)	1	6	7
Whittier College (Whittier)	1	..	1
	4	159	163
COLORADO			
Regis College (Denver)	..	2	2
University of Denver (Denver)	..	2	2
	..	4	4
CONNECTICUT			
Yale University (New Haven)	..	1	1

	Women	Men	Total
DISTRICT OF COLUMBIA			
Georgetown University	..	2	2
George Washington University	..	34	34
	..	36	36
IDAHO			
University of Idaho (Moscow)	..	12	12
ILLINOIS			
Chicago Medical School (Chicago)	..	4	4
Chicago Technical College (Chicago)	..	1	1
Illinois College (Jacksonville)	..	1	1
Knox College (Galesburg)	..	1	1
Lake Forest College (Lake Forest)	..	1	1
Lewis Institute (Chicago)	..	73	73
Loyola University (Chicago)	..	1	1
National Kindergarten and Elementary College (Evanston)	1	..	1
Northwestern University (Chicago)	..	19	19
Union Theological College (Chicago)	..	1	1
University of Chicago (Chicago)	..	17	17
University of Illinois (Urbana)	2	18	20
	3	137	140
INDIANA			
Indiana University (Bloomington)	..	3	3
Notre Dame University (Notre Dame)	..	1	1
Purdue University (West Lafayette)	..	9	9
Tri-State College (Angola)	..	4	4
	..	17	17
IOWA			
Cornell College (Mt. Vernon)	..	1	1
Drake University (Des Moines)	..	1	1
Grinnell College (Grinnell)	..	2	2
Iowa State College (Ames)	..	7	7
State University of Iowa (Iowa City)	..	10	10
Iowa State Teachers College (Cedar Falls)	..	1	1
	..	22	22

	Women	Men	Total
KANSAS			
Kansas State Agricultural College (Manhattan)	..	4	4
University of Kansas (Lawrence)	..	26	26
	..	30	30
KENTUCKY			
Asbury College (Wilmore)	..	1	1
Louisville Presbyterian Seminary (Louisville)	..	2	2
University of Louisville (Louisville)	..	2	2
	..	5	5
LOUISIANA			
Louisiana State University (Baton Rouge)	1	15	16
MARYLAND			
Johns Hopkins University (Baltimore)	..	2	2
MASSACHUSETTS			
Boston University (Boston)	2	1	3
Gordon College of Theology (Boston)	..	1	1
Harvard University (Cambridge)	..	2	2
Massachusetts Institute of Technology (Cambridge)	..	7	7
New England Conservatory of Music (Boston)	..	2	2
Northeastern University (Boston)	..	1	1
	2	14	16
MICHIGAN			
Calvin College (Grand Rapids)	..	1	1
Hillsdale College (Hillsdale)	..	1	1
Michigan State College (East Lansing)	1	1	2
Michigan State Normal College (Ypsilanti)	..	3	3
University of Michigan (Ann Arbor)	1	21	22
	2	27	29
MINNESOTA			
College of St. Theresa (Winona)	1	..	1
College of St. Thomas (St. Paul)	..	2	2
University of Minnesota (Minneapolis)	1	23	24
	2	25	27

	Women	Men	Total
MISSOURI			
Drury College (Springfield)	..	2	2
Southwest Baptist College (Bolivar)	..	1	1
St. Louis University (St. Louis)	..	2	2
University of Missouri (Columbia)	..	3	3
Washington University (St. Louis)	..	2	2
William Jewell College (Liberty)	..	1	1
	..	11	11
MONTANA			
Intermountain Union College (Helena)	..	1	1
Montana State University (Missoula)	..	5	5
	..	6	6
NEBRASKA			
University of Nebraska (Lincoln)	..	28	28
NEW MEXICO			
University of New Mexico (Albuquerque)	..	1	1
NEW JERSEY			
Drew University (Madison)	..	1	1
Princeton University (Princeton)	..	1	1
Princeton Theological Seminary (Princeton)	..	1	1
	..	3	3
NEW YORK			
Biblical Seminary in New York (New York)	..	1	1
College of the City of New York (New York)	..	1	1
Columbia University (New York)	7	16	23
Cornell University (Ithaca)	1	4	5
Elmira College (Elmira)	1	..	1
New York University (New York)	2	9	11
Pratt Institute (Brooklyn)	..	1	1
St. John's College-Fordham University (New	..	1	1
York)	..	1	1
Syracuse University (Syracuse)	1	1	2
Union Theological Seminary (New York)	..	4	4
	12	38	50
NEVADA			
University of Nevada (Reno)	..	2	2
NORTH CAROLINA			
University of North Carolina (Chapel Hill)	..	1	1

	Women	Men	Total
Ohio			
Bonebrake Theological Seminary (Dayton)	..	2	2
Denison University (Granville)	..	1	1
Ohio State University (Columbus)	..	6	6
University of Cincinnati (Cincinnati)	..	2	2
	..	11	11
Oklahoma			
Oklahoma Agricultural and Mechanical College (Stillwater)	..	1	1
University of Oklahoma (Norman)	..	2	2
	..	3	3
Oregon			
Albany College (Albany)	..	3	3
Columbia University (Portland)	..	1	1
Eugene Bible University (Eugene)	..	4	4
Linfield College (McMinnville)	..	6	6
Oregon State College (Corvallis)	..	17	17
University of Oregon (Eugene)	..	39	39
Willamette University (Salem)	..	3	3
	..	73	73
Pennsylvania			
Drexel Institute (Philadelphia)	..	1	1
Hahnemann Medical College (Philadelphia)	..	1	1
Philadelphia General Hospital (Philadelphia)	1	..	1
Temple University (Philadelphia)	..	4	4
University of Pennsylvania (Philadelphia)	..	2	2
University of Pittsburgh (Pittsburgh)	..	3	3
	1	11	12
South Dakota			
South Dakota College of Agriculture and Mechanical Arts (Brookings)	..	1	1
State College of Mines (Rapid City)	..	1	1
University of South Dakota (Vermilion)	..	1	1
	..	3	3
Texas			
Baylor University (Waco)	..	1	1

	Women	Men	Total
Utah			
University of Utah (Salt Lake City)	..	11	11
Utah State Agricultural College (Logan)	..	1	1
	..	12	12
Washington			
College of Puget Sound (Tacoma)	..	19	19
Seattle Pacific College (Seattle)	..	8	8
State College of Washington (Pullman)	1	62	63
University of Washington (Seattle)	2	45	47
Washington State Normal School (Ellensburg)	..	3	3
	3	137	140
West Virginia			
West Virginia University (Morgantown)	..	2	2
Wisconsin			
Marquette University (Milwaukee)	..	1	1
University of Wisconsin (Madison)	..	6	6
	..	7	7
Wyoming			
University of Wyoming (Laramie)	..	1	1
Total	30	866	896

II. COURSES OF STUDY

Agriculture	51
Architecture	4
Biology	5
Botany	3
Business Administration	31
Chemistry	6
Civil Engineering	10
Commerce	55
Dentistry	2
Economics	6
Education	94
Electrical Engineering	10
Engineering	59
English	20
Foreign Service	2

Forestry	3
Genetics	3
History	6
Household Economics	1
Latin	1
Law	15
Letters and Science	99
Liberal Arts	113
Library Science	1
Journalism	5
Mathematics	5
Mechanical Engineering	19
Medicine	15
Mining	10
Music	4
Naval Architecture	1
Not Reported	147
Nursing	1
Pharmacy	4
Physical Education	1
Physics	1
Philosophy	4
Political Science	11
Pre-Medical	15
Psychology	1
Public Health	1
Railway Engineering	1
Science	10
Social Science	12
Theology and Religion	19
Veterinary Medicine	5
Zoology	4
Total	896

APPENDIX G

THE PULL OF PREVIOUS EMIGRANTS AS A FACTOR IN FILIPINO EMIGRATION

To throw light on the part which personal contact with previous emigrants plays among the motivating causes of Filipino emigration, O. H. Charles, District School Superintendent of Pangasinan Province, distributed questionnaires among teachers and students of the local High and Normal School. The following facts are taken from 131 returns to the teacher questionnaire and 163 returns to the student questionnaire. The province, and particularly the immediate region where the great majority of teachers and students have their homes, is typical for the western coast of Luzon from which a majority of Filipino emigrants originate.

Of the teachers 64, or 49 per cent, have at least one friend or relative in Hawaii, the mean being 2.9 and the median 2; all but one have at least one friend on the mainland of the United States, the mean being 4.9 and the median 3. Of the students, 56, or 34 per cent, have at least one friend or relative in Hawaii, and 149, or 91 per cent, have friends or relatives on the mainland.

Owing to an unfortunate lack of clarity in the questionnaire, no complete reply is possible to the question, how long these friends and relatives have been in Hawaii and on the mainland respectively. However, for the friends and relatives of those teachers whose answers could be included, both the mode and the median of length of residence was two years for Hawaii and four years for the mainland. For the friends and relatives of students, the median was three years' residence, both in Hawaii and on the mainland.

Of the 131 teachers, 36, or 27 per cent, had friends who had been to and returned from Hawaii, the mean being 1.5 of such friends; and 62, or 47 per cent, had friends who had returned from the mainland, the mean being .8. Both the mode and median stay in Hawaii for those who had returned was three years; the mode for those returned from the mainland was seven years' stay, and the median six years. Of the 163 students, 37, or 23 per cent, had friends who had been to and returned from Hawaii; and 95, or

58 per cent, had friends returned from the mainland of the United States. Eliminating a number of doubtful answers, we find that for those friends who had returned from Hawaii the median stay was four years, and for those who had returned from the mainland five years—the respective mode being three years' stay in both cases.

Since many of the teachers and students unquestionably have the same friends, and duplications cannot be eliminated, a statistical record of the occupations held by these friends in Hawaii and on the mainland of the United States may be misleading, particularly also as in some cases there is reason for doubt as to whether the information furnished refers to one person or more. However, assuming that where numbers are not given, the answer refers to one friend, we find that out of 59 friends *in* Hawaii whose occupations were specified by the teachers, 27, or 46 per cent, were "on sugar plantations," 7, or 12 per cent, were "laborers," and 21, or 36 per cent, simply stated to be "earning." It may be inferred that almost 100 per cent of these friends are plantation workers. This is also true of 33 friends *returned from* Hawaii, whose occupation is given. Similarly, of 50 friends of students for whom this information is given, 28 are on sugar plantations, 4 on pineapple plantations, and 13 "earning," the remaining 5 being respectively goldsmith, aviator, soldier, musician and "self-supporting student."

Of 129 of the teachers' friends on the mainland of the United States, 62, or 32 per cent, are earning and studying at the same time, 26, or 20 per cent, studying, and 7, or 5 per cent, earning. Only two occupations are specifically named, each four times: hotel work and Navy. Of 58 friends returned from the mainland whose occupation is specified, 20, or 35 per cent, had studied, 17, or 29 per cent, had studied and earned at the same time, the remaining 21 having "labored" and "earned"—4 of them in the Navy. Of 151 friends of students on the mainland for whom this information is given, 52, or 34 per cent, were both studying and earning, 27, or 18 per cent, were studying, and 72 earning—specific occupations named being fruit-picking (6), waiter (6), sailor (6), workers in salmon canneries (5).[1]

Concerning the reasons for going to Hawaii and the mainland of the United States, the following figures assume that each answer, unless otherwise stated, refers to one friend who has gone.

[1] In the student questionnaires this information refers both to friends still abroad and to those who have returned.

Out of 49 friends of teachers whose motives for going to Hawaii are named, 40, or 82 per cent, went to "earn." This motive is associated with that of adventure and travel in 5 additional cases. Study as a sole motive is mentioned twice, in association with adventure once; adventure alone is mentioned only once. Almost the same proportions hold good for the friends of students who have gone to Hawaii. Out of 48 whose motives are reported, 40, or 83 per cent, went solely to "earn." This is also part of the remaining motivations, in association with a desire for better living and working conditions (4), for travel and adventure (3), and for study (1).

For the teachers' friends who went to the mainland, the motives are stated in 102 cases: 34, or 33 per cent, went to study, another 37, or 36 per cent, to study and earn, 6 to study and adventure, 6 to study, adventure and earn, and 11 merely to earn. Out of 151 friends of students whose motives are specified, 48, or 32 per cent, went to the mainland to study and earn at the same time, 29, or 19 per cent, simply to study; in 12 cases a desire for adventure is mentioned, and in another 10 a desire for travel.

The teachers' questionnaire distinguished from the question of motives a question as to the conditions which seemed most to have attracted their friends to Hawaii and the mainland of the United States. For all of the 51 migrants to Hawaii for whom this information is given, high wages formed an attraction. This cause stands alone in 40, or 78 per cent, of the replies. In five it is associated with the opportunity for adventure, in one each with favorable reports from friends and with the expectation of good living conditions, and in three cases with the stimulus of money sent back by other friends. Of 106 friends of the teachers on the mainland, 19, or 18 per cent, are said to have been attracted by educational opportunities; in 40 cases, 38 per cent, high wages are an additional attraction, and in 7 cases opportunities of adventure —making a total of 63 per cent of cases in which educational opportunity played a part. Only for 11, or 10 per cent, are high wages named as the sole attraction. Steamship advertisements and reports of friends are named five and four times respectively.

These proportions of mention in reply to specific questions may be checked against the mention of motives for their friends' emigration in brief essays attached by 75 of the teachers to their questionnaires. The desire to earn money here appears 64 times, in 85 per cent of the essays; but only 16 times (21 per cent) as the only motive. The desire for education here occurs 53 times, in 71 per cent of the essays; but only 6 times (8 per cent) as the only motive. Twenty-five, or one-third, mention love of adventure, but never by itself alone. It must be concluded that, with much inquiry into this subject, the replies have become somewhat stereotyped, for the three motives named are the only ones mentioned in the essays.

The teachers were asked to state whether their friends liked it in Hawaii and on the mainland of the United States. In tabulating their answers it is assumed that their replies either refer to all their friends in these two countries or represent their general impression from correspondence with them, except where specific mention is made of the attitudes of several individual friends:

Do the Friends Like it?	*Teachers Reporting*		*Friends Abroad Reported Upon*	
	Number	*Per Cent*	*Number*	*Per Cent*
IN HAWAII				
Yes	52	81	126	67
Fair	6	9.5	20	11
No	..	..	..	..
Doubtful	6	9.5	41	22
Total	64	100	187	100
ON MAINLAND				
Yes	115	88	462	74
Fair	11	9	136	21
No	..	..	..	..
Doubtful	4	3	32	5
Total	130	100	630	100

Noteworthy in this table is not only the complete absence of wholly unfavorable reports but also the fact that, evidently, the less favorable reports have less influence on public opinion: In regard to both Hawaii and the mainland of the United States the proportion of teachers reporting favorable attitudes on the part of their friends is larger, and the proportion of teachers reporting only moderate satisfaction on the part of their friends smaller than are the respective proportions of the total number of emigrants reported upon. The following table gives the same information for friends who have returned from Hawaii and the mainland of the United States:

Did the Friends Like it?	*Teachers Reporting*		*Returned Friends Reported Upon*	
	Number	*Per Cent*	*Number*	*Per Cent*
IN HAWAII				
Yes	28	78	44	80
Fair	2	5.4	5	9
No	3	8.3	3	5.5
Doubtful	3	8.3	3	5.5
Total	36	100	55	100
ON MAINLAND				
Yes	57	92	100	92.5
Fair	1	1.6	4	3.7
No	2	3.2	2	1.9
Doubtful	2	3.2	2	1.9
Total	62	100	108	100

A comparison of this table with the one previously given, if any reliance may be placed upon them, would seem to illustrate the fact that a slightly larger proportion of those who "have made good" and who therefore report favorably return home, so that the influence of satisfactory experiences abroad on public opinion is greater than that of average experiences. Or it may be that in retrospect hardships are forgotten. However, the often subjectively colored nature of the reports and the relatively small number of experiences reported upon hardly justify definite conclusions.

Both teachers and students were requested to state their reactions to the information given, the latter specifically as regards the effect of their friends' reports on their own plans. Of 153 students who answered this question, 55, or 36 per cent, plan to teach after graduation; 8 others (5 per cent) definitely state that they do not intend to go abroad; 26, or 17 per cent, plan to go to the United States for further study; 5 plan to go to the United States without specifying their purpose. In the more general essays, the proportion of those students who "wish to go to the United States" is much larger, namely, 88, or 62 per cent of a total of 143, while the proportion of those wishing to stay at home coincides with the proportion (but not the actual number) of those who stated they were going to teach after graduation—51 out of 143, or 36 per cent. Of the 88 who wish to go to the United States, 77 (48 per cent) desire to study, 35 of them (40 per cent) mentioning at the same time their purpose of earning money in the United States. Only two out of these 88 would-be emigrants mention the purpose of earning without naming education as an additional purpose. Fifty-eight of them indicate the amount of time they wish to stay in the United States, ranging from a minimum of three years (4) to a maximum of 20 years (1), a five- or ten-year period being most frequently mentioned. (The tendency of such estimates to cluster around digital figures is well known to statisticians.)

Somewhat stereotyped, it would seem, are the references of 68 out of the 88 students who wish to go to the United States to their probable career upon their return to the Philippine Islands: 34, or 50 per cent, desire to "serve their country"; 13, or 19 per cent, more definitely state that they are going to teach, and 8 that they will seek a government position. Three of the last-named and four others naïvely state that on their return they will invest their earnings. Four wish to go into business, three to develop food preservation (a promising Philippine industry much discussed in the schools), and one to "uplift the women of the Islands."

Both teachers and students in their brief essays give their observations and conclusions regarding the general effects of emigration. Of 38 teachers who comment on its benefits, 8 mention savings accumulated in Hawaii and on the mainland, 7 refer to the hardness of the work. Five give it as their opinion that the moral character of emigrants is destroyed by temptations far from their homes, 4 that emigrants were maltreated because of prejudice against them, 3 that they did not earn much money anyhow, 2 that it was very difficult for them to find jobs in the United States. On the other hand, 5 of the essays point to the good education that may be obtained in the United States, 2 to improvement of character through work abroad, and 2 to the value of widened experience through travel. Twenty-four speak of the great help of the emigrants to their families by sending money home, only 4 of the breaking up of families occasioned by the emigrants' departure.

Both students and teachers express themselves on the general advantages and disadvantages of emigration to the community, but the latter in many more instances and at greater length. Of 143 student essays, 9 disapprove emigration, 7 approve it, and 10 approve it for students only. Emigration is both approved and disapproved on patriotic grounds and on grounds of personal fortune. Of 75 essays by teachers 38 deplore the loss to the Philippine Islands of labor needed to develop the national resources; on the other hand, 11 place a high value on the training received in the United States, especially by future educators; 6 hold that returned emigrants promote the economic and social welfare of the community, and others single out for special commendation the importance of new capital saved by emigrant workers, the buildings erected with money earned abroad, the value of farming experience gained, training for future leadership in the community, and the contributions made by emigrants to better interracial understanding.

Ninety-two of the teachers' essays contain suggestions for dealing with emigration problems: 43, or 46 per cent, favor restriction; 15 of these, or 16 per cent of the total, specifically add their desire for student exemption from such restriction; 9 (10 per cent) favor a serious attempt to reduce the volume of emigration through the improvement of work and wage opportunities in the Islands; while another 6 (6 per cent) in general terms recommend the discouragement of emigration. In contrast, 8 of the writers (9 per cent) oppose restriction of emigration and 19 (21 per cent) wish to see it further promoted. Other specific suggestions are for laws to protect Filipinos working in the United States, for additional health examinations of those who go to the mainland, for literacy tests.

A partial attempt at correlating attitudes favorable to emigration with favorable reports from friends in the United States, by assigning a score between 1 and 10 to each answer in these question categories, resulted in the positive but low correlation of .25. Unfortunately, the data do not lend themselves to a more definite correlation between influences and opinions.

APPENDIX H

THE HAWAIIAN SUGAR PLANTERS' ASSOCIATION'S METHODS OF LABOR SELECTION AND MANAGEMENT[1]

I. ORGANIZATION

THE Hawaiian Sugar Planters' Association, referred to in brief as the H.S.P.A., with headquarters in Honolulu, is an organization of, at present, 43 plantations for the purpose of studying the technical needs of the industry, of carrying on technical experiments, of conducting for the membership firms a joint system of labor selection and distribution, of providing uniform systems of labor contract, and of assisting in the development of effective methods of labor management.[2] Apart from its experiment station, which does not concern us here, the association's most important and costly operations are the maintenance of a system of direct hiring of labor in the Philippines, with four receiving stations or *cuartels* where the workers employed and members of their family accompanying them are medically examined and kept under observation before sailing, and the receiving station in Honolulu, where a second medical examination takes place before distribution to the plantations. The Philippine agencies of the H.S.P.A. employ sub-agents who are paid a fee of ₱3.50 for each laborer finally accepted by the physician of the H.S.P.A. About nine such agents are working in the provinces of Ilocos Norte, Abra, Ilocos Sur, and La Union. As the number of steerage passages sold is regulated by the labor requirements of the plantations, the activity of these agents is more one of encouraging and helping those likely to pass the tests (see below) than of stimulating a general desire to go to Hawaii. And this they accomplish by home visits in those communities, more especially, where previous contract workers, who have returned from Hawaii, reside.

[1] Mainly from material supplied by the H.S.P.A.

[2] The joint transportation and marketing of the produce, shipped by the Matson Line—financially controlled by the planters—and refined, for the most part, at Crockett, near San Francisco, is organized through separate concerns.

2. SELECTION AND HEALTH SUPERVISION

There is no longer any "recruiting" of labor by the H.S.P.A. in the Philippine Islands, in the aggressive sense of that term. The association's agents are engaged, rather, in a careful selection of workers from among those who voluntarily present themselves for examination, of signing labor agreements with those hired and seeing to their safe passage under conditions ensuring their welfare and contentment. The number of laborers sent is kept as nearly as possible even with the plantations' requirements as presented in the monthly statements.

Under an agreement of the H.S.P.A. with the Philippine Government, legalized by Act 2486 of the Philippine Legislature of February 5, 1915 (see Appendix I, p. 392), the Association is entitled, for payment of a license fee of $3,000, to recruit laborers in the provinces of Manila, Cebu, Bohol, Oriental Negros (including Siquijor), Ilocos Norte, Ilocos Sur, Abra and La Union, Pangasinan and Tarlac[3]; but its activities—no longer through private Filipino agencies but through sub-agencies—are now even more closely limited.

The criteria of selection are largely physical. Men over 35 or under 20 years of age are only exceptionally employed. Those with the more obvious debilitating physical defects, especially tuberculosis and any kind of heart trouble, are rejected. At the large receiving station in Manila, a further and more complete medical test, repeatedly applied during a period of isolation, further eliminates the unfit and those likely to prove unfit, for plantation labor. In addition, the federal health service here applies its customary tests for steerage passengers from the Orient—including a cholera stool test and, since the cerebral meningitis epidemic in the spring and early summer of 1929, also special bacteriological examinations of mucus. Workers with small temporary ailments, such as influenza or common colds, are detained for later sailing.

Each worker (who has paid his own transportation and that of members of his family) is provided with a full suit of clothes, a pair of shoes, socks, underwear, blue denim shirt, hat, sweater, blanket, cup and plate, at the Association's expense. The purpose of this equipment is to protect the worker against changes of

[3] Under the latest agreement with the Philippine government, Tarlac is excluded from these operations.

temperature and possibility of infection through the loaning of such articles during the passage.[4]

Under an arrangement with the Dollar Line, all steerage accommodation for plantation workers, contracted for in bulk, is kept separate and subjected to special sanitary control: All bunks are freshly painted and covered after each trip; women and children are segregated. Exercise on deck, when the weather allows, is insisted upon; cathartics are regularly administered. The ship's surgeon and the steward are giving special instructions to those seemingly in need of precaution, a Filipino-speaking nurse is in attendance; the food is prepared by a Filipino cook. At the end of the trip, the ship's doctor hands to the medical staff of the association's receiving station in Honolulu a list of those requiring a new medical test or special care.

After the official medical examination by the Public Health Service in Honolulu, all arriving passengers destined for the plantations are again examined by the association's own physicians. Those found in need of special medical care are sent, at the association's expense, to one of the local hospitals; others are retained for observation and rest at the station itself. If a worker is found unfit for plantation labor, in spite of the earlier precautions, he and his dependents are sent back to their home town at the association's expense. The station itself is a modern structure, excellently equipped and not lacking in facilities for outdoor and indoor recreation, including moving pictures.

Distribution from Honolulu to the plantations, at the association's expense, is in accordance with the needs of the various plantations which are filled in the order of the number to which the various groups of plantations may be entitled on the basis of their proportion of the total tonnage produced during the preceding year. The cost of this as of all other H.S.P.A. activities is financed by assessments on the plantation companies on a per tonnage basis. Each plantation contributes in proportion of tonnage of sugar produced in the previous year.[5]

After having worked, according to the terms of his contract, in

[4] In the spring of 1930, the Dollar Line in cooperation with the H.S.P.A., inaugurated a new, direct steamship service between Manila and Honolulu, avoiding the trip of steerage passengers through the cold northern climate; but the measures taken for the protection of their health are continued.

[5] A plantation favorably situated in close proximity to an urban community may get most of its labor force from those migrating to the city for a visit and then seeking reemployment close by, or from those moving directly to the plantation from one more remote. Such a plantation may receive from the H.S.P.A. few laborers during the

the plantation assigned to him, for no matter how short a period, the laborer is entitled to a transfer to some other plantation of the association without losing his right to free return passage on the ground of discontinuity of service.

On the completion of his contract, the Filipino worker is given a certificate, bearing his finger prints, which serves as a means of identification if subsequently he desires to re-enter the services of the H.S.P.A. A large proportion of new workers, in the last two years, engaged and examined as above described, consisted of men previously employed.

3. CONDITIONS OF EMPLOYMENT

The labor agreement signed by the assistant director of the H.S.P.A. and by the prospective laborer (whose finger prints also are attached to the document) is in effect a unilateral affair; for under the existing law it is impossible to compel the laborer to fulfill his part of the contract; and, unless it can be proved that he has means, civil proceedings are useless.

The association binds itself to assign the laborer to a sugar plantation and to have work given him there for a period of not less than three years from the date of arrival, at the prevailing rate of pay. Actually, the minimum wage for those on daily pay is $1. The normal day's work is of ten hours, without extra pay for night work. In addition to his wage, the laborer receives a suitable house or living quarters for himself and his family, water and fuel (wood or kerosene) for household purposes, free medicine and medical attention and hospitalization. If he works on an average not less than 20 days per month for the full period of the contract, the laborer is given free return transportation from Honolulu to Manila at any time, in his choosing, within three years after the termination of three years of employment. He is also given free transportation to Manila if he should become permanently incapacitated during the term of the contract.

The stipulated wage, it should be noted, is only a minimum. Much of the work is done on a contract basis for a given operation performed by a crew of men over a given length of time—

year; but this fact would not be considered in assessing tonnage for the total upkeep of the association. The labor cost is distributed in this way on the theory that it is necessary to have the labor reservoir filled to equal the total demand rather than the demands of any specific plantation.

such as ditching, irrigation, plowing and cultivation of a sugar field, laying portable tracks, cutting and loading cane. This work is on an individual piece-rate basis per row, per acre or per ton. Only from 5 to 15 per cent of the workers are on day wages—mostly newcomers who have not yet been assigned to the more difficult, specialized or responsible work, convalescents, and men who have finished a long-term contract (see below, p. 389) and are waiting to be assigned to another.

In order to encourage regularity of work, a bonus system has been introduced to which particularly Filipino workers respond favorably: For a work performance of no less than 23 days per months, ten per cent is added to the basic wage, whether it be on a time or piece rate. About four out of every five workers earn this bonus. An additional bonus is in the nature of profit sharing: For every one-tenth of one cent above 5 cents in the price of raw sugar for the month, 1 per cent is added to the earnings for the month. Thus if by piece work a man earns $1.50 a day (a frequent figure), an additional 15 cents is paid for work performance and, assuming the price of sugar to have been 6 cents, an additional 10 per cent of $1.65, or 16.5 cents, making the total daily earnings $1.815.

Average earnings for short-time contracts for the month of June, 1930, on all Hawaiian plantations, amounted to $1.82 per day, exclusive of the turn-out bonus which might be roughly figured at 10 per cent, making approximately $2 cash earnings plus the value of perquisites, estimated at $1 per day.

For a comparison of wages with American standard wages, we may leave out of account the fact that earnings on the plantations are regular whereas those on the mainland for work of this character are often irregular, and we may further guard against too favorable a picture of Hawaiian conditions by assessing the value of the Hawaiian perquisites at only 70 cents per day. What, then, is the mainland equivalent of this daily wage of $2.70? The rate of wages per day, without board, for male farm laborers for the United States in 1929 averaged $2.34 for the quarter ending January 31, $2.34 for the quarter ending April 30, $2.43 for the quarter ending July 31, and $2.46 for the quarter ending October 31.[6] The averages for the eight South Atlantic states were $1.69 per

[6] Year Book of Agriculture for 1930. U. S. Department of Agriculture, table No. 537, p. 1000.

day for the quarter ending January, $1.66 for the quarter ending April, $1.70 for the quarter ending July, and $1.71 for the quarter ending October. For the eight South Central states the averages were $1.68, $1.65, $1.71, and $1.72. For the North Atlantic states the averages varied from $3.42 to $3.63, and for the Western states they varied from $3.21 to $3.39. It appears, therefore, that the average wages of plantation workers on short contract in Hawaii, conservatively estimated, are higher than those in sixteen of our states.[7]

Piece rates are arranged separately by each company in accordance with the special conditions of its fields. They are applied to the great majority of large-scale operations, including cultivation, plowing, cutting and piling, and are received by 80 to 95 per cent of the common laborers. That is, a separate work record is kept for each man, and he is paid accordingly.[8] A piece rate, once set, is always paid for that month. Rates for cutting and piling remain current for a long time; other rates vary with field conditions.[9] The average earnings of laborers on piece-work are $1.70.[10]

[7] See also Clarence Heer, Income and Wages in the South. University of North Carolina Press, 1930.

[8] In former times some of this work was contracted out to contractors who then were responsible for paying each worker his share. This system did not work well, especially with Filipino foremen—contractors who could not be educated away from traditions, yet largely current in the Philippine Islands, that are unfair to the workers.

[9] One of the largest plantations has a few years ago introduced a system which, in addition to other advantages, insures the workers of fairness in the calculation of their earnings. Under the *luna,* or foreman, each crew is headed by a straw-boss, or "number one man," one of the workers, who acts as its spokesman and is responsible for the turn-out and for the execution of the *luna's* orders. He receives a bonus of 30 per cent of the average daily earnings of the crew. Out of this class the regular foremen are recruited who are on regular salary. The "number one man" is informed of the piece rate and watches closely over its fair application to individual earnings. He also takes up with the management any questions that may arise over the setting of new piece rates in relation to other rates current. Under this system, errors both in the setting of piece rates and in the computation of earnings have been reduced to a minimum, likewise, complaints of individual workers which used to be frequent, often arising from misunderstanding. This system especially has done away with complaints that the workers had no opportunity of checking up on the weight of cane credited to them.

[10] A detailed account of wage rates for different plantation occupations, not quite up-to-date but indicating the large variety of rates in force for different operations, will be found in the excellent report made in 1926 by Hermenegildo Cruz, director of the Philippine Islands Bureau of Labor, on a tour of inspection of the Hawaiian sugar plantations, at the request of Governor-General Leonard Wood: Bulletin of the Bureau of Labor, Manila, vol. VII, No. 25, March, 1926. Incidentally, this report contains a comparison of daily earnings in different occupations in the sugar industry for Hawaii and the Philippine Islands, indicating for the more common forms of field labor differences ranging from 150 to over 400 per cent of the earnings in the Philippines. (Page 6.)

4. LONG-TERM AGREEMENTS

It has been found increasingly worth while to divide responsibility with the workers themselves by signing agreements with selected crews of them under competent straw-bosses (see note 9, p. 388) for the care of a field which may be anything between 50 and 250 acres. The work contracted for usually includes keeping irrigation ditches clean, fertilization and cultivation. Separate records are kept of the time spent by each man on the job—usually at the rate of 20 for a hundred-acre field—and, when the crop is harvested, each gets his pro rata share on the basis of the final product. The rates vary with soil and water conditions. Since the total operation takes from eighteen to twenty-four months, each worker is advanced for living expenses a minimum wage of $1 a day (in addition to the other perquisites to which he is entitled under the general agreement). The price paid at the end of the operation is on the basis of an agreed rate per ton of cane produced. The workers thus take some chance on their earnings, but they like the system. It gives them an added incentive in achieving the highest possible yield of cane. Since this work under agreement—usually called long-term contract—does not necessarily fill the crew's whole time, they are entitled as individuals to secure assignment also for part of their time on piece-rate work in other parts of the plantation. The average earnings for workers on long-term contract are $2.35 per day. Since experienced ditchmen and irrigators are valuable, the employer is interested in keeping them on the job rather than in cutting wage rates. On "big payday," usually at the end of two years, individual earnings of $600 and $800 are common; and the larger part of these amounts is usually sent or taken home to the Philippine Islands for permanent investment.

5. WELFARE WORK

The housing of the plantation workers is the first care of the welfare departments on all the plantations. Grouped in villages large enough to permit the establishment of common features, such as stores, churches and recreation halls, the colonies of workers of different racial groups are usually kept together but not separate. The houses of more modern construction, now outnumbering those of a more primitive type, usually consist of four rooms for families and of four or eight rooms for two persons each in bachelor quarters. They are provided with running water and sanitary facilities—these of a simple type preventing misuse. Each house has adequate yard space and, usually, an outside laundry and shower bath. Fuel is furnished free, but electric light is charged for at cost price. These homes often are well planned on high ground facing adequate roads, set back behind strips of lawn or gardens in the care of which the tenants are instructed. Usually the yard space suffices to keep a few chickens. Often garages for the tenants' automobiles take up some of the space.

Outdoor recreation is fostered by the provision of playing fields and, on the larger plantations, by the employment of social workers who organize games and also manage the indoor recreation halls. These halls often are large, dignified structures, containing reading and pool-rooms and facilities for holding parties. They usually also contain the dining halls for unmarried laborers. All plantations have moving picture theaters and company stores, in addition to which private stores are permitted in the larger colonies.[11] The plantation stores are stocked, according to the racial composition of the plantation population, with a large variety of necessities and luxuries. Staples are sold at cost price. Community churches, usually with a minister of their own nationality, are maintained by the different national groups. Through cooperation with the territorial government, good schools for the children of plantation workers often are provided on company land in the plantation villages.

On an average each plantation has hospital facilities at the rate of one bed to each hundred of the plantation population. The total number of surgeons employed is thirty. Not only the laborers but also their dependents are entitled to free medical and surgical treatment—including medical and nursing care in childbirth—to a limit of an expenditure of $100 per family a month, which may include support of the family while the breadwinner is under medical care. Modest fees for medical treatment and hospitalization are charged to employees with cash earnings exceeding $100 a month, except where large families are dependent upon them. Some of the hospitals and clinics provided are as complete in modern equipment as such institutions can be. Where the need for additional treatment or specialist services seems indicated,

[11] In one or two instances, where the plantation management does not operate a company store, an independent store may operate under an agreement permitting the plantation company a control over prices similar to that exercised in company stores.

Above: HAWAIIAN PLANTATION VILLAGE OCCUPIED BY JAPANESE AND FILIPINO LABORERS
Below: VISIT OF PHILIPPINE LABOR OFFICIALS WITH A FILIPINO PLANTATION WORKER AND HIS FAMILY IN HAWAII

Above: KINDERGARTEN FOR JAPANESE AND FILIPINO CHILDREN ON A HAWAIIAN SUGAR PLANTATION

Left: TYPICAL FILIPINO CLUB HOUSE ON A HAWAIIAN SUGAR PLANTATION

patients often are, at the company's cost, removed to one of the larger institutions in the nearest city. Visiting nurses treat minor ailments and instruct women in the care of children.

The plantations maintain their own systems of policing. One object of a careful watch over outsiders visiting the plantations is to keep out solicitors, labor agitators, and immoral women. There are also occasional minor clashes between neighbors which usually are quickly adjusted owing to the common confidence in the welfare director or the plantation manager. The relationship between the workers and these officials in most cases is a very happy one, fostered by a close personal interest in the welfare of individuals and their families. Great care is exercised that neither these special officials nor foremen ever exceed their authority and that their tone toward the workers is friendly. Personal troubles, however trivial, receive courteous attention; and workers are free to take to the manager himself any grievance for which they cannot get redress.

A service greatly appreciated by the Filipino workers is the provision, in cooperation with territorial banks, of savings facilities —with a uniform interest rate of 4½ per cent—and safe transmission of payments to relatives in the Philippine Islands—at the constant rate of two pesos to the dollar, irrespective of fluctuations of the money market. Moreover, to protect from possible losses those who have finished their contract and return to their home town with considerable savings, the H.S.P.A. arranges for the transfer of these sums in the depositor's name to its branch office in Manila. In 1928, Filipinos returning to the Philippines took out savings deposits to the amount of nearly two million dollars, approximately $300,000 of which were deposited in the H.S.P.A. office for cash transmittal. Not content with guarding their ex-employees against theft, the H.S.P.A. has an arrangement with local mayors and other officials throughout the Ilocos country to advise these men on the investment of their funds, especially where land purchase is under consideration.

For the return trip to the Philippines, the H.S.P.A. renders its workers services similar to those which the American Express Company or a tourist bureau renders American tourists—without charging for them: It handles their baggage, clearance of taxes, purchase of tickets, and arranges matters so that no man need leave his work until the last moment necessary to catch the boat.

APPENDIX I

PHILIPPINE LAW PROVIDING FOR THE CONTROL OF LABOR CONTRACTS

ACT NO. 2486—AN ACT FIXING A TAX UPON EVERY PERSON OR ENTITY ENGAGED IN RECRUITING OR CONTRACTING LABORERS IN THE PHILIPPINES . . .

Section 1. Every person or entity who, directly or indirectly, shall engage in the Philippine Islands in contracting, enlisting, recruiting, or shipment of laborers, shall pay annually, as a tax, to the provincial treasurer of each one of the provinces where laborers are contracted or recruited, and if in Manila, to the Collector of Internal Revenue, the sum of five hundred pesos, which fund shall be subject to the conditions expressed in the following sections: *Provided,* That when such contracting, enlistment, recruiting, or shipment of laborers is made in representation of a corporation or person, said tax shall be paid by the same and not by each one of its agents or employees: *Provided, further,* That nothing contained in this Act shall be interpreted or construed in such a manner as to permit any contract or recruiting of individuals of non-Christian tribes for the purpose of exhibiting same in the Philippines or in any other foreign country, which is hereby declared prohibited and unlawful: *And provided finally,* That nothing contained in this Act shall be applied to persons who contract individuals for other personal service or to make up the crew of a vessel.

Section 2. Any company or entity engaged in the industry mentioned in the next preceding section shall be obliged to furnish free passage upon the return to these Islands of the laborer or laborers contracted, so soon as the time stipulated in the contract made with him shall have expired in case they shall have complied with the terms and conditions of the contract on their part to be kept and performed, or in case they shall have later become unfit for work on account of physical incapacity.

Section 3. Any person or entity referred to by this Act shall annually provide himself, before engaging in the industry referred to by this law, with a license issued by the Director of the Bureau of Labor and approved by the Secretary of Commerce and Police, in which shall be expressed the name of the province or names of the provinces where he is to exercise such industry. For the issuance of said license, the Director of the Bureau of Labor shall collect the sum of six thousand pesos annually which shall be covered into the Insular Treasury.

Section 4. The Governor-General, with the advice and consent of the Commission, shall from time to time appoint a commissioner or commissioners for service outside of the Philippine Islands, whose duty it shall be to receive and hear the complaints made by Filipino laborers, to arrange the differences between the latter and their employers, to see to the compliance of the contracts made with said laborers, and to look after their interests in general, making a report of the condition thereof to the Governor-General . . .

Section 5. All of the contracts made with laborers shall be supervised by the Director of Labor, whose duty it shall be to permit no contracting of minors . . .

Enacted, February 5, 1915.

APPENDIX J

PHILIPPINE INTER-ISLAND MIGRATION

By Frederick V. Field and Elizabeth Brown Field

1. HISTORICAL BACKGROUND FOR MODERN MIGRATIONS

It is only within the last forty or fifty years that population movements in the Philippines have become a public problem, and only a hundred years since they have assumed significant proportions. Yet, in order to understand modern tendencies of the Filipino people to redistribute themselves more evenly over the Islands it is necessary to turn to the conditions attending the prehistoric settlement of the archipelago. The causes which produced the emigrations from what is now the mainland of Asia to the Philippines, the various cultures of the early and later settlers, the prevailing currents and winds, and the land and water formations which in large part determined the course of the emigrants' voyages, geological and geographical features of the Islands, the results of the impact of later upon earlier settlers are all items which directly or indirectly have affected the modern migratory movements. The conditions which forced large groups off what is now the Asiatic mainland in prehistoric times, for instance, are in general still operative. Today they are pushing thousands of Chinese annually into the Philippines and other islands of that region, and those Chinese are affecting the racial, cultural, and economic make-up of the people among whom they are settling and are thus an indirect factor in the present population movements within the Philippines Islands. Geographical features of the archipelago are still of basic importance in understanding both the present distribution of population and its future possibilities. The situation which existed many centuries ago, moreover, when groups with a more developed culture reached a region inhabited by people of an earlier culture and either forced these back into the hills, mixed with them, or retreated before their barbaric customs, is being re-enacted today in parts of Mindanao and other places when colonizers and homesteaders come into contact with more primitive peoples.

An important characteristic of the prehistoric settlement of the Philippines bearing directly on our topic was the diversity of the settlement both as to time and place. Professor H. Otley Beyer, of the University of the Philippines, has estimated that ten per cent of the present population of the Islands are Pygmies of paleolithic origin, thirty per cent Indonesian of neolithic origin, and forty per cent Malay, who reached the Archipelago during the Iron Age. In general, each successive migratory wave pushed the previous ones further back toward the headwaters of the rivers and into the mountainous regions, reserving for itself the fertile broad valleys at the lower end of the rivers. The settlement of the Islands, however, was by no means so simple as that, for each of the successive waves just mentioned took centuries, was extremely complex in itself, and merged into others. In spite of continuous racial and cultural mixture, groups in various parts of the Islands nevertheless settled and developed in practical isolation from each other. This was largely due to the fact that besides the long period of centuries during which the settlement of the Philippines was taking place, there was great diversity and comparative isolation among the various regions in which the immigrants settled. The diversity of settlement may be illustrated by the immigration of one of the large groups, the Indonesians, for example. One type of Indonesian migrated from what is now the Asiatic mainland to the East Indies and from there spread northward into the Philippines. Some entered the southern islands of the Archipelago, others of this type were carried by ocean winds and currents up the east coast. A second type of Indonesian migrated southward from Indo-China. During this migration, however, many were caught in ocean currents which carried them up to the western coast of Luzon.[1] This diversity of settlement, common to each of the migratory waves, resulted in the practical isolation of the various groups due to the inability of their simple culture to break down local boundaries formed by geographical and institutional barriers.

As the successive invasions of the Philippines covered several centuries, the people exhibit marked differences in language, manners, customs, laws, and degrees of civilization. . . . Lack of homogeneity arises also from the inade-

[1] Steiger, Beyer, and Benitez, History of the Orient. Ginn & Co., 1926.

quate land and water communications among the widely scattered groups and from the many different languages and dialects spoken.[2]

As a result of this characteristic of the prehistoric settlement of the Philippines, certain inhabited regions became, in the course of centuries, heavily overpopulated, while other regions, untouched by the early migrations, remained entirely unpopulated or very sparsely so. A century or more ago, the pressure of population in the congested districts became so great that many inhabitants were forced annually to look elsewhere for sustenance. Some left their homes for good, others for the planting or harvesting season when they could get a share of the product from a more sparsely settled community in return for the labor they offered. As the problem became more acute, the migratory movements within the Islands became of greater importance numerically and more complex in their directions and nature. During the last forty or fifty years, these population movements have become a matter of public concern in the Philippines, and more recently in Hawaii and the United States to which many thousands of Filipinos have migrated.

For an understanding of the modern migratory movements in the Philippines we must present further details concerning the present distribution of population in the Islands, as well as briefly discuss the geographical and institutional factors hindering the breakdown of local physical and cultural barriers. It will also be necessary to review the conditions of land tenure in pre-Spanish and Spanish days, and to describe them in greater detail as they exist today under the American régime.

2. CONGESTED AND SPARSELY SETTLED DISTRICTS

Out of a total area of 114,360 square miles, a little less than a third is suitable for cultivation or pasturage. Of this third only two-fifths is now occupied by the twelve million odd inhabitants. The Philippines is capable of supporting a vastly larger population than at present, an additional eighty million according to one authority,[3] particularly if the timber, fishing and other resources of the Islands are exploited. Today, nevertheless, with only twelve million people inhabitating two-fifths of the cultivatable area, there

[2] Survey of American Foreign Relations, 1930. Council on Foreign Relations. Yale University Press, 1930, pp. 258, 259.

[3] W. Cameron Forbes, The Philippine Islands. Houghton Mifflin Co., 1928. See also George W. Goddard, The Unexplored Philippines from the Air. *National Geographical Magazine,* September, 1930, p. 310 *et seq.*

is serious population congestion leading the Philippines into national and international complications.

The principal congested areas are found on the Ilocos Coast and in Cebu, Bohol, and Iloilo in the Visayan Islands. (See map, p. 232.) The cultivatable area of the Ilocos Coast is a narrow strip of lowland between the sea and the high mountain range which runs through the center of the island of Luzon. The population is so heavy that the average landholdings are the smallest in size in the Philippines, in the worst districts, Ilocos Norte for example, being one-half hectare or about one and a quarter acres. To make matters worse, owing to a very definite dry season and an equally well marked period of rainfall, the former including the winter and spring months, the latter the summer and autumn, only one crop can be produced a year. The conditions in Iloilo are less serious than on the Ilocos Coast, Cebu, and Bohol largely because of substantial rice and sugar crops and good means of transportation. Cebu, however, consisting of a very poor rocky soil and being subject to an annual dry season and frequent droughts, makes that island a very poor region for habitation. The conditions in Bohol are similar, although the soil could be cultivated profitably more easily than that of Cebu if irrigation systems were introduced.

On the other hand, the immense territory of Mindanao, considerable portions of the Sulu Archipelago, the Islands of Samar, Leyte, Mindoro, Palawan, and the Cagayan Valley are very sparsely settled. The Island of Mindanao, the second largest in the Philippines, is one of the most fertile and at the same time the most thinly populated. Rice, coconut, hemp, cattle, sugar, pineapples, coffee, rubber are among the products that can be raised there. In addition, there are vast extents of valuable lumber and some mining possibilities and developments. A great portion of Mindanao, including the provinces of Lanao, Cotabato, the western part of Davao, Misamis, and Zamboanga, is in the region in which there is no period of very pronounced maximum rainfall and no absolutely dry season. A great portion of the eastern half of the island, that facing the Pacific, receives a very pronounced maximum rainfall in winter and has no dry season. The eastern part of Misamis, Agusan and Bukidnon, and the central and eastern regions of Zamboanga have a dry season of only one to three months with no very pronounced rainy season. Mindanao is, furthermore, completely out of the typhoon district. It is, therefore, an ideal region for habitation and development.

Basilan Island, in the Sulu Archipelago, is thinly populated and could be exploited for lumber, copra, and abaca. Zamboanga Peninsula is also good for these products and has fertile land on which rice could be grown intensively. The warm, moist climate of Sulu makes it an area suitable for a great variety of crops, including fruits.

Samar and Leyte have for many years received Visayan migrants; they are still, however, very poorly settled. Practically the whole of Samar and the eastern part of Leyte receive abundant rains and have no dry season. Western Leyte has rains of less intensity with no dry season.

Palawan is another large island, ranking near the bottom of the list of provinces arranged according to population density. There are great possibilities in the coconut, fishery, lumber and orange business, which have scarcely been touched. The grassy plains of the islands could be used for cattle raising.

Mindoro has large forests, good grazing areas, and fertile soils. The western half of the island has a wet and dry season, the eastern half constant rain. Abaca, rice, corn, and sugar are grown in Mindoro, as well as coconuts.

There is, finally, the Cagayan Valley, a large district of great importance, particularly as it is situated on the island of Luzon other portions of which are very much overpopulated. The Cagayan Valley is hemmed in on both the east and west by mountain ranges, being open to the sea only at its northern end. The river, by bringing down new soil every year, makes the land unusually fertile. The western part of this valley receives moderate rains except for a short dry season; the eastern part has no dry season. The valley is protected from the excessive rains common to most of the provinces facing the Pacific by the coastal mountain range.

3. GEOGRAPHICAL AND SOCIAL FACTORS IN POPULATION DISTRIBUTION

Geographical barriers between the congested and sparsely populated regions have played an important part in preventing an easy flow of population from one to the other. This is well illustrated in northern Luzon where the overcrowded Ilocos Coast is all but adjacent to the thinly inhabited provinces of Cagayan, Isabela and Nueva Vizcaya, but where the high mountain range between these areas has hindered travel. In spite of difficulties, however, before the days of modern roads, the migrations of Ilocanos followed three somewhat indefinite routes over and around this mountain barrier. One led the migrator around the northern end of Luzon and into the lower end of the great Cagayan river system. But as a map suggests, this route must have been very perilous for two reasons, first that the mountains go to the edge of the sea and force the migrant to cross over them in what is usually unfavorable weather, and second that just beyond the mountains to the east are vast swamps which can be traversed only during a few weeks of the year. A second way which Ilocanos took started across the mountains at Tagudin and after an arduous journey deposited them in Isabela. The third route lay southward into Nueva Ecija and then north into the headwaters of the Cagayan river system. There were, then, major difficulties for the Ilocanos to overcome purely on account of the physical lay-out of the island. In the congested areas of the Visayan Islands the physical barriers, instead of being mountains and swamps, were waters of unknown extent which made emigration away from a particular island a hazardous undertaking, and mountainous, rocky territory which prohibited easy redistribution within a particular island.

In addition to these geographical conditions there were certain habits, customs, and superstitions which played and still play a large part in hindering migrations. The Ilocanos, for instance, knew that in the mountains which they would have to cross to reach the fertile valleys of the Cagayan dwelt primitive and unfriendly tribes. Cebuans who had landed on the shores of Mindanao had returned with discouraging tales of their experiences with the "uncivilized and hostile Moros." There was nothing in the family or *barrio* background of these adventurers to provide them with the type of experience or fortitude required of a pioneer. In addition, many of the Ilocanos who had taken up land in Nueva Vizcaya had after clearing it been dispossessed by a rich and powerful man who had suddenly arrived with papers and lawyers proving ownership. Many others had found it necessary to borrow a small amount of money to start out with in the new territory and, before they were able to repay the full amount, had been tricked out of all their possessions. In these thinly inhabited regions of Luzon and Mindanao, settlers were lonely, disease was too often rampant, there was no way of borrowing money at reasonable rates, there was no way of getting the advice so much needed in settling a new area. All these and further experiences were carried back to the Ilocos Coast, Cebu, Bohol and the other overpopulated regions, passed rapidly by word of mouth from family to family, from *barrio* to *barrio,* until few dared to start out on such an uncertain adventure.

Geographical and social barriers, however, are gradually being overcome or broken down. Railroads now run on the islands of Luzon, Cebu, and Panay, a total distance of approximately 790 miles.[4] The Manila Railroad Company, owned and operated by the government, has tracks which run north from Manila to San Fernando, La Union, northeast to Cabanatuan in Nueva Ecija, south to Batangas, southeast through Tayabas with a continuation line from Pamplon, Camarines Sur, to Albay. The lines in Cebu and Panay are operated by the Philippine Railway Company for a little over 130 miles, the line in Cebu running along the east coast and that in Panay going from Iloilo to Capiz. Roads have increased steadily in mileage and improved in condition during the last few years in the well populated regions where production is good. A continuous good road runs from Manila to a point a little north of Laoag on the west coast of Luzon and another up the northeast section. Most of the Visayan Islands also are fairly well equipped with roads. The vast areas of Mindanao, however, the Sulu Archipelago, and Palawan have scarcely been touched in this respect. Even in Luzon the fertile, thinly populated valleys along the Cagayan River suffer from lack of proper means of communication. The absence of roads in these regions, as well as of roads crossing Luzon Island, has retarded the movement of homesteaders, for instance, from Ilocos Sur to Cagayan, or into any portion of Mindanao, just as the building of roads into Nueva Ecija greatly speeded up its settlement. Water transportation is, of course, the outstanding means of transportation for many of the islands and important for all of them. The inter-island steamship service has not developed rapidly, though there are indications that within a year or two it will offer a greatly improved service.

In dissolving certain provincial limitations in the geographical category, the building of roads and railways, and the improvement of inter-island shipping will also help do away with social habits and institutions which have depended for their growth and maintenance on extreme provincialism. This is certainly true when the improvement of lines of communication is concurrent with the establishment of a widespread school system, with the decline of evil

[4] Statistical Bulletin of the Philippine Islands, 1928.

practices, such as land grabbing and usury, and the beginnings of a rural credit system, and of at least some possibilities of securing reliable land surveys. For present purposes, it is perhaps sufficient merely to indicate that at least a start has been made toward breaking down the social and geographical barriers which have for so long hindered Filipino migrations.

4. LAND TENURE

The protection or lack of protection which the Filipino migrant has had from the government in respect to his property has naturally been an important factor in either promoting or discouraging settlement in new regions. The customs and laws in regard to land titles, and the stipulations regarding the methods of settlement, have had an important bearing on the redistribution of population.

In the fifteenth century and before, lands were divided among the families inhabiting a *barangay*.[5] Unless by purchase or inheritance no one could occupy or cultivate the land in any but his own *barangay*. Certain portions of each *barangay*, however, were not divided but were held in common, and these portions were available to any member of that particular *barangay* who wished to cultivate them. After clearing and sowing part of this commonly owned land the farmer would obtain possession of it, and his ownership would be respected by the others.[6] Lands outside the areas controlled by existing *barangays* were also taken up. Migrants in groups of from five to twenty, each under a headman, would take possession of a certain amount of public land. When this territory was cleared and ready for cultivation, it was divided among the group. The headman played an important rôle; it was he who often took charge of the combined savings of the group members and who retained the title to all their land.[7]

The Laws of the Indies which the Spanish introduced into the Philippines enabled the Spaniards who had assisted in the discovery and conquest of the Islands or who wished to leave Spain and join the colony to secure free grants of land. After four years of residence and cultivation absolute ownership was conferred. The Laws protected the native owners and cultivators of property and

[5] Appleton's New Spanish-English Dictionary, 1916, defines a *barangay* as a "ward of fifty families into which a Philippine village is divided."

[6] Conrado Benitez, History of the Philippines. Ginn & Co., 1926, p. 65.

[7] Hugo H. Miller, Economic Conditions in the Philippines. Ginn & Co., 1925, p. 224.

also reserved portions of the public lands for their use.[8] That the Spanish way of dealing with this problem was not altogether satisfactory is evident from the present-day heritage of many of its unfortunate characteristics. Conrado Benitez, a Filipino historian, says:

> In spite of legislative protection, the question of land ownership has from this early period been the source of conflict. This has been due chiefly to the fact that lands claimed by individuals and granted by the government were not first surveyed, but their areas were only roughly estimated and their boundaries described in terms of adjoining lands. Thus confusion arose.[9]

Ex-Governor-General Forbes reaches the same conclusion:

> The Spanish system of land titles, admirable as provided by law, in practice has created a most unfortunate situation. Of some 2,300,000 parcels of land claimed to be privately owned, relatively few were represented by title deeds acceptable for transfers of ownership, mortgage purposes, or as collateral for bank credits. A more serious feature of the situation was the lack of exact definition of metes and bounds, even in the instances of royal grants or other recorded titles, due either to vague descriptions of natural boundaries or faulty surveys. The boundaries were sure to be disputed sooner or later, and such disputes were likely to run for generations, giving ground for much ill-feeling, controversies between neighbors, and, as sometimes happened, serious infractions of public order, including crimes of violence.[10]

It is interesting to compare these criticisms of the Spanish system with those of the American system suggested later in this paper, particularly to notice how many of the characteristics of the former system have persisted.

Upon their assumption of power in the Philippines, the Americans devoted considerable attention to the question of land ownership. By Act of Congress of July 1, 1902, the regulations for the disposal and administration of public lands were provided. By Act No. 496 of the Philippine Commission in November of the same year, it was provided that after compliance with requirements for proper surveys and proofs of ownership, titles would be granted to real estate and land ownership registered under the Torrens system. On November 29, 1919, the Public Land Act of the Philippine Islands was approved and thereafter provided for the disposal and administration of public lands. Land which is dis-

[8] Conrado Benitez, *op. cit.*, p. 65.
[9] *Ibid.*, p. 66.
[10] W. Cameron Forbes, The Philippine Islands. Houghton Mifflin Co., 1928, vol. I, p. 314.

covered to be more valuable for its timber or mineral products than for agricultural purposes is not included among the disposable agricultural public lands. The Public Land Act, as it stands today with amendments, provides among other things for the disposal of unreserved, unoccupied, unappropriated, agricultural public land as follows:

a. *By Homesteading.*

Citizens of the Philippine Islands or of the United States are entitled to apply for a portion of this land not exceeding 24 hectares in area. Within six months of the date of the approval of the application, and upon the payment of ₱5, the applicant must begin to work his property. One year (and not more than five years) from the date of the approval of the application, if the homesteader can prove that he has improved and cultivated at least one-fourth of his homestead area and upon paying another ₱5, he shall be entitled to a patent.

b. *By Sale.*

Citizens of the Philippine Islands or of the United States, corporations and associations of which at least 61 per cent of the capital stock belongs to citizens of the Philippine Islands or of the United States, and corporate bodies organized in the Philippine Islands may purchase disposable land up to 144 hectares in area in the case of an individual and up to 1,024 hectares in the case of a corporation or association.

c. *By Lease.*

Citizens of the Philippine Islands or of the United States, and corporations and associations of which at least 61 per cent of the capital stock belongs to citizens of the Philippine Islands or of the United States may lease any tract of disposable land not exceeding an area of 1,024 hectares. The lease may be renewed after 25 years.

d. *By Free Patent.*

Any native of the Philippine Islands who is not the owner of more than 24 hectares and who since July 4, 1907, has continuously occupied and cultivated, by himself or through his predecessors in interest, a tract of disposable land shall be entitled to have a free patent issued to him for such land not to exceed 24 hectares.

The law also prevents partners, or stock holders, or directors, or others interested from holding land individually and pooling it in excess of 1,024 hectares. Recent alterations in the Corporation Law make it possible for a member of an agricultural corporation to become interested in other agricultural corporations, provided his interest in any one corporation does not exceed 15 per cent of the capital stock. These laws, however, which attempt to prevent the exploitation of the land by strong financial interests, are very difficult to enforce. Many ways have been found of dodging them.

Changes which have been made in the public land law which are interesting in view of the frequently heard criticisms are: the increase in the maximum holding allowed a homesteader from 16 to 24 hectares;[11] the reduction of the residence requirement from two to one year; the reduction in the fee required for the approval of an application and for the issuance of a patent; and the reduction of the area the applicant must cultivate before he may apply for a patent from one-half to one-fourth the area of his homestead.

5. TYPES OF MIGRATION AND NUMBERS INVOLVED

For many decades population pressure has made it necessary for about 25,000 people annually to emigrate from the Ilocos Coast and a similar number from the congested districts in the Visayas. In addition, a much larger number has migrated seasonally. At first these migrations were an indigenous readjustment of population distribution unaffected by influences either outside the Islands or from Manila. With the growing acuteness of the situation, however, and with the general development of the people and resources of the Philippines, the migration movement has become increasingly complex. One may now distinguish the following types of migration: (1) a natural permanent migration; (2) a seasonal labor migration, as yet only slightly affected by government aid; (3) a government-stimulated migration to unsettled public agricultural lands; (4) emigration to Hawaii, mostly sponsored by the Hawaiian Sugar Planters' Association; (5) emigration to the United States. The last two types of migration are dealt with in the text of this book, and need not be discussed in this appendix. The first three types we shall discuss below topically, the last being divided into two parts, one dealing with agricultural colonies and the other with homesteading.

[11] A holding of 24 hectares (59.3 acres) of tropical land should not be compared, as regards remunerative cultivation, with a similar holding in our country of large farms. Tropical land is harder to clear and make arable than land in temperate zones—at least with such tools and resources as are available to the ordinary Filipino. In many parts of the Islands a man cannot clear more than 2 hectares a year. Moreover, where rainfall permits, two crops per annum are possible.

a. *Natural Migration.*

We have already seen how migrants moved into new territory in early days in groups under a headman. Another method was to send out scouts in parties of two or three to look over the new land and report on conditions. When the scouts discovered a promising looking region they sent for the others, and a group of friends and relatives would set out together and settle. Friends and relatives, already in the new country, would often send back word; in that way also those back home would learn of the country over the mountains or across the waters. Game laws, enacted in 1916, put a stop to the scouting parties who could no longer wander through the mountains and thus found themselves unable to secure food. The building of roads also greatly altered the migrations. The completion of the road leading through Nueva Ecija and Nueva Vizcaya to the Cagayan Valley has shifted the bulk of the movement from the Ilocos region to that route. A road into the mountains from Tagudin has also facilitated that pathway. The road around the northern end of Luzon is not yet completed, and so migrants travelling in that direction have still to face the hazards of climate and swamps.

The traditional natural migration of the Visayans has gone along these routes: from Panay and Iloilo to Occidental Negros; from Cebu to Oriental Negros; from Cebu and Bohol to western Leyte. More recently, Masbate has become the meeting ground of migrants from Cebu in the south and from the Bicol Peninsula and Tagalog country in the north. Masbate is now, however, nearly saturated. The movement from Cebu and Bohol to Misamis and Davao on the great island of Mindanao has recently become the most important migration in the Visayans. People from these congested islands may now be found all along the eastern and northern coasts of Mindanao. They have crossed the water in small boats and landed wherever the boats could take them.

Upon arriving at their destination, migrants have taken up homesteads, or if conditions were less favorable they have become tenants. The numbers involved will have to be considered under the topic of homesteading, there being no statistics available to show the number of migrants in each type of migration, nor indeed of all the types taken together. All that can be done at present is to suggest the magnitude of the movements.

The natural migration movements going on at present may be summarized as follows: from Batangas and Pampangas to Mindoro; from Tayabas and Marinduque to the Bicol Provinces (Camarines Norte, Camarines Sur, Albay, Sorsogon); from Cebu and Bohol to Mindanao; from the Ilocos provinces and La Union to Cagayan, Isabela, Nueva Vizcaya, Nueva Ecija, and Mountain Province.

b. *Seasonal Labor Migration.*

The major places of origin and destination of seasonal labor may be summarized as follows: Ilocos provinces to the tobacco region, composing the provinces of Cagayan and Isabela; Ilocos provinces and La Union to the rice region in central Luzon, consisting of the provinces of Pangasinan, Nueva Ecija, Tarlac, and Bulacan, and the sugar *haciendas* in Pampanga and Laguna; Iloilo, Antique, and Cebu to the sugar district of Occidental Negros; Cebu, Bohol, and the subprovince of Sequijor to Mindanao; Capiz and Pampanga to Mindoro; and Batangas to Mindoro, Laguna, and Tayabas.[12]

The Bureau of Labor believes that the Islands have a floating agricultural population of 600,000. It is not quite clear whom the Bureau means to include in this number, but presumably it intends the figure to cover migrants of all sorts. Until more detailed statistics on population movements are available, however, no estimated total can be relied upon. In regard to the numbers involved in the seasonal migrations we may refer to a carefully made estimate of 221,742 as the number of laborers available in the Philippines. This number of migratory laborers could, it seems, be procured for work in districts away from their homes; they represent, in other words, a surplus labor supply. In presenting this estimate, the Bureau of Labor suggests that, were systematic methods of recruiting and better care of the laborers and their families established, the number obtainable would exceed this figure. In view of the existing haphazard methods of recruitment and care, it is reasonable to assume that the number of laborers migrating seasonally is considerably under the number available. What data there are, though very incomplete, are perhaps worth presenting: The planting and harvesting seasons for the tobacco grown in Cagayan and Isabela, January to June, require an additional two thousand laborers. Rice harvesting and planting in central Luzon employs about five thousand extra workers. The sugar plantations in Occidental Negros hire about fifteen thousand laborers for the milling

[12] Bulletin of the Bureau of Labor, Labor Conditions in the Philippines, March, 1927.

season from November to April. In regard to other major and minor movements of labor no figures are available.[13]

c. *Agricultural Colonies.*

In 1913 there was passed an Act[14] appropriating the sum of ₱400,000 in order "(a) to increase the production in these Islands of rice and other food cereals which at present are imported in large quantities for local consumption; (b) to equalize the distribution of population of these Islands; (c) to afford opportunity to colonize, to become landed proprietors, and to bring under cultivation extensive wild public lands." This fund was at the same time put under the control of the Governor-General. In subsequent years more funds were appropriated for the same purpose. These funds were spent in the recruitment and transportation to Mindanao of colonists and in the establishment and maintenance of agricultural colonies. The greatest expense was incurred in the loans made to colonists to assist them in the early cultivation of their homesteads.

Up to 1918, 8,774 colonists had gone to the agricultural colonies, and 12,888 hectares were cultivated. Of these colonists only 700 had come from Luzon, 4,878 from the Visayas, and 3,088 from the Moro regions. Thirteen colonies had been established, eleven of which were in Mindanao or Sulu. While considerable corn and rice were produced, the amount of indebtedness incurred by the colonists and their inability to pay, the large number of colonists who gave up the adventure and returned home, and the generally discouraging outlook for the plan were important factors in influencing the Legislature to alter its methods of stimulating migration.

d. *Homesteading.*

At the end of 1917, the Legislature in making the appropriation for inter-island migration put it under the jurisdiction of the Bureau of Labor.[15] The scheme of directly promoting agricultural colonies was abandoned, and efforts were thereafter concentrated upon the recruitment and shipment of homeseekers. Money was no longer loaned to colonists by the government.

The Bureau of Labor reports[16] that "recruitment was limited

[13] *Ibid.*
[14] Act No. 2254, Philippine Legislature.
[15] Act No. 2727, Philippine Legislature.
[16] Labor Conditions in the Philippines. Bulletin of the Bureau of Labor, March, 1927.

to the densely populated provinces like Cebu, Antique, Capiz, and Iloilo, in the Visayan Islands; Ilocos Norte, Ilocos Sur, and La Union, in northern Luzon; and Pangasinan, Tarlac, and Nueva Ecija, in central Luzon." It continues:

> The following have been declared places for settlement: first, the different colonies of the Government in order to reinforce them with homeseekers; second, those places in Mindanao containing public lands, properly delimited, surveyed, subdivided, and classified as agricultural lands; third, in regularly organized provinces, such as Tayabas, Mindoro, Isabela, Cagayan, Camarines Norte, and Camarines Sur . . . whenever public lands therein are available.

From the time the Bureau of Labor took over the task until the end of 1929, 21,482 homeseekers had been dispatched, of which much the greatest number went to Mindanao, much smaller numbers going to Mindoro, Nueva Vizcaya, Isabela, Tayabas, and other destinations not worth mentioning. Ilocos Norte and Ilocos Sur together furnished only 785 of these homeseekers. La Union and Pangasinan, however, with 2,158 and 1,589 respectively, ranked high in the list. Cebu, with 10,003, provided by far the greatest number of homeseekers of any province. In addition, the Bureau of Labor sent 8,708 contracted laborers between 1918 and 1921, of whom 5,833 went to Mindanao, particularly for the abaca [17] plantations and public works in Davao and the rubber plantations in Basilan, the remainder going to the sugar plantations in Occidental Negros, Mindoro, Pampanga, and Laguna, timber concessions in Nueva Vizcaya, and abaca plantations in Albay. After 1921, contract labor fell off suddenly due to the economic crisis. In 1922 and lasting for four years, there was a sharp falling off of the number of homeseekers which is explained by the Bureau of Labor as having been caused by a decrease in appropriations, the greater expense of transportation, and less cooperation among the officials in charge. The lack of funds seems to have been the result of Governor-General Wood's attitude toward inter-island migration. He felt that the work was not being properly carried on, and that the results were of insufficient value to warrant so large an annual expenditure. In 1926, the homesteading movement recuperated to a certain extent, though the figures for 1918, 1920, and 1921 have not since been equalled. The small success which has attended this endeavor may best be explained by indicating the prevalent public attitudes toward it:

[17] Manila hemp.

6. PROBLEMS OF MIGRATION

From official reports, newspapers, periodicals, and individuals we have collected a mass of criticisms directed at the conditions under which the natural and seasonal labor migrations are carried on and at legislation and lack of legislation which have produced an unfavorable setting for colonizers and homesteaders. Inasmuch as these criticisms indicate the fundamental problems which the Philippines face in attempting to redistribute its population and open up its unsettled areas we may beneficially mention a number of them.

Governor-General Wood, who in 1922 and 1924 recommended the curtailment of recruiting and shipping of homesteaders, gave these reasons for his action: first, that there was a lack of proper preparation for the reception, care, and temporary maintenance of the newcomers; second, that this had resulted in sickness and loss of life among the colonists; and third, that the region to which the emigrants were sent acquired a reputation highly prejudicial to its future development.[18]

Newspaper files and conversations revealed the following attitudes toward the question: that insufficient or no selection goes into the recruitment of homesteaders; that as a result the majority of homesteaders are drifters who have not done well at home and who would do well nowhere; that insufficient protection against physical and social hazards is given the settler during the first months and years on his homestead; that the homesteader is not given proper advice in regard to the clearing of his land and the cultivation of his crops; that the residence requirement isolates him on his homestead and causes him to become lonely and discontented; that the homestead method is unsuitable for a people for whom *barrio* and family life is so deep a tradition and custom; that the Moros have shown considerable antagonism to the Christian newcomers; that it is almost impossible for the homesteader to secure the small amount of capital necessary to start on; that transportation to the homesteading regions as well as communication facilities there are inadequate; that many of the lands have not been properly surveyed; that as a result landgrabbers secure an advantage over the colonists; that usury is permitted to exist; that landholding is limited to a certain area; that there is a general lack of supervision and intelligent advice and direction. It is also frequently stated

[18] Labor Conditions in the Philippines. Bureau of Labor, March, 1927.

that the political situation is such that those who should be responsible for the welfare of migrants are too often motivated by unsocial political considerations.

The following extract from the Report of the Director of Lands brings out further points:

> During the year covered by this report, there were 91,775 applications, covering 1,738,953.1969 hectares, pending action in this office. . . . This unusually large number of pending applications represents 41 per cent of the total number of applications received from 1904 to 1928, and was due to various causes, among which may be mentioned the limited appropriation for hiring the services of men exclusively for investigation work, the failure of applicants to remit their homestead dues, delay in the receipt of certification from the Bureau of Forestry as to the agricultural fitness of the land, and to the certificate of the Provincial Treasurer as to the extent of the land privately owned by the applicant. Another important reason is the failure of the applicants to appear on the premises when the time set for investigation comes, either because the applicant resides in a distant municipality, is sick, or because he cannot be located. The filing by a great many public land applicants of applications for lands already covered by subsisting applications, a practice which gives rise to inevitable controversies and long-drawn conflicts requiring tedious and frequent field investigations and a corresponding extra work upon the limited personnel in the Central Office, may also be mentioned as among other causes responsible for the large number of pending applications.[19]

In a recent report, the Director of the Bureau of Labor suggests that the proper flow of seasonal labor is often hindered by inadequate recruiting methods.[20] He feels that there is not the proper anticipation of labor needs nor the coordination necessary for successful recruiting of laborers.

It must not be inferred, however, from this long list of criticisms that the attitude of Filipinos and Americans toward the efforts which have been made to promote and facilitate migrations is wholly unfavorable. The measures which have been taken to survey public lands, to settle property disputes, to aid colonizers financially, to eliminate usurers and landgrabbers, to provide technical assistance, or to build roads and promote inter-island boat service, many persons hold to be fundamentally sound. At the same time most critics suggest that in none of these or similar efforts has the government gone sufficiently far. Roads, they point out, have been built in those parts of the Philippines already well populated, but

[19] Report of the Director of Lands, December 31, 1928.
[20] Bulletin of the Bureau of Labor, March, 1927.

few or no roads have been provided for the unsettled regions. In like manner, a great deal of survey work has been done in crowded regions but little in the lands still unoccupied. Land disputes, moreover, have been judicially settled in various heavily populated districts, but they have not been anticipated in those areas to which migrants, if properly protected, would swarm. Certain students of the problem feel that the methods employed by the government in dealing with the redistribution of the population and the opening up of new territories has been too paternalistic, and too little informed of the indigenous habits of the people. Ilocanos or Cebuans, they point out, have for over a century solved their own population problems by establishing definite routes of natural and seasonal migrations and by working out methods for settlement in new country. Only when these migrants clashed with other interests and when the congestion of population became acute did it become necessary for the government to step in. The government's mistake, they say, was that, instead of studying the course and method of these indigenous migrations and then facilitating and protecting them and adjusting them to the twentieth-century situation, it attempted to establish entirely new migratory movements novel to the people and unsuited to their experience.

On the side of the government, it must be emphasized that many of the methods suggested by all these criticisms involve a financial burden which the receipts of the insular treasury would not permit. Ex-Governor-General Forbes tells in detail of the proposed cadastral law which was framed in 1910 for the purpose of surveying all occupied lands in the Archipelago and settling all disputed titles and land boundaries.[21] After indicating that the additional cost to the government for the first few years was estimated at about $500,000, he says:

> It was not practicable to put this system into effect immediately, as the government at that time had very little financial margin above the amount absolutely necessary to maintain its existing activities, and it was difficult to see where an additional half million dollars a year was to come from.

7. SUGGESTIONS

The opinions held by those persons who write or speak on this subject do not lack in constructive suggestions. The range and

[21] W. Cameron Forbes, The Philippine Islands. Houghton Mifflin Co., 1928, vol. I, p. 315 *et seq.*

scope of these suggestions may be gathered from the following samples.

One student of the problem, Professor Toribia Vibar, of the College of Agriculture, University of the Philippines, after estimating that, at the rate unsettled land was taken up in 1926, three hundred years would be required for all the public lands suitable for cultivation to be settled, goes on to make several suggestions.[22] The public land act "provides for the disposition of public lands," he says, "but it does not provide intelligent direction for the development of the lands disposed of, much less does it provide for the organization, social, and economic improvement of the settlers." These tasks could be accomplished if the Bureau of Lands could have more men to check the lands applied for, settle disputes, supervise and direct homesteading, and push the work of recruiting. The creation of a land-settlement office under the bureau to take care of the settlement of lands would be a great help.

Another suggestion calls attention to the methods employed by the Dutch in facing similar problems.[23] District banks advance about ₱250 to each colonizer; colonizers are recruited from one locality where they are related and acquainted and sent to one locality where again they can live together continuing the communal life to which they are accustomed; there is no restriction on the amount of land a colonist may acquire after he has paid his initial debt.

The foreign capital controversy is raised by several persons interested in this question. If the bars were lifted and foreign capital allowed to enter, one writer suggests, Mindanao would soon be opened up, and to the advantage not the detriment of Filipinos.[24] This writer, an official of several plantations in Mindanao, claims that for every hectare developed or opened by foreigners, ten are developed and settled by Filipinos. To prove this, he cites the 10,000 acres that have been developed around the property of the American Rubber Company by laborers and ex-laborers of that company; the 15,000 acres occupied in the lands surrounding the Basilan Plantation, also by those employed or formerly employed by the plantation; and, again, the 20,000 acres that have been taken up around the Basilan Lumber Company reservation.

22 *Philippine Free Press,* July 14, 1928.
23 *Ibid.,* October 20, 1928.
24 *Ibid.,* September 15, 1928.

Allow foreigners to own larger tracts of land, he concludes, and they will employ more Filipino laborers, and the more Filipinos who are induced to come to Mindanao, the sooner that island will be opened. These laborers working on large plantations have been able to take up homesteads on surrounding land largely because it was easy for them or their families to fulfill the residence requirement at the same time that they were saving sufficient capital to give themselves a start. These two advantages are also shared by several teachers in Misamis province who have successfully homesteaded on land near the schools.

We have already mentioned the suggestion made by the Bureau of Labor regarding the more systematic selection and care of migratory laborers.

A suggestion that is made with great emphasis is one which has been touched upon previously in this appendix, namely, that migration that is initiated and sponsored by the government has not and will not succeed, that instead the government should study the natural migratory movements of the people and facilitate and encourage migration along those indigenous lines. The quality of those who will set out on their own initiative, it is pointed out, is far superior to the quality of those who accept government aid and who become almost wholly dependent. The energetic will migrate from congested areas whether the government steps in or not. A number of specific suggestions are made in this connection. Prominent among them is the building of roads into unoccupied regions. This question, however, has an unfortunate political aspect in that it is not a vote-getting project. A representative or senator pushing through such legislation could expect little thanks in the nature of votes from the benefited constituency. Such legislation is, therefore, we were repeatedly reminded, a concern of the insular government. Strengthening of the Bureau of Lands would be another thing the government could do to facilitate natural migrations. The settlement of questionable land titles, the efficient handling of applications for public land, and the proper surveying and making known of public lands are needed improvements.

Usury and the activities of many members of the *cacique* or wealthy land-owning class are severely criticized. Many persons feel that only through a strong policy on the part of the insular government carried out in cooperation with those citizens who would be willing to take a definite stand on the subject can these evils be eradicated.[25] It is generally believed, we must add, that education is gradually wiping out these unfavorable conditions, but that more drastic action than the slow progress of education must be employed. Advocates of such a positive policy constantly warn of the difficulty of divorcing questions of domestic conditions from the independence issue. It is largely for that reason that they look to the insular government for initiative. Aside from the negative aspects of this suggestion are proposals for the further encouragement of rural credit societies and a wide extension of the banking system to the smaller towns and rural districts.

In a recent commencement address delivered at the University of the Philippines [26] Governor-General Davis made a strong plea for constructive pioneering in all parts of the Philippine Islands and in all phases of its life. He made especial mention of the development of Mindanao, increasing the yield per hectare of crops throughout the Archipelago, and the improvement of the inter-island shipping service with respect to cheaper freight rates and cheaper and pleasanter third-class passages. This program, along with his recent appointment of a committee to study the populating of Mindanao, Sulu and other sparsely settled regions, indicates that action along the lines suggested by various persons quoted above may be shortly forthcoming.

[25] It may be pointed out, however, that a high interest rate may be necessary even with government credits unless part of the overhead cost is to be carried at a loss. The Dutch government in Java has to charge from 12 to 18 per cent on many loans so small as to occasion a disproportionate cost compared with farm credits in countries with larger farm units.

[26] *Commerce and Industry Journal,* published by the Bureau of Commerce and Industry, Philippine Islands, June, 1930.

APPENDIX K

SOCIAL AND ECONOMIC BACKGROUNDS OF FILIPINO EMIGRANTS

By Frederick V. Field and Elizabeth Brown Field

THE Filipinos are a group of about twelve million people, pagans, Mohammedans, and Christians, primitive and civilized, who speak forty languages divided into eighty-seven dialects, whose traditions and customs today represent a selection and synthesis of primitive, native, Spanish, Chinese, and American cultures with minor influences besides. Following the classification of the 1918 census, about 10 per cent of the people of the Islands are Mohammedans, pagans, Buddhists, and adherents of local sects.[1] According to another classification made in 1927 by H. Otley Beyer, Professor of Anthropology and Ethnology at the University of the Philippines, 9,500,000 people speak one of the seven Malay languages, all of which are real languages, as distinct as English is from Dutch or Italian from Spanish, having their own printed literature.[2] At the same time it was estimated that between 15 and 20 per cent of the population can read Spanish or English, this figure corresponding to the educated class.[3]

I. SOCIAL AND ECONOMIC DIVISIONS OF THE POPULATION

Since Spanish days and earlier there have been two major classes —chiefs and followers among the primitive peoples, *datos* and their subjects among the Moros, *caciques* and *taos* among the Christian Filipinos.[4] Since the last group, the Christian Filipinos, comprise so large a part of the total population and are the only class from which emigrants come, we shall confine ourselves to them.

[1] Census of the Philippine Islands, 1918.

[2] Estimate printed to accompany "Letter from the President of the United States to the Governor-General of the Philippine Islands, Containing the President's Reasons for Vetoing the Plebiscite Bill," April 6, 1927.

[3] For origins and migrations of the present Filipino population, see Appendix J.

[4] Only Sulu has a sultan, and there are four nominal sultans in Lanao.

a. *The Cacique Class.*

When the Spaniards arrived in the Philippines, they found the people living in groups related by blood. A family of parents, children, relatives and their slaves made up a group which was ruled by a chief. The group might occupy twenty or a hundred houses. Many of these family groups might live in one village, under ten or twelve chiefs. Among these chiefs, the richest was the one whom all others obeyed. These chiefs made the laws, judged the people, and imposed penalties on wrongdoers.

The Spanish rule in the Philippines imposed a central political and judicial organization on top of this native one, but local and less important affairs were left in the hands of the chiefs. The Spaniards did not deliberately strengthen the local organization, indeed with the help of the Church they in large measure destroyed it. But the wealthy native families held their place at the top, at present comprising about 7 or 8 per cent of the total native population. When the Spanish officials and missionaries needed local native leaders either for small political positions or to gather the people about the Church, they naturally turned to this native aristocracy. In the later days of the Spanish administration, this class was no longer purely native, for there had for generations been intermarriage between the wealthy Filipinos and the educated Spaniards.[5]

In speaking of the political importance of the *cacique* class, Benitez says:

> What is today known as caciquism ("boss rule" in the United States) may be regarded as a survival of the recognition granted by the Spaniards to the Filipino chiefs, who were the leaders of their people at the time of the arrival of the Spaniards.[6]

With the coming of the Americans and the subsequent attempt at democratizing the Islands, it was inevitable that this same class should again assume political leadership. Today the government is more democratic, but the *caciques* still have the power of wealth and landed ownership, of higher education, and of tradition. One hears it frequently said that the two houses of the Philippine Legislature are made up of members of this class.

The *cacique* class established and to a great extent still sustains

[5] Summarized from Conrado Benitez, History of the Philippines (Ginn and Co., 1926, chapter VII, "Government, Religion, Education, and Social Life"), using Blair and Robertson, The Philippine Islands, 1493-1898, as chief source.

[6] *Ibid.*, p. 128.

the standard which gives the greatest prestige to the man who owns land but does not work it, or who holds a governmental, professional, or clerical position.

In the past, the landowning class did not participate in the cultivation of their lands beyond an occasional visit or the appointment of someone to watch over the work. Little attention was paid to bettering the conditions of laborers. Until recently relations between owner and laborer conformed to the old tradition which Hugo H. Miller describes in this way:

> It is evident that the ignorance of the agricultural classes, their lack of initiative, and their inability to care for themselves, together with the ancient custom of loans, high interest rates, and honor connected with debt, place a considerable amount of power in the hands of large landowners and persons of intelligence. In the Philippines the possessor of such power is called a cacique. The control which the cacique may exercise over his tenants or even over peasant proprietors . . . applies not only to agricultural affairs but to everyday private and public matters. Often so complete is the control of the cacique that he can use his power to his own advantage and to the detriment of the tillers of the soil. It is such abuse that has attracted odium to the word. During the last ten years the power of this class of men has waned with the increase of education and the greater initiative and independence of the people.[7]

b. *The Tao Class.*

This group comprises virtually all the rest of the people in the Philippines with the exception of foreigners and possibly those who have a little capital and some small business. They are the men and women who live in the thousands of small villages throughout the Islands, who gain a meager living from their own small piece of land or from working for someone else, whose children attend the public schools, and who with but few exceptions are the ones to emigrate in search of new and better opportunities.

2. THE VILLAGE COMMUNITY

Manila in 1918 had a population of 285,306, which exceeds by over two hundred thousand the population of the next largest city, Cebu.[8] Some one hundred and ten cities (exclusive of Manila and Baguio) are listed as having a population of 18,000 or over, and a combined population of about three million. Obviously,

[7] Economic Conditions in the Philippines. Ginn and Co., 1920, p. 267.
[8] Census of the Philippine Islands, 1918.

there can be no comparison between our cities with their concentration of population and any city in the Philippines. Nor do the Philippine cities, with the exception of Manila, perform the same functions as an American city. They are not industrial centers, for there are virtually no factories in the Islands; they are not important distributing centers, for what little produce is imported or exported must travel diverse courses by cart and automobile and railroad or boat to get from one place in the Islands to another; transportation is still too undeveloped for the existence of huge arteries of communication which converge at certain intervals for distribution and reshipment. For education, Manila and the largest provincial towns serve as centers. Manila alone has a government university, although branches are planned for Vigan, Ilocos Sur, and Cebu. Normal schools, and usually high schools, are located in the largest town of each province.

On the other hand, one must not imagine the Philippines a country in which each family lives on the land which it works. The basic unit is the *barrio,* a village which may have only ten or fifteen houses or as many as a hundred or more. If you drive along a provincial road you notice the continuous alternation of a stretch of fields, a tiny village, again fields, and another village.

While technically a *barrio* is a political subdivision of a provincial township, sometimes in turn divided into smaller villages, colloquially the term is applied to all the villages in a province except the two or three larger towns. One might use any small town in the Ilocos provinces as an illustration. Such a town would have a post office, a market—usually a plot in the center of town protected by a roof—, one or two small retail stores, a large church now fallen into disrepair, a house or small building given over to municipal affairs, one or two simple school buildings, and perhaps a small farm school with a household economics building or department, and the surrounding houses.

The houses are close together, interspersed with a few banana and papaya trees and occasionally a small garden. They stand high above the ground on wooden posts, leaving space below for rambling pigs and chickens, consist of one or two or even three rooms and sometimes an open porch. The sides and roof are made of bamboo or nipa thatch, and the floors of slender split bamboos, laid side by side. This type of house is found throughout the Islands. It is cheaply built, easily repaired, and serves admirably to keep out sun and rain. In the larger towns, especially those which have sent successful emigrants abroad, there is an increasing number of wooden houses with concrete foundations and galvanized iron roofs, built by the more prosperous members of the community.

The grouping of houses in *barrios,* however small, is no mere result of immediate or chance circumstances. Economic conditions alone do not demand it. True, the land used in lowland rice cultivation is not suitable for dwelling, but this would account for only a small part of the country. Land has not been owned communally since before the arrival of the Spaniards, and so this cannot be the causal factor. On the contrary, land is privately owned and is often far away from the village; and if a man owns more than one small parcel, his holdings may be far distant from each other. In the past, the Islands were divided into countless units, each largely self-sufficient, and all raising very much the same few crops. Division of labor in the primitive and semi-civilized groups is still common among the members of a family or among those who live and work together. Only comparatively recently has communication between groups within the Islands and with the rest of the world permitted and encouraged a larger exchange and interdependence. Not more than twenty-five years ago, it was a common necessity for people to band together for protection. As yet without communications, without trade and the development of larger specialization and division of labor, without education and wider knowledge, the small local units were held together by bonds of religion, language and customs.

In such relatively isolated and self-sufficient communities, a strong, traditional social organization has developed which starts with the family, encompasses immediate relatives and neighbors, and is bounded by the village. The whole is sustained by dependence and obligation, and bound together by the degree of experience and development of the particular community.

a. *Family Organization and the Position of Women.*

Some years ago, a study was made of the Ilocanos and their customs and literature which included a summary of a scene in an Ilocano novel.[9] A son asks his father and mother to permit him to go with a friend to Manila to continue his education. He is refused by his parents, who dwell on the perils that might befall

[9] Emerson Brewer Christie, Notes on Iloko Ethnography and History. In H. Otley Beyer's Collection of Manuscripts on Philippine Folklore, Customs and Beliefs, vol. X, "Pangasinan and Iloko."

him away from their care, on their desolation if he were far away, and on the uselessness of thinking any more about education anyway. Filial duty keeps him at home. A very recent sociological study also discusses this matter:

> Family ties are also very strong among the Filipinos. A painful test for a Filipino is to part with his home and leave his family for other countries. . . .
>
> We must also not be deceived too much by the idea that filial love in the Philippines has no selfish motive behind it. Children are accustomed to look up to their parents for support up to the age of majority, in contrast to the American who, after graduation, unless the father is very wealthy, will have to earn his way through college and make good "on his own hook." With the Filipinos, therefore, the spirit of dependency creates a liking for the parents, while the individualistic attitude of the American parents toward their children lessens the family ties.
>
> It is just as true, however, that the old take good care of their children in the belief that children are their old-age pensions. It is not very infrequent that Filipino parents, after their children have attained a certain degree of affluence, keep away from productive work. It is this spirit of dependency of the parents upon their children in their old age that creates a strong family solidarity.[10]

Many of the difficulties of Filipinos in Hawaii have been attributed to the abnormal social life, not merely the absence of women of the same age as the laborers but of the older members of the family who at home exercise a very strong influence on the ideas and activities of the younger members.

The dependence which Macaraig describes applies not only to parents and children but to aunts and uncles and cousins as well. A young Filipino said that his father had become separated from the rest of his family by his conversion from Catholicism to Protestantism; but, he added, if they were in any serious trouble they could count upon these same relatives to take them in and support them. At New Year's we visited a Filipino family of six, living many miles from the main road and the nearest large town. They celebrated the holiday by having thirteen of their relatives visit them! Financially, this bond between the members of a large family often means a severe tax upon one who is earning something above his immediate needs, regardless of the possible earning capacity of the rest; it places upon him the entire burden of support-

[10] Serafin E. Macaraig, Social Problems. Educational Supply Co., Manila, 1929, p. 103.

ing those who elsewhere would be cared for by charity or by the state.

The position of women is one of the outstanding features of Filipino life. In the villages, women help in the planting and harvesting, and carry on many household industries such as hat-making, embroidery, and cloth-weaving. They manage the family income and do the marketing, and very often own and manage the small local stores.

> There is practically no social activity in the Philippines today in which the Filipino woman does not play an important rôle. The great influence that she exercises in home and community life makes her contribution very significant for Philippine social progress.[11]

> The Filipino woman today is a strong and dominant influence in every home and community; she is modest, loyal, hard-working, and while not much in evidence, she is nevertheless always to be reckoned with. She is the strong conservative influence which keeps together the home, saves money, and is the foundation of the success of many families.[12]

Nor is this situation a new development, for since earliest times have Filipino women carried on these same activities and been recognized as having independent legal rights, for example of inheritance and property-ownership.[13] However, it is only since the beginning of the American administration that girls, whether rich or poor, have had opportunities for education equal with those of boys. Together with the diminution in power of Catholic and Spanish customs which tended to limit the scope of women's activities, this means far greater opportunities for women who wish to enlarge their field of activity and learn to support themselves. The provincial normal schools are crowded with young men and women preparing to be teachers. It is still true, however, that girls are sheltered and protected far more than boys. Far fewer girl students than boys even consider going abroad to study, and they almost never leave without careful and definite plans and enough money for their needs.

It is interesting to note that, although many Filipino women are active in business, in education, in community and club work, there

[11] The Philippine Situation, by Philippine Delegation to Conference, Institute of Pacific Relations, October, 1929, p. 20.

[12] *Ibid.*, p. 20, quotation from the Report of the Leonard Wood-Cameron Forbes Commission.

[13] Dr. Maria Paz Mendoza-Guazon, The Development and Progress of the Filipino Women. Bureau of Printing, Manila, 1928. "Pre-Spanish Time" and "Spanish Régime," pp. 8-35.

is no strong agitation either for or against suffrage for women. One reason is the fear in many quarters that women voters, more attached to the Church than men, would strengthen the power of the Church. The Philippine delegation to the Kyoto Conference of the Institute of Pacific Relations said:

> It is the consensus of opinion in the Philippine Legislature that suffrage will be extended to women the moment a majority of them feel a need for it.[14]

b. *Group Functioning.*

It has long been customary for the families of a village to work together at many tasks, the range and importance of which are well shown by the following quotations from Hugo H. Miller:

> In the Philippines labor in common is often put on a permanent basis of reciprocity into which the elements of lottery, insurance, and banking enter. The most common form is in connection with many of the village economic activities, such as making kaingin [temporary clearings]; plowing, planting, harvesting, threshing, and husking; building houses; making hats; in fact, doing any work which the member whose turn it is wants done. The "turnuhans," for such we shall call them, are not regular associations with formal rules and regulations. They are simply spontaneous associations of persons with a common aim to help each other, and different places have different practices in regard to details. . . .
>
> Another common form of group labor in the Philippines is in connection with social activities, as distinguished from the economic activities mentioned above. These activities partake of the nature of mutual insurance in the help rendered the members of the community. Help is given at baptisms, weddings, and burials. In the case of funerals the work involved is the making of the coffin and the preparation of the food for the friends. . . .
>
> The courtship of a woman is frequently the cause of many forms of group labor, and the activity that results therefrom may be classed as economic. A group of young men may decide to help the woman husking rice. Here we have the beginning of a socializing activity, for usually the person helped prepares something to eat, and everybody has a merry time, especially when there are music and singing to keep time with the pounding. . . .
>
> An interesting form of group labor in connection with either death or marriage is that performed by young men. If any member dies or marries, the others contribute a sum of money previously agreed on. Besides the money, they give commodities, such as wood for fuel, and render service at the feast, such as getting water and waiting on the table. . . .
>
> Still another form of group labor in the village is the banding together

[14] The Philippine Situation, by Philippine Delegation to Conference, October, 1929, p. 21.

for protection against fire and robbers. This was common during the Spanish administration; it is still found in its original form in many towns.[15]

To some extent these practices remain unaltered, as for example at harvest time when it is common to see a group of twenty or thirty, both men and women, at work in one field, or on the occasion of a *barrio fiesta* when the work of preparation is shared by everybody. There are other instances when much the same group combine for a new task, such as building a school. There is, however, a new factor, introducing both new activities and new groupings: In the northeastern provinces of Luzon where tobacco is grown a farmer can no longer simply follow the local customs of harvesting, curing, grading and marketing tobacco; if he wishes to make a living from his crop he must follow the requirements of the government in every one of these steps and learn to seek help and advice from the government agricultural agents. Another illustration of work once done by group initiative and now done most frequently by the government is the laying out of large irrigation projects. For such projects to be successful there must be not only good engineering and construction, but an agreement mutually satisfactory between the government as financier and the people of the district involved as taxpayers and consumers. Whereas some 55 per cent of the cultivated land is still worked by hired labor or tenants, the number of peasant proprietors, each caring largely for his own fields, is growing every year, and the old system whereby a large landowner could call upon his tenants and their families to help in building a house or making repairs, in addition to cultivating their share of the land, is gradually disappearing in favor of a more definite and businesslike stipulation of duties.

Certain relationships of long standing between the leading families and the less wealthy ones have interfered in the organization of rural credit societies. A typical instance was one where the farmers of a certain village had organized themselves into a cooperative association and obtained a loan for the purchase of machinery needed in harvesting. At the time of granting the loan it was assumed that the group as a whole would benefit by the machinery, each farmer using it in turn as his crop ripened. Actually, as the time of harvesting approached, it appeared that the president of the association, a *cacique,* was to have first use of it, and after him his brother-in-law, and so on down the list of

[15] *Op. cit.,* pp. 279-282.

village officials, without regard for the needs of each member's crop, and with the ultimate result that a few benefited and the poor man had gained nothing.

c. *Contacts with the Government.*

Under the present system of government, there is one man in each *barrio* who represents the government.[16] He is not elected, but appointed by the larger municipality to serve in the following capacity:

> The lieutenant of a *barrio* . . . must enjoy the respect of the people as a man of experience and knowledge of their customs and of the laws and ordinances of most direct and frequent interest to the masses. This "head-man," or *pangulo,* as he is termed in many of the dialects, is the point of contact, the connecting link, between organized government and people. He communicates the laws and orders of government to the people, and they look to him in the first instance for advice and protection in all matters beyond the power or knowledge of the family council. He is the first responsible authority in the maintenance of public order, but is not required to collect taxes as was the case under the Spanish régime.[17]

The American system of government depends for its success upon a growing comprehension of certain principles and attitudes—free vote and equal representation and opportunity, responsibility to a political community as well as to oneself and one's family, legislation and taxation for the public good—and the responsibility for

[16] The organization of the government of the Islands falls into three major divisions. Briefly, there is the central government, headed by the Governor-General, appointed by the President of the United States, and a legislature consisting of an upper and a lower house, both elected by popular vote, except for two senators and seven representatives appointed by the Governor-General to represent the Moros and tribal peoples. In addition, there are seven executive departments. In the second division are the provincial governments. There are forty-eight provinces, ten of them inhabited by non-Christian peoples under special jurisdiction, and Manila (which ranks as a province under separate jurisdiction). The thirty-eight regular provinces have as chief officer a governor, elected by the councillors of the provincial municipalities. Legislative and administrative affairs are handled by the Provincial Board, consisting of the governor, the treasurer, who is appointed, and a third member, chosen by popular election. This board exercises supervision over the administration of municipalities and over the collection of revenue. The third division is into municipalities. A municipality is not merely a town, but all of the villages and scattered dwellings within a given geographical area (corresponding roughly in area to a township or county in the United States), functioning under a popularly elected municipal president and council, each member of which is in charge of one district of the municipality. These districts are made up of *barrios,* each with its lieutenant appointed by the municipal councillor of the district. The functions of the municipality are to collect revenue under the supervision of the provincial authorities and to attend to local matters requiring control.

[17] W. Cameron Forbes, The Philippine Islands. Houghton Mifflin Co., 1928, vol. I, pp. 151, 152.

this cannot rest upon the contact between the people and a particular government official; rather, it must come with a long process of education and practice.

One of the obstacles to a change from an older system of government to the new is the traditional prestige of the *cacique*. It is repeatedly pointed out that the grasping and unscrupulous *cacique* is a disappearing type, but while this is true, certain corollaries of *caciquism* persist. For instance, a man who thirty or forty years ago would have had complete and arbitrary control over the people of his vicinity, may today be a duly elected or appointed official of government. In this we find simultaneously a long step toward improvement and two factors slow to change—the first a condition, that those who can afford to take public office are the more wealthy members of the community, and the second a tradition, that the rich and educated must govern. When we visited the capital of one province, we heard frequent mention of the governor, who had been in office several months, for he was the first man in eighteen years to defeat the candidate of the *cacique* party. No one attacked the integrity of previous governors, but everyone waited expectantly for the actions of a man without special interest in or responsibility to the privileged class.

Furthermore, people who have long been accustomed to get help and advice from the leading man in their village cannot suddenly change their habits. A short while ago, an article was published describing the growth of a middle class in the Islands. In discussing its political power, it was pointed out that even the members of this class have little direct contact with the government and still turn to some influential individual rather than seek help directly from the appropriate government official or by discriminating vote.

One of the most interesting illustrations of the relation of the people to government is found in the making of laws and their enforcement. People have always known that the Moros had their own customary law, decidedly different from that adopted by the other Filipinos, and adjustments have been made accordingly in the application of Filipino law; but very few people realize that in one province after another the civil statutory law is fundamentally different from the prevailing common law as it is practised in all but criminal cases. For example, in Ilocos Norte the written law regarding dowry is exactly opposite to local custom and practice, and the law requiring equal division of property among the legitimate heirs of a deceased person is ignored in favor of a tradition which gives the largest share to the oldest son or daughter and a larger proportionate share to daughters than to sons.

Probably the most important and universal contact which a Filipino family has with the government is through the schools. As early as 1900, at the time of the Schurman Report, mention was made of the eagerness of Filipinos for educational opportunities.[18] In describing the situation today W. Cameron Forbes says:

> The Filipinos are in no sense apathetic toward education but on the other hand show genuine enthusiasm. Nor is the desire for learning confined to any class. It manifests itself alike among the sons of the wealthy and socially prominent, the children of the middle classes, and throughout the rural and laboring communities. It has found expression in the voluntary contributions for support of additional teachers, purchase of equipment, in the gift of land for school sites, and of money, material, and labor for construction of school buildings.[19]

Although the school accommodation is sufficient for only about a third of the children of school age, almost every village has a school.

The public schools are so much a part of everyday life that they exert a wide, general influence, growing steadily with the increase in the number of schools and of teachers. The farm schools, successful or unsuccessful, bring into a community new ideas of farm methods and possibilities in production and marketing. Every school tries to teach children, and through them the large community of their parents, fundamentals of cleanliness and hygiene, improvements in diet, a democratic attitude toward work. The schools are the largest factor in acquainting Filipinos, especially in the rural districts, with government—not politics, but the underlying principles and aspirations of the system.

d. *Religious Organization.*

If it is through the schools that the American régime in the Islands gets its most intimate contact with the mass of the people, it was through the Roman Catholic Church that the Spanish achieved the same contact. Immediately upon their arrival in the Philippines in the sixteenth century, the Spaniards began a rapid and wholesale conversion of the population, until about 90 per cent belonged to the new faith. Many of the institutions and

[18] W. Cameron Forbes, The Philippine Islands, vol. I, p. 419.
[19] *Ibid.*, vol. I, p. 473.

customs of today were either initiated or maintained by the Church, among them the attitude toward divorce and toward the limitation of the size of families, the solidarity of the family, the position of women. The priest in Spanish days was the most influential citizen in every community. Besides fulfilling the functions of spiritual leader,

> He was inspector of primary schools; president of the health board and the board of charities, president of the board of urban taxation, inspector of taxation, honorary president of the board of public works; he certified the correctness of the *cedula* or poll tax; he was the president of the board of statistics; he was president of the census taking of the town; he was censor of the municipal budgets, president of the prison board and inspector of the food provided for the prisoners; he was a member of the board for partitioning crown lands.[20]

This list suggests rather than completes the range of his duties and spheres of influence. With the arrival of the Americans, a complete separation of Church and State was made, and the priests' powers were strictly limited to spiritual affairs. In consequence, the influence of the priests greatly diminished, and the Church ceased to be an agent of the government for contact with the people.

With the American régime was also introduced (unofficially, of course) the Protestant Church with its many denominations. Though the Protestants have made some converts from the Roman Catholic fold, they have concentrated their attention more on the small element in the Philippine population that had never been reached by the priests, and on establishing hospitals, clubs and schools.[21]

3. THE ECONOMIC BASIS OF RURAL LIFE

The majority of Filipino people earn their living, or the greatest part of it, from agriculture, supplemented according to the season and the skill of the various members of the family by fishing, lumbering, running a small store, or carrying on a small trade, such as carpentry or silver work. A small percentage of the people earn

20 W. Cameron Forbes, *op. cit.*, vol. II, p. 55.

21 According to the Census of 1918, the latest reliable source of information, 90.5 per cent of the total population of the Islands were Christians. Roman Catholics come first, with 75.5 per cent; Aglipayans (Independent Catholics) 13.7 per cent; Protestants 1.3 per cent.

their living working at mechanical or skilled jobs in the modern sugar, rice and coconut mills, or in some one of the small factories and industries in Manila. These latter include the tobacco factories, the building and clothing trades, and a list of great variety. The number so employed in Manila was 44,820 in 1928.[22] In addition, some 20,000 held positions in the Philippine civil service as teachers, clerks, etc.[23]

a. *Land Tenure.*

Some time ago it was estimated that 10 per cent of the agricultural land was cultivated by hired labor, 45 per cent by tenants, and 45 per cent by peasant proprietors.[24] Large plantations are usually worked by a system under which the owner superintends directly or through a manager the work of laborers who receive a wage. Such laborers may be hired seasonally or be established permanently on the plantation. Large plantations are also cultivated on the share system, whereby the tenant works the land and receives a certain share of the produce. Occasionally large plantations are rented for a definite sum. Small or medium-sized farms, from one to five hectares, by far outnumber any others—for a number of reasons. In the first place, lowland rice cultivation calls for the division of land into small plots for the purpose of irrigation; second, settlers have been accustomed to clear and cultivate only as much land as they and their families can manage; third, large plots of land are divided generation after generation by inheritance; finally, the desire to own land is so great that a man will buy a small plot rather than have none at all. Consequently, small plots are found where there is much new or unoccupied land and in regions long settled in which the system has come about through wide distribution of wealth. In more densely populated regions the proprietor usually owns more than one plot. It is estimated that a man with one *carabao* (water buffalo) can work about one hectare, while with the help of his family a man can work from one to five hectares. In the Visayan Islands it is more common for the owner of a few hectares to cultivate them by hired labor while he works for the government, or a large company, or at fishing, or trading. In other places it is customary to lease land for a definite sum of money or for a definite amount of produce, the

[22] Statistical Bulletin of the Philippine Islands, 1928, Table 73.
[23] *Ibid.*, Table 75.
[24] Hugo H. Miller, *op. cit.*, p. 256. Much of the following description of the Philippine land system is summarized from the same source.

amounts depending upon the size of the holding, its fertility, and its nearness to town. Land is also leased to tenants on a share system in which the three important factors are ownership of the improved land, ownership of the *carabao,* and labor. A common division of the crop is: one third to the landowner, one third to the man who has cultivated it, and one third to the person who owns the animal.

It might be well to summarize the status of these different classes of farmers: The large landowner is in a position where he is financially independent, and the lender to his tenants and laborers. He is often accused of having no appreciation of modern methods or requirements and of not paying sufficient attention to the land. The absentee landowner is apt to find that his obligations are rapidly exceeding his income. Except on up-to-date plantations, hired labor is the most inexperienced, and the most lacking in initiative or responsibility. Tenants live with greater independence and security than hired labor; but they, too, are forced to accept advances from the landlord, often have additional obligations to him, and live under a highly paternalistic system. In speaking of the small peasant proprietors, Hugo H. Miller says:

> The condition of the Philippine peasant proprietor is better than that of any other tiller of the soil in the Islands. His position is more stable; for he owns property which protects his creditors from loss. He is not often an habitual gambler or a permanent borrower. His intelligence is greater than that of hired or share laborers, since his self-reliance and initiative are more developed. His income is greater because he obtains the total crop from the land which he works.[25]

b. *Methods of Farming.*

Farming methods and even the choice of crops are matters of long standing, having changed but little since before the arrival of the Spaniards. Economic development in general, the improvement of crops, intensification of production, improvement in methods of work and of distribution, has proceeded very slowly.

> At the time of the arrival of the Spaniards, agriculture in the Philippines was in a comparatively prosperous condition. Of the principal staple crops of today, the pre-Spanish Filipinos cultivated rice (which was even then their chief article of food), sugar cane, coconuts, and hemp . . . It has been truly stated that the centuries of Spanish sovereignty have affected the Filipino far less on his material side than on his spiritual side. As we

[25] *Op. cit.,* p. 234.

read the early accounts of agricultural life at the time of discovery and settlement, and compare it with that of two decades ago, we do not find any marked change or advance.[26]

Benitez quotes former Secretary of Commerce Charles B. Elliot who said:

The American government entered upon the work of rehabilitating and stimulating agriculture with great enthusiasm, but the results of fifteen years' labor have not been very satisfactory. The comparative failure has been due in part to bad administration, but principally to the inherent difficulties of the situation. In the early days the Bureau of Agriculture misjudged the problem, and by the time it learned that the natives must be taught to produce more of the staple products of the country by the use of modern machinery and better methods of cultivation and that this can be accomplished only by actual demonstration on the ground, it was engaged in a struggle with animal diseases which absorbed much of its funds and energies.[27]

Other students of the subject are more optimistic and point out that under American influence there has actually been a great increase in the yield per hectare of such crops as rice and coconut.[28]

The leading crops are rice, sugar, abaca, tobacco, coconuts and corn. Each of them is in need of better cultivation with proper implements, of scientific seed selection and care, of better harvesting methods, and more efficient marketing. In a few cases, these needs have partly been met, and in others persistent efforts are being made to do so. For example, large companies can afford to use machinery and modern methods in certain sugar cane mills, and the contrast, in both quality and quantity, between the sugar produced by small farmers in the Ilocos provinces and the high-grade centrifugal sugar sent out from the big centrals is striking. In another case, increase in export business has clarified the demands of the market and accordingly improved the supply of tobacco. In this the government has taken an active part. Machinery suitable for small farms and within reach of the purse of the small farmer—or a group of small farmers—is being put on the market, instances being steel-tipped plows which can be drawn by *carabaos,* and machinery for milling rice which can be operated by some company for the benefit of a particular community or by a group of farmers themselves. The government is also establishing experiment stations

[26] Conrado Benitez, *op. cit.,* pp. 56, 59.

[27] *Ibid.,* pp. 432, 434.

[28] See also W. Cameron Forbes, *op. cit.,* vol. I, p. 558. Frank F. Bunker, Hawaii and the Philippines. J. B. Lippincott Co., 1928, p. 137.

and disseminating their results and products—seed which will withstand local weather conditions, suitable methods of curing tobacco, and the like. The farm schools train students in improved methods and offer practical demonstrations of results to the surrounding community. The public schools, beginning with the first grade, give practical instruction in gardening and the cultivation of vegetables and fruits.

However, developments requiring large-scale activities, such as irrigation for example, or business organization, as in running a community rice mill, often fail. Certain districts have been accustomed since earliest times to form cooperative associations to install and operate rather large irrigation works; on the other hand, in parts of the Islands the government meets so much opposition to an irrigation program that it cannot proceed. (Of course, there are many causes for such opposition, including previous experience with high taxation or mismanagement; but in some instances the major cause has been general distrustfulness on the part of the farmers.)

In summarizing his chapter on developments in agriculture, Hugo H. Miller says:

> The farming districts of the Philippines differ in the character and intelligence of their population. In the wealthiest and most progressive communities a considerable advance has occurred in the last few years.
>
> Three factors that are bringing about general improvement in agriculture warrant special mention: First, the prosperity of the Philippines in recent years has increased the purchasing power of agriculturalists and given them the funds necessary to improve their lands and purchase machinery. . . . Secondly, the government control of grading tobacco and abaca has encouraged better methods in these crops. Thirdly, special schools exercise an ever-widening influence on agriculture. By 1918 there had been established in the Islands twelve agricultural schools and fifteen farm schools.[29]

c. *Methods of Marketing.*

About fifteen years ago, studies were made by Emerson Brewer Christie of some of the local industries in the Ilocos provinces, which offer interesting material on the older customs respecting marketing and distribution. For example:

> Just as the manufacture of pottery is strictly a household industry, so the distribution is usually a family affair. . . . Speaking broadly each family

[29] *Op. cit.*, p. 215.

that makes pottery sells it to the ultimate consumer. . . . It often takes a whole day to dispose of 50 centavos worth of pots. . . .

The distribution of the [stone] product is effected with the same slackness as the production . . . There is at San Esteban no public market, nor is there any other place where a stock of articles is kept for sale. . . .

Occasionally a buyer comes to San Esteban with the intention of purchasing stone articles to the value of 50 or 100 pesos, but in such cases he usually has to wait in the town for two or three weeks until the workers have made the required amount. No one keeps a large stock on hand.

[In the wood-working industry.] The material for making boxes is bought in the most expensive way. This statement applies also to all the wood manufactures of San Vincente. Each worker in the business does his buying independently of the others. He buys from time to time the small amount of wood which he can use wherever he can find it. Sometimes he gets it from a Vigan shop; sometimes he wanders about the country till he finds a suitable tree of the kind wanted, and buys it of the owner. In either case he brings to San Vincente only his own wood, when, in some cases, he could without any larger expenditure of time or money transport to his town enough for several woodworkers at the same time. In other words, there is none of the economy that comes from combination.

The disposal of the product is done in the same individualistic way. When the head of a family workshop has a dozen or so small boxes on hand, he or one of his family usually goes on the road to peddle them.

Professional brokers in San Vincente manufactures of wood do not as yet exist, but there is reason to think that they are being developed. I know several men who at times buy boxes and other things by the dozen, advancing all or part of the price.[30]

Unfortunately, we had no opportunity to discover the changes in these particular industries and towns since Christie wrote. However, it is evident that communications, especially in that part of the Philippines, have very much improved in the last fifteen years. There has also been a growth of middlemen handling the distribution of wholesale goods to the village retail stores.

Markets are held once or twice a week or oftener in all of the towns and in many *barrios*. The smaller sell rice, corn, vegetables, and sometimes meat in small quantities. The largest carry meat, fish, vegetables, minor household necessities, domestic and imported cloths, chickens, eggs, bread, kerosene, rice, corn, pottery, cutlery, hats, mats, native sugar, tobacco, rope, fruits, salt,

[30] Notes on the Pottery Industry in San Nicolas, Ilocos Norte; The Stone Industry at San Esteban, Ilocos Sur; Notes on the Wood-working Industry of San Vincente, Ilocos Sur. H. Otley Beyer Collection of Manuscripts for an Ethnography of the Iloko People.

beverages, and canned goods (chiefly fish and milk). In addition, there are markets for export in the producing centers: Aparri sells tobacco grown in the Cagayan Valley, Cabanatuan rice, and so on. Supplies are usually bought where they are produced by merchants and middlemen and resold to various markets. Some marketing is done by small traders who carry a small quantity of goods and cover a limited district. Often these traders are landowners who can leave their farms in charge of someone else for a few weeks or months at a time. Sometimes they finance themselves, but more often they are financed by a wealthy man in the community or by the Chinese whose goods they sell.

In addition to the public markets, retail goods are bought at the small stores in provincial towns and in the *barrios*. The town stores are usually owned and managed by Chinese, while those in the *barrios* are usually run by Filipinos.

d. *Rural Credits.*

Even brief mention of business and farming in the Philippines would be incomplete without reference to the systems of obtaining credit. The first step in the direction of rural credits was made in 1915, when a law was passed enabling the people in each community to organize a rural credit association by incorporating under the Corporation Law. The capital was provided by the sale of shares at ₱2 each. Many of these associations worked effectively; but they were hampered by lack of larger capital, and so the Legislature in 1919 appropriated ₱1,000,000 to be loaned on approved real estate security to associations which in turn made loans to members. At the present time there are 550 associations with 90,843 shareholders, 30,285 borrowers, 2,198 depositors; ₱2,585-873.64 outstanding loans.[31] In December, 1929, the Manila *Bulletin* published an editorial under the caption, "Spoiled with Money." It claims that the earlier form of association worked on a small scale but was effective and self-reliant; that the present associations are subject to abuse, often give no help to the small farmer who lacks political influence; and that no ultimate good can come from an institution which so completely depends on the government. The officials of the Rural Credit Division of the Bureau of Agriculture say about the same thing, but they are more optimis-

[31] Philippine Rural Credit Associations. Manila *Bulletin,* February 1, 1930.

tic about the fundamental value of rural credit associations. Arthur W. Prautch, Chief of the Rural Credit Division, says:

> A beginning has been made in 550 municipalities of the 840 in the Philippines to teach the elements of simple banking and how to meet the needs of agriculturalists who have seasonal crops and continuous expenses throughout the year. It is clearly impossible for the Government to supply all the capital necessary to agriculture, therefore the lesson must be learned that all that can be expected is for the Government to help organize their own resources by producing more, diversifying and growing crops which yield a better income, and selling these at the best price, and that they must cooperate to provide the money necessary for these operations. It is impossible to open branch banks in small towns because there is not enough business to pay their expenses; therefore, this Rural Credit System is the only banking hope for the small farmer . . . In these rural credit associations the directors have the opportunity to advise borrowers not to borrow unwisely, as this will only burden them with unproductive debts. They can advise a borrower how to improve his crops and get a better income by better farming, etc. The possibilities are limitless as to what these associations can accomplish.[82]

Disregarding plans and hopes, the situation is such that there is not an industry in the Philippines free from the practice of advances, either of food or cash, at exorbitant rates of interest, and of selling in advance at a price far below the market value of the product. Even those who may have gone through the growing season without such advances must usually sell immediately after harvest when the market price is lowest. It is common for rice growers to sell all of their harvest as quickly as possible at the lowest price of the year and within a few months to start buying back rice, not only for food but for planting, at higher and higher prices as the next harvest approaches. Lack of storage space is often one of the difficulties. Lack of rural credit facilities is a very serious one, for there are few farmers who could afford the trip to Manila even if they could meet the exacting requirements of the banks with respect to collateral. Hugo H. Miller speaks of the difficulty of obtaining credit and the high rates of interest, and attributes them to the following causes: (1) The amount of capital in the Philippines is not great. (2) Much wealth is borrowed for consumption rather than for production. (3) Money lenders take advantage of the ignorance and antipathy of the borrowers. (4) The lack of clear title to lands, the chief form of wealth in the Philippines, prevents land from being good security

[82] Philippine Rural Credit Associations. Manila *Bulletin,* February 1, 1930.

for loans. (5) The lack of a banking and credit system results in people hoarding wealth instead of using it to finance productive enterprises.[88] The wasteful and expensive methods of marketing have much to do with the first and second points.

By far the most common way of obtaining credit is borrowing from wealthy individuals, regardless of the rate of interest. At the present time, there is a law fixing legal rates of interest at 6 per cent unless otherwise stipulated, 12 per cent for loans secured by real estate mortgage, and 14 per cent for unsecured loans, and providing a penalty for anyone charging more than this amount. However, the penalty is not very severe and enforcement of the law a practically impossible task when ignorance on the part of the borrower is combined with skill and long practise in evasion on the part of the lender. The average person in need of a loan is not familiar with the law and with the technique of making a contract which will protect him, and if he were he would probably not be able to secure the money needed. As Hugo H. Miller has pointed out, money is too often needed not for investment but for immediate and necessary expenses, and the borrower is in no position to bargain. Needless to say, the rural credit societies can lend money only for productive purposes. The result is that interest rates may be anywhere from 30 to 150 or 200 per cent per year, payable usually in kind; and often the debt so nearly approaches or even exceeds the earning capacity of the borrower that he is permanently obligated to the lender.

4. CONDITIONS OF LABOR

a. *Wages and Cost of Living.*

Wages and income in the Philippines are extremely small, and when this condition is combined with usury and poor credit facilities and with the tendency to live from day to day, spending anything extra on clothes or cockfighting, the result is that many people are perpetually in debt and few have any surplus money to save or invest.

To illustrate the income of a rural family, suppose that a farmer and his family live in Ilocos Sur, and that they own a hectare of land and a *carabao*. Only one crop of rice is possible, and the average yield for this district is a little less than twenty *cavans* of rough

[88] *Op. cit.*, p. 430.

rice per hectare.[34] According to the best available estimates, this amount would be just a little more than sufficient to feed a family of five.[35] Whatever surplus there may be over the needs of the family would either be used for seed or sold at ₱3 or possibly ₱3.50 per *cavan* of rough rice. What are the ways in which the family income can be supplemented? If all of the family help him, the farmer can rent another hectare or so of land and receive a portion of its produce. After the harvest at home, he may go south and work there for a few months. He can plant a few banana trees around his house, keep some chickens and a pig, and perhaps raise some vegetables. His wife can do weaving and help in the fields at planting and harvesting time.

Statistics show that the wage for agricultural laborers in all provinces is between ₱.63 and ₱.1.37 per day for men, or an average of ₱.98; ₱.65 per day for women; and ₱.43 a day for children.[36] A laborer hired for daily wage is often transient and consequently has much less opportunity to supplement his earnings with food raised at home, and is apt to be unemployed for long stretches of the year. On the modern plantations where daily wages for permanent employees are being substituted for the share system this is, of course, not true.[37]

Tenants are more sure of their earnings and have more chance to supplement them, but they receive only a portion of what they produce.

The expenses of people living in the country are even harder to estimate than their incomes. To go back to our example of a small independent farmer in Ilocos Sur: Probably fish is the only article of food which he buys; his wife makes the clothes and

[34] Statistical Bulletin of the Philippine Islands, 1928. Table 39. A *cavan* of rough rice averages 43 kilos or 94½ pounds in weight. 2.05 *cavans* of rough rice are needed to make one *cavan* of cleaned rice.

[35] The average consumption per capita for the nine years 1910-1918 was about 85 kilos; in 1918 it was about 112 kilos. . . . Hugo H. Miller, *op. cit.*, p. 54.

[36] Statistical Bulletin of the Philippine Islands, 1928, Table 71.

[37] Wages in Manila are between ₱25 and ₱40 a month for unskilled workers, ₱30 a month being the most common; and they are from ₱100 to ₱200 a month for skilled workmen, such as mechanics, the most usual wage being around ₱125. Of course, a worker in the city must buy all his food, and a working day of nine or ten hours rarely permits of outside work, but his wife may either do work at home or in one of the factories. An article in the Manila *Herald* on December 1, 1929, stated: "By common consent, it is considered that a laborer earning ₱1.20 a day, for that is the rate of wage of some government-employed laborers, can maintain a family. A rate of wage of ₱2 a day places a laboring family, then, well above the line of minimum existence. This is sixty pesos a month or seven hundred and twenty a year. In Manila, this is not an unusual wage, being approximately the average of semi-skilled labor and minor clerks in business houses."

may even weave the cloth for them; his children must pay a few pesos a year for books; and there are taxes and miscellaneous expenses for *fiestas,* etc. The Bureau of Labor estimates that in 1927 the average expenses for a family of two adults and three children for the Philippines as a whole were ₱2.42 a day for the items of rent, food, clothing, light and fuel, primary school and miscellaneous.[38] This is unquestionably more than many people actually spend, either in cash or in kind, especially in the congested regions. We were told that in the coconut provinces of Southeastern Luzon a family which owns five hundred trees and earns approximately ₱600 from their four crops each year can live with a minimum of comfort.[39]

b. *Standards of Living.*

i. *Clothes.* Men and women wear a shirt or blouse, trousers or a skirt, and a large straw hat to keep off the sun when they are working in the fields. Many wear shoes, but the majority are bare-foot or wear native shoes like carpet slippers except that they have wooden soles. In the towns and cities the children wear a school uniform such as American children might wear, and men and women dress more elaborately, the women in net blouses with puffed sleeves and fitted skirts, and the men in white suits. The Ilocanos still weave cotton cloth, and in the southern islands cloth is woven from pineapple and other fibers, but with these and a few other exceptions, cloth is imported.

ii. *Food.* Rice and fish, or in some regions corn and fish, are the main articles of food. Bananas are the most common fresh food. Almost no milk is used. Occasionally the diet is varied by chicken or a little pork or perhaps sweet potatoes. In 1920, Hugo H. Miller wrote that "with improvement in economic conditions in the Philippines the amount and quality of food have increased to less extent than other factors in the standard of living." To remedy

[38] Nineteenth Annual Report of the Bureau of Labor, 1927.

[39] The Bureau of Labor places the estimated cost of living for a family engaged in industry in Manila at from ₱1.92 to ₱2.43 a day for common and skilled labor respectively. (Nineteenth Annual Report, 1927.) However, we were told of a family of eight living in Manila whose monthly earnings are ₱30 for the father who works in a candy factory and an occasional peso or two for the children. They eat rice, dried fish, beans and only occasionally some fresh vegetable. The children do not attend school. In another family of eight, the father earns ₱150 a month and the children occasionally a few pesos. They own their own house and pay ₱5 a month in taxes; they spend from ₱100 to ₱150 a month on food, depending on the other demands of the month, and they eat a varied diet of bread, rice, fresh fish, vegetables and fruit, and buy artesian well water. The children are all in school, paying a fee of ₱4 each a year and about ₱20 a year for books in the higher grades.

this, children are being taught home economics, and the government Bureau of Science has done a great deal of research on the best methods of preserving fruits and vegetables. Its methods and recipes are taught and demonstrated throughout the Islands. The work of agricultural experiment stations and farm schools toward improvement in quality of rice, corn, stock, etc., will eventually improve both food and diet. There is definite need for a better balanced, more varied, and more nourishing diet, to build up resistance to illness and fortify men for hard work. In the past Filipinos were often characterized by American observers as victims of tropical indolence and inertia or of innate inability to perform arduous work; but the success of Filipino laborers in Hawaii, where they have been taught how to nourish themselves properly, and gradually to form habits of working hard and steadily, have forced people to drop the old characterization and to consider the importance of health, diet, and controllable factors of environment—particularly the elimination of hookworm.

iii. *Recreation.* Recreation varies greatly according to the isolation and modernization of a particular community. In olden times and today in the poorer communities, virtually the only amusement is an occasional *fiesta* held on the anniversary of the patron saint of the town or in celebration of a wedding or the completion of the harvest. In these public *fiestas* everyone takes part, preparing the food or helping to serve it, and it is far more than a feast—it is an occasion for high spirits, forgetting cares, and gaiety. It is a form of celebration dear to the hearts of Filipinos. In January, 1930, when all the resources of the central government were being taxed to combat the leaf miner pest which was jeopardizing the coconut trees in several provinces, when people throughout the Islands were being called upon to help in the work of extermination, a three days' *fiesta* was held in the capital of one of the stricken provinces! [40]

With the coming of the Spaniards, cock fighting and new forms of gambling were introduced, and much effort and skill are needed today to eliminate them. As Professor Macaraig points out, conditions combine to give the average Filipino unusual leisure at the

[40] The educational opportunities of the public holiday are not being overlooked. There is, for example, the Manila Carnival, held annually for many years with increasing success. The carnival is open for two weeks, and the daily attendance in 1929 averaged 60,000. The carnival is a combination of pure recreation and education, a stand for cold drinks being side by side with a booth for the demonstration of seed selection, model irrigation projects and an orchid exhibit being announced simultaneously with the opening of the roller-skating rink.

same time that there are few constructive recreational opportunities to lessen the monotony of rural life.

> Illiteracy is the great handicap of our common *tao* for mental recreation; and among those who can read, their sources are limited by the scarcity of books written in the vernaculars. . . . The amusements of the rural districts are either vicious or expensive. They are gambling, *fiestas,* dancing, and *moro-moro* performances. . . . With the exception, therefore, of the *barrio* schools, where occasional musical and literary programs are held, there are no institutions for moral advancement in the rural districts. There are also no churches, societies or any other public agencies which can make rural living more agreeable.[41]

Among the new forms of amusement in the Philippines, the chief ones are athletics and movies. Athletics are an integral part of the school programs. The Philippines are represented at the Far Eastern Olympics and won second honors at the last meet in Japan in the spring of 1930. Even the older people take an interest and give their support. Manila compares in the number of movie houses with cities of its size in the United States, and many of the provincial towns have shows once or twice a week.

[41] *Op. cit.,* p. 319.

INDEX